THE STORY OF HEREFORD

The Story of Hereford

Edited by
Andy Johnson & Ron Shoesmith

Logaston Press

LOGASTON PRESS
The Holme, Church Road, Eardisley
Herefordshire HR3 6NJ
www.logastonpress.co.uk

First published by Logaston Press 2016
Reprinted 2020
Advantage has been taken of this reprint to incorporate results of recent research and make minor editorial changes. However, these are not of an extensive nature, and the main text remains essentially as it was when first published.
Copyright text © author of each chapter
Copyright illustrations © as per credits and acknowledgements

All rights reserved. No part of this publication
may be reproduced, stored in a retrieval system,
or transmitted, in any form or by any means,
electronic, mechanical, photocopying, recording
or otherwise, without the prior permission,
in writing, of the publisher

ISBN 978 1 906663 98 8

Typeset by Logaston Press
Printed and bound in Poland by
www.lfbookservices.co.uk

Logaston Press is committed to a sustainable future for our business, our readers and our planet. The book in your hands is made from paper certified by the Forest Stewardship Council.

Front cover: All illustrations appear in the book with a full caption to each.
Rear cover: Looking up King Street to Hereford Cathedral in the early 1960s.
(Photograph by Donovan Wilson)

Contents

	Preface and Acknowledgements, with Details of Contributors	*vii*
1	Prehistoric and Roman 'Hereford' by Keith Ray	1
2	Anglo-Saxon Hereford by Keith Ray	11
3	The first years of the Norman Conquest by P.J. Pikes	29
4	The early Castle, the City Walls and Gates by Ron Shoesmith with P.J. Pikes	35
5	The Castle post Anarchy to the eve of the Civil War by David Whitehead	51
6	The Norman Cathedral, Bishops and Churches by Ron Shoesmith with P.J. Pikes	61
7	Hereford as a Centre of Medieval Learning and Art	81
	Cathedrals as centres of learning by Christopher Pullin	81
	The Hereford Mappa Mundi by Sarah Arrowsmith	85
	The Cathedral library and other ecclesiastical libraries by Rosemary Firman	89
	Hereford Cathedral; the Romanesque and Early Gothic Sculpture by Malcolm Thurlby	93
8	Trade and Commerce in the Middle Ages by David Whitehead	101
9	The Medieval Buildings of Hereford by Pat Hughes with Ron Shoesmith	115
10	The Civil War by Ron Shoesmith	143
11	Faith and Religion by Ken Hylson-Smith with Andy Johnson	165
12	Georgian Hereford by David Whitehead with Heather Hurley	187

13	Victorian Hereford by John Eisel	221
14	Literature and the Arts by John Eisel	245
15	Hereford in the 20th and 21st centuries by Derek Foxton with Graham Roberts	263

References	291
Index of Personal Names	311
General Index	316

Preface and Acknowledgements

For a while we have felt that Hereford deserves a new book about its history: much information has been brought to light through research and archaeological excavation in recent years, whilst recent books have dealt with specific aspects of the city's history rather than trying to draw it all together. Several years ago Ron Shoesmith and Graham Roberts started on the task of writing this history, but Ron's workload, not least in completing years of research into Goodrich Castle for English Heritage, then Graham Roberts' ill health and subsequent death, necessitated a rethink. As a result we worked out a synopsis for a book divided into chapters with specific themes or periods that we hoped would appeal to historians and archaeologists who might be tempted to write them. We were almost too successful, for a bidding war all but broke out to author some chapters. That keenness shows through in the final text, which makes for a lively read.

In devising the structure of the book and its chapters, we wanted the end result to cover the city's history in both depth and breadth, to bring out the results of recent research and to include some less well known aspects of that history. In addition we wanted to use colour to make best use of the range of illustrative material available. To prevent the book from becoming too large (and therefore expensive), some aspects of the city's history have been covered only briefly – there is little on the city's churches (other than the cathedral), for example, and even less on education, while sport is barely mentioned.

The contents page gives the sole or main author of each chapter, and also acknowledges others who have either provided much help or written some of the sections within a chapter, as well as Graham Roberts, on whose work Derek Foxton based much of the text in chapter 15. We also know that the following have been of assistance to one or more of the contributors, and would like to thank them: Rosalind Caird, former Archivist at Hereford Cathedral Library, Richard Hyde of Hereford New Cattle Market, Bill Jackson of Rotherwas Enterprise Zone, Malcolm Jones, Scott Lahive of the Old Market Shopping Centre, Dr Noel Meeke of the Waterworks Museum, Jean O'Donnell, Cllr Roger Phillips, Stephen Phillips of Herefordshire Housing, Nigel Sweet of Western Power and Margaret Thompson of the Cider Museum.

Not only has it been enjoyable to work with all the authors, each known personally to us before the project began, but we have appreciated their enthusiasms and suggestions. We are also indebted to numbers of people for help concerning illustrations, notably Catherine Willson of Herefordshire's Museum Service for helping source and then providing several images; Malcolm Thurlby for taking additional photographs of the cathedral in addition to those he already offered us; Rosemary Firman for allowing us access to the cathedral's own collection of images and Derek

Foxton for access to his huge archive. Thanks are due to Jon Backhouse and the staff of Hereford Library for access to the local collection and maps over a long period. The source and copyright of many illustrations are acknowledged in their caption. In addition it should be noted that the paintings by James Wathen featured in the book have been made available by Herefordshire Records and Archive Centre and Hereford City Library, and many of the photographs by Alfred Watkins have also been made available by Hereford City Library.

Andy Johnson & Ron Shoesmith
March 2016

Details of Contributors

Sarah Arrowsmith has worked in the Education Department at Hereford Cathedral since April 2005. She is the author of *Mappa Mundi, Hereford's Curious Map*.

John Eisel has lived most of his life in Herefordshire, although he is a native of County Durham. Having been a pupil at the Cathedral School he subsequently lectured in mathematics at the College of Technology. He is deeply interested in the history of his adopted city and county, and has been involved in several books on different aspects of these, as well as a number of articles published in the *Transactions* of the Woolhope Club. He is also an authority on the history of church bells and change ringing.

Dr Rosemary Firman is Librarian of Hereford Cathedral.

Derek Foxton has lived in Hereford all his life, bar a few months after he was born in RAF Cranwell Hospital, just after the outbreak of the last war. Educated in the city and county, he graduated in Dentistry at London University in 1964. After running a multi surgery practice for 35 years, he retired and concentrated on his hobbies. A collection of Hereford photographs, postcards and books were accumulated over these years and have been the source for several new books. He also has a collection of very early motor vehicles.

Pat Hughes has been researching the archives of both Herefordshire and Worcestershire for many years, and is constantly finding additional stories about people and buildings. She is the co-author of *The Story of Ross* and also *The Story of Worcester*.

Heather Hurley worked in public and college libraries and is the Hon. Librarian at Herefordshire Archives. Her books include *The Old Roads of South Herefordshire*, *The Story of Ross*, *Landscape Origins of the Wye Valley*, *The Green Lanes of Herefordshire*, *Herefordshire's River Trade*, *Harewood End Agricultural Society* and three social histories of pubs.

Kenneth Hylson-Smith has degrees in sociology and theology and doctorates of Leicester University and King's College, London. His published works include *Christianity in England from*

Roman Times to the Reformation (in 3 vols), *The Churches in England from Elizabeth I to Elizabeth II* (3 vols), *Evangelicals in the Church of England 1734-1984, High Churchmanship in the Church of England,* and *Bath Abbey, A History*. He lives in Bath.

ANDY JOHNSON established Logaston Press in 1985, and the press has now published over 300 books on the central Welsh Marches and adjacent areas, the majority on what he has long considered his home county of Herefordshire.

P.J. PIKES is a freelance archaeologist with field experience dating from the 1970s, when he worked on excavations of Bronze Age, Iron Age, Romano-British and Medieval sites, including Maiden Castle, Hadrian's Wall, Stonehenge and London's riverside. He has worked for the National Maritime Museum and English Heritage, among other organisations.

CANON CHRIS PULLIN has been Chancellor of Hereford Cathedral since 2008. With degrees in theology and philosophy, he has studied the life and work of Dante for 35 years, calling this 'an indispensable introduction to medieval thought', which illuminates much of his current work, including the Mappa Mundi and the subject matter of much of the Chained Library.

KEITH RAY achieved a first degree and a doctorate in archaeology from Cambridge University before embarking upon an archaeological career. He was Herefordshire's County Archaeologist between 1998 and 2014, and is currently Honorary Secretary of the Herefordshire Victoria County History Trust. He is a Fellow of the Society of Antiquaries of London and a full Member of the Chartered Institute for Archaeologists. In 2007 he was awarded an MBE for services to archaeology in Herefordshire.

GRAHAM ROBERTS was a civil engineer who moved to Hereford in the 1960s, becoming the city's chief surveyor. In this role he worked on the Maylord Orchards shopping centre and Greyfriars Bridge. He was chairman of Herefordshire Nature Trust for eight years, wrote a guide to the city of Hereford and, in retirement, *The Shaping of Modern Hereford* followed by *Around and About Herefordshire and the southern Welsh Marches*. He died in 2012.

RON SHOESMITH is a Fellow of the Society of Antiquaries of London and a Member of the Chartered Institute for Archaeologists. For many years he was Director of the City of Hereford Archaeology Unit and Hereford Cathedral Archaeologist. He has written several books on Hereford and its county.

MALCOLM THURLBY teaches in the Department of Visual Arts, York University, Toronto. He specialises in Romanesque and Gothic art and architecture, and 19th-century architecture in Canada.

DAVID WHITEHEAD is the present Hon. Secretary of the Woolhope Naturalists Field Club and the Vice-Chairman of the Trust for the Victoria County History of Herefordshire. He has lived and taught history in Herefordshire for most of his life.

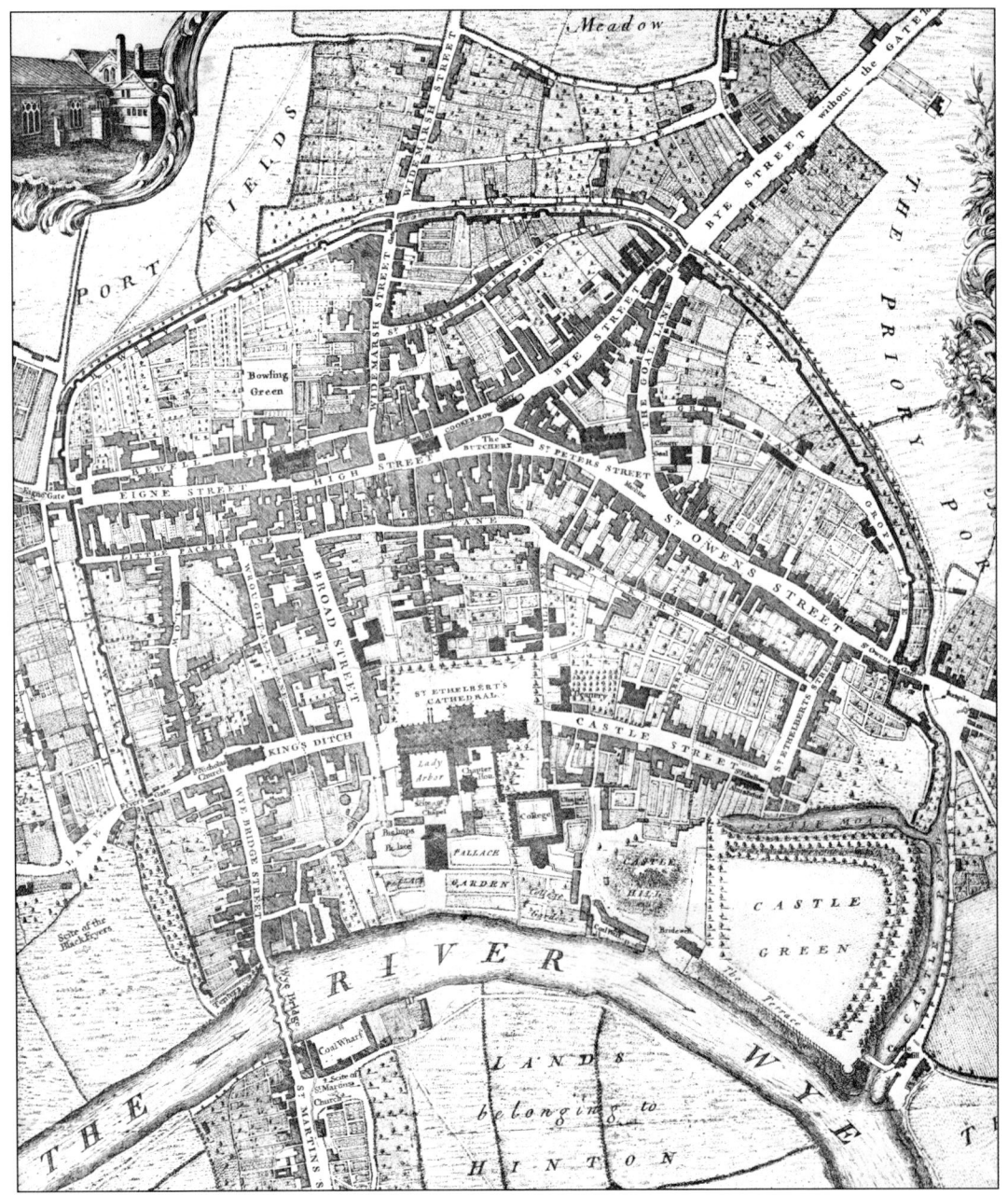

Hereford in 1757 as depicted on Isaac Taylor's map

1   Prehistoric and Roman 'Hereford'[1]

THE CENTRE of the historic city of Hereford occupies a broad gravel terrace overlooking the River Wye from the north, on the outer flank of a northwards-trending bend of that river. On the south-facing side of this 30-40m high terrace, two springs rise close to the western and eastern heights and flow down two narrow combes towards an upstream and a downstream fording-point of the river. The potential of the location for pre-urban settlement is very clear when the modern buildings are 'stripped away' from the underlying topography (Fig. 1.1): in addition to the resources of the Wye floodplain, the Eign Brook provides a parallel floodplain to the north where it flows east and then southwards to join the Wye. This tributary brook, which descends its valley steeply beneath the heights of Aylestone Hill to the east, also in effect makes the terrace a peninsula of higher ground, with lower areas to north, east and south. The steeply

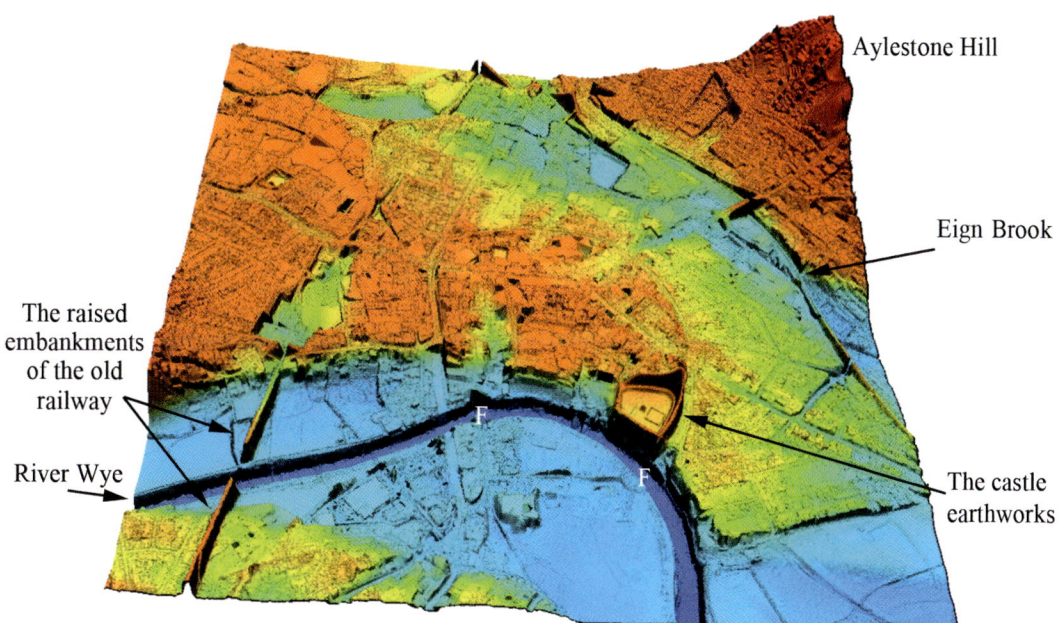

Fig. 1.1 LIDAR image showing Hereford without its built urban topography[2]
Blue: Lower ground/floodplain   Orange: Higher ground
Yellow: Intermediate elevations

descending and narrow westerly combe containing the 'Pipewell' lies to the west of the cathedral and Bishop's Palace. It once extended (all the while becoming shallower in profile) as far north as West Street. This served further, if subtly, to isolate the promontory of land upon which the city later developed, although a considerable distance of apparently quite level ground separated its most northerly point from the Eign Brook valley and its 'Wide Marsh' to the north.

Envisaging 'remotest' Hereford: before the Bronze Age

Only with the greatest difficulty can we imagine the landscape of the environs of today's Hereford as it was 300,000 years ago. Elsewhere in the county, as in the vicinity of Mathon north of Ledbury, there were 'palaeo-rivers' which joined riverine systems with much larger principal rivers than today flowing eastwards to the great plains now covered by the North Sea, or southwards towards a 'Severn' estuary many miles south-west of the present estuary. The 'palaeo-Wye' must have drained in the same direction, but its exact dimensions and course are unknown. There is, however, some evidence of the presence of the earliest people to inhabit the terrain of 'remotest' Hereford, in the form of a stone hand-axe discovered by chance in the course of casual digging in the garden of a house in Tupsley, close to the Ledbury Road in the eastern suburbs (Fig. 1.2). Although originating many thousands of years earlier, the axe was found in clay and gravel deposits that had been sorted by the action of ice, probably during the period from around 26,000 to 11,000 years ago in the last Ice Age when the river-terraces took their present form.

The centuries after the final retreat of the ice saw relatively rapid changes in the environment. Tundra-like conditions gave way to birch and pine woodlands, extensive scrub and dense grasslands. In turn this was followed by a 'boreal climax' vegetation in which a more varied and more strikingly deciduous woodland cover developed. This woodland cover was gradually becoming sparser by around 6000BC, but there are few traces of the presence of people at Hereford at that time. Very small worked flint objects termed 'microliths' of likely Later Mesolithic (*c*.6000-4000BC) date were found during excavations in the 1960s at Berrington Street and at Victoria Street. These were not used individually, but were hafted in series along wooden shafts and were used for a variety of purposes, including fishing and as arrows, and for cutting plant stems.[3] In addition,

Fig. 1.2 A replica of the late Acheulian flint axe found in Seaton Avenue, Tupsley, Hereford, probably dating to 300,000-250,000 years ago, during a warmer phase between glaciations. (Hereford Museum accession no. 2004-43. Photograph: Adam Stanford, Aerial-Cam Ltd)

a bladelet core (from which small parallel-sided flint blades had been struck) that is also of likely Late Mesolithic date, perhaps around 5000BC, was recovered (along with a burnt blade) from a probable late 14th century AD pit at the Trinity Almshouses site on the north side of Commercial Street just within the former Bye Street gate.[4]

From this limited data, it is clear that there was Mesolithic activity at more than one location within the 'promontory' between the Wye and the Eign Brook. Some of these finds may be associated with temporary periods of occupation by groups of mobile hunter-gatherers. The small posts of simple houses, shelters, or 'benders', could be (but have not yet been) found in central Hereford where early land-surfaces have been preserved, either in highly localised hollows or where later peat deposits may have sealed the relevant levels over larger areas. Circumstances such as these have been recorded at King Street, where the land surfaces have been dated to at least the Bronze Age and in the area to the east of Widemarsh Street and north of the former Blackfriars monastery.

Hereford in the Neolithic period and the Bronze Age

As for the period during which the earliest farming in Britain began, the Neolithic (4000-2400BC), numbers of individual worked flints have been found during excavations in the city centre. As far as can be established, however, all such finds were made in 'residual' contexts: that is, not where they were originally deposited, but rather, mixed with artefacts belonging to (mostly) the medieval and later periods, in the infilling of rubbish pits dug in the 2nd millennium AD. For instance, a Neolithic flint blade, scrapers and flakes were found along with flint working debris at Victoria Street. Two such re-deposited flint flakes were nonetheless found in pristine condition in two different locations within each of two sites excavated at the west end of Bewell Street, and a flake and a blade were found at Wall Street (Tesco exitway) adjacent to the inner ring road and just to the west of Widemarsh Street.[5] The latter find, close to the northern part of the medieval city wall, needs to be considered in reference to the discoveries of later Neolithic/Early Bronze Age material from the Old Market site (see below).

A total of 24 flint flakes and 4 blade fragments were retrieved from the two trenches excavated in 1985-6 at the Sack Warehouse site directly upon the south bank of the Wye just to the east of old Wye Bridge. These were either found in the riverine silts, or in features dug into them.[6] They are matched by finds from the exploratory excavations at the Asda (Causeway Farm) site just upstream. Here, further worked flints were found in alluvial deposits, and a single pit/shallow scoop sealed within a sequence of alluvial deposits produced several large and well-preserved sherds of Early Neolithic 'plain bowl' pottery and many cereal grains. A mixed charcoal sample from the same feature produced a radiocarbon date of 3800-3510BC.[7] Just to the west, also south of the Wye, a Neolithic polished axe was found in Hunderton. Taken together, these finds beneath the city centre and along the south bank of the Wye indicate a significant level of Neolithic activity in and around the city. This suggests at least periodic and episodic use of the riverside and adjacent areas in both the 4th and the 3rd millennia BC.

Some of the individual flint flakes found in the city centre may be of later 3rd or early 2nd millennium BC date, not least since there is a fragmentary barbed and tanged arrowhead likely to be of this period among the Victoria Street finds. Another similar arrowhead was found at Cantilupe Street (again re-deposited in a secondary context). More certainly from the Early Bronze Age was a pit containing a Beaker sherd from the Old Market excavations, close to the western end of Blackfriars Street. A series of pits directly across that street to the north, found in a subsequent evaluation on the site of a proposed Hereford United south stand, may also be of this date.

The basal peats in the deeply buried sequence infilling the shallow natural combe traversed by King Street, and the broad peat deposits at the former West Mercia Police training ground east of Widemarsh Street, are broadly dated to the Middle Bronze Age, around the mid-2nd

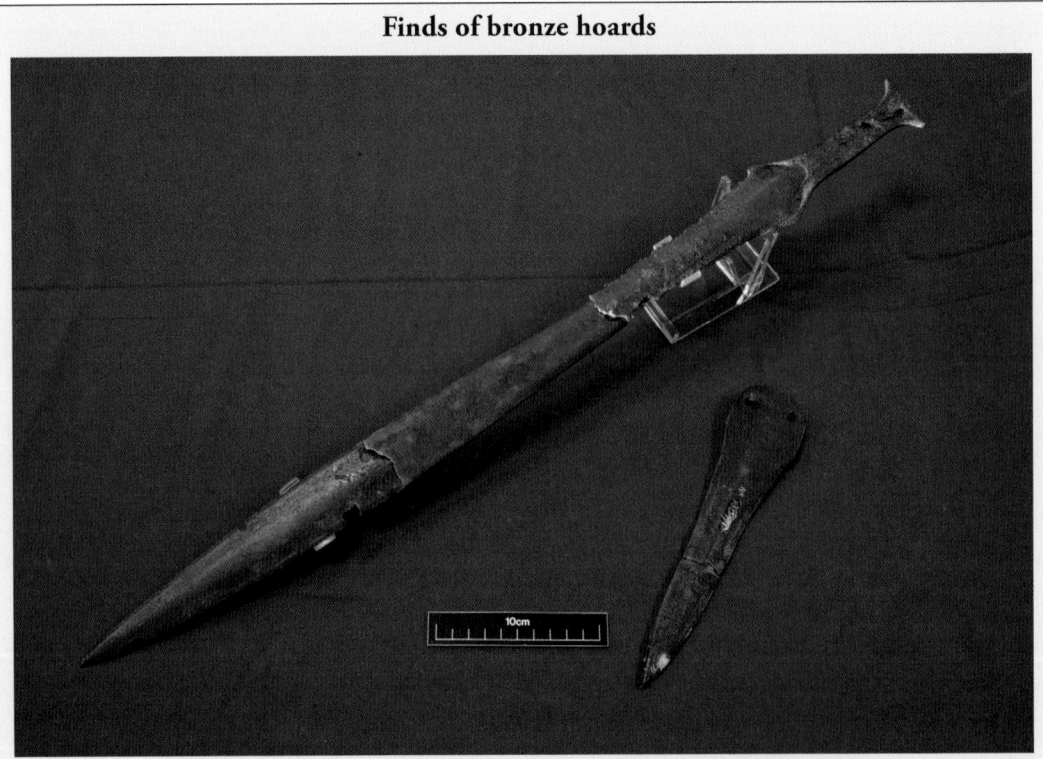

Fig. 1.3 Fayre Oaks (Whitecross) bronze sword and dagger-blade.
(Hereford Museum accession no. 1307. Photograph: Adam Stanford, Aerial-Cam Ltd)

A number of deposits of Middle to Late Bronze Age objects such as cast axe-heads have been discovered by chance in the Hereford region. Some of these objects were found complete, and some broken. Some were apparently placed into shallow scoops, or pits, while others appear to have been put into watery or boggy places. A group of bronze swords and daggers, some complete and some fragmentary, was discovered in the late 19th century at Fayre Oaks adjacent to King's Acre near Whitecross, 1.5km to the west of the city centre.

The above artefacts, now in Hereford Museum, are typical of such groups of bronze objects from the borderlands of Wales, which regularly feature swords and spear-heads. Such groupings have often been interpreted as 'founder's hoards', the trade stock of itinerant smiths awaiting re-casting. Some such objects, however, were deliberately broken. The groups concerned may therefore have been intended as gifts to the gods, to the ancestors or to the spirits of the place concerned.

millennium BC. However, no cultural remains have yet been found in direct association with, or beneath, these deposits. A paved or cobbled surface was found sealed beneath mixed deposits at a depth of 1.5m just to the south of the new Royal Mail Hereford Delivery Office towards the western end of Station Approach. This probably represents a trackway similar to the street discovered beneath Maylord Orchards.[8] However, given the existence of similar paved areas dated to the Early Bronze Age at Redhill and at Rotherwas (The Rotherwas Ribbon), only 1.5km south and 2.5km south-east of the city respectively, a similar origin for the Station Approach surface cannot yet be ruled out entirely.

A pond barrow was excavated at Redhill at the Bradbury Lines development (renamed Stirling Lines in 1984) east of the A49. This featured a circular hollow 18m in diameter, hollowed out to a depth of nearly 2m, with a raised platform in the centre on which had been placed a rectangular oak structure, on top of which had been placed a deposit of cremated bone and pottery sherds of Middle Bronze Age form. The timber produced a date of *c.*1500BC. At the Hereford Academy site nearby, at Bullinghope just to the south, and at Rotherwas industrial estate, sites featuring burnt stone spreads or dumps have been dated to broadly the same period. These stones were broken as a result of having been heated ('burnt') and then placed in cold water to heat it. The purpose behind this is unknown, but the sites may have been used for cooking (historically documented in Ireland), or were where plant fibres were retted, preparing them for use in fabrics to be used for example to make clothing. More unusually, it has been suggested, on analogy with the documented practices of North American First Peoples, that the sites were used for sweat-lodges or simple saunas.

From excavations in a dry-valley or combe leading down from the hill towards the Wye valley near Green Crize just to north of Dinedor, organic deposits preserved in peat have been sampled. This has revealed that much of the landscape in the environs of Hereford has been maintained as open farmland, either cultivated or grazed, since the Middle Bronze Age around 1200BC, and this is borne out by other organic samples taken from hand-coring of river silts close to Mordiford Bridge.[9]

'Dun(b)re': an Iron Age centre and its northern hinterland

In the Domesday Survey of England in 1086, the most prominent feature of the Hereford district is named for the first time as 'Dunre', the hill we know today as Dinedor. This hill, featuring an elongated ridge aligned south-west to north-east, and located 4km to the south of the cathedral, is the most prominent topographical feature in close proximity to Hereford. Whereas Aylestone Hill rises to 83m OD at its highest point at Eign Hill, the eastern end of Dinedor Hill by Rotherwas Park Wood is 137m OD, and the south-western end of the hill peaks at 182m OD. The oval, nearly flat-topped, natural knoll at this end of the hill is surrounded by the earthen ramparts of Dinedor hillfort, comprising a single circuit of bank with an external ditch.

The north-eastern part of the circuit that faces along the ridge (and towards the Wye as it glides below Hampton Park) is a very considerable earthwork, with a height differential of between 5 and 10m from bank-top to ditch-bottom, even in its eroded state. This part of the bank both provided a solid defence against attack along the ridge, and a fine look-out point across the Wye floodplain and the site of Hereford itself. It also overlooked the single entrance into the fort enclosure, placed on the south-east angle of the circuit, which features out-turned banks flanking (what must be assumed from the evidence of other such Herefordshire forts) the heavily fortified gateway. An embanked hollow-way or trackway still descends the hillside in the direction of Dinedor village south of the eastern end of the hill.[10]

Even very exploratory excavations at Dinedor Hill undertaken in 1951 by the famed excavator of the Biblical site of Jericho, Dame Kathleen Kenyon, produced considerable quantities of Iron Age objects, and indications of occupation including the post-holes of houses. In contrast, only a single, late, find of certain Iron Age date has been found within, or close to, the city centre. This is a gold coin of the Dobunni kingdom, found at Greyfriars Avenue in 1981. Although it is difficult to interpret the significance of a single stray find in a built-up area of the city, its location, not far from a possible fording-place across the River Wye (see below), could indicate that its presence is not simply accidental. Nor is the proximity of the find to an area that might well have witnessed religious activity in the Roman period potentially unimportant. The Greyfriars Avenue coin is the easternmost find in a distribution that extends westwards to Kenchester, where several Dobunnic coins have been found.

The Bartonsham Rowe Ditch, a straight linear earthwork bank running east-west and with no obvious associated ditch, is of some potential interest in this context. It extends from Bartonsham Farm eastwards towards the mouth of the Eign Brook (to the west of which its continuation is obscured by the Cardiff-Manchester railway line as it crosses onto the north bank of the Wye and approaches Hereford station from the south). In doing so the linear earthwork cuts off the Bartonsham loop of the River Wye, in a similar manner as does the Dyke Hills (a proven late Iron Age earthwork) a loop of the Thames at Dorchester south of Oxford. However, the Bartonsham Rowe Ditch earthwork marks the edge of higher ground at the northern edge of the floodplain, and perhaps makes more sense as an earthwork built to defend Saxon Hereford on its vulnerable south-east flank. The western end of the 'Ditch' meets the left bank of the Wye only 200m south of the point that the Hereford 'Rowe Ditch' (in this

Fig. 1.4 Dinedor hillfort seen across the roofs of the city centre, with Widemarsh Street in the foreground. The fort crowns the western summit of Dinedor Hill. (Photograph: Keith Ray)

case an east-west bank with a southern ditch, at least one phase of which has been dated to the mid-11th century; see chapter 2) meets the right bank.

Several later prehistoric and early Romano-British farmsteads, often enclosed within simple banks and ditches, most frequently roughly square or circular in plan, existed near Hereford, although only two settlements – near Stretton Sugwas to the west and at the former Bradbury Lines site at Redhill to the south – have been examined through excavation. The site near Stretton Sugwas featured a circular hut, and may have formed part of a broader settlement beneath the eastern fringes of what became the Roman town at Kenchester (see below). Looming above it to the north was the massive hillfort crowning the hill by Credenhill, and giving its name to the place. This may have been the chief-place of the Herefordshire sub-region during the period from around 650 to at least 100BC, but what exactly its role was remains uncertain (see below).[11]

A minor strategic and religious focus in the Roman world
Much discussion has taken place, but no real evidence has emerged, concerning the presence, let alone the disposition, of Roman roads in the vicinity of Hereford: apart from the east-west road, still called 'Roman Road' today, which marks the northern limit of the 19th-century racecourse. This road runs east from Kenchester, the deserted Roman walled settlement of *Magnis*, and heads towards Stretton Grandison, where it meets another road running north from Dymock and Gloucester.[12]

A well-known Roman road approached Hereford from the north, having traversed the countryside southwards from Wroxeter near Shrewsbury, through Leintwardine, Aymestrey and Canon Pyon. Since it is aligned, broadly, upon the site of Hereford, it might be expected to have continued towards the city and a crossing of the Wye there. However, this road (known as 'Watling Street West' because it linked the important legionary and ex-legionary centres at Chester, Wroxeter and Caerleon-on-Usk) appears to have made instead a sharp turn to swing around Badnage Hill and proceed south-westwards towards (and beyond) Kenchester, south of which there was a definite crossing-place at Old Weir. Despite the fact that no trace of a road has been found south of the Wye near Hereford, it is still plausible that a 'Watling Street West extension' did once exist, crossed today's 'Roman Road' at Holmer, and continued from there towards a crossing of the Wye close to the Bishop's Palace in Hereford.[13]

Although a number of individual sherds of Romano-British pottery have been found across Hereford, only at Victoria Street have they been retrieved in any quantity. However, even here, where the assemblage dominated by Severn Valley ware nonetheless also included a Samian ware bowl fragment, their location shed no further light on life in Hereford. The Victoria Street excavations also produced the earliest Anglo-Saxon remains, buried beneath the first phase (mid-late Saxon; probably late 8th or early 9th century) of the rampart (see chapter 2, Fig. 2.3). These remains included corn-driers or ovens, which were built from rubble including re-used Romano-British stonework (used also in the foundations of the 10th-century wall facing the earlier rampart), and pieces of two stone altars. It has been assumed that these re-used altar stones, and the other Romano-British stonework found at the site, were transported from Kenchester to Hereford. Besides the Romano-British pot-sherds, however, there were also several pieces of ceramic building material, including both roofing tiles and hypocaust flue-tiles, and this strongly indicates that substantial Roman period buildings once existed in the near vicinity.

A series of individual finds have been reported from Blackfriars Street and from the nearby Coningsby Hospital east of Widemarsh Street.[16] This concentration, like another in the Hunderton area, may suggest that a farmstead or similar domestic settlement once existed in the vicinity. In addition to coin finds at various sites in the city centre, there have been two reported discoveries of Romano-British bronze items. The first, and simplest, found along with a coin during the Bewell House excavations, was a fibula brooch of 2nd-century date. The second was in Eign Street (on the site of Eign Chapel), where a bronze figurine of Hermes was found in 1829. Romano-British quernstone fragments were also found among the rubble re-used in the Saxon stone wall excavated at Victoria Street. This is of particular interest given also the reported discovery of a 'Roman' quernstone during the construction of the Woolworths store in Eign Gate.

The available evidence therefore points towards the existence of a modest Romano-British settlement, probably once located on either side of the head of the narrow valley to the west of the later cathedral precinct. No excavations have taken place directly in, or around, Broad Street in recent years on a scale sufficient to uncover undisturbed traces of the earliest occupation of the area. The discovery of an altar and fragments of altars in and around this part of Hereford suggest the former existence of at least one temple in this location, of which the building remains located at depth in Broad Street may have been the foundation; the existence of a ritual complex near a significant river-crossing is a common occurrence in the archaeology of Roman Britain. An example is the site at Frilford west of Abingdon in Oxfordshire, where a temple in its own precinct, close to a minor settlement with an amphitheatre associated with fairs held at the site, existed to the east of a road crossing the River Ock.[17] Hereford, located equidistantly between the walled settlement at Kenchester (to the west) and what is emerging as having once been a significant centre at Stretton Grandison (to the east), is therefore a candidate for having been a ritual complex such as are typical of such border locations between two secular marketing centres.

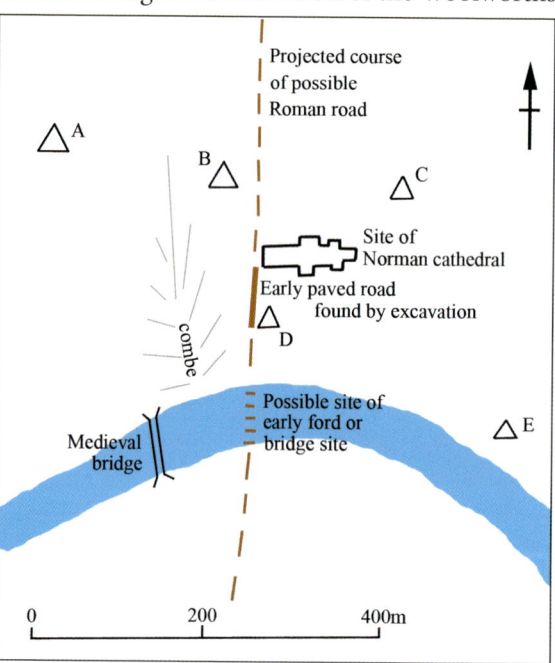

Fig. 1.5 A plan showing the location of a possible Roman-period river crossing at Hereford.
A: Berrington Street site where fragments of Roman altars and dressed stone were found.
B: Broad Street where Roman mortared structures have been found.
C: Appx. position where the St John Street altar was found (see Fig. 1.6).
D: Mappa Mundi building site where Roman tile was found from roadside ditches.
E: Site of Castle Green inhumations.
Something of a pattern is indicated in the concentration of Roman finds either side of a known routeway to the south of the medieval All Saints church.

A Roman settlement at Hereford?

The Victoria Street altar fragments mentioned opposite are of greater interest due to the discovery of a nearly complete Roman altar in sandstone found at some depth in 1821 beneath a garden to the east of St John's Street (Fig. 1.6). This large stone object, standing over a metre high, has traditionally been assumed to have been transported to Hereford from the ruins of Kenchester, given the cartloads of masonry that were said to have been removed from the site when it was cleared for cultivation in 1808. However, in view of the concentration of what appears to be occupation debris at Victoria Street, this now appears doubtful. Moreover, linear trenching for water-mains replacement in Broad Street in 2000, made subject to archaeological monitoring, produced further potential insights into activity in the near vicinity. On the west side of the street south of the Green Dragon Hotel, the lowest levels uncovered in the service trench intercepted significant deposits sealed beneath a series of medieval gravelled street surfaces. These lowest deposits, which the works did not penetrate into, appear to have comprised building debris with much mortar, potentially Roman cement or *opus signinum* (an unpatterned pavement of gravel or fragments of stone or terracotta cemented in lime or clay). It was not possible to establish whether this represents a floor level, a dump of rubble, or the remains of an *in situ* building.

That these remains might relate to buildings standing close to the western side of a north-south road approaching a ford (or bridge) over the Wye is further hinted at by the group of 11 fragments of Romano-British tile found, together with animal bone waste, in one of the earliest features investigated during the excavations undertaken in 1993 next to Palace Yard in advance of the building to house the Hereford Mappa Mundi.[14] The pieces concerned were retrieved from the surviving southernmost 2m length of a ditch aligned north-south. This 2m wide ditch, traced also at the northern limit of the 18m long excavation area, just might, therefore, be the eastern flanking ditch of a Roman road that aligned northwards upon what is today Widemarsh Street.[15]

Fig. 1.6 Roman altar, found in 1821 during the digging of foundations in St John Street. The largely obliterated inscription reads 'Deo Siluano…S' ('To the god Silvanus…'). It stands some 1m high with smooth sides, but the rear is rough, suggesting that it once stood against a wall.
(Hereford Museum accession no. 9318. Photograph courtesy of Judy Stevenson)

Credenhill fort and Kenchester Roman town as precursors to Hereford

Fig. 1.7 The eastern suburbs of Kenchester Roman town, overlooked by the hillfort at Credenhill. The excavations pictured were undertaken by Worcestershire Archaeology in advance of the Eign Brook flood-alleviation scheme.

Geographically speaking, Herefordshire is coherent. Hereford is located at the centre of the county, with distances to the borders to north, south, east and west of the city being broadly equivalent at 18 miles or 28 kilometres. Situated 4 miles (6km) to the north-west of Hereford, Credenhill fort is the largest of the county's Iron Age hillforts and the most centrally placed. The walled Romano-British 'small town' of *Magnis* (at Kenchester) is located only half a mile south of Credenhill Fort, on a broad knoll with wide views up and down the valley. As such it has become a commonplace belief that, in turn, Credenhill fort and Kenchester town were the lineal predecessors of Hereford as 'capital' of the wider district.

Inevitably, the reality is not quite so simple. Although Credenhill fort was surrounded by massive defences, it was nonetheless no metropolis: the interior appears to have been but sparsely occupied. Not long after the Roman invasion in the time of the Emperor Claudius, the fort was apparently converted into a military supply-base for the Roman army for its campaigning further up the Wye valley. Meanwhile, some years before that invasion, the focus of 'late Iron Age' activity in the 1st century BC was instead located in the valley to both east and west of the later Roman crossroads just to the east of the Roman town. The western half of that town, with a bustling, partly porticoed, main street, and with its temples, hotels, and eye-doctors, was later equipped with a military-style stone-fronted and bastioned wall (see Caerwent near Chepstow for a well-preserved example). There were cemeteries outside the walls and the former east end of the site, now outside the town but still centred upon the crossroads, became an industrial and commercial centre.

2   ANGLO-SAXON HEREFORD

THERE ARE reasonable grounds to believe that Hereford had emerged as an Anglo-Saxon ecclesiastical centre, and as a frontier settlement perhaps with something of a military character, by the end of the 8th century AD. It is not until the 10th century, however, that there is sufficient surviving contemporary documentary evidence, and a requisite density of archaeological finds, to identify its key features. By this time there was a monastic establishment, with a church dedicated to St Guthlac, on a site that later became occupied by the outer bailey of Hereford Castle. Nearby, to the west, there was also a cathedral situated on the same gravel terrace directly overlooking the River Wye. And around this there was a settlement located mostly within a circuit of defences which, during the same century, featured a stone-fronted earthen rampart.

This chapter focuses upon what can be gleaned about Anglo-Saxon Hereford from what is by now a reasonably extensive record of excavation[1] and the few surviving historical references. Concerning the latter, the documentary evidence for the cathedral in the later Saxon period is poor as compared with the episcopal community at Worcester, and the exact location of the pre-Norman cathedral buildings remains elusive (although see below).

The lack of documentary information is due largely to the loss of so much of what no doubt once existed. Any early records belonging to St Guthlac's monastery were lost either during the destruction of Hereford in 1055 (see p.22), or as a consequence of appropriation of the site and most of the monastic estates by the Normans in the years immediately following 1066, or during disturbances in the castle precincts during the 12th century.[2] The early records of the cathedral chapter and diocese are also likely to have been destroyed when the church was burnt in 1055. Furthermore, other Mercian sources are limited due to catastrophic fires in the major monasteries at Peterborough, Evesham, Winchcombe and elsewhere, again mostly in the 12th century. Nevertheless, important shrines are likely to have existed during the late Saxon period, dedicated to St Ethelbert (at the cathedral) and to St Guthlac (in the principal monastic church). Hereford was not only significant as a cult centre, but also for its continuing contribution to the military and economic security of the Anglo-Saxon state.

While there has been a divergence of views about the exact dating of the sequence of development of the Saxon defences of Hereford, and concerning the early planned elements of the intra-mural settlement, there have been recent tangible advances in knowledge of the Saxon town from archaeology. These latter include indications of high-status secular activity just north of the early cathedral, of early extra-mural activity, and of intensive iron-working in several places across the settlement.

The early post-Roman centuries
If there was ever any 'sub-Roman', British, occupation of the site of medieval and later Hereford, it has yet to come to light. As was evident from John Leland's entry for the city in his *Labouriouse Journey* (presented to Henry VIII in 1545, and known in recent times as his *Itinerary*), human remains were from time to time seen in the bank above the River Wye at Castle Cliffe (present-day Castle Green), due to erosion, at least since the late medieval period. Some early radiocarbon dates from excavations in 1973 suggest that the first inhumations examined nearby could be as early as the 6th or 7th century AD. This led to speculation that an early Christian, pre-Saxon, British monastic community might once have existed there.[3]

When a cathedral community developed at Hereford, either at the same time as or soon after the monastic one, the chosen location was a site less than 300m to the north-west of this early cemetery. The cathedral area was also just to the east of a north-south road comprising a well-metalled surface that appears to have replaced an earlier one dating from Roman times.[4] The metalling has now been traced further north by the west front of the cathedral, and its alignment would project it northwards to Widemarsh Street and southwards to a crossing of the River Wye.[5] If this siting of road and precinct was deliberate, it may have been the result of royal policy, not least because the area of the Anglo-Saxon town located to the west of this north-south road was to an extent, and from a certain point in time, laid out to a grid plan.

Moreover, at a site 250m again to the north-west of the cathedral precinct site, archaeological evidence has been found for settlement from broadly the same period as the ecclesiastical sites appear to have developed into substantial establishments, namely, the late 8th to mid 9th century AD. The excavation concerned, now known by the generic name 'Victoria Street', took place in 1968, just before the building of the western arm of the Hereford city inner ring road north of the then new Greyfriars Bridge (opened in 1967).[6] A full sequence of activity was revealed here, at the rear of the rampart into which the western line of the medieval city wall was subsequently inserted, the earliest traces being sealed beneath the rampart and later wall.

The sequence began with two corn-drying ovens, each L-shaped in plan, and each of which 'consisted of a combined firing chamber and stoke pit with a long, lateral, stone-lined, horizontal flue'.[7] Broken Roman stonework was re-used in the flue linings.[8] These ovens have been regarded as 'isolated structures in an otherwise rural scene', and as existing on a site 'that probably then lay in fields outside the settlement'.[9] However, there is no good reason to accept either of these judgements: there are no demonstrably contemporary deposits known anywhere within the present city centre that would indicate that 'the settlement' then existed at any other location.

What may be most significant is the ordered character of these remains: not only were the two ovens identical in form, but they were clearly a pair, oriented such that they precisely mirrored one other. It is plausible, given the regular east-west/north-south layout of the kilns and the considerable investment involved in their construction, to interpret these structures as indicative of the exercise of royal authority, or even as having been built to assist the provisioning of an army on campaign. It is tempting to link such possible deliberate planning to what some Welsh sources have recorded as the military intervention successively of the Mercian kings Aethelbald and Offa hereabouts, including a battle fought between British and English forces near Hereford in or around 760AD, close to the beginning of Offa's reign in 757.[10]

Although not entirely satisfactorily dated, the primary sequence of activity on the Victoria Street site remains crucial to an understanding of the early development of Hereford. This is because there were at least two, and possibly three, phases of activity *before* the earliest gravel rampart was built there. After the corn-dryers had gone out of use, a light post-built rectangular structure was erected. This two-roomed building, measuring 9m east-west by 7.5m/8m north-south, was built on exactly the same orientation as the two kilns. It is undated, but may have been contemporary with a small bank and ditch, again sharing the same orientation, located immediately to the west. After an unknown interval, a 'gravel rampart' (only the very rear of which survived within the excavated area) was piled up over the site of the building and the earlier bank and ditch, on exactly the same orientation as all the earlier features.[11] This gravel bank was the first in a series of banks (later ones being much larger) that were built on this alignment. The consistency of orientation of all the primary features (up to and including the gravel bank) strongly suggests that they were all part of the same scheme of operations.[12]

One possible reading of this evidence is, therefore, that all these earliest features relate to mid 8th- or early 9th-century activity on the site, and that this activity, far from being 'domestic' in character, instead reflects the presence of the military apparatus of successive Mercian kings. This presence at the 'army ford' (Old English, *Here-ford*) might date initially to the latter part of Aethelbald's reign, when he is known to have been campaigning across the Wye southwards into the British kingdom of Ergyng, and then across the 40 years of Offa's involvement in this part of the western frontier.[13]

Fig. 2.1 Victoria Street: section through the defences looking north (corn-drying kilns from the earliest levels, in the foreground)

Two sites recently discovered not far to the south of the Wye have provided further tangible evidence for early Anglo-Saxon settlement, and perhaps also military presence, in the near environs of Hereford. The first site, located to the north-east of the medieval village of Bullinghope, comprised a series of ditches and pits, presumably from a small settler community. The finds included bun-shaped loom-weights and metal items dated provisionally to the late 6th to mid-7th century due to their similarity to other such material from secure contexts elsewhere in England.[14] The second site was more enigmatic. It consisted of a length of ditch around a metre deep that defined the curving south-eastern angle of a large enclosure, the extent of which is presently unknown, located on the edge of the Wye floodplain underneath what is now the Rotherwas Industrial Estate. Radiocarbon dates place its construction in the late 6th or early 7th century.[15]

The Castle Green cemetery and the pre-Conquest St Guthlac's monastery
A series of parch-marks in the grass on Castle Green, outlining the position of stone walls of long-vanished buildings, was, like the burials along the slope above the river, first noted many years ago. While several of these lost structures were clearly contemporary with the outer bailey of the Norman castle, others on a different alignment were explored briefly in archaeological investigations in 1960 (to the south-west of the Nelson memorial) and in 1973 (to the south of the bowling-green). Burials and parts of buildings were uncovered in both excavations, with a timber structure succeeded by stone foundations in the 12th century in the former case and two successive stone-founded structures in the latter.[16]

The sequence of burials on both sites, and elsewhere in the Castle Green cemetery, may have extended from as early as the 6th century through to the 12th century, when St Guthlac's

Fig. 2.2 Excavations at Castle Green in 1973: the northern end of Area 2.

monastery was transferred to a new site on Bye Street (now Commercial Road, where the Bus Station and County Hospital are located). The best recorded and reported part of this cemetery was in the northern end of 'Area 2' of the excavations carried out in 1973 (Fig. 2.2), within and immediately to the north of the stone foundations of two successive rectangular buildings. The burial sequence began with simple burials that established the practice here of east-west interment without grave goods (and with heads to west) in the standard Christian manner. These were succeeded by a group of burials surrounded by charcoal. These in turn appear to have been followed by 'coffin' burials that were loosely dated to the early- to mid-9th century. A subsequent, second, series of 'charcoal' burials was of likely 10th-century date, and early in the 11th or early 12th century there were burials interred within stone-lined cists.[17]

The rectangular timber building excavated in 1960 had an apse at its eastern end and was built upon an elevated gravel platform, at a place where a chapel of St Martin was located in the medieval period. It therefore seems likely to have been an Anglo-Saxon predecessor. Only the south-western angle of either of the successive and superimposed stone-founded buildings to the south, closer to the river-bank, was uncovered within Area 2. The earlier of the two buildings, 'Building A' (see Fig. 2.3), was a lightly-built structure, within the inner face of the western wall of which the early series of four or five charcoal burials had been carefully placed. One of these charcoal burials produced a 9th-century date.[18] This stone-founded structure was likely originally to have been a mortuary chapel, but its relationship to the extensive remains of structures evident (both from parch-marks and from geophysical survey: see panel on the following page) immediately to the north is not clear. However, all these remains are most plausibly interpreted as comprising earlier and later phases of the monastic buildings of St Guthlac's, including an apparently aisled building that may represent the monastic church.

Important questions concern the status of St Guthlac's as a monastic establishment: under whose patronage did it emerge, and was it *de novo* dedicated to St Guthlac? One suggestion is that the first dedication of the monastery was to St Peter, and that this was why the later church built at the eastern end of the medieval market-place was also dedicated to St Peter, and why the later monastery off Bye Street had its double dedication.[19] It has also been plausibly argued that St Guthlac's was, or became, a royal foundation, and that this most likely stemmed from Aethelbald's involvement in the frontier and his well-documented 'mentored' relationship to Guthlac.[20]

The Saxon defences of Hereford and the early growth of the town

To recapitulate, the first earthen bank recorded at Victoria Street comprised a broad dump of gravel and was plausibly created as part of a deliberate operation by King Offa late in his reign, towards the end of the 8th century, to raise Hereford to the status of a defended strongpoint, market-centre and deliberately 'frontier' bishopric, in parallel with the creation of Offa's Dyke and possible intended annexation of the northern part of the kingdom of Ergyng. The early gravel bank was observed to turn sharply to the east just to the north of West Street, so defining the north-western limit of a fortified rectangular enclosure. The eastern arm of the gravel rampart has not been established but could be just to the east of the cathedral precinct.[21]

A deliberate foundation of Hereford as a market settlement and fortress during the period of Mercian hegemony from around AD780 to 820 might well provide the historical (and economic) context for the construction of the earliest buildings in the area to the west of

Castle Green: under the turf

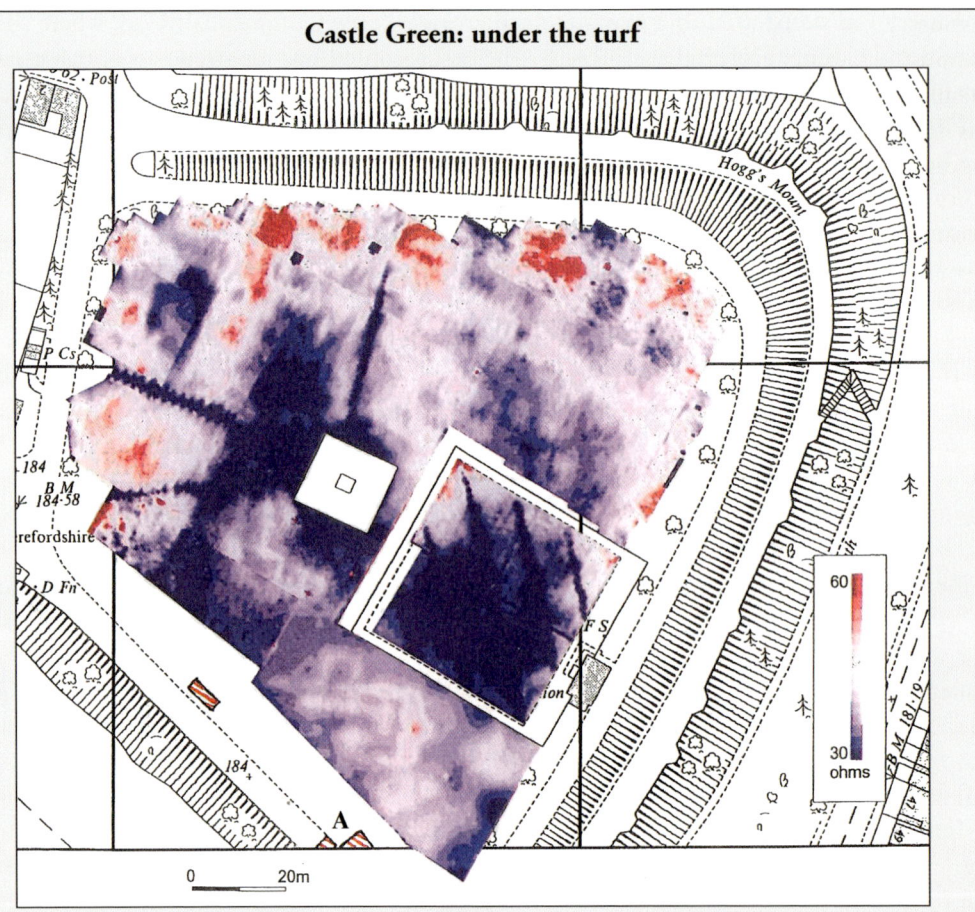

Fig. 2.3 Geophysical survey of Castle Green. 'A' marks the site of building 'A', the south-eastern corner of which was revealed in the 1973 excavation.
(Reproduced courtesy of A. Boucher and Headland Archaeology)

In dry summers, the grass on Castle Green parches differentially. As the grass becomes drier, the position of former walls becomes evident as lighter lines showing up against the darker green background; this fact was first pointed out in the 19th century.[22] The positions of these parch-marks have never been closely mapped, but their approximate locations were indicated on a plan.[23] An electrical resistance (resistivity) survey was carried out by Archaeological Investigations Ltd (now Headland Archaeology) in 2009, and this provides a more accurate mapping of these remains. Areas in red represent high resistance areas, in blue lower, in white, intermediate. It seems likely that those remains (probably including heaps of masonry rubble that are evident in red and below them in white) lying parallel to the northern embankment that retains the line of the north wall of the outer bailey of Hereford Castle, are from buildings formerly lining the inside of that wall. In contrast, there are two groups of structures to the south, each of which have slightly contrasting alignments. It is these latter buildings that were partly investigated in 1960 and 1973, and that appear to be the focus for burials dated to the Anglo-Saxon and Anglo-Norman centuries.

Berrington Street, to the south of the Victoria Street site and also within the earliest rampart. The presence there of burnt daub and post-holes in lines running north-south next to a linear metalled surface on the same orientation, and with some lines of posts running east-west from this 'frontage', indicates that several of the structures were built along the eastern side of what appears to have been an intra-mural street. On the opposite (eastern) side of the area examined at Berrington Street between 1972 and 1976 only a small area of the early activity survived later disturbance (lower right area in Fig. 2.4). However, here a series of structures were also aligned east-west, seemingly onto a road immediately to the east.

In this period, up to the mid-late 9th century, 'the buildings were all of post-hole construction and were well separated from their neighbours although they were all close to parallel north-south roads. There was only slight evidence of laid floors and hearths'.[24] The four buildings from this phase for which ground-plans were recoverable were rectangular in plan, were oriented east-west, and were spaced around five metres apart, in two cases with paved access-lanes running eastwards off the north-south street to which their western gable-ends were aligned. Three of them had north-south subdividing walls. At least two structures from this phase had been destroyed by fire. The rectangular plans and careful east-west orientation of buildings sited adjacent to the streets indicate a markedly regular settlement organisation.

The early bank at Victoria Street was superseded, after some considerable interval, by a turf and clay rampart, strengthened by timbers laid east-west in rows through the thickness of the bank. On the top of the primary bank was built a light stone wall. What is understood to be early 11th-century pottery found in a subsequent soil layer was interpreted as demonstrating that a period of collapse and disuse of the earlier defences was likely to have continued into that century.[25]

Fig. 2.4 Berrington Street Site 4, from the south

It has been suggested very recently that the 'secular' settlement at Hereford dating to the 8th century and bounded by the early gravel rampart covering the corn-drier related structures enclosed only a small area to the west of the valley that the present-day King Street traverses (which valley extends from the Aubrey Street area to the north down to the Wye just east of Bridge Street). There are strong indications that the first-phase gravel bank is present for the whole of the 150m length of the western defences between the Victoria Street and Friars' Gate sites.[26] However, the course of the gravel rampart on the north was also seen in 1965 at excavations on the site of the King's Head on the corner of West Street and Broad Street and again in the subway excavation across East Street at the rear of Marks and Spencer.[27] No adequate opportunity, however, has arisen to test the idea that an original enclosure extended as far east as the former Milk Lane (St John Street).

Topographically, despite the presence of the hollow that descended towards the Wye west of the cathedral precinct, it seems most likely that the original defensive enclosure around Hereford did extend this far to the east. As such it would have included the site of the middle to late Saxon cathedral located within part of the original south-eastern quadrant. The eastern side of this probable early enclosure corresponds both to a change in the alignment of East Street at what would have been an original north-eastern angle of the defences, and to the historic eastern boundary of the parish of St John.[28] This line extends southwards down the course subsequently followed by Quay Street. There is a continuous scarp across the grounds of the Vicars Choral and the Bishop's Palace, and the top of this slope to the river could mark the line of the southern defences. Alternatively, a parch-mark observable directly opposite Quay Street on the Bishop's Meadow aligns exactly with the course of this eastern defensive line, taking it across the Wye onto its south bank and extending south as far as the Rowe Ditch. This raises

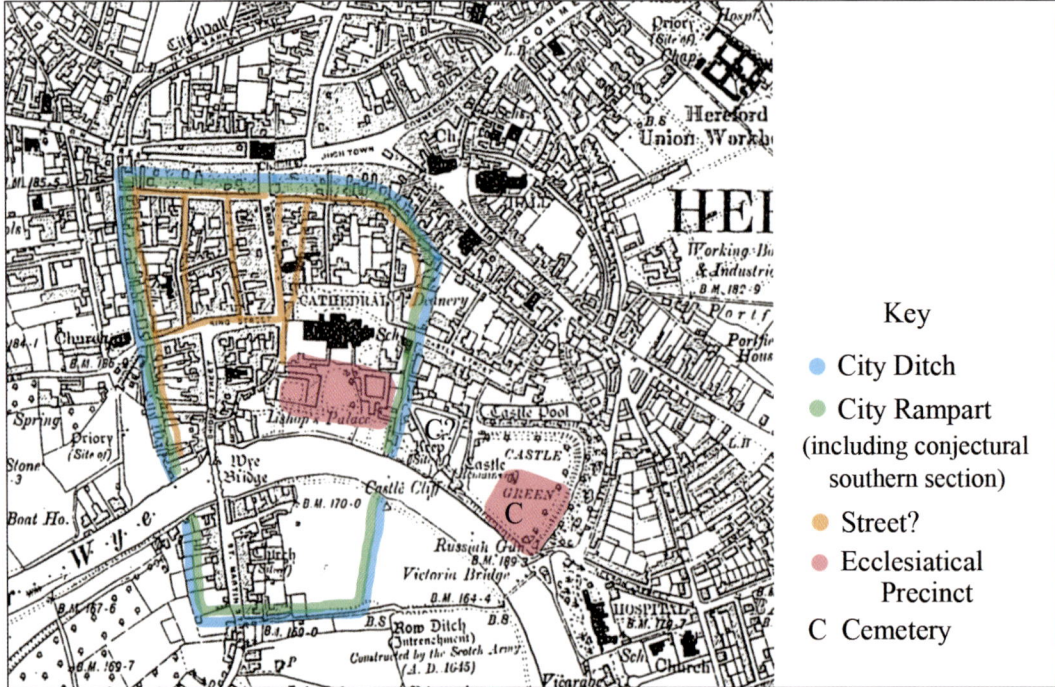

Fig. 2.5 The first Hereford

the possibility, which can be little more than a conjecture at present, that from the outset the vulnerable south bank may have received some protection.[29]

The Saxon cathedral and diocesan centre

The episcopal list for the diocese begins in the late 7th century, but it is not certain that the centre of the see was fixed at Hereford before 800.[30] Circumstantial evidence nonetheless indicates the likelihood that Bishop Cuthbert headed a cathedral community at Hereford by the 740s.[31] The first definite reference to a bishop at Hereford was when Wulfheard was appointed in 800; three years later, in October 803, he attended a council of the Mercian church presided over by King Coenwulf. At that council, Wulfheard defended a claim concerning dues from the minsters at Cheltenham and at Beckford in Gloucestershire, disputed by the bishop of Worcester. Wulfheard was succeeded in October 824 by Beonna, possibly formerly the abbot of Peterborough Abbey.[32]

Cuthwulf, bishop in the mid-9th century, issued a charter that specified the terms of a three-year lease of an estate on the River Frome by the minster at Bromyard to a certain Ealdorman Aelfstan. This is exceptional only in the survival of the document in its original form. The 10th-century bishops are little more than names appended as witnesses to charters, but of Aethelwulf, who had a particularly long episcopate from around 970 to 1015, the biographical detail shows that he had formerly been a monk at the Old Minster at Winchester. The equally long tenure of Bishop Athelstan, Aethelwulf's successor, between 1015 and his death at his manor at Bosbury in February 1056, is the first to be well attested in surviving documents. The engagement of the Anglo-Saxon bishops in the affairs of the eastern areas of Herefordshire is further underscored by Athelstan's involvement in a dispute over land at Wellington and at Cradley resolved at the shire-meeting held at Aylton.[33] His death followed soon after the at least partial destruction of his fine new minster at Hereford, built sometime between 1020 and 1040. According to John of Worcester, the Anglo-Welsh horde, having summarily seen off Earl Ralph's lightly-armed forces, 'went back to the town and burnt it with the glorious minster which Aethelstan the venerable bishop had had built. They stripped and robbed it of relics and vestments and everything …'.[34]

The response by Harold Godwinson to this political setback was to reinforce the defences of the city (see below), but arguably the cathedral community itself did not recover until later in the century: between 1056 and 1060, for example, the diocese was held in plurality by the bishop of Worcester. This may have been because the Hereford community, being non-monastic, was more fragile when exposed to events such as that which occurred in 1055 and required the initial support of a monastic community to help rebuild itself. Hereford had from the outset been served by a community of clerks (canons), having not been influenced by the 'monastic reform' of the 10th century which saw Canterbury, Sherborne, Winchester and Worcester become serviced by cathedral monasteries.[35]

It appears probable that the first cathedral was dedicated to St Mary, and that only after the execution of King Ethelbert of East Anglia, upon the order of King Offa in 794 (and according to local tradition recorded in the 12th century, at Sutton in the royal manor of Marden on the River Lugg north of Hereford), was the dedication of the cathedral 'expanded' to embrace a new royal saint's cult. The key question, of course, is where the early cathedral might have been located. As with Lichfield Cathedral, it is not impossible that the Anglo-Saxon structures were simply levelled and buried beneath the Norman structure. However, it is equally plausible that the Norman cathedral was built on an entirely different footprint. This possibility is given some support when the orientation of two structures south of the Norman cathedral is compared with its own orientation. These structures are the episcopal double-chapel built by Bishop Robert de Losigna (1079-1095) before work on the new Romanesque building began; and the southern wall bounding the Chapter House Yard.[36]

Fig. 2.6 (above) St John's Quad excavations of 2010 viewed from the south. The row of excavators standing at the rear of the site mark the line of the foundations of the timber building shown in Fig. 2.7. Four staff members stand at the corners of one of the rectangular industrial structures. In front of them, but obscured from view, lie the robbed foundations of the massive stone-built possible late Saxon cathedral.

Fig. 2.7 (left) The foundation trench for the large early timber building on the northern side of St John's Quad viewed from the east. Post-holes along the outer, southern, side of the trench (at left here) indicate that the building was located mostly northwards from the excavated area. The line of stones further left may represent the site of a porch or lean-to structure. (Courtesy of A. Boucher, Headland Archaeology)

The shared orientations of buildings to the south of the Romanesque and later cathedral are most likely indicative, at Hereford as elsewhere, of the anterior presence of the Anglo-Saxon cathedral in this part of the complex. Nor should we necessarily assume that this comprised a single church, given the agglomerative nature of the structures belonging to major Anglo-Saxon episcopal establishments as described by medieval writers for places such as Glastonbury.[37] Investigations underneath Lichfield Cathedral have indicated the kind of structure to be expected at Hereford, with a succession of builds in timber on stone foundations, and a series of structures added cumulatively, in that case focused around the shrine of St Chad.[38]

In this light, the recent discovery of part of a major east-west robbed foundation in St John's Quad to the south of the Lady Chapel of the cathedral at Hereford, and directly east from the former chapter house, may well be a first glimpse of the otherwise fugitive remains of the Anglo-Saxon cathedral.[39] The foundation trench concerned, the robbed-out footings of which contained some finely carved stonework, may mark the course of a former length of a north wall belonging to one part of Athelstan's stone-built cathedral. It is significant that it shares the same orientation as the two other structures to the west of this point, but it is potentially equally significant that this foundation trench is located in the very area in which Silas Taylor was said to have observed in 1650 or thereabouts 'stupendous foundations', 'capitals and pedestals', 'well-wrought bases for arches', and 'mouldings of friezes' which he presumed must have come from the early 11th-century cathedral.[40]

An equally complex question arises in reference to the location of the origins and site of the cathedral cemetery. Twelve either 'late Saxon' or post-Conquest burials, and a charnel pit (possibly originally dug as a source of gravel for building the new Norman cathedral) containing the disarticulated remains of around 5,000 people assumed mostly to have been from an Anglo-Saxon cemetery, were found during the 1993 excavation on the present site of the new cathedral library building (south of the former west end of the Norman cathedral).[41] It was thought at first that the location of the early burials formed part of the late Saxon cathedral graveyard, and that the charnel pit was created when the Norman cathedral foundations carved through the northern part of that cemetery. However, the extensive, if minimally intrusive, excavations to the east, north and west of the cathedral have failed to locate any trace of such a cemetery, and the charnel deposit has been tentatively explained, instead, as deriving from disturbance of St Guthlac's cemetery during the anarchy of Stephen's reign in the 1130s.[42]

Hereford in the later Anglo-Saxon period: defences, ironworking and more

Documentation for the burgeoning town is almost non-existent during much of the 9th century, across the period when Hereford passed from the control of the later Mercian kings to the West Saxon dynasty under King Alfred and then Edward the Elder. The entry for the year 914 in one of the extant versions of the Anglo-Saxon Chronicle mentions the involvement of men from Hereford in a fight against a Danish force on the middle Severn. This implies that there was a defended centre at Hereford at that date, and this impression is strengthened by the fact that there is no mention of Hereford as having been newly fortified by Ealdorman Aethelred of Mercia or his wife Aethelflaed (daughter of King Alfred) in the period 902-18.

According to the 12th-century writer William of Malmesbury, King Aethelstan (924-39) received the homage of the princes of 'the people of north Wales' specifically at Hereford in the year 930. The 10th-century history of the city is poorly documented, but both Aethelstan and King Edgar (957-75) may have taken a particular interest in Mercia and its western provinces given that the former kingdom provided each of them with a power-base early in their respective reigns. Aethelstan inaugurated a mint in the city, and by 958, early in Edgar's reign, Hereford had a well-organised market.[43]

For the rest of the century and into the early years of the 11th century, little is heard of Hereford other than ecclesiastical events and the rise of the cult of St Ethelbert. The mint continued to flourish, including under Cnut (1016-35), and moneyers were producing coin for both the king and the bishop by the mid-11th century.

The events of 1055 cast a long shadow over the development of late 11th-century Hereford and it is therefore worth examining the circumstances and consequences of the sacking of the city in a little more detail. In 1052, Sweyn, Earl Godwin's son, died on pilgrimage to Jerusalem, and it was probably at that time that King Edward the Confessor appointed his nephew, Ralph, son of the Count of Vexin (a province of Normandy on the north bank of the River Seine 20km upstream from Rouen), to Sweyn's Earldom of Herefordshire.[44] Ralph had returned with Edward from his exile in France in 1041, and this move demonstrates both the extent of royal interest in the city, and the need King Edward felt to keep close control of events there.

Edward in turn banished Earl Godwin and his sons into exile in 1051, and Aelfgar, the son of Leofric of Mercia and Queen Godgifu (Godiva), was appointed to the earldom of East Anglia in place of Godwin's son Harold. Earl Godwin and King Edward were nonetheless reconciled in 1052, and as a result Harold regained East Anglia. However, when Godwin died in 1053, Aelfgar resumed control of that earldom while Harold assumed control of Wessex. Tensions between Edward and Aelfgar (as the impatient 'heir apparent' also to Mercia) in 1055 resulted in Aelfgar being exiled. He immediately went to the Scandinavians in Ireland and raised 18 ships to oppose the king, and then marched into Wales to join forces with Gruffudd ap Llywelyn. Gruffudd was the most powerful king in Wales for several generations, and the pact was sealed with the marriage of Gruffudd to Aelfgar's daughter Ealdgyth. The combined forces then advanced to within two miles of Hereford, at which point Ralph at last acted.[45] He gave battle on 25 October, but his army largely deserted him. As a consequence, the town was overrun, and the cathedral community suffered the loss of books and vestments, the relics of King Ethelbert, and much of its building fabric was damaged. According to John of Worcester, three canons and their supporters were killed defending the doors of the cathedral. The impact on the rest of the town is difficult to assess, but the damage is likely to have been considerable.

King Edward responded by appointing Earl Harold's chaplain, Leofgar, as bishop, and the latter, clearly of a military mind-set, regarded it as his mission to seek immediate revenge. Leofgar led a force which, in June 1056, attacked Gruffudd's army at Glasbury, west of Hay-on-Wye, where he was killed along with further cathedral canons, Aelfnoth, sheriff of Herefordshire, and 'many good men'.[46] Earl Harold realised the imminent danger of another attack on Hereford and beyond, and himself put in train the necessary further response. He began by repairing Hereford's neglected defences (which is now understood to have included re-cutting substantial parts of the city ditch, including the part south of the river) and simultaneously assembled an army at Gloucester 'from very nearly all England'.[47] War was, however, averted and peace negotiated at 'Bylgeslege', probably Billingsley, a place near Bolstone, at the southern limit of today's Holme Lacy parish, on what had been the border between (English) Archenfield and (Welsh)

Ergyng. In 1057, having secured Herefordshire, Harold went on campaign into Wales, building a fortress 'beyond the Golden Valley', according to one version of the Anglo-Saxon Chronicle. Meanwhile, Ralph's son Harold was given lands in the most eastern district of Ewyas, and is likely to have sponsored the building of an 'earthwork castle', apparently on the site of the present Ewyas Harold castle.[48]

The clearest picture of late Saxon Hereford is that provided by the Domesday survey of 1086, with its record of the situation in King Edward the Confessor's reign (1042-66). At this time there had been a clear distinction between the 'Civitas', presided over by the secular authority of King and Earl, with 103 royal and 27 comital burgesses owing quasi-military services (and who probably continued to occupy the northern districts), and the 'port' (or market) with its traders and craftsmen (specifically not burgesses) under the bishop's authority. The king had six moneyers in Hereford, the bishop one, this total of seven being equivalent to the situation under royal and under arch-episcopal patronage in contemporary Oxford and Canterbury respectively. Six smiths were mentioned, specifically retained to make horseshoes using the king's iron (see below).[49]

Cantilupe Street and the eastern extension of the defences

The remains of the massive defensive rampart in clay and timber that was seen in excavations at Victoria Street as a rebuilding phase of the earlier gravel rampart formed the earliest component in the sequence of Saxon town ramparts that was subsequently encountered in excavations at 5 Cantilupe Street to the north-east of the site of St Guthlac's monastery. These latter excavations also showed that the defences went through at least two further phases of augmentation. The evidence survived at Cantilupe Street, and not at Victoria Street, because here the medieval city wall circuit was built on a different course, beyond the line of the Saxon defences.[50] The

Fig. 2.8 Cantilupe Street excavation: the imprint of the wooden facing replaced in stone

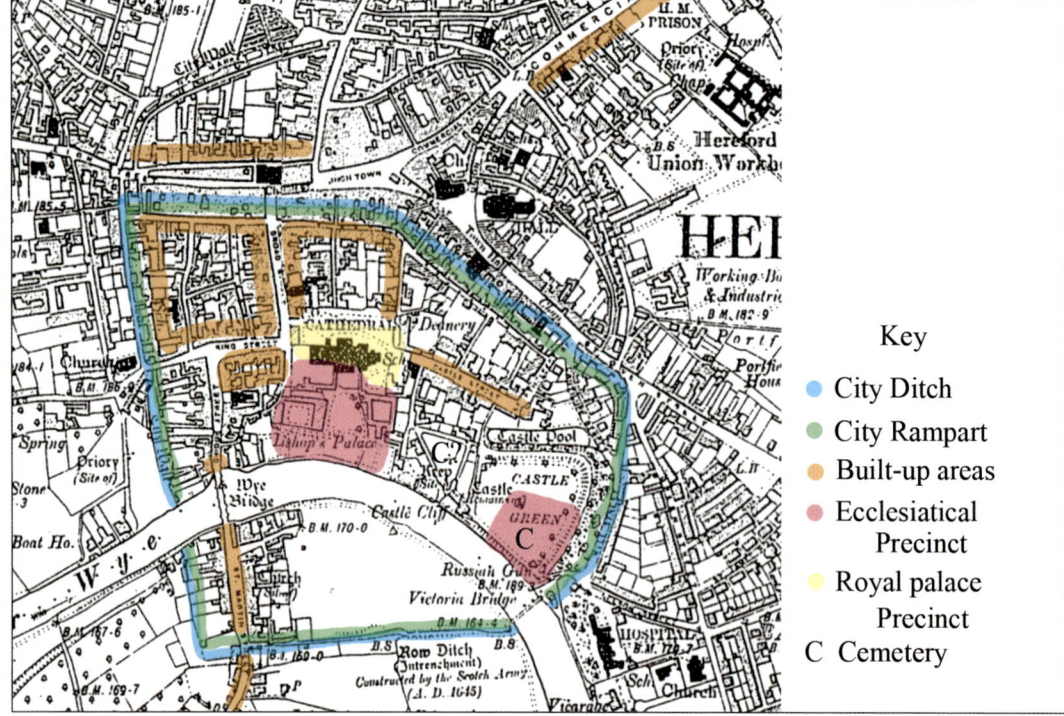

Fig. 2.9 Later Saxon Hereford

initial timber revetment at the front of the rampart was found at this site, in the form of the imprint made by the former vertical timbers and horizontal bracers in the face of the gravel bank butting up against them.[51]

The first of the two later phases saw the construction of a substantial dry-stone wall inserted in front of the timber revetment, supported by a mass of stones to fill the gap between that revetment and the new wall. Subsequently, another stone facing was added to this wall before the whole became decayed. The dating of the 'stone wall facing phases' is as problematical as that of the gravel bank (elsewhere on the defensive circuit) and timber turf and clay rampart phases that preceded them, but a best estimate is that the first phase was of early 10th-century origin, and that the stone wall phases belong later in that century.

Excavations across the Rowe Ditch which crosses the Bishop's Meadow (King George VI's Playing Fields) have in recent years produced firm dating evidence for at least one phase of ditch cutting in the mid-11th century. Not only does this indicate that Earl Harold's refurbishments affected this area, but it also allows for the suggestion that this was a rebuilding of an existing line of defences that could have had its origins as far back as the middle Saxon period.[52]

Domestic settlement

Within the Saxon walls, the timber buildings found at Berrington Street indicate the bustling nature of this part of the settlement. The pottery associated with the later phases, and dating from the mid-late 10th century through to the mid-11th century, marks a period of significant change in the form, construction methods and disposition of the structures in use. The later

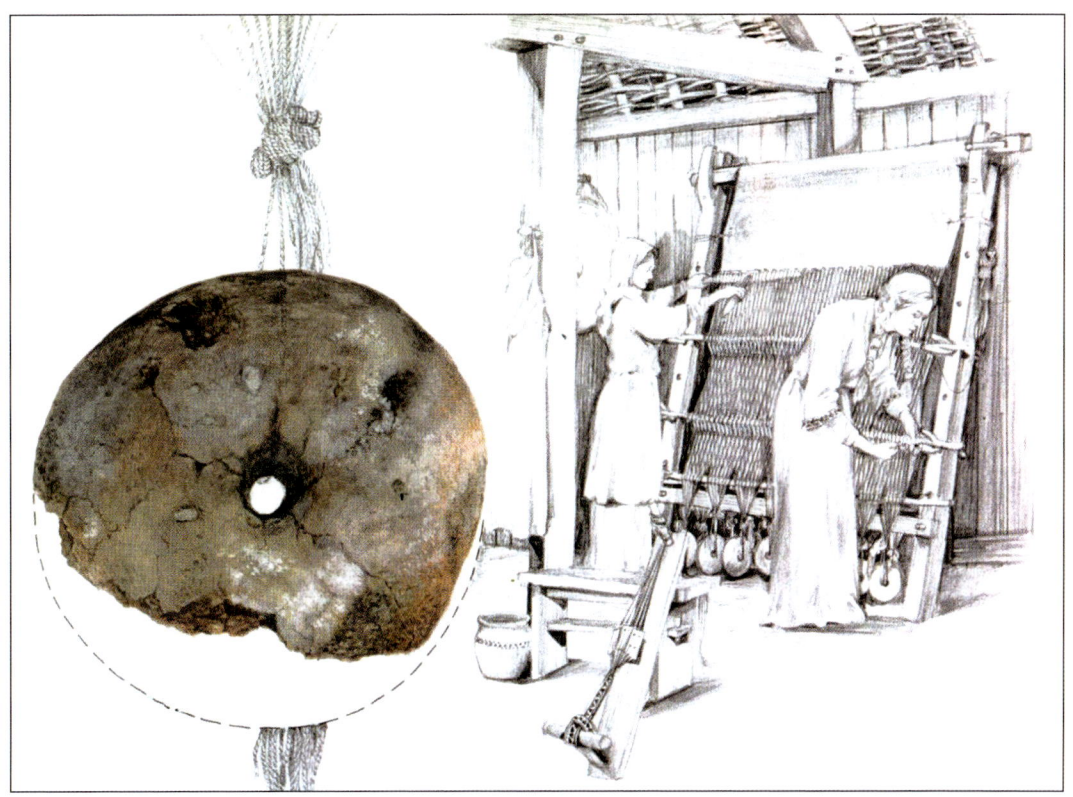

*Fig. 2.10 One of the loom weights found at the site near Castle Street with a drawing showing how the loom and building in which it was housed may have looked.
(Drawing by Brian Byron, provided courtesy of Hereford Archaeological Trust)*

phase buildings on this site were all apparently built either upon sleeper-beams set horizontally in narrow shallow gullies, or had posts inserted into such gullies, perhaps implying plank-built walls, or box-frame construction, as compared with the earlier post-built structures. All of these buildings had 'laid clay or packed earth floors', and several possessed hearths.[53] At least three buildings (of nine) had been destroyed by fire. Through time these buildings became associated with metalled areas approximating central courtyards, and the surfacing comprised pebbles but increasingly also deposits of smithing slag. Other finds included spindle whorls and clay loom weights indicative of weaving, and a variety of objects in bone, iron, copper and glass. Pottery associated with these later buildings included sherds from pots imported from as far away as Stamford (Lincolnshire) and Stafford.

Few other buildings have been recorded elsewhere in the late Saxon settlement, largely due to the destructive effects of later development upon the relevant Saxon levels, and partly due to the lack of large areas available for archaeological excavation. Another building that was destroyed by fire was intercepted in a small excavation off Castle Street. This comprised a structure with a clay floor and hearth, upon which among the ashes was found a complete loom represented by a line of clay weights (Fig. 2.10). The site concerned lay next to a north-south road, later St Ethelbert Street, that led into St Guthlac's monastery precinct (and later to the north gate of the medieval castle).

In addition to the roads already mentioned, observation of a service trench cut along the south side of King Street in 1980 produced evidence for an east-west roadway of likely late Saxon date. This comprised a timber causeway with whole tree-trunks and poles (an outer ring of one of which was radiocarbon dated to between AD 990 and 1155) laid north-south across the line of the roadway over the peaty deposits in the slight valley separating the site of the Bishop's Palace from the Wye Bridge, to link the road along the eastern side of Broad Street with the street on the line of Berrington Street. Another line of timbers at a lower depth appears to suggest that this dated surface was but one in a series of such causeways built here.

Ironworking
Traces of Anglo-Saxon ironworking have been found on a number of sites in the city, but it has only been recently that the scale of this industry has become appreciated. In addition to the sites already mentioned, substantial debris from smithing, including slag and hammer-scale, has been retrieved from two sites in Bewell Street north of the medieval All Saints church (see below). Although smithing debris was found right across the northern areas of the cathedral precinct during the recent investigations, only at the St John's Quad excavation have remains associated with this activity been found *in situ*, and they provide a window on industry in the late 10th and early 11th centuries in Hereford. A series of smithing hearths and associated light rectangular buildings were found to the north of the robbed foundation that was possibly part of a contemporary phase of construction of the cathedral itself. The location of this activity is the more significant when put together with the Domesday reference to the king's smiths, and the possible identity of a building just to the north of these hearths, which continued in existence despite their presence.[54]

A royal residence?
That there were stone buildings in late Saxon Hereford, or at least stone-founded structures, is evident from the discovery of a stone-walled basement of a building on the new cathedral library building excavation site. This was a high-status structure not far from the west end of the present cathedral, and it was clearly aligned so that its western gable-end faced onto the street running north and south. This alignment is shared with the Bishop's Palace, and it may be simplest to view it as having formed part of the Anglo-Saxon episcopal palace complex.

Around 100m due east from this stone-lined basement, excavations in 2010-11 in St John's Quad produced tantalising evidence for the presence of a former major timber-founded building. This was the earliest structure on the site, and may have featured a deliberate young male 'foundation burial' – the earliest-dated inhumation uncovered anywhere in the precinct during this work.[55] Only a 7.5m length of the southernmost wall of this building was revealed in the excavated area, but enough of its construction method and scale was evident in the length concerned to achieve an appreciation of its character. The location of a series of posts along one side of the foundation trench was complemented by a 1m diameter 1.9m deep post-pit at the western end of the exposed length. The focus for the posts-in-trench was in the centre of the length of former foundation, and a line of stones possibly representing the housing for a buttress was found to parallel this just to the south. This raises the possibility that this was the gable wall of a massive structure aligned north-south.[56] Its build method is strongly reminiscent of the contemporary royal hall at Cheddar, and it is worth noting that at major late

Fig. 2.11 Stafford-type ware of 11th-century date from the Berrington Street area (Hereford Museum Acc. no. 1987-108; photograph by Adam Stanford, © Aerial-Cam Ltd)

Saxon centres such as London and Winchester, cathedral church complexes and royal palaces co-existed side by side.

Two further groups of finds from the recent investigations reinforce the possibility of a 'royal precinct' here, referred to in the Domesday Survey of 1086 which mentions the existence of a royal hall in Hereford during Edward the Confessor's reign. The first is that animal bone finds from the levels at St John's Quad associated with this structure included both significant amounts of pig bone (indicative of feasting) and the extremely rare find of an eagle bone (eagles being associated with Anglo-Saxon kingship). The second is that not only were no definitely Saxon burials found anywhere on the northern and eastern sides of the modern cathedral precinct, but finds of domestic pottery ('Early Cotswold ware' of late 9th to early 11th century date; Stafford-type ware of the 11th century), food waste, spindle-whorls, and more metal-working hearths and debris right across the northern and western areas indicate the essentially secular but relatively high-status nature of activity here in the relevant centuries.

Such a reading of the results of the recent excavations runs counter to another line of thought that the royal precinct may have lain to the east of the cathedral, between it and the precinct of St Guthlac's, in the area where the castle motte was subsequently built. The western boundary of the St Guthlac's site is unknown, but it could well have been to the east of the site of the subsequent castle motte approximately where the present path that separates Castle Green from Redcliffe Gardens now runs. Such a location for the royal precinct would allow for what are now King Street and Castle Street having been one street running through what is now the Close and under part of the Norman cathedral. This street, on the edge of the Saxon cathedral precinct, would have been well sited to be the location of the market area or 'port' under the bishop's authority. This is not a theory especially favoured by this author as no excavation in the area of the Close has yet unearthed any evidence for such a road. Nonetheless it is appreciated that the building of the Norman cathedral would have destroyed most of the evidence, whilst the recent finds do suggest a royal rather than secular presence north of the site now identified as probably being that of the Saxon cathedral in St John's Quad.

Beyond the town walls
A quantity of 10th- and 11th-century pottery has been found at the two Bewell Street sites already mentioned, and at sites within the north-eastern angle of the medieval defences nearby (an area presently occupied by the Tesco supermarket near Bewell House). The distribution of this material, and of iron-smithing debris, points to the existence of an extramural street running east-west to the north of and parallel with the northern defences. However, this was not the only suburban activity that has come to light, with a significant concentration to the north-east, halfway down the former Bye Street (Commercial Road). Perhaps more surprising still is the late Saxon pottery that was found at Drybridge House, to the south-west even of the medieval St Martin's area. This is some distance south of the city, and is perhaps simply related to the causeway across seasonally flooded land here. However, if the southern circuit of defences is factored in from the 8th or 9th century onwards, the 'Drybridge' activity can be seen as resulting from a simple suburban expansion beyond the likely gate here.

Conclusion: towards a simplified developmental model for Saxon Hereford
Debate will no doubt continue for some while regarding the historical development of Hereford during the centuries covered in this chapter. However, some definite progress is being made towards resolving what have appeared to be contradictions in the story. The model presented here simplifies the developmental sequence of the defended settlement.[57] A possible early phase, belonging to the period of Mercian hegemony in the late 8th and early 9th century, could have featured a rectangular fort-like enclosure focused upon the river-crossing, with a partial planned settlement grid within the northern quadrants of the defended enclosure and an extramural monastic establishment to the east (Fig. 2.5). A later sequence then began in the late 9th or early 10th century, with an extension eastwards of the defended area possibly promoted by Aethelred or Aethelflaeda (Fig. 2.9). A strengthening of the defences then occurred, perhaps in Aethelstan's reign (924-35) or in that of King Edgar (957-75). After nearly a century of neglect, Harold Godwinson then refurbished the existing course following the devastation of the 1055 raid. There is now mounting evidence that, despite the lack of documentary evidence, Hereford became important during the 10th century both as a military base producing iron goods and as a royal centre with a possible palace similar to that at Cheddar, located to the north, or east, of the early cathedral.

3   The first years of the Norman Conquest

It cannot have been clear in Hereford, far from the events which had figured so largely in 1066 and where the threat from nearby Wales had always been much more immediate, that a new king at Westminster presaged any major shift in the order of things.[1] Many of William's acts in the first months of his reign were designed to emphasise the legitimacy of his position and its continuity from the reign of the Confessor. The Godwins, and all who fought with them at Hastings, were rebels; all other English were the new king's subjects as they had been Edward's. Edwin (son of Aelfgar and grandson of Leofric) remained Earl of Mercia, his brother Morcar, Earl of Northumbria.[2]

However, without the Godwins, the earldoms of southern and eastern England stood vacant, and the void was rapidly filled by King William.[3] William fitz Osbern, whose father had been King William's Steward in Normandy, was granted the great earldom which had been held by Harold, essentially the old kingdom of Wessex with the addition of Herefordshire which Harold had acquired on the death of Ralph of Mantes.[4] Early in 1067 the new king built a castle in Winchester where he installed fitz Osbern who from then on used it as his base.

Although the majority of the English leaders had quickly submitted to the new regime, there were pockets of discontent. In the Marches this burst into open warfare between two of the largest landowners. One, Eadric *Cild*, an English nobleman, often now referred to as Eadric 'the Wild' or *Sylvaticus*, was a younger kinsman of the great Mercian magnate Eadric Streona, and had extensive possessions in north-west Herefordshire and south-west Shropshire.[5] The other was Richard Scrob, a Frenchman, not necessarily a Norman, who had arrived in England as a follower of Edward the Confessor, had married the daughter of another French immigrant, Robert the Deacon, and had built at his manor of Auretone, later known as Richard's Castle, one of the first castles in England.[6]

It is in the account of this conflict that the first reference to a castle in Hereford is found. The D-version of the Anglo-Saxon Chronicle, the 'Worcester' Chronicle, records that in 1067 Eadric and the Welsh rose in rebellion and attacked the 'castelmenn' of Hereford.[7] John of Worcester is more informative, recounting that Eadric was a powerful 'minister' (thegn) whose lands were frequently attacked by the garrison of Hereford Castle (*Herefordenses castellani*) and forces of Richard Scrob. These attacks apparently were costly to the Normans, who lost many knights and 'squires'.[8] In mid-August Eadric the Wild retaliated and, allied with the Welsh leaders Blethyn and Rhywallon, laid waste to Herefordshire 'as far as the bridge over the River Lugg'.[9]

Throughout the summer of 1067, while the king was in Normandy and Eadric was raiding in Herefordshire, fitz Osbern was in Norwich,[10] watchful for invasion from Denmark. In 1068 he and the Breton Count Brian led an army against English rebels at Shrewsbury and at Exeter, and he attended the Easter Feast in Normandy in 1069. A charter granted at or shortly after the Whitsun Council of 1069 was signed firstly by the king and queen, then the clergy present, and then the laity beginning with Earl William, followed in order by the English Earls Waltheof and Edwin. Often deputising for King William in England, sometime after Christmas 1070 fitz Osbern was sent to govern Normandy. While he was leading a handful of knights to intervene in a war in Flanders, he was ambushed and killed at Cassel on 20 or 21 February 1071.

Despite his other responsibilities, fitz Osbern seemed to have paid close attention to the southern Welsh Marches, aiming to establish a firm Anglo-Norman presence on both sides of the Wye from bases at Hereford and Chepstow.

There is no doubt about the importance of fitz Osbern, although the English and the Normans had rather different views of him. For William of Poitiers, a Norman and an ex-soldier, both Earl William and Bishop Odo of Bayeux (the Conqueror's half-brother who was given control in Kent) were virtuous and pious, and while the king was in Normandy in early 1067 'burned

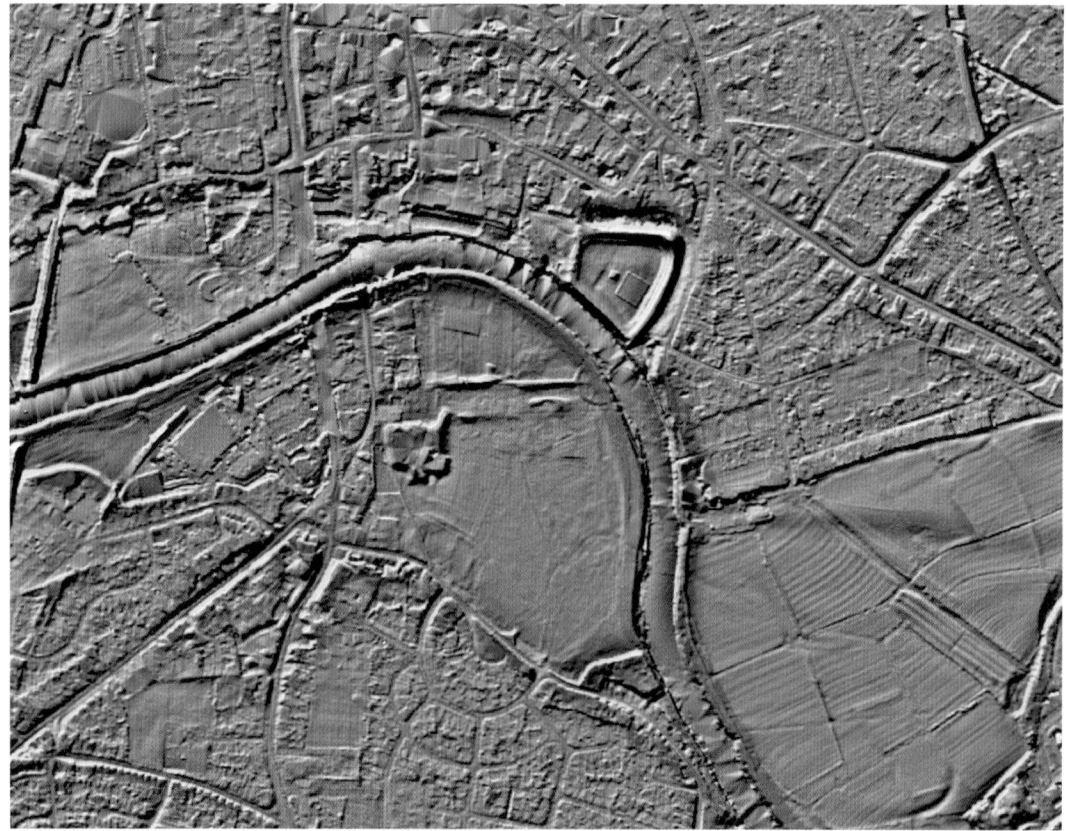

Fig. 3.1 LIDAR image showing medieval strip fields to the south-east of Hereford. Such fields once surrounded the city in the areas named Portfields, Westfields and Moorfields.

with a common desire to keep the Christian people in peace. They paid the greatest respect to justice, as the king had admonished, so that fierce men and enemies might be corrected and brought into friendship.' The partly English Orderic Vitalis presents a somewhat modified view of the conditions in England during the Conqueror's absence: 'Meanwhile the English were groaning under the Norman yoke, and suffering oppressions from the proud lords who ignored the king's injunctions. The petty lords who were guarding the castles oppressed all the native inhabitants of high and low degree, and heaped shameful burdens upon them. For Bishop Odo and William fitz Osbern, the king's vice-regents, were so swollen with pride that they would not deign to hear the reasonable pleas of the English or give them impartial judgement. When their men-at-arms were guilty of plunder or rape they protected them by force, and wreaked their wrath all the more violently upon those who complained of the cruel wrongs they suffered.'

Fitz Osbern's son, Roger of Breteuil, inherited the Hereford part of his father's earldom, a much less powerful position than his father had enjoyed. In 1075, together with his brother-in-law, Ralph, Earl of Norfolk and Waltheof, Earl of Northumberland, he rebelled against King William. Moving east to join Ralph, Roger was captured and tried. Deprived of his lands and earldom, he was sentenced to spend the rest of his life in prison, and the recently created earldom of Hereford was forfeit to the crown.

The Expansion of Hereford

In his brief four years as earl, Domesday records that fitz Osbern established and garrisoned a castle in the city and took steps to develop trade. He acquired the land 'where the market now is' from Bishop Walter in exchange for the manor of Eaton (Bishop) and some land at Lydney. The land he acquired in Hereford from Bishop Walter is almost certainly the area immediately to the north of the Saxon defences, where the market (in what is now High Town) has operated for centuries, and still does. Although the creation of this new market is not explicitly attributed to the earl, and there may have been other reasons for this land exchange (Domesday was 15 years after fitz Osbern's death) there is sufficient reason to believe that the creation of a 'new town' for Norman-French settlers was planned from the early days of the Conquest. Such new towns were a feature of the Conquest and are found at Northampton, Norwich, Nottingham, Wallingford and York.[11] Prior to 1066 it is likely

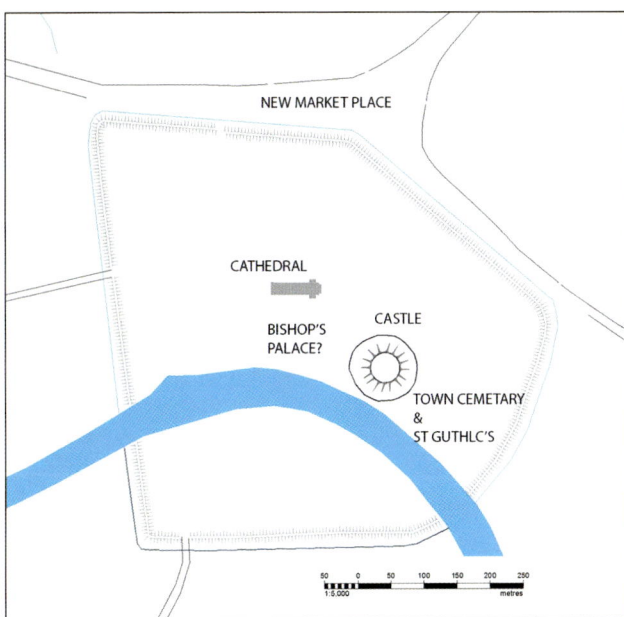

Fig. 3.1 An outline plan of early Norman Hereford. Later, a new cathedral would be built a little to the north of the Saxon one and the defensive line moved to encompass the new market area.

that markets and fairs were held in an area adjacent to the Saxon cathedral, to its west and/or north-west and possibly around a road that connected present King Street to Castle Street, though the existence of such a road is far from certain (see p.28).

The large new market-place was triangular, as was the market-place in fitz Osbern's home town of Breteuil-sur-Iton in Normandy. This coincidence has led to speculation that the shape is a deliberate copy. Triangular market-places, though, are not uncommon and occur in English towns without a Breteuil connection, such as Swaffham,[12] Worcester[13] and St Albans. At Hereford the triangular lay-out was dictated by the three roads which met to the north of the Saxon town defences: one leading west towards Wales, one south-east towards to a crossing of the River Lugg at Mordiford, and one north-east to the old Roman road where it crossed the Lugg at the place later known as Lugg Mills. These three roads converged at the North Gate of the town. The north road – the later Widemarsh Street – may have joined up with a road to the west of the cathedral. Widemarsh Street, so-called because it crossed the Wide Marsh where the Eign Brook meandered through a pre-glacial course of the River Wye, may only have been created after the establishment of the market-place and possibly after the construction of All Saints church. A study of the development of Widemarsh Street in 1997 concluded that there was no archaeological evidence for occupation earlier than the 12th century.[14] The large new market place was cobbled; the original topsoil being stripped away in order to lay the cobbles on the underlying fluvioglacial gravels.[15]

The ends of the town's strip fields next to the new market appear to have been converted to burgage plots, to accommodate a planned expansion in the population. The strip-burgages gave the 'new town' a distinctive character, quite different from the sub-rectangular plots of the bishop's part of the town. Despite this new market-place, it is not evident that the late 11th century was, in the end, a period in which Hereford saw much expansion. Although in 1067 Hereford's defences would still have been formidable (it was after all only 11 years since they had been rebuilt by Harold Godwinson), the town itself had not recovered from the devastation of 1055; a layer of burnt debris found in an excavation in Broad Street suggests the town suffered serious damage at this date.[16]

Although the market-place was the site of metal working prior to 1055, so far little archaeological evidence has been found for activity here in the late 11th or early 12th centuries. In this the archaeological record supports William of Malmesbury who, in about 1125, described Hereford as not being very big but said that it 'had once been something great'.[17] Nevertheless, Domesday records a rise in the city's render to the king to £60 by 1086, as opposed to the pre-Conquest £18, which must reflect increasing prosperity within the city. Perhaps this was due in part to the rebuilding of the cathedral by then underway, and in part to the arrival of the new French burgesses from Breteuil. These simply paid a rent of 12d per annum for their burgages, unlike their English counterparts, who lived according to their pre-Conquest customs, which carried burdensome military duties, and their arrival may have stimulated a rise in commercial activity.[18] The arrival of the French was marked in the names of two streets at the western end of the market-place, in the area of All Saints church: Bewell Street (*beau-val*) and Frenchman's Street (*vrenchemannestrete*), possibly a continuation of Eign or Bewell Street.[19]

Hereford also became the principal service centre for south Wales, and the Domesday Book mentions that the king had six moneyers in the city, who, 'when the king came to the city, …

made him as much pence as he wanted ...'.[20] Such activity and the demands from south Wales would also have stimulated Hereford's commerce.

One of the few demonstrable projects of the immediate post-Conquest period was the construction of a new house of secular canons within the new market-place. This was dedicated to St Peter and the builder was Walter de Lacy, who allegedly died falling from scaffolding during the building work.[21] Walter de Lacy, who held extensive lands in Herefordshire, also founded a secular church, St Owen's, immediately to the east of the town defences.

In *c*.1150 Osbert, son of Theobald, presumably one of the French settlers in the city, left some tenanted houses and land in Hereford to the monks of Great Malvern. This generous gift may have been related to the construction of a stone bridge over the Wye a few years earlier, under the supervision of the first prior of Great Malvern, Aldwyn, whose skills as an architect had been tested in the erection of both Great Malvern and Little Malvern priories. Matthew Paris, a century later, mentions the tradition that he was the 'surveyor' in *c*.1120 of the new Wye Bridge at Hereford.[22] It is possible that the new bridge replaced an older one, but the evidence for this is rather circumstantial. However, there can be no doubt that a new stone-arched bridge was of considerable value to the burgeoning merchant community in Hereford, whose commercial aspirations looked, particularly, towards the undeveloped hinterland to the west.

The Citizens of the new Hereford

Although Norman and French soldiers and churchmen settled in Hereford after the Conquest there was some continuity of people holding official positions from the reign of Edward the Confessor. The most prominent of these was Bishop Walter of Lorraine. Walter was one of the English leaders who had submitted to William at Berkhamsted in December 1066 and would have worked closely with fitz Osbern as the new regime settled in.[23] He attended ecclesiastical councils held at Windsor in May 1072 and at London a few years later. Little is known of Walter's activities otherwise and no charters of his survive. Walter's place of burial is not known and the only account of his death is in William of Malmesbury's *Gesta pontificum*, which recounts that Walter was killed by a seamstress for whom he had developed a long-lasting passion and had finally attempted to rape, whereupon she had stabbed him with a pair of scissors. The king is alleged to have endeavoured to suppress the story. Malmesbury qualifies the story with 'if rumour is to be believed', though the silence of other sources on Walter's death may perhaps suggest that his decease was not wholly respectable.[24]

Other officials who remained in post from the reign of Edward included moneyers. Earnwig, who had struck coins in Hereford for Harold I Harefoot of the Fleur-de-lys type in 1038-40, coins of Edward's 'Sovereign / Eagles' type dated to 1056-59 and of Harold II's Pyramid' type in 1066, would continue at the Hereford mint after the Conquest, striking coins of the 'Bonnet type' (1068-70) for William. Other moneyers who continued striking coins under the new regime included Eadwig, Aelfwig and Æthelstan.

The Governance of the City

The city was divided into four fees, those of the King, the Bishop, the Dean and Chapter and, as from the mid 12th century, the Hospital of St John in Widemarsh Street Without (i.e. outside the walls). The king's fee, the 'civitas', which was the largest, contained the castle and the area occupied by the burgesses. This was separated from the bishop's fee by the King's Ditch and included the area close to the cathedral. Those that lived in each fee owed their rent or other duties to the respective owner of that fee. In practice the owner would 'farm' out the collection of any rents and dues (which would also include market tolls and court amercements or fines) to the highest bidder, who in turn would gather in and administer the monies payable. As the person who had the 'farm' would aim to make as much profit as possible, by fair means and sometimes foul, the city sought its own charter so as to be able to manage affairs for itself on payment of a fixed fee. This came with the grant of a charter by Richard I in 1189 (see pp.38-9). However, the charter could not grant self-government to those men who lived in the bishop's fee, and the difference between the two sets of city dwellers would cause contention for years. Subsequently arrangements, for example, had to be made between the citizens and the bishop's men about which parts of the city wall would be the responsibility of which group and whose courts had jurisdiction at different times and in different parts of the city. Richard's charter was, however, the foundation of the city's self-government.

Subsequent charters gave rights to those who lived in the area of the king's fee to hold specific fairs, refined the administration of justice, gave protection to the goods of those who died intestate, allowed the use of tolls to repair the city defences, and created the right to have a merchant guild, the right to elect a mayor rather than a chief bailiff, and the right to acquire a house for use as a court house.

Tolls were kept at a low level so as not to discourage trade, and the records that survive of the amounts collected in September 1264-5 and again in May 1299 show that the Wyebridge Gate was the most heavily used by traders, supporting the case that Hereford was a service centre for south Wales. On each occasion the next gate most used by traders was St Owen's Gate, which was at the end of the road from Gloucester across Mordiford Bridge. During some weeks the other gates on the east and the north collected no tolls.[25]

4   The early Castle, the City Walls and Gates

The walled Saxon city enclosed an area of some 21 hectares on the northern bank of the Wye and 7 hectares on the southern. Although these early defences had been damaged during the Welsh invasion of 1055, restoration works including, at the very least, the deepening and widening of the city ditch, had been carried out by Harold Godwinson shortly before the Norman Conquest (see chapter 2).

In the north of the settlement the old Saxon defensive wall, rampart and ditch ran parallel and just to the south of the new Norman market-place (see chapter 3) so it would not have been long before the redundant defences were dismantled. The embankment would have been gradually levelled, eventually narrowing the ditch until it became little more than an open sewer. The situation was different on the eastern side of the city where the Saxon defensive works were incorporated into the embankment that surrounded the bailey of the expanded castle following the Anarchy and St Guthlac's move to the Bye Street suburb. Indeed, the old defences presumably still lie buried beneath the eastern embankment of Castle Green. On the western side of the Saxon city the defences probably fell into disuse as the stone wall gradually collapsed under the pressure of the embankment piled up behind it. Although the defensive line was still recognisable as including a wall at the time of the Domesday survey, it continued to deteriorate thereafter. It is therefore not surprising that early in the 12th century William of Malmesbury should mention 'the ruines of many broken ditches'.[1] This comment may also indicate that the grand design of William fitz Osbern had not been as successful as had been intended and that the city had tended towards stagnation following his death in 1071.

It is apparent that, by the beginning of the 12th century, the castle was the only strongpoint – the contemporary accounts of the fighting during the Anarchy in 1138-40 (see pp.36-37) make no mention of there being any city defences and it was only the castle that was besieged. The lack of defences in this period is not particularly surprising as the 12th century does not seem to have been a period when town fortifications were considered to be of any great importance.[2]

The early Castle
As noted in chapter 3, the first reference to a castle in Hereford is in the post-Conquest feud between Eadric the Wild and Richard Scrob, when the 'castlemenn' of Hereford are mentioned, and there had been several raids on Eadric's lands by Normans based in Hereford by early August 1067 at the latest. It follows that the garrison must have been established in the city by late spring or early summer, when they would have set about constructing a safe fortification

– the beginning of the castle. Of this first structure there are neither any documentary references nor archaeological evidence.

The most likely position for Hereford's first castle is where the motte was later known to have been, in the area between the precincts of the cathedral and St Guthlac's. A similar development of a royal site is believed to have occurred at Wallingford, where the Norman castle was built on a site where, before 1066, Edward the Confessor had held 15 acres of land on which his housecarls used to dwell.[3] It may also have occurred at Stamford where a substantial enclosure pre-dated the Norman castle.[4]

It has long been considered that the earliest Norman castles built in England were earth and timber fortifications of the motte and bailey type.[5] However, analysis in Normandy shows that many castles constructed in the early 11th century were simple enclosures, and it may have been that the first castle at Hereford took this form.[6] Although the design of the earliest Hereford castle is unknown, it would not have been long before the classic motte was built in the city.

The Anarchy: Stephen and Matilda

Henry I, the fourth son of William the Conqueror, ascended the throne in AD1100, succeeding his brother, William Rufus. Henry died at his hunting lodge at Lyons-la-Forêt in Normandy on 1 December 1135, having sworn his barons to accept his daughter, Matilda, as his successor, but the decision was not popular in the Anglo-Norman Court. Thus, as soon as he had news of Henry's death, his nephew, Stephen of Blois crossed the Channel to claim the throne, being crowned by the archbishop of Canterbury on 22 December 1135.

On 1 January 1136, with Stephen's uncle not yet buried, the Welsh of Glamorgan annihilated a Norman force in north Gower and the situation rapidly deteriorated in Wales. However England was beset with its own problems – in April 1138, in one of the first acts of the rebellion which later historians would call 'The Anarchy', Geoffrey Talbot overwhelmed the garrison and seized Hereford Castle for Matilda. Stephen immediately led an army to Hereford and besieged Talbot in the castle. The castle soon fell, but Talbot had moved to the de Lacy castle at Weobley where Stephen pursued him. Talbot again slipped away, back to Hereford where he burnt the suburbs south of the Wye. This event may have had important consequences for Hereford's subsequent development, as the defences that had given some protection to the southern suburb were never repaired (see below). At Whitsun 1138 – Sunday 22nd May – Stephen wore his crown in the unfinished Hereford Cathedral.

Meanwhile the rebellion spread. Earl Robert of Gloucester declared for Matilda during the summer of 1138 and Miles of Gloucester, sheriff of Gloucester, in the autumn of 1139. In December, Miles laid siege to Hereford Castle, turning the cathedral into a stronghold. During this period, Stephen seems to have approached Hereford twice, both times from the north. The first occasion was late in 1139, when a truce was arranged so as not to conduct warfare during Advent, which gave those besieged in Hereford Castle some respite. The second time was in January or early February 1140, when he made a grant to Robert, Earl of Leicester of the castle, borough and county of Hereford.[7] However, Stephen was in no position to fulfil this grant, soon withdrawing for a second time.

In the late spring of 1140 Miles tried again to take Hereford Castle, this time enlisting the support of Geoffrey Talbot, who used his recent experience of being besieged in the castle. The description of the siege by Robert de Bec, one of Stephen's adherents, may be an eyewitness account:

> Geoffrey Talbot ... endeavoured to besiege the soldiers whom the king had left in the town of Hereford as defenders of the country and ministers and guardians of his right. And entering into the church the episcopal seat, dedicated to the Mother of God, and irreligiously driving away the ministers of God's table, he ... turned the house of prayer, the place for the propitiation of souls, into a den of war and blood. It was really horrible, and not to be borne by persons of pious dispositions, to see the abode of life and salvation changed into a retreat for plunderers and fighting men; the citizens in tears uttering loud cries, either because the burial-place of their friends was thrown up against the ramparts of the castle, and they saw the bodies of their relations, some half putrefied, others very lately buried (a cruel spectacle), drawn without remorse from their graves; or because on the tower, whence they used hear the sweet and peaceful summons of the bells, they now saw engines erected, and missile weapons thrown against the king's men. Geoffrey, therefore, from the church vehemently assaulted the king's soldiers, who were shut up in their castle; and Milo of Gloucester, on another side, carrying on the siege with machines, very much straitened them so that at last they were forced to surrender the castle of Hereford.

The burial place which was 'thrown up against the ramparts of the castle' was presumably the one which surrounded St Guthlac's monastery on Castle Green. The description indicates that it was still in use although it was abandoned shortly afterwards when the St Guthlac's community moved to their new site outside the city about 1143.

One of the most enigmatic features of Hereford Castle is the prominence known as 'Hogg's Mount' sited at the north-east corner of Castle Green and still visible although heavily landscaped. This has been sometimes interpreted as the first motte at Hereford, dating from fitz Osbern's time, only later being superseded by a later motte to the east of Castle Green, (long known as Castle Hill until it was demolished in the mid 1650s).[8] Robert de Bec's description may help our understanding of the origins of Hogg's Mount. The 'engines' erected on the cathedral tower were probably trebuchets, capable of slinging heavy stones (probably those not yet used in completing the building of the new cathedral) as far as the castle and causing considerable damage, but incapable of throwing such missiles as far as Hogg's Mount. It may therefore be that Hogg's Mount was constructed as a siege castle, built to mount an additional trebuchet or similar weapon to attack the castle from 'another side'.

No mention is made of the defences of the city itself in the, admittedly sparse, accounts of these actions, and it is a reasonable inference that they had not been repaired since William of Malmesbury had observed their ruinous condition a few years earlier. But Miles of Gloucester was a serious soldier, and having improved the defences of the castle and borough of Gloucester it is not improbable that, in order to secure his rear during the siege of Hereford Castle, he improved the defences of the town. It is possible that news that Hereford had been placed in a strong defensive posture might have deterred the royalist army.

In 1141 Matilda created Miles of Gloucester, Earl of Hereford, granting to him and his heirs 'the castle and moat of Hereford'. Miles died in 1143 and was succeeded by his son Roger as Earl of Hereford. Hereford, like Gloucester and Bristol, was to remain an Angevin city until the Treaty of Winchester in the summer of 1153 which effectively ended the war and settled the succession on Henry, Matilda's son. Stephen died in 1154 and Henry II granted 'the motte of Hereford with the whole castle' to Roger, but resumed possession of it when Roger rebelled in the following year, and for the rest of its history Hereford remained a royal castle.

The extended Gravel Rampart
The initial impetus for the construction of new extended defences for Hereford must have taken place during the Angevin period, probably carried out by Miles of Gloucester or his son Earl Roger, as there is a mention of St Owen's Gate (doubtless a wooden structure) by 1155 in a charter of Roger.[9] The limited amount of pottery which has been found sealed underneath the extended rampart during archaeological excavations is of early to mid-12th-century date and earlier and tends to suggest that the bank was indeed built some time about the mid 1100s. The new enclosure consisted initially of a gravel embankment made from material excavated from the external ditch. Although the prime need would have been to incorporate the Norman market-place and the new town with its French settlers within the defensive circuit, it was apparent that some parts of the earlier defences were able to be reused. On the western side of the city there had apparently been no expansion beyond the line of the Saxon defences and it would have been a relatively simple matter to strengthen and reuse these earthworks. To the east of the Saxon town the castle and St Guthlac's monastery formed the premier line of defence and nothing more was required (Fig. 4.1).

The main difficulty would have been to the north where there would have been several problems to overcome. The new defensive line would have had to be designed so as to be as short as possible because of the cost and the difficulty of defending a large enclosure. Even so, it would have to enclose all the buildings of importance in the market-place and as many of the burgage plots on the approach roads as practicable. In addition, it would have been essential to ensure that the defensive capabilities of the new works were not compromised by existing buildings. Finally, the extended defensive line would have needed access roads and additional gates.

This extended northern defence was doubtless the gravel rampart and ditch examined in several excavations in the 1960s and '70s.[10] There is no evidence for any facing to the embankment in this earliest phase. An indication of the size of the earthworks has been obtained from archaeological investigations.[11] Allowing for a 3m wide berm – the area between the bank and the ditch edge, necessary to prevent rapid erosion and the consequent silting of the ditch – the rampart was probably about 12m wide and a maximum of some 3m high. The ditch was probably a similar width to the rampart and the whole defensive feature would therefore have been some 27m wide. It is assumed that from the beginning the intention was for the ditch to hold water around the whole circuit, although this cannot be demonstrated. If this was the case there would have had to be a reliable source of water and bridges would have been needed in front of each gate. To form the bridges the ditch would probably have been narrowed on its approaches to the road lines. Adjustments may also have been made to the width of the ramparts at these points, resulting in a decrease in the total defensive width to perhaps 20m or less.

In 1189, in part to pay for his campaigns overseas, Richard I gave a charter to the city which includes:

> Richard by the grace of God King of England Duke of Normandy and Aquitaine and Count of Anjou, to the archbishops, bishops, abbots, earls, barons, justices, sheriffs, ministers, and all his faithful subjects both French and English throughout England, greeting. Know that we have granted to our citizens of Hereford in Wales the town of Hereford to hold for ever for £40 to be paid yearly to the Exchequer. So that they shall give help

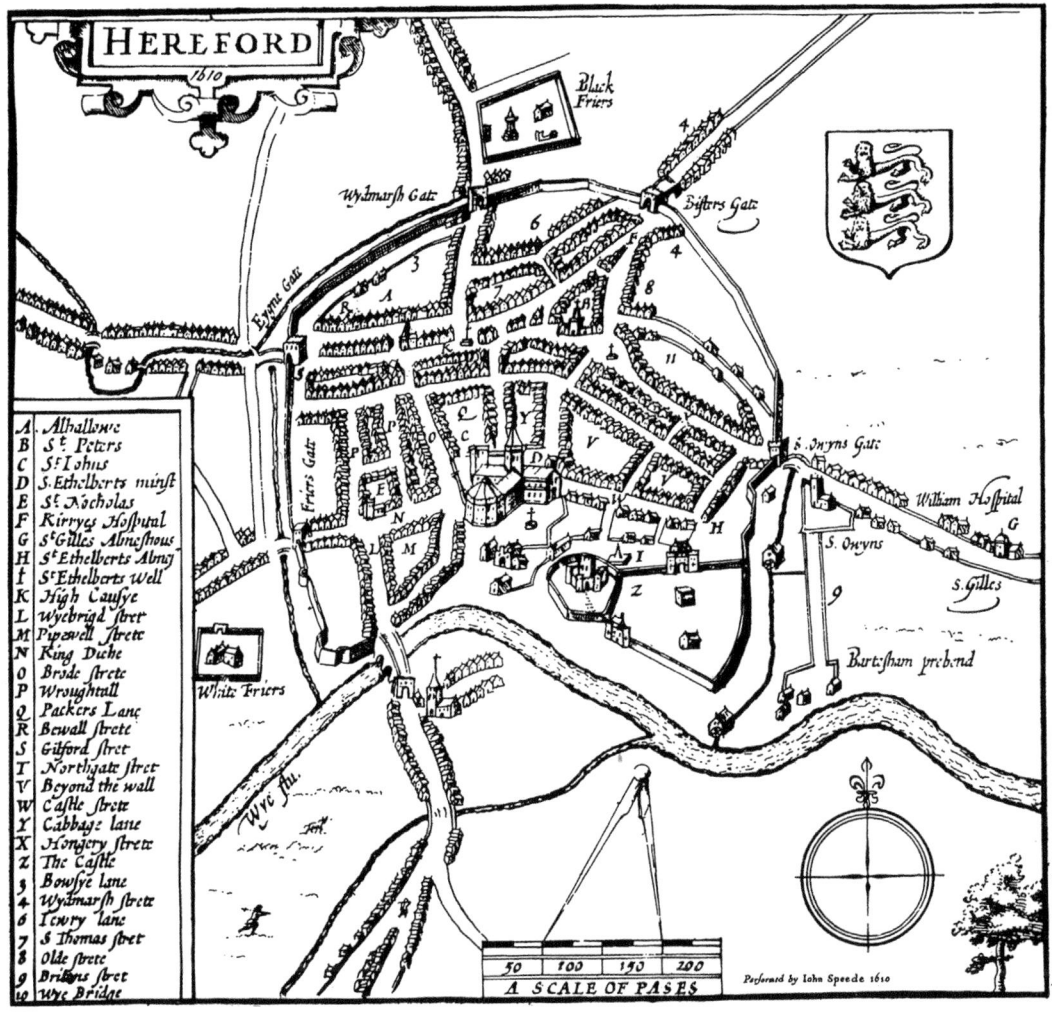

Fig. 4.1 John Speed's map of Hereford of 1610, showing the line of the city walls, the position of the various gates and how the wall linked to the castle.

in fortifying the town. And they have given us 40 marks of silver for this grant. And so we order that they shall have and hold this said town for ever for the same rent with all its liberties and free customs with all its appurtenances. So that none of our sheriffs shall impose his administration on them in any plea or suit or dispute or in any matter appertaining to the town.[12]

In addition to the encouragement to improve the defences of the city, this charter was the foundation of Hereford's independence as an incorporated borough, with the administration of law being carried out by officers appointed by the people.

Towards the end of the 12th century the increase in tension on the Welsh border may also have encouraged work on the defences. Rhys ap Gruffydd raided Painscastle in 1195, so if they had not already completed the new fortifications for the city, this event would doubtless have been of sufficient concern to the burgesses to persuade them to take rapid action. In addition, by the beginning of the 13th century, England was faced with the possibility of invasion from France. With this dual threat it is not surprising to find Richard of Devizes commenting that, during the absence of King Richard, 'castles were strengthened, towns were fortified, and moats were dug'.[13]

It may well be that the gates were the first parts of the defensive circuit to be rebuilt, for it was in 1190, the year after the charter was granted, that the sheriff had an allowance of £56 0s 8d 'for the making of four city gates, and one gate at the castle'.[14] On the west was Friars' Gate, surviving from the old Saxon defences, and in the northern extension Eign Gate, Widemarsh Gate, Bye Street Gate and St Owen's Gate. This may well have been the occasion when the timber gateways were replaced in stone.

Before murage grants (licences which allowed the citizens to levy a toll on goods coming into the town for sale in the market, monies which were then to be spent on the building and repair of the town's defences) first appeared in 1220, several towns received gifts in cash or kind to help with the construction of defences. This may have been the reason that the bailiff of Hereford was allowed to keep the 100 marks due to the king in October 1215 for having their city 'at farm'.[15] It is also significant that the city had a grant of timber in 1216;[16] a similar grant of timber to Winchester in the previous year had been specifically for making the 'turrets of the city and to make the wall walks'.[17] Certainly by 1223, when Henry II visited Hereford, the embankment must have been substantially complete, for they received an additional defence of brushwood and thorn palings.[18]

The Defences south of the river

A rampart and ditch was built on the south side of the river, probably before the Conquest (see p.24) and, at a later date, would have been used to protect the St Martin's suburb and the approaches to Wye Bridge. This Saxon earthwork shows no sign of any stone facing but excavations have shown that the ditch was cut or re-cut in the mid 11th century, probably as part of the repairs works of Harold Godwinson.[19] It may, however, have been abandoned after the Conquest, although Taylor's map of 1757 does show an enigmatic feature called 'The Wall'. The condition must have been poor in 1138 when Geoffrey Talbot burnt the town 'beyond the River Wye' as mentioned above. The embankment and associated ditch, together known as Rowe Ditch, crosses Bishop's Meadow and excavations have been carried out on the ditch line at Drybridge House indicating that it was water-logged, some 4m deep and up to 12m wide.[20] The external ditch was probably filled in during the Civil War when the embankment was used in reverse by the besieging Scots army in 1645.[21] The bounds of the royal forest of Haywood which had extended to South Bridge (later called Drybridge) were extended to the banks of the Wye to include the vacated part of the town (see also p.52). When the town defences were improved by stone walls in the 13th century, the severance was made explicit by the construction of a stone gateway at the southern end of the bridge.

The addition of the stone face to the Defences

The first murage grant to the city was in 1224 and may have reflected the inadequacy of the existing defences. The money raised was to be used to face the whole of the defensive circuit with stone and to build or repair the gates. The grant was renewed regularly, but even so the work was to take at least 40 years to complete. The lack of progress was such that a special mandate was issued to the mayor in 1251 to complete the work,[22] at a time when Henry III was waging an increasingly fierce war against the Welsh and was frequently in Hereford, where his royal castle was being almost totally rebuilt (see chapter 5). It would seem that the ramparts to the south of the river were largely abandoned and an effort was made to build a wall on the north bank of the Wye. This was apparently completed from the Wye Bridge westwards and there are traces underneath Wyebridge House, but there is no indication of a wall, or indeed any defensive feature, upstream of the Wye Bridge as far as the castle.

In 1262 Llywelyn ap Gruffudd ravaged Herefordshire as far as Weobley, and the burgesses of Hereford must have realised that their city could be in some danger. The work of strengthening the defences in stone was probably completed around the whole 1,645m circuit by 1265. Hereford was then considered to be as strong a walled town as any in England (Fig 4.1).

The methods used in constructing the wall, which followed the line of the earlier gravel rampart, differed from place to place around the circuit. To the north and south of Friars' Gate, the earlier defences were cut back to a vertical face and a 0.7m thick stone wall was built in front of it. Around the northern part of the circuit, the wall was built free-standing on the berm and was 0.8m wide. Along the excavated section behind what is now St Owen Court, the 2.4m wide foundations for the wall were built into the re-cut Saxon ditch.

The wall included 17 semi-circular towers of which two remain. They were apparently built at the same time as the defensive wall and had walls varying from 1.3 to 2m in thickness. In places, where the wall was built on the berm, the towers had to be built down into the face of the ditch.

The surviving Saxon defences, the mid-12th century gravel rampart, and material thrown up from widening and deepening the ditch, provided a substantial embankment within the wall line. This embankment provided both a fighting platform and an easy means of access around the wall. Several sections of this intra-mural access eventually became formal roads, other parts being assimilated into the properties which backed onto them.

The sections of city wall which survive are of many periods and it is difficult to isolate any parts which can be conclusively defined as original.[23] Even the two surviving bastion towers (one near the old bridge, Fig. 4.4, the other in the stretch of wall to the north of where Friars' Gate stood) are of differing sizes and design suggesting either different constructional dates or substantial modification and repair. Where the foundations of sections of the wall have been examined archaeologically, additional evidence of rebuilding has been established.[24]

The City Gates

The city gates, all demolished before 1800, were the most significant features of the defences. Fortunately drawings, sketches and paintings survive of most of the gates and, allowing for a measure of artistic licence which is apparent in some of the pictures, they can be used to add a considerable amount of information to the defensive story.

There were six main gates into the city (including the one on Wye Bridge) and at least three postern gates – the latter being apparently of 15th-century date.[25] The only gate position re-used from the Saxon defences was on the western side where the minor road from Breinton approached the city. This was Friars' Gate, used by the monastic settlement at Greyfriars and the least used of the six gates. It is the only gate for which no illustrations have been found apart from the schematic illustration on Speed's 1610 map of the city (Fig. 4.1) and the west prospect of 1721 (Fig. 4.2).

Fig. 4.2 The west prospect of the city in 1721 showing Friars' Gate on the left.

There was a gate on the southern end of the Wye Bridge but this was very badly damaged during the Civil War and although it is shown partially on Speed in 1610, there is no indication of it on Taylor's 1757 map. The only illustration with any detail is a sketch drawn in 1685 with the archway only barely surviving and the rest of the gate in ruins (Fig. 4.3). There are no means of dating this gate but it may well have been built or rebuilt at the same time as the main part of the bridge in 1490.

To the south of the river there may have been an outer gateway where the line of Rowe Ditch crossed the road running southwards from the bridge. This is shown on Taylor's map as Dry Bottom and as a bridge over a stream on Speed. The lack of any indication of a gate on the latter puts its existence in some doubt, although it may, together with the defences on the south side of the river, have fallen into disuse and been demolished well before the Civil War.

Eign Gate was of some considerable importance for it guarded the road leading into the city from the west; the direct road from Wales. The only sketch that has been found is one

Fig. 4.3 A sketch of 1685 showing the bridge with a ruined gate at its southern end.

Fig. 4.4 The remains of the bastion to the south of Friars' Gate (see Fig. 4.2).

Fig. 4.5 A drawing of Eign Gate made in 1784.

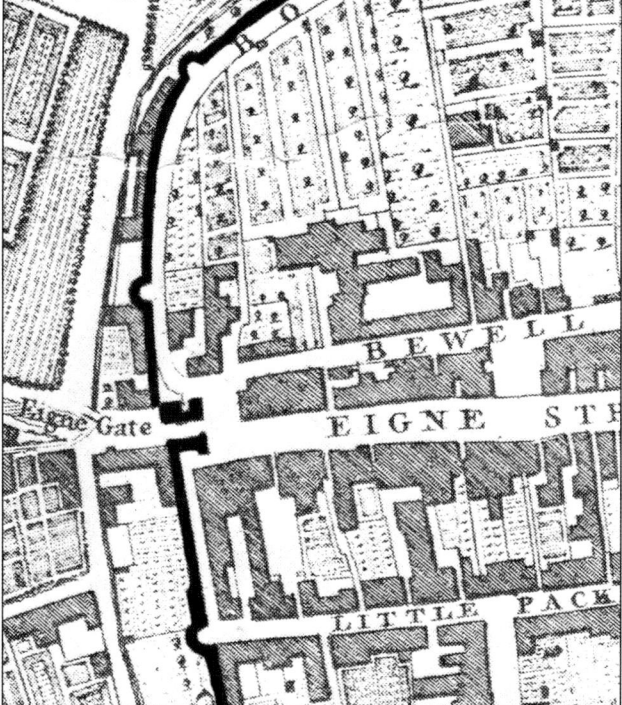

Fig. 4.6 Taylor's map of 1757 showing the offset in the city wall at Eign Gate.

drawn in 1784 (Fig. 4.5). Only the outer arch and the flanking towers survived – the upper portion had completely gone. However, it has similarities with Bye Street Gate, with a two-centred arch of several moulded orders not continuing down the jambs. The drawing does not show that the approach walls on each side of the gate are offset, the one to the north being set forward, but the extent was sufficient to be indicated on Taylor's map (Fig. 4.6).

Widemarsh Gate provided the access into the city from the north. Although originally designed to be defensive, by 1634 the only means of blocking the arch was 'a little iron chaine, knee high on the outside'.[26] A painting by George Samuel and a series of watercolours by James Wathen show the internal and external aspects, one of the latter showing demolition taking place (Figs. 4.7, 4.8 and 4.9). The gateway was not very tall, and had a two-centred head. Above the gateway was a first-floor chamber, lit on each side by a tall, central window which could have been original. Above the outer window was a horizontal string course, above which was a series of projecting corbels that may have been associated with a former machicolation that was destroyed when the upper parts of the gatehouse were rebuilt and reroofed probably in the 17th century. Flanking the gateway were two narrow projecting towers topped by the remains of a parapet, presumably part of former battlements. At ground-floor level in the eastern tower was a mullioned and

44

*Fig. 4.7 (top left) Widemarsh Gate c.1795 by George Samuel.
(© Herefordshire Museum Service, ref.1552)*
Fig. 4.8 (lower left) Widemarsh Gate by James Wathen showing demolition underway.
Fig. 4.9 (above) Widemarsh Gate from inside the walls by James Wathen in June 1798.

transomed window, presumably inserted for the benefit of the gatekeeper. On the inner face of the gatehouse there was a doorway immediately west of the passage and a niche containing a statue above it (Fig. 4.9).

The wall approaching the gatehouse from the west was offset to the south by some 5m from the line of the wall on the east. On the eastern side of the gate passage was a timber-framed building. It may have formed part of the gatekeeper's lodgings and would originally have been protected by the wall. In 1582, Thomas Church, a dyer, who lived adjacent to the Widemarsh Gate, asked permission to 'make one little doore through the Towne wall so thend [then] your said orator may the better washe his coloured clothes … And for the same wilbe glad to keepe one lowpe [?loop or stretch] of the said wall, in sufficient reparacons'. He promised to keep the door in 'suche sorte that it should not by any means be prejudiciall or hurtfull to the citty'.[27] The door still survives with Thomas Church's initials carved on the lintel. His house still stands, with parts dating back to the 16th century, on the corner of Widemarsh Street and the inner ring road.[28] The dating of the gatehouse from the surviving illustration is difficult, but the rectangular design and corbelling along the external face would suggest a 14th century date. On the western side of the gateway there was sufficient room between the set-back wall and the ditch for a narrow building – an inn – to be built, which is reflected in the position of the present late 19th-century Wellington Inn. An inserted doorway led through the wall from the inn into the city.[29]

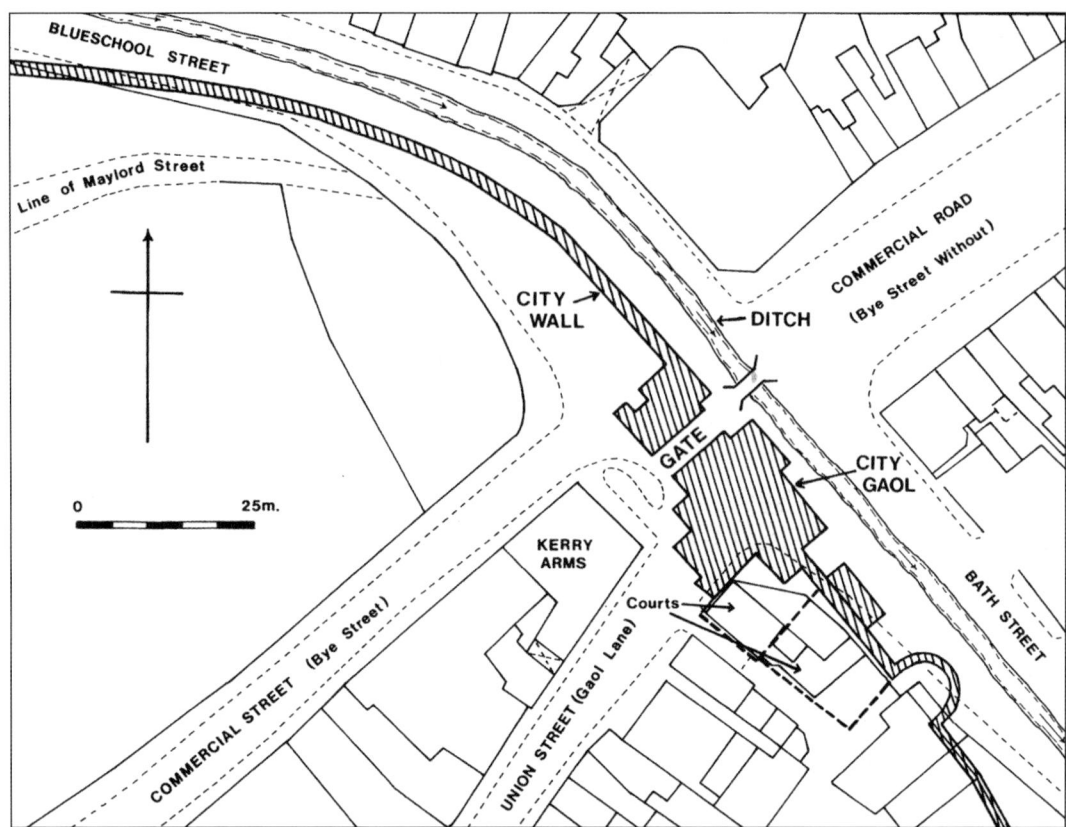

Fig. 4.10 A plan showing the approximate positions of Bye Street Gate, city gaol and the city wall under what is now the junction of Blueschool Street, Bath Street, Commercial Road, Commercial Street and Union Street.

The most important entry into the city was from the north-east, the approach from Worcester, and it was here that the most impressive gateway stood. The Bye Street or Byster's Gate had a dual function, to defend the entry into the city, and to serve as the city gaol (Figs. 4.10 & 4.11).

There are several similarities with the Widemarsh Gate – once again the walls were offset, the western part being set forward. It also had a tall, two-centred arched gateway which was flanked externally by attached towers, the one to the north being slim like those at Widemarsh Gate whilst the southern one was much wider. The external window, lighting the room above the passage, was quite ornate, with a two-centred head and a drip mould with decorated terminals. The two statues which stood in the niches above the gate passage have recently been found and sold by auction (Fig. 4.13). Although the evidence is fragmentary, it is likely that there were machicolations on top of the gatehouse with parapets around the flanking towers. However, the building had been reroofed by the 18th century, destroying many of the defensive features.

To the south of the gate the buildings that comprise the city gaol appear to envelop the wall for a distance of some 20m and were probably later additions. Small timber-framed buildings had been erected some time after the Civil War on the berm on both sides of the entrance

Fig. 4.11 Bye Street Gate shortly before its demolition as painted by George Samuel.
(© Herefordshire Museum Service, ref.1553)

Fig. 4.12 The demolition of the city wall adjacent to Widemarsh Gate photographed by Alfred Watkins in the 1930s.

Fig. 4.13 The figures of two knights that were set in the niches at first-floor level on the outside of Bye Street Gate (see Fig. 4.11).

The Prison at Byster's Gate[30]

At the beginning of the 16th century, and probably much earlier, the city gaol was situated within the southern part of the Byster's Gate complex. In the early 17th century the gaol had a rather dubious reputation; it was recorded that in a nine-month period during 1624/5, 12 prisoners died there. However, the verdict of 15 jurymen was that nine of them died from God's visitation; one poisoned herself; one was drowned in the River Wye; and one 'did casually fall out of the gallery of the Boothall'.[31]

The gaol continued to be notorious into the latter part of the 17th century. In 1691, in a booklet entitled *The Cry of the Oppressed*, Moses Pitt described the actions of the gaoler, one William Huck, 'a common lewd person, a swearer, curser, liar, drunkard ... a common hunter of whore houses' etc. who 'murthered one Mary Bar[n]ard, a prisoner, that was under his care ... by knocking her on the head with the gaol keys'. As for the conditions, 'The said gaoler keeps his swine, geese, ducks and hens, stinking, and breeding diseases among the prisoners'.

Summary punishment for offenders was normal. Thus in 1699, the town council ordered the chief gaoler and his deputy to 'cause the several bodies of seven people [including women] prisoners, committed to your custody, to be duly whipt as usuall in such cases and that then after you immediately set their bodies at liberty'.[32] It would seem that the late 18th-century Acts of Parliament regarding the care of prisoners did not worry the council too much. However, in November 1792 they did note that the prison 'is at present in a very ruinous and bad state of repair and very insecure and incommodious for the confinement of prisoners'.[33] Although they accepted an estimate for alterations and repairs in 1797,[34] the works were apparently not extensive. Byster's Gate was demolished the following year, but the gaol buildings remained and continued in use,[35] as illustrated in a letter from one James Nield to a Doctor Lettson of London in 1803. At that time there were only four prisoners and a lunatic in the gaol.[36]

> This gaol is in the Bye Street Gate, in which one room is called the Bridewell. It has a small Court with a sewer in it, and the Whipping-post. For Common-side Debtors here is a Free Ward, to which the Corporation allows straw: they have a little Court, about 15 feet square, with a sewer; and it is well supplied with water. Master's-side Debtors have two Rooms in the Keeper's house, for which they pay 2s. 6d. per week each single bed; or if two sleep together, 1s. 6d. each. For Felons here are two small Court-yards, about 15 feet square, with a sewer in each, and well supplied with water.
>
> In one of the Courts, down eleven steps, are two horrid dungeons totally dark (apparently no longer used). The Felons have also three close offensive Sleeping-rooms, which I found scattered over with loose straw on the floor, dirty, and worn to dust. Here is likewise one room, justly denominated 'The Black Hole', which, if not impenetrably dark, has no light or ventilation, save what is faintly admitted through a small aperture in the door: it is supplied with a barrack bedstead and loose straw; and in this wretched sink-hole was a poor deranged man, in the most filthy and pitiable state that it is possible to conceive.

Nield was a supporter of the prison reformer John Howard, and his criticisms clearly had some effect for a later visitor to the gaol described the conditions as much improved.[37] By 1827 the gaol contained four cells for men and three for women, all for felony and misbehaviour; there were also three sleeping rooms for debtors. In 1842 it was finally replaced by new buildings on the north side of Gaol Street and the old prison was demolished shortly afterwards.

roadway. The building to the north of the gatehouse, between the wall and the berm, is set forward from the passage and could possibly have provided some defensive flanking fire for any attack on the gateway. It is suggested that the gateway was of mid-13th century date with additions in the following century and alterations through to the 18th century. The gate was demolished in 1798, but the gaol buildings continued in use.

The eastern gate to the city was in St Owen Street. This part of the defensive circuit must have been the most difficult section to design. The basic problem was not just the extent of the existing burgaging; rather it was the presence of St Owen's church on the south side of the gradually widening St Owen Street. If this building was to be included within the defensive circuit there would have had to have been a large semi-circular bulge in the line to create a return to the north-eastern corner of Castle Green – the only feasible point to complete the enclosure as the river bends abruptly south from the south-eastern corner of the Green, the castle's bailey. A decision must have been made to leave the church and any surrounding buildings outside the defences. Had St Owen's Gate been positioned a little further to the east, still leaving St Owen's church outside, the defensive line could have achieved a smooth curve. However, the main objection to such a solution would have been the potential use of the church and especially its tower, in any attack on the Gate.

The final solution was a compromise. A short length of the Saxon defences, where it curved round from the castle earthworks, was repaired. The new defensive line then took a course at right angles to join up with St Owen's Gate. Although such a re-entrant was a very poor defensive feature, it must have been assumed that the adjoining St Owen's Gate would give the necessary protection (Fig. 4.14).

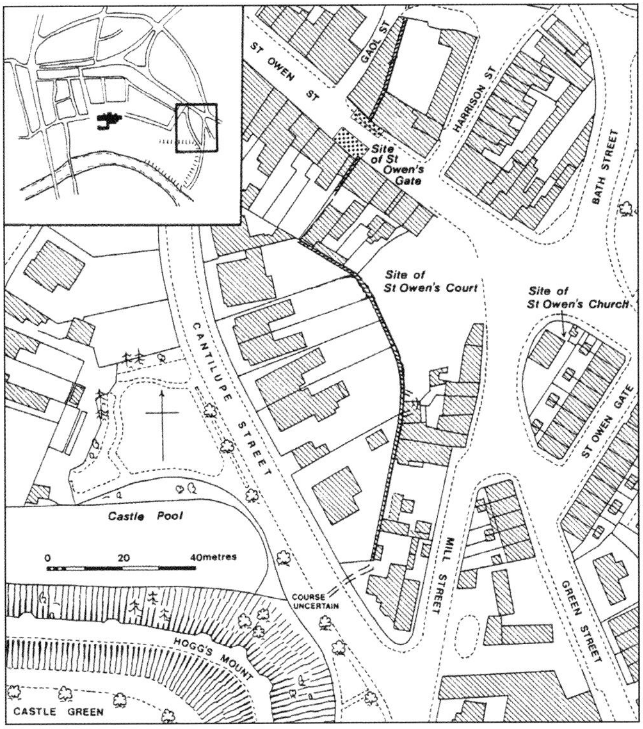

As with Widemarsh Gate and Bye Street Gate, the walls of St Owen's Gate are offset, the southern part being set forward. Some illustrations survive, one of which is a watercolour painted from inside the gate (Fig. 4.15). Like the other gates it was rectangular in shape and had two projecting buttresses to the front and rear. The gate passage had a two-centred head of two orders with a drip mould. According to the 1732 Buck panorama (Fig. 12.3) and the 1790s sketch of the exterior (Fig. 4.16), the gateway arch was recessed beneath a shallower segmental archway. Above was a first-floor chamber lit on the inner side by what appears to be a window of two, tall, round-headed lights under a two-centred relieving arch. This room was used by the

Fig. 4.14 Map showing the location of the city wall in relation to St Owen's church and also to the castle.

Fig. 4.15 The inside of St Owen's Gate c.1890s by Emily Eyton. (© Herefordshire Museum Service, ref.6219)

Fig. 4.16 Sketch of the outside of St Owen's Gate in the 1790s.

militia to store the armaments at the outbreak of the Civil War.[38] The inner parapet had battlements and was pierced, below the merlon level, by several loops. There is a hint of a plinth on the south side. The external illustration includes a hanging sign for an inn on the right, doubtless a predecessor to the Barrels, earlier the Lamb.[39]

Immediately to the left of the gatehouse on the internal illustration (Fig. 4.15) is a small stone-built lean-to that replaced a flight of steps up to the first-floor room. It was built on the inside of the wall and at a late period may have been the Porter's Lodge, including the stair. This single-story building which fronts onto Grope Lane, the narrow intermural roadway (now Gaol Street) still survives. It is only at this gate that the medieval layout and the wall offsets can still be fully appreciated.

The overall sizes of the gates are rather difficult to judge from the illustrations, but an attempt has been made to take basic measurements from Taylor's map and check these against all other available data. The passageways appear to vary in width from 3m to 4m, whilst the lengths of the passageways vary from a 6m passage at Friars' Gate to 14m passages at Eign and Bye Street Gates.

It is unfortunate that there has been no opportunity to examine or excavate the buried foundations of these two gates; when service tranches have been dug by utility companies, they have usually taken the easy course directly through the gate passage. The footings of the various buildings which comprise the gates and the foundations of the bridges over the city ditch must survive in places and are an important part of the archaeological resource of medieval Hereford.

5   THE CASTLE POST ANARCHY TO THE EVE OF THE CIVIL WAR

THE CASTLE that Miles of Gloucester captured in 1139 was described as a *motam* or 'motte' – a vague term, which suggests that it was still an earthwork and timber structure. It is unlikely that Miles or his son Roger, who lost the castle to Henry II after his rebellion in 1155, would have rebuilt it. When the castle appears in the pipe rolls in 1163, still in the hands of the king, the main feature on the motte is still referred to as the *domus* or 'house' – the living accommodation used by its lord or castellan.[1]

It is clear from the small sums spent on the castle recorded in the pipe rolls during the 1160s-70s that only minor work was taking place. The records show, however, that there was a bridge (1165), gate (1174) and walls (1173), which were provided with *breteschiarum* – 'brattices' – wooden parapets or additional towers, added to the palisades.[2] In 1177 the 'king's house in Hereford castle' was put into repair, at a time when Henry II was conducting a series of negotiations with the leaders of the Welsh. The work was extensive and special attention was paid to the 'council chamber', which suggests a building in the new bailey of the castle that superceded St Guthlac's rather than on the motte. Indeed, this public building was presumably the successor to the Saxon hall and was also the county or royal hall mentioned in 13th-century documents. A further not inconsiderable sum was spent upon the 'king's house' in 1178-9.[3]

Although the pipe rolls indicate a growing interest in Hereford Castle by the first Angevin king, there is little indication that Henry made substantial additions in stone, albeit that a limekiln is referred to in 1181-2 and money was spent on repairing a stretch of defective wall. Elsewhere in England, timber towers survived in royal castles until the early 13th century, as at Shrewsbury and Clifford's Tower, York.[4]

Hereford hardly impinged upon Richard I's consciousness, apart from when he sold the citizens a charter in 1189 (see p.38).[5] On Richard's return from crusade and imprisonment in 1194 work commenced on 12 brattices at the castle,[6] but Richard left England again in May that year to recover his continental possessions from Philip Augustus of France. He never set foot in England again.

His successor, John, was regularly found at Hereford. In the Autumn of 1200, having signed a peace treaty with Philip Augustus and married his second wife, Isabella of Angoulême, John made a tour of his English possessions, during which he visited Hereford Castle. He instructed the sheriff to make sure there was plenty of wine available and, following the visit, some minor repairs were carried out. In 1202 some serious work took place on the *turris* – 'tower', and the following year work was undertaken on a 'small tower', accompanied by major work on the 'king's house'.[7] The appearance of the term *turris* suggests either that the timber structures on the motte were being replaced with a stone tower or else this was a mural tower, perhaps built by his father.[8] Certainly the sums involved, when compared to what is known to have been built in other places for similar expenditure, suggests that a major round stone tower, then becoming fashionable in place of square towers, could have been under construction. On the other hand, the 'king's house' and its associated apartments may still have been present in the bailey of the castle. Within a few years, however, the public activities within the castle were taking place in a 'shire hall' within the bailey, whilst some of the private apartments created by Henry III, John's son, were certainly located in the tower. This separation may have started in John's reign.

One of the repeated criticisms of the chroniclers is that John eschewed the public life in the great hall, and preferred the company of his young wife and a few intimates in the privacy of his *camera* – 'withdrawing room'.[9] The building work certainly suggests that Hereford Castle was becoming more like a residential palace than a fortress, perhaps as a result of John's love of hunting. Though the focus of the royal forest of Haywood to the south of Hereford had been Kilpeck Castle, it is possible that John saw Hereford as an alternative base. John certainly extended the boundaries of the forest to the 'Southbridge' (Drybridge today) of Hereford, within a bowshot of the castle. John took full advantage of this closeness on his visits to Hereford where he stayed at least three times in 1211, 1213 and 1214.

One of the other amenities of the castle, 'the king's garden', was also on the other side of the Wye, squeezed between the river and the royal forest. This first appears in the records in the early 12th century, in the possession of Hugh de Lacy, when at least apples, hay and flax are recorded as growing here.[10] Clearly then productive rather than ornamental, its role seems to have changed by 1256 when it was referred to as a 'herber' or flower garden. Ownership of the

Fig. 5.1 The shell keep at Chateau Gaillard on the Seine gives an indication as to how that at Hereford would have appeared.

garden passed between the castle and St Guthlac's, to whom it was granted or restored in return for services carried out by the community in the king's chapel within the castle. In a rental of the priory for 1456 the garden is said to extend to 10 acres and is described as the *Kyngisorchard*.[11]

At the beginning of the reign of John's son, Henry III, the situation in Wales and the Marches was in a state of flux, in part due to the fall of the de Briouzes, who had clashed with John and whose demise left the southern Marches particularly vulnerable. By the 1220s a royal presence in the southern Marches became essential, and Henry turned his attention on Hereford, lavishing expenditure on the castle and making it into a fortress-palace and one of the 'key points in the military geography of England'.[12]

During 1239 and 1240 the tower on the motte was reconstructed, perhaps with the addition of an outer chemise approached by a stone staircase from the inner bailey.[13] The steps are indicated on Speed's drawing of the castle on his map of the city for 1610 (Fig. 4.1). This sketch, together with the description of John Leland early in the 16th century, brings us as close as we can expect to the Angevin castle. What we see appears to be a modified shell keep. The outer wall of the tower is constructed either as a circular or flat-sided ring-wall, rather typical of the mid- to late-12th century, but still being constructed in a modified form in the early 13th century. To this outer wall there has been added ten semicircular half-turrets – according to Leland – and in the centre a freestanding round tower, with space between the two for an open courtyard. The clustering of the turrets around the shell keep is reminiscent of the most famous castle of the age – Chateau Gaillard in southern Normandy where, being integral to the wall, they achieve a corrugated effect (Fig. 5.1). Speed's sketch (Fig. 4.1) only shows five but even if we assume a fairly extended circumference for the wall, the ten turrets noticed by Leland must have been fairly close together achieving the same effect as Chateau Gaillard, which also has

Fig. 5.2 A reconstruction drawing by Brian Byron showing how Hereford Castle might have looked in the late 13th century. (Courtesy of Monica Heijn)

a square gate, like Hereford. Leland was impressed by the great tower, which he describes as 'highe and very stronge' but he does not explicitly state that it was round. Speed's plan is also rather unhelpful but in the early 13th century a square keep, in a land of round towers, would have been very regressive.

In 1239-40 other towers around the bailey were either renewed or built for the first time. One on the north side, presumably close to the gate, became the county gaol. The gate itself received attention, as did a small tower near the great tower, together with its passages. Timber and stone for this work came from Haywood Forest. The king's great chamber, presumably in the bailey, was panelled and whitened, ready to be coloured with diaper patterns. The roof was covered with wooden shingles. Nearby was the queen's chamber, but the assertive Eleanor was less happy with this and asked that it be lengthened by ten bays. Adjoining the royal apartments was a new private chapel, which the sheriff had been ordered in 1233 to construct 'at the head of the oriole in the king's chamber', and was to be 'a decent chapel of the length of 25 feet'.[14] (This was a separate chapel to the free-standing de Lacy chapel of St Martin built in the bailey in the early 12th century; services in both chapels were carried out by the monks of St Guthlac's.) The majority of this work was presumably completed when Henry met some of the Welsh leaders at Hereford in February 1241 – a sensitive moment, only a year after the death of Llywelyn the Great and with the kingship of north Wales disputed between his two sons.[15]

Work went on at the castle throughout Henry's reign. Much of it was designed to improve its comforts rather than reinforce its military potential. Repairs to the great gate and the bailey gate are referred to in 1251 when work was also required on 'the house in the great tower'. The gravel banks, first thrown up, perhaps, to define the precinct of the minster and graveyard, provided poor foundations for the outer walls of the castle, which were constantly in need of repair. In 1254 the sheriff was allowed £60 to build a stone quay on the riverside to prevent the castle wall slipping into the Wye.[16] As new royal castles were built in Wales, Hereford became a centre of supply. Grain and salted meat were sent from Hereford to Builth and Painscastle and the 'quarrels' (iron bolts) of crossbows were stored here and distributed around the southern Marches. Occasionally 'engines of war' such as mangonels and trebuchets were mentioned, either being stored or repaired.[17] By the end of Henry III's reign a distinct impression is gained from the records that Hereford was no longer a front-line castle.

As detailed opposite, for a while in 1265 Hereford Castle became both the headquarters for Simon de Montfort, and a prison for Henry III and his son, Prince Edward, and city and castle held off an assault by Roger Mortimer (d.1282). Three months after the Battle of Evesham that saw the death of de Montfort and the release of Henry III, a commission of three barons was established to enquire into the 'robberies and other trespasses committed in the city and suburbs of Hereford' by Roger Mortimer. As a result, the citizens were granted £100 'for their expenses in the amendment and defence of the town'. The commissioners were also asked to view the defects of the castle, which resulted in a long list of instructions to the sheriff who was required to:

> fit the tower with joists and roof it with lead, make a bridge to the tower, repair the king and queen's halls, chambers, kitchens, the larder, the knights' chamber, the king's chapel, the stable and two turrets; finish a chamber lately begun for the king's clerks, make a bake house, repair the walls descending from the tower to the city and Wye; repair the king's

hall belonging to the almonry, the halls where the county courts are wont to be held, the Exchequer chamber in the inner bailey; to make a building for housing engines, the gate beneath the tower, the swing bridges there and prison within the castle with all necessary repairs.[18]

This must represent the best description of the castle at its zenith, but there is little evidence to suggest that the comprehensive refurbishment planned here ever took place. Ironically the

---

Simon de Montfort and Hereford

Henry III had campaigned against the Welsh with minimal success, but with growing criticisms of his arbitrary rule and perceived preferment of his Savoyard cousins and their kinsmen rather than the English barony, he needed to turn his attention to unrest within the latter. He therefore negotiated a series of truces with Llywelyn ap Gruffudd, but matters with the barons turned to civil war and in May 1264, Simon de Montfort, who had emerged as the leader of the baronial party, took Henry and his son Prince Edward prisoner at the Battle of Lewes in Sussex.

The citizens of Hereford took Simon's side in the affair and on 10 November 1264, one of Simon's bitterest enemies, Roger Mortimer (d.1282) of nearby Wigmore Castle, moved against the city. The outlying hamlets of Lower Bullingham, Putson, Hinton, Tupsley, Widemarsh and Huntington were pillaged and that night the priory of St Guthlac's was despoiled. That night too, the inhabitants pulled down houses outside the walls which might have provided cover to the enemy.

The following morning the assault on the city began in earnest but by now, although not complete, the defences were of sufficient strength to repel the attackers, and Mortimer's army had to be content with ravaging the suburbs. Having burnt down the houses outside the Bye Street Gate, the attackers withdrew.

In January 1265 Simon summoned to Westminster his famous parliament, which included two knights from each shire and two burgesses from each borough. On 6 May 1265 he arrived in Hereford bringing Henry III and Prince Edward with him, but some of the barons were now deserting de Montfort and, in a weakened position, he had come to seek an alliance with Llywelyn. Hereford at this time had a wealthy Jewish community, but de Montfort was no friend to the Jews, and some were expelled from their houses in order that these should be given to citizens whose own houses outside the walls had been pulled down to improve the city's defences.

On 28 May, as the result of a conspiracy, Prince Edward escaped from his escorts while riding in the outskirts of the town. He galloped to the Mortimer stronghold at Wigmore and thence to Ludlow and was soon in the field at the head of a loyalist army. In late June, Simon moved the court to Monmouth but, prevented from crossing the estuary to Bristol, returned to Hereford. From there he marched east to the Severn and, having forded it, was defeated and killed by Edward and Mortimer at Evesham on 4 August. Hereford was fined 500 marks for its support of de Montfort, at the same time that Henry III paid compensation to the citizens for their losses sustained in Mortimer's attack and also reducing the annual tallage paid under the city's charter.

sheriff was Roger Mortimer, who in 1269 found himself very much out of pocket, claiming £445 10s 3d for 'munitions at Hereford Castle including the wages for serjeants and knights dwelling within the garrison at Hereford Castle'. Apart from the citizens, only the prior of St Guthlac's seems to have received adequate compensation. In 1266 he was allowed to 'raise again a mill below the castle of Hereford' and provided with sixteen oaks from Haywood Forest to repair the priory in Bye Street.[19]

With Edward I's conquest of Wales between 1277 and 1282, Hereford Castle slipped from the purview of the government. In 1281, for reasons unknown, the sheriff allowed the military stores in the castle to be destroyed by fire. Perhaps they were old and redundant – like the castle.[20]

Late medieval decline

In 1316 Edward II instructed a commission to view the defects of the castle but when his wife, Queen Isabella, arrived in Hereford in 1326 for the trial of Hugh Despenser the Younger, she was persuaded to take lodgings at the Bishop's Palace. The security was poor and she lost four bags of account rolls and inquisitions, carried off from her chamber by three knights.[21] The weakness of the castle was also apparent in 1344 when the justices conveyed certain felons

Fig. 5.3 A rather fanciful illustration of Roger Mortimer (ex.1330) greeting Isabella, wife of Edward II, in front of Hereford in 1326. Hugh Despenser the Younger is being led away to execution by the gateway into the city. (British Library MS Roy 15 E IV f 316v)

A late flourish under Roger Mortimer (ex.1330) and Queen Isabella

Hereford briefly flared into prominence at the end of the reign of Edward II. Edward had a number of favourites over the years who used their position to increase their status and land-holdings, few more so than Hugh Despenser the Elder and his son, Hugh the Younger. Hugh the Younger had married a sister and co-heiress of Gilbert de Clare, Earl of Gloucester, who had been killed at the Battle of Bannockburn in 1314. As from 1320, not content with this inheritance, he set his sights, in particular, on increasing his influence in the Marches, and so came up against Roger Mortimer. Mortimer and his allies were outmanoeuvred by Edward and the Despensers, and in 1322 Mortimer was imprisoned in the Tower of London. The following year he managed to escape, possibly aided by Bishop Adam Orleton of Hereford (see p.72) and fled to France. Here he began a liaison with Isabella, the wife of Edward II,

Fig. 5.4 Illustration of the execution of Hugh Despenser the Younger, from a manuscript of Froissart. (Bibliothéque Nationale MS Fr. 2643, folio 197v)

> who had been allowed to go to France to negotiate with her brother, the French king, over a dispute between the two countries, and who then refused to return to England. However, in September 1326 she and Mortimer returned to England with a small force of mercenaries, their numbers soon swelled by disaffected nobles. In November Edward and Hugh the Younger were captured in Glamorgan and became prisoners of Isabella and Mortimer. Edward was sent first to Kenilworth and then to his doom at Berkeley Castle, while Hugh was brought to Hereford. On 24 November, after a show trial before Mortimer and the queen, Hugh was hanged from a gallows some 50 feet high, quartered and beheaded.[22] Some accounts say he was taken down from the gallows before he died and his entrails and heart removed.
>
> Mortimer was soon to rule England as regent of the young king Edward III, in conjunction with Isabella. He now proved as corrupt as Hugh Despenser the Younger and accumulated territory and finance. With the latter he remodelled Ludlow Castle, but also seems to have spent money in Hereford. On 31 May 1328 the city celebrated the wedding of two of his daughters, Joan and Catherine, to James Audley and Thomas de Beauchamp, Earl of Warwick, respectively. But by the end of November 1330 Mortimer was dead, executed after a coup in support of the young king.

to the castle for hanging but a 'multitude of people' laid siege to it, broke in and carried off the prisoners, and this despite the gaol having been rebuilt in 1291 at the county's expense.[23] References to delivering prisoners to the gaol in Hereford Castle continue throughout the Middle Ages and in the 17th century the gaol was said to be within the gatehouse overlooking the Castle Pool.[24]

The castle continued to be inhabited by a keeper and porter, but references to their appointment become intermittent as the Middle Ages progressed. The saviour of the castle should have been John of Gaunt (1340-99) who in c.1390 became its governor and began to assemble building materials, intending to make the castle his 'chief abode'. Unfortunately, Richard II, suspicious of his over-mighty uncle, restored royal custody. As a result, Gaunt turned his attention to Kenilworth, where his apartments, including a magnificent great hall, are regarded as one of the climaxes of domestic architecture in the Middle Ages.[25] Back under royal control, Hereford Castle continued to decay.

Among the facilities provided by Henry III for the local community within the castle was a county hall. This provided a courtroom for the activities of the sheriff and the itinerant justices. As late as 1381 rent from the royal estates in the county was being paid to the sheriff in 'the king's castle at Hereford' but soon after this the county hall became untenable and in 1393 Richard II granted a licence to the citizens to acquire a messuage valued at 60s. as 'they have no house within the castle and the city to hold their sessions and assizes'.[26] The Booth Hall in High Town (see pp.134-7), which came into existence at this time, presumably provided a venue for these occasions.

The declining state of the castle is epitomised by the regular grants of herbage for sheep and cattle within the 'king's castle and the king's orchard' which occur from the late 14th century.[27]

In 1396 Richard II reminded the prior of St Guthlac's that the monastery was to celebrate divine service in the king's chapel within the keep of the castle three times a week. Richard was also sensitive about encroachments upon the entrance to the castle. In front of the great

Hereford and the fight against Owain Glyn Dwr

A last Welsh threat arose when Owain Glyn Dwr was proclaimed Prince of Wales and took up arms against the newly installed Henry IV. In the Battle of Bryn Glâs (or Pilleth to the English) on 22 June 1402 a large force under Edmund Mortimer, consisting mainly of men from Herefordshire, was heavily defeated by a Welsh army, and by early August many towns in south-east Wales were under attack. On 7 August orders were sent out to collect troops in Hereford to form an army under the earl of Warwick as part of a triple assault on Wales. The advance began at the end of the month, but was thwarted by bad weather and poor tactics.

The following March, the king put Prince Henry in overall command in Wales and the Marches. Whilst the prince focussed his attention on north Wales, Owain moved his campaign to south Wales. In July Brecon was besieged, a siege broken by the sheriff of Herefordshire, John Bodenham. Bodenham then returned to Hereford where he heard alarming news of Welsh risings in Carmarthenshire, Carmarthen itself falling on 6 July. Four days later Harry Percy, also known as Hotspur, son of the earl of Northumberland, angered by what he saw as Henry IV's treatment of him after the support he had given in helping Henry obtain the throne, rose in rebellion. Events followed quickly. The king was already en route to Scotland with an army when he heard the news, and now brought his army to Shrewsbury and battle with Hotspur on 21 July. The resulting royal victory did little to quell the rebellion in Wales. Only two days later Welsh forces were east of the Black Mountains. By September there were many reports of widespread depredations in Herefordshire and even though the king led an army to recapture Carmarthen that month, the picture remained bleak. During the following year, 1404, reports of Welsh burnings and lootings in Herefordshire continued, and by midsummer Owain was in charge of most of Wales; in north Wales the English retained control of just eight castles.

It was at this point that Prince Henry based himself and his household in Hereford and Leominster, his household remaining here into 1405. Tit for tat victories by the English at Grosmont and the Welsh near Monmouth, in the late summer and autumn of 1404, were followed by two victories by the English in March and May 1405, at Grosmont for the second time and at Usk. These appear to have been secured by the use of mobile companies of troops operating in concert, a new tactic perhaps inaugurated or at least developed by Prince Henry, then still based at Hereford. King Henry joined his son in Hereford in May intent on another invasion of Wales, only to be diverted north by the rebellion of the earl of Northumberland. Owain, meanwhile, had obtained the support of a small French army numbering some 2,500 men which landed in Pembrokeshire in August. The combined Franco-Welsh force of some 12,500 men then advanced into England, passing to the south of Hereford and reaching the edge of Worcester. Here, there was a stand off with an army under the command of King Henry, till the Franco-Welsh force about faced and returned to Wales. The king was in Hereford once more in September having marched to relieve Coity Castle in Glamorgan, although again he had been partially thwarted by the weather. Over the winter Owain was left largely in peace and some of the French force returned to France in November, the rest the following Lent. From 1406 war weariness, an increasing English determination and an appreciation that events elsewhere were leaving Owain without any international allies, gradually meant that Wales returned to English control, and Hereford could return to being a sleepier backwater.[28]

bridge, on a site occupied today by St Ethelbert's almshouses and Castle House Hotel, there was clearly an open space – large enough it seems for a market-place. In 1395 a commission was established to inquire into the buildings erected by the tenants of the Dean and Chapter, which prevented access to the land adjoining the fosse and bridge of the castle 'where the corn market has long been held'.[29] Richard's interest in Hereford Castle suggests that in different circumstances, the crown may have restored it as a royal centre.

Significantly, it was one of the royal castles ordered by Henry IV to be refortified during the Glyn Dwr rising in the early 1400s (see previous page). Unlike many in the list, work actually seems to have taken place. The roof of the great tower was repaired, corner towers were refurbished and, where the riverside wall had collapsed, oak paling was erected. In all £100 was spent.[30] This was the last time before the Civil War that the military potential of Hereford Castle was taken seriously.

John Leland's description of the castle in *c*.1540 states that the 'great bridge of stone archis' was already in ruins and the water, which enclosed both the 'dungeon' (great tower) and the two 'wardes', no longer flowed through the castle although the water powered a mill 'within the castle'. He did notice, however, that the 'dungeon' was in relatively good condition – 'high and very stronge, havynge on the upper waull or warde 10 towers *forma semicirculari*' – and one great tower in the inner ward. There was also a 'faire chepelle' with a circular apse standing in Castle Green, probably the 12th-century chapel of St Martin, and not St Cuthbert (St Guthlac) as Leland believed. He also made the famous assertion, with a certain amount of exaggeration, that Hereford Castle 'be of as great a circuite as Windesore'.[31]

The gaol continued to be used and in 1513 it was full of recruits who had fled from the royal army on its way to France, while in 1536 Thomas ap Hugyn was incarcerated for expressing, in public, sympathy for the 'rebels in the North' – the Pilgrimage of Grace.[32]

6   The Norman Cathedral, Bishops and Churches

Following the attack on the city by the Welsh in 1055, the damaged Saxon cathedral, built by Bishop Athelstan some time between 1020 and 1040, still stood, somewhat nearer the river than the present building.

With the arrival of the Normans it must have soon become apparent that a new cathedral was needed. Athelstan's cathedral would still have been used for services, so a completely new site had to be found. The solution was radical. If, as has been suggested on page 28, there was an east-west road joining Castle Street to King Street, this would have been closed in an eastward direction from its junction with Broad Street. Any market stalls and buildings in the area would have been pulled down and the businesses relocated to the new market in the High Town area. It would have taken some time, but with all this clearance there was sufficient space to build a Romanesque cathedral fit for this important border city.[1]

There is debate about the date when work started on the new cathedral. Bishop Reinhelm (1107-15) is called *fundator ecclesie* in his obit, and he is usually therefore seen as responsible for overseeing much of its construction, but work probably began earlier. Whenever started, consecration did not take place till the 1140s under Bishop Robert de Béthune (see The Bishop Builders p.65). It was de Béthune who formed a chapter of canons under Ralph, the first dean, with a treasurer, chancellor and precentor.

The Herefordshire Domesday records that an anonymous mason (*cemtarius*) was rewarded by Robert de Losinga, Bishop of Hereford (1079-95), with half a hide and half a virgate at Eastnor.[2] This may be compared with the two priests at Fownhope (Herefordshire) with half a hide of land. Rather than being involved in the construction of the cathedral, however, the mason may have built Bishop Robert's chapel. Unique in England and similar to Charlemagne's chapel at Aachen (just 40km from Bishop Robert's home town of Liège), this was a *Doppelkapelle* – a two-storey chapel with the ground floor for the servants and the upper one for the family. The two chapels were connected by a central well on four cruciform piers (Fig. 6.1). The chapel was demolished, apart from its north wall, which backs onto the south wall of the Lady Arbour, by Bishop Egerton *c*.1737.

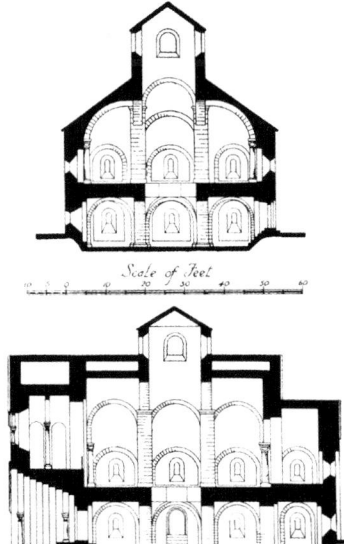

Fig. 6.1 Section drawings of the demolished Bishop's Chapel.

Fig. 6.2 The east wall of the south transept. The south transept is mainly of early 12th-century date. The east wall is of four storeys, the ground with plain recesses with round arches (and a modern opening into the south aisle). The two middle storeys correspond with the triforium. 15th century. (Photograph by Gordon Taylor, © Hereford Cathedral Library)

Parts of the original Norman cathedral still survive, but the east end (shown by excavation to have had three apses) has been replaced by the structures between the choir and the Lady Chapel (see Fig. 6.3).³

The chancel or choir is of three bays with aisles; the Norman work surviving up to the springing of the clerestorey. It originally had towers above the eastern ends of the aisles. Of the Norman transepts only the south one survives (Fig. 6.2) although the arch between the north transept and the choir aisle indicates its original presence. There is a small chapel, with two original Norman bays on the east side of the south transept adjoining the south choir aisle, which was once the treasury but is now the vestry. The bays are groin-vaulted in stone.

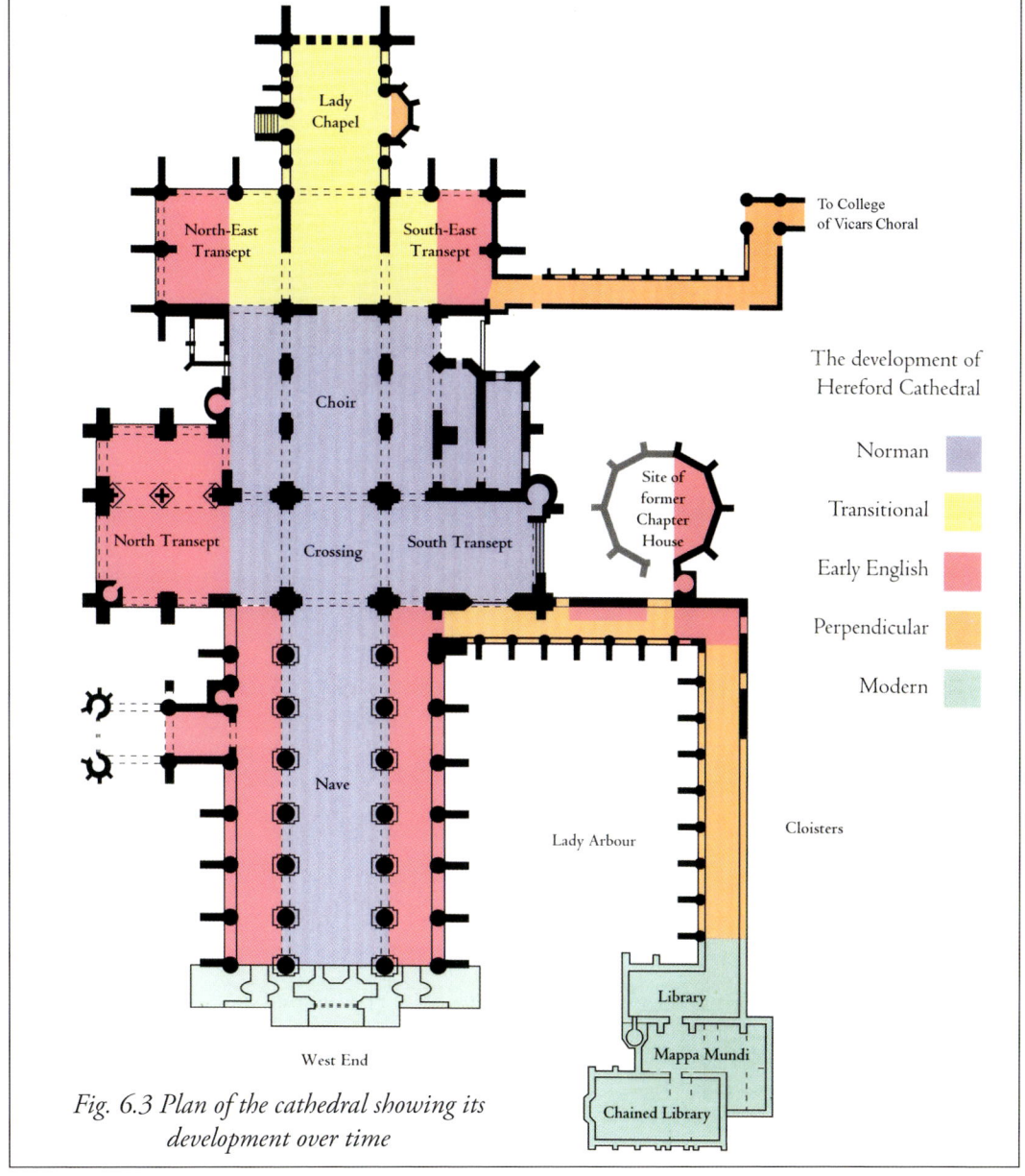

Fig. 6.3 Plan of the cathedral showing its development over time

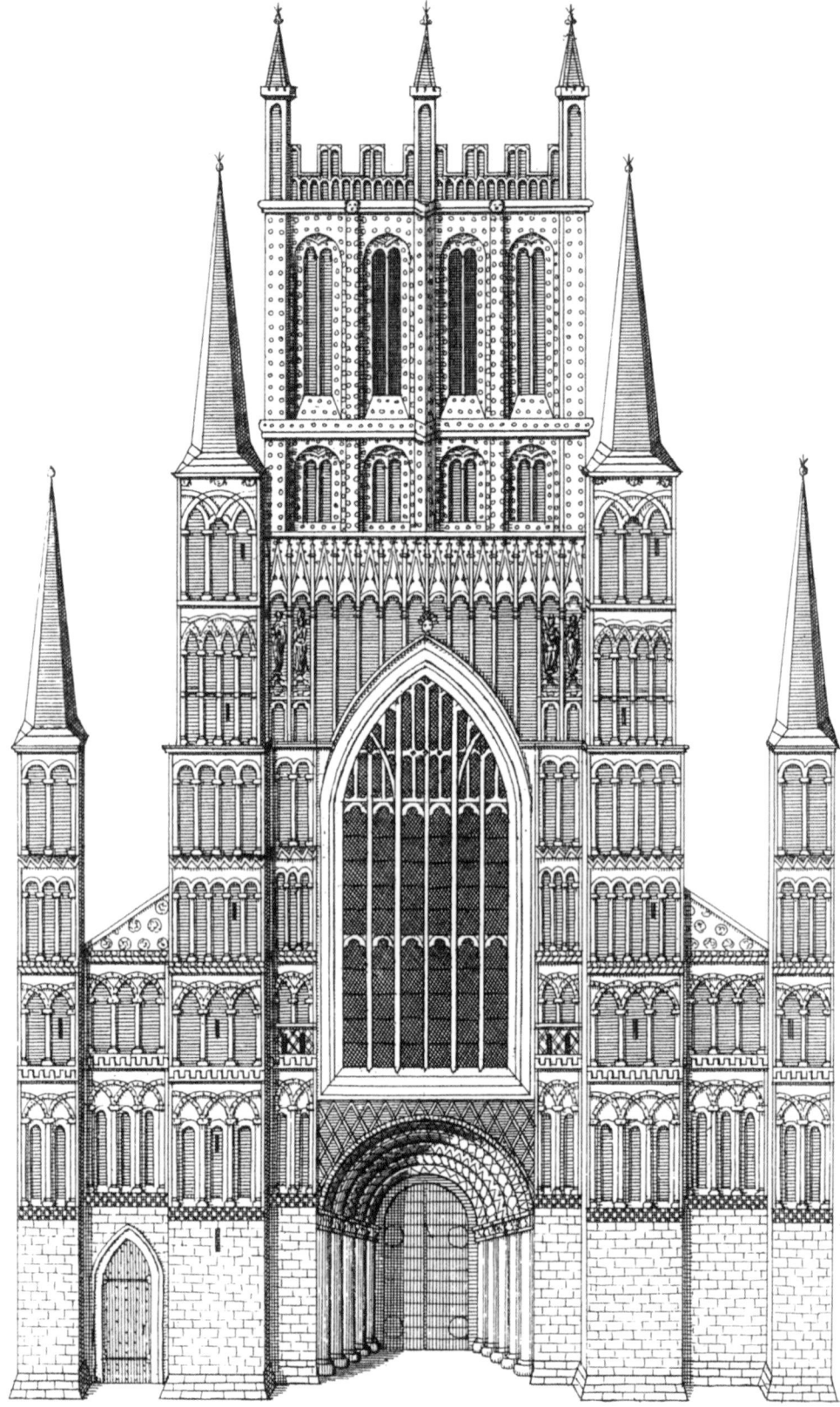

Fig. 6.4 The Romanesque west front of the cathedral

The Norman crossing, with its tower, was rebuilt in the 14th century. The nave, of eight bays, had a tower at its western end (Fig. 6.4) with turrets flanking the nave and aisles. There is some decorative work on the nave columns and arches. The columns rest on square bases and double semi-cylindrical shafts run up their north and south faces, ending in small double capitals. On the south side of the nave is the Norman font (Fig. 6.5), a circular bowl large enough to allow the total immersion of children.

Fig. 6.5 *The Norman font. (© Malcolm Thurlby)*

Scarcely 50 years after the completion of the Norman cathedral, Bishop William de Vere (1186 to 1199) altered the east end by replacing the three eastern apses with an eastern transept (now called the retrochoir). It is apparent that this was built with the intention of extending the central section eastwards, but it would seem that the work was not completed.

The Bishop Builders

Planning for the new Norman cathedral might have been started by Walter of Lotharingia, formerly chaplain to Edward the Confessor's wife, Edith, who was consecrated bishop in 1061. It was Walter who granted land to the north of the Saxon town to William fitz Osbern for a new market-place. In 1079 Walter was followed as bishop by Robert de Losigna, also known as Robert of Lotharingia. Though born in Lorraine, Robert was, like Walter, in England before the Norman Conquest where he was ordained by Bishop Wulfstan of Worcester. He was a skilled administrator and was one of William I's commissioners of the Domesday Survey and it is he who is usually credited with commencing the rebuilding of the cathedral. The work may have paused under his successor, Gerard, who was bishop for just four years between 1096 and 1100, and for the following seven years when the see was vacant. In 1107, Reinhelm, formerly chancellor to Matilda, wife of Henry I, was consecrated bishop and it was he who oversaw the completion of the east end of Norman cathedral. Reinhelm died in 1115, and it was only in the 1140s, under the austere Bishop Robert de Béthune, that the completed cathedral was consecrated. Béthune came from a knightly Flemish family that had settled in Buckinghamshire and he had been prior of Llanthony in the Black Mountains before becoming bishop. On his deathbed he admitted his affection for the storks and peacocks he kept at Hereford. An unofficial cult flourished at his tomb following reports of miracles, but attempts to have him canonized proved unsuccessful.

Fig. 6.6 Four examples of Norman decoration on the pillars in the nave and the arches between the pillars. (© Malcolm Thurlby)

Bishop Giles de Briouze (or Braose)

Giles de Briouze was Bishop of Hereford from 1200 until his death late in 1215. His father, William, had been one of King John's foremost counsellors at the start of his reign, rewarded with castles, lands in the Welsh Marches and Ireland, and high office. Possibly because of William's perceived proud independence in Ireland whilst John was trying to assert his kingly authority there, John turned against him and his entire family and set about destroying them. In 1207 William was deprived of his office as Sheriff of Gloucester and of his lands and castles. His wife Maud and eldest son (also William) were imprisoned by John and starved to death. Giles was the only bishop required to pay scutage (a type of tax) in 1214 – other bishops were all let off the heavy charge because of their loss of income between 1208 and 1213 when England had been under a papal interdict. When Giles' father died in 1211 John demanded a vast sum of money from Giles to allow him to claim his inheritance. (Four years later Giles was still trying to regain the castles his family had lost, the draining effort of which was a contributory factor to his death at the end of 1215; his tomb effigy in Hereford Cathedral rather poignantly shows him cradling a castle in his hand.) In late 1214 Giles was forced to act as a witness to a charter in which John deprived his widowed sister of all her proper inheritance from her husband.

Following eight years of John's persecution of his family it is small wonder that Giles joined the rebel barons in 1215; he was the only bishop who did. On 5 May 1215 the rebel barons announced their rejection of allegiance to John, and on 10 May Giles represented them in negotiations with the king at Windsor. The bishop and his supporting barons extracted a promise from the king in advance that 'he would not arrest or disseise them or their men nor would he go against them by force of arms except by the law of the land and judgement of their peers in his court'. In that promise is a powerful foreshadowing of clause 39 of Magna Carta and it is tempting to wonder whether that charter's most famous words might have been penned originally by Giles de Briouze.

Fig. 6.7 Hereford Cathedral's copy of Magna Carta dated to 1217. (© Hereford Cathedral Library)

It was around the beginning of the 13th century that work started on the Lady Chapel and its crypt. What was there beforehand is unknown, but the new extension to the cathedral could have replaced an earlier detached chapel.[4] If the walls of the crypt were completed before Bishop de Vere died in 1190,[5] any remaining work would have been suspended during the time that the Papal Interdict was in force (1208-14) and the king was taking all episcopal revenues. Work would have either resumed or possibly started in 1217 and was completed about 1225. However, it should be appreciated that as late as 1274 money was still being sought to furnish the Lady Chapel (Fig. 6.9). The main part of the chapel is of three bays standing on an unusually deep moulded plinth. The vault of the Lady Chapel is strengthened by two substantial stage buttresses, but even so the walls have been pushed out of the upright. The crypt fills the space below the main part of the Lady Chapel (Fig. 6.10). It is five bays in length and three in breadth with a quadripartite vault that has plain chamfered ribs and carved bosses at the intersections in the middle alley only. There is an external entry on the north side and an internal flight of 20 steps from the Lady Chapel vestibule. It has been suggested that the crypt originally provided space for worship for the cathedral parish of St John the Baptist.[6] This could possibly explain the external entry by way of the north door. However, by the 14th century, St John's 'church' had been established in the cathedral nave and the crypt gradually became a charnel house.

It was around the middle of the 13th century that the clerestorey, and vaulting of the choir, were rebuilt, having probably been damaged by the settling of the central tower. Under Bishop

Fig. 6.8 (left) The nave looking east.   Fig. 6.9 (above) The Lady Chapel.
(Both photographs © Malcolm Thurlby)

Fig. 6.10 The crypt under the Lady Chapel. (Photograph by John Stevenson)

Aquablanca (1240-68), one of Henry III's foreign favourites, the rebuilding of the north transept and north aisle was begun. The new transept has been described as 'the finest architectural set-piece in the present cathedral',[7] and was largely completed by the time of d'Aquablanca's death in 1268 as he is buried there. The style of the new transept is copied from Henry III's rebuilding of Westminster Abbey.

It was during Holy Week in 1287 that the bones of St Thomas Cantilupe were translated to the north transept which rapidly became a destination for pilgrims (see chapters 8 and 11). Pilgrims' contributions, as a result of Cantilupe's shrine, provided for the completion of the rebuilding of the transepts and the nave aisles as part of the pilgrim route to and from the shrine. The latter work included Gothic rib-vaults and large new windows, both in the nave aisles and in the choir. The great crossing tower was built *c.*1310, replacing a Romanesque one. The inner north porch was also constructed around this time with its frieze of figures, some humorous and indecent.

Bishop Robert de Melun

Robert of Melun was bishop of Hereford between 1163 and 1167. His name belies the fact that he was an Englishman, Melun being a small town near Paris where he stayed whilst he was teaching at the school of St Geneviève, a forerunner of the University of Paris. He was known as a philosopher, logician and theologian and was bishop during the period when Hereford was known as a centre of learning and science (see chapter 7). He was a friend of Thomas Becket, who had encouraged his return to England, and was present at the stormy meeting between Henry II and Becket at Northampton in 1164. In 1167 the pope asked him to visit Becket and attempt to reconcile him with the king, but Henry prevented him going. He died shortly afterwards in Hereford, it is said of grief at his failure to heal the rift between the two men.

> ### Bishop Peter of Aigueblanche, also known as Peter d'Aquablanca
>
> Peter d'Aquablanca was bishop of Hereford between 1240 and 1268. He had accompanied Henry III's wife, Eleanor of Provence, when she came to England, spoke no English and is noted as having been very fat. He appointed his Savoyard relatives to any offices he controlled and reputedly became the most hated prelate in England; Matthew Paris said 'his memory exhaled a sulphurous stench'. He was often absent from the diocese, Henry sending him both on diplomatic missions and on ones for raising money, and he is said to have been the prelate captured by Robin Hood in Barnesdale and held for a ransom. The cathedral was neglected and hatred of him put his staff at risk; in 1252 his chaplain Bernard was murdered while saying Mass in the Bishop's Chapel. When Henry III arrived in Hereford to organise the city's defences against the threat posed by Llywelyn ap Gruffudd, d'Aquablanca fled to Gloucester and had to be ordered to return to the city. In 1262, when he was in Hereford, he was seized by Roger Clifford and supporters of Simon de Montfort, who detained him at Eardisley Castle. After his release had been negotiated, he fled to Savoy, but in 1268 he returned to his see, made his will and died at his favourite palace of Sugwas on 27 November. His heart was sent to Aigueblanche in Savoy for burial, but his body was interred in a tomb in the north transept which had been rebuilt under his patronage in mid-13th-century French fashion.

The decagonal Chapter House, which was started about 1340 and completed in 1370, was probably the earliest building in Hereford to include a decorative vault. It was built on the south side of the south transept and approached by a covered cloister with a first-floor room for storing chapter records. It was probably not until the latter part of the 15th century that the cloistral walks were completed.

The crossing and its tower was eventually completed with a lead and timber spire in the 15th century. This work, being prominently visible from both the city streets and the whole neighbourhood, proclaimed to the world the greatness of the shrine and the cathedral as a whole. The Romanesque west tower of the nave was also heightened at this time. Both towers were decorated with ballflowers – one of the earliest examples of the use of such ornament in the country. It was probably towards the end of the 14th century or early in the following one that the nave vault was replaced and Perpendicular windows inserted in the clerestorey.

The south transept was restored by Bishops Trefnant (1389-1404) and Spofford (1421-48) during the first half of the 15th century with a new south wall, windows and vault, the monument to Trefnant being clearly part of this new architecture.

> ### Bishop Thomas de Cantilupe
>
> Thomas de Cantilupe was bishop of Hereford from 1275 to 1282. Simon de Montfort, a relative, made Thomas Chancellor of England during his ascendancy in 1265. When Prince Edward escaped from Hereford Castle (see p.55) and Montfort was killed at the Battle of Evesham, Thomas discreetly went to Paris, where he met St Thomas Aquinas, before returning to England and becoming bishop in 1275. An ascetic, he also took firm control of affairs in his diocese, visiting most of his parishes and defending the diocese's lands. He was described as having a ruddy complexion, red hair and a temper which he occasionally lost. For the story of his canonisation see pp.165-8.

Fig. 6.11 The arch at the end of the nave south aisle leading to the south transept as it would have appeared when painted

Fig. 6.12 (right) The screen to the Audley Chapel, with the Traherne windows by Tom Denny showing beyond (see p.267). (Photograph by Gordon Taylor, © Hereford Cathedral Library)

Bishop Adam Orleton

Adam Orleton was born in Hereford, where his father was mayor, and was bishop of Hereford between 1317 and 1327. Edward II tried to have the pope remove Adam from office, accusing him of taking the barons' side in their struggles with the king. In 1320 Adam allowed Queen Isabella and the 14-year-old Prince Edward (the future Edward III) refuge in Hereford Palace at a time of unrest. He supported Roger Mortimer (ex.1330) in his conflicts with the Despensers, the king's favourites, helping Mortimer escape from the Tower and negotiating with the French for their backing of Isabella and Mortimer's invasion of England. Orleton joined the queen at Hereford for the execution of Hugh Despenser the Younger (see p.57), and was prominent in the arrangements for the deposition of Edward II, haranguing him angrily and requiring his abdication. He presented Edward III as king to the lords in parliament on 7 January 1327 and to the enthusiastic Londoners outside. He is supposed by Marlowe in his play *Edward II* to have assisted in Edward's murder. Certainly his support of Mortimer earned him translation to Worcester in 1327. He survived Mortimer's fall and execution and in 1333 became bishop of Winchester, where he died in 1345.

> **Bishop Thomas Trefnant**
>
> Thomas Trefnant was bishop of Hereford from 1389 to 1404. A noted theologian and lawyer, Trefnant is remembered both for the role he played in the abdication of Richard II, encouraging him to take this step, in conjunction with Archbishop Courtenay, when Richard was held in the Tower of London, and for his pursuit of Lollards in his diocese. It was also during his time as bishop that the College of Vicars Choral was instituted, and the south wall of the cathedral's south transept was rebuilt in a late Perpendicular style.

On the outside of the north choir aisle is the chantry chapel dedicated to Bishop Stanbury (1453-74) but not completed until 1491. Bishop Audley (1492-1502) was responsible for the two-storey chantry chapel, built on the south side of the Lady Chapel, that bears his name (Fig. 6.12).

The outer porch, on the north side of the nave, was probably started by Bishop Mayhew (1504-16) and completed in 1518 by his successor, Bishop Booth (1516-35), after whom it is named. It contains two polygonal stair turrets leading to the magnificent glazed first-floor chamber, which also led to the room above the inner porch, previously only accessed by a spiral stair in the north nave aisle.

Bishop Booth's porch was the final medieval enrichment of the cathedral before the Protestant Reformation. Little work was done to the cathedral during that period, but the Reformation did involve the destruction of the main Cantilupe Shrine in the choir, although the earlier one, in the north transept, survived with only slight mutilation (Figs. 11.1 & 11.2). There seems

Fig. 6.13 The cathedral from the north in 1786, after its partial collapse, showing the many graveyard monuments and the Booth Porch completed in 1518.

> **Bishop Thomas Mylling**
>
> Thomas Mylling was bishop of Hereford from 1474 to 1492. When Abbot of Westminster he was a patron of Caxton. It was whilst abbot, in October 1470, that he took Edward IV's queen, Elizabeth, and her daughters into sanctuary from Henry VI's vengeful Queen Margaret, and when Elizabeth gave birth to her first son Edward, Mylling became his godfather. When Edward IV returned as king after the Battle of Tewkesbury he showed his gratitude by appointing Mylling chancellor and bishop of Hereford.

to have been little other damage to the cathedral at that time. During the reign of Elizabeth I (1558-1603) work to the cathedral consisted of routine repairs, but included much whitewashing of the walls of the choir to remove wall paintings. Routine repairs remained the order of the day up to the Civil War, with general repair to the Close paths, the bells and the clock.[8]

The Civil War was a disastrous time for the cathedral: neglect, and not wilful damage, posed the greatest threat to the fabric, following the abolition of the Dean and Chapter in 1649. The main casualty of this period was the Chapter House which was stripped of its lead for use in the castle. Following the restoration of the newly-established cathedral chapter, small amounts were spent on repairs, but it was not until the latter part of the 18th century that major works were carried out.

One of the main events was the collapse of the west face on Easter Monday 1786 (see p.204 and Figs. 6.13 & 12.15). It was rebuilt to a design of William Wyatt (Fig. 15.2) which was modified by John Oldrid Scott in the early 20th century (Fig. 15.3). Further repairs took place throughout the century and into the present one (see pp.263-6).

The Cathedral Close

The extent of the cathedral precinct in the latter part of the Saxon period is somewhat uncertain. Figure 2.5 gives an indication of the probable extent of the ecclesiastical precinct between the river and the site of the present cathedral. The western boundary could be either the 'combe' or the early paved road (Fig. 1.5); the northern one was possibly the southern side of any properties on the putative west-east road joining King Street and Castle Street; and the eastern on the suggested early eastern defence of the city (Fig. 2.5).

Radical changes must have occurred after the Norman Conquest with the construction of the Bishop's Chapel (Fig. 6.1); the new Bishop's Palace (pp.121-23) and the new cathedral. Speed (Fig. 9.14) shows a precinct wall enclosing a smaller area than the present-day limits. It was during the Cathedral Barn restoration in 2010 (pp.129-30) that archaeological excavations exposed a stone wall that ran underneath the southern side of the barn and turned northwards underneath the west wall, perhaps indicating an opening. A similar wall, on a north-south alignment, was uncovered to the south of the barn during service trench work, just to the east of the Old Deanery,[9] and aligning with the south-eastern corner of the barn. Both walls were almost 1m thick and may well have formed a precinct boundary to the Close. There was no firm evidence to date the construction of this wall apart from the indication from the earlier layers that it was of early 13th-century date or later and is therefore believed to be part of the precinct wall built in 1389 to protect the graveyard from the depredations of roaming pigs and dogs and to prevent the unlawful burial of unbaptised infants.[10] The gradual build-up of the ground level adjoining the wall (that occurred throughout the Close mainly due to many burials) gives some indication of the length of time that it was in use. This 0.4m thick layer indicates that the wall was probably used until the 16th or early 17th century when the above ground parts were demolished.

The present Close is very similar in shape and size to that of the early 17th century with houses and other buildings to the north and east, all associated with the cathedral (pp.123-31). To the south-east of the cathedral the College of the Vicars Choral balances the grounds of the Bishop's Palace to its west. On the western side of the Close, facing King Street, various buildings were gradually erected, to be demolished in 1935 (Figs. 15.5 & 15.6).

The Lady Arbour

The Bishop's Cloister or Lady Arbour lies to the south of the cathedral nave. The eastern cloister walk may well have started its life in the 12th century as a corridor or pentise connecting the cathedral with the Bishop's Palace and later providing a covered link to the 14th-century Chapter House. In the early 15th century, the passageway was radically reconstructed to become the eastern range to the cloister. The western arm of the cloister was attached to the western bay of the nave, as is shown on Taylor's 1757 map (see p.*x*).

Between the western range and the precinct wall was an area used as a timber yard during the middle part of the 18th century. In 1760, the west range, which had been used for a time by the Free Grammar School, was totally demolished and the timber yard was moved into the Chapter House Yard. The range was replaced by a new, much more spacious Georgian brick building called the Music Room, which was designed for use during the Three Choirs Festival as well as by the School (see Fig. 12.15). The area to the west was laid open in order to form a more commodious way to the Music Room. Although it suffered only a little damage when the cathedral west tower fell in 1786, by 1835 the Music Room had been demolished and the space was left empty (as shown on Curley's 1858 plan and the 1888 Ordnance Survey map). Throughout this time the west end of the cloister remained open until the southern part of what had been the west range was filled by the Dean Leigh Library, constructed in 1897. The library building, which is of similar style to the rest of the cloistral ranges, was designed to have a northern extension that would join it to the cathedral. In the event, the new library building, completed in 1996, was positioned to the west and parallel to the Dean Leigh building to which it was joined by a wide corridor. The 15th-century south and west cloistral ranges still survive although there have been some alterations from time to time. The Lady Arbour was used as part of the cathedral cemetery until the general closure at the end of the 18th century. It was then presumably levelled down and laid mainly to grass. Curley shows what appears to be a tree in the middle and the Ordnance Survey mark the site of a cross more or less centrally. This was apparently a preaching cross, approached by steps and with a short, rather stumpy steeple-like roof, which was taken down in 1762.

Burials round the Cathedral

The earliest Christian burial ground for the city was within the St Guthlac monastic precinct in the present Castle Green area, where burials dating from the 7th to the 12th centuries have been found (see pp.14-15). The Norman Conquest changed things and well before 1140 the cathedral was claiming exclusive burial rights not just in the city parishes but in several outlying ones as well. From then on, for several hundred years, burial fees generated much income for the cathedral.

Excavations to the south-west of the main cathedral building, in advance of the new building to house the extensive cathedral library and archives, exposed many burials.[11] Although some were initially classified as pre-Conquest, further research has indicated that all were post-Conquest. The excavations also encountered a large pit containing the bones of perhaps 5,000 people. The excavators pointed out that 'all but 23 of the individuals represented by the enormous quantity of human bone which had been dumped in this charnel pit in the early 12th century had originally been buried elsewhere and had been placed in the pit as disarticulated bones.'[12] A possible explanation for the charnel pit is that when the town's original cemetery at St Guthlac's was desecrated by the siege works of Miles of Gloucester, the remains that could be recovered from the old cemetery were reinterred in the new one (see p.21).[13] Radio-carbon dating from burials found during the excavations in St John's Quad and various other areas in the Close were mainly 12th-century or later. None were pre-Conquest.[14]

The Close, in the modern and later medieval sense, would not have existed at this period. Nonetheless, the erection of a house on the burial ground in the second half of the 12th century suggests that it took some time for the bounds of the new cemetery to become an established fact on the ground.[15]

Some more unusual burials were found during the excavations for foundations and services for the new toilets in the north-eastern corner of the Chapter House Yard in 1999. The remains of ten skeletons were found, but only one was completely exposed due to the small size of the excavation. There were several layers of burial, including some that inter-cut others. Some of the burials were within stone-lined cists; others with simple non-inscribed headstones. Several of the burials included additional bones, arranged around the latest burial, occasionally in a rather macabre way – thus there were skulls supporting each side of the head of one burial. There were no remains that were definitely female and several had been buried with a base-metal chalice and paten. Burials with chalices tend to be priests, or possibly priestly pilgrims. The people represented did not have an easy life; there was much degenerative joint disease present, particularly in the spine. In addition, four of the bodies showed evidence of trauma – a very high proportion. In two cases there was minor damage to the frontal lobe of the skull; one also had rib fractures and the loss of some of his upper teeth. Deliberate violence is indicated. Dating of such burials is always somewhat tricky, but most of these are likely to date to before the mid-12th or 13th century.

Parts of three large pits on the western side of the new library building site contained large numbers of individuals who had obviously been buried in great haste. As these pits were dated to the late 14th to mid-15th centuries, the most likely cause was the Black Death, which arrived in Hereford in 1349 and again in 1361-2 (p.174).[16]

The constant use of the limited area of the Close for large numbers of burials meant that, as it was filled and refilled with monuments and coffins, the level of the ground gradually rose. The level then was much greater than it is at present, for various old deeds describe the ascent to it from different sides. In 1520 the Close was approached from Church Street by several steps. Steps at the entrance from Castle Street are also mentioned in 1699, and others from Broad Street. By the end of the 18th century the situation had become so serious that on 11 September 1790, the Dean and Chapter wrote to the several parishes in the city and suburbs to the effect that: 'after March 25, 1791, no bodies can be admitted for sepulture here, except such as shall happen to die within the Precincts'.[17]

In 1796 it was noted that all the tombstones and gravestones in the Cathedral yard (Fig. 6.13) were levelled and removed, causing both grief and outrage. Burials continued to take place from time to time in the early years of the 19th century, apparently of those who died within the precincts. At least one such burial was close to the east face of the Lady Chapel – a lead plaque on a coffin exposed following minor subsidence during the recent work on the east face recorded one Mary Powell who was buried in 1823. It was not until 1850-51 that the ground level in the Close was lowered, in some places by several feet, and all the remaining tombs and headstones were taken down. Some of the gravestones were moved to Chapter House Yard, including the one for Mary Powell. Of the remainder, the earth, including fragments of coffins and bones which were discreetly overlooked, were carted away and deposited in a pit somewhere in the 'Barton', presumably in the Barton Road area.

Churches and Religious Houses

One consequence of the Anarchy was the removal of the minster of St Guthlac's from the Castle Green area. In 1140, an exchange of 8 acres of land alongside Bye Street held by Geoffrey Talbot (see pp.36-37) and land held by Bishop Robert de Béthune near the city ditch, meant that St Guthlac's had a new site to which it could move.[18] Meanwhile St Peter's, the house of secular canons founded by Walter de Lacy, had been given to Gloucester Abbey by his son, Hugh, in 1101.[19] A location within the market-place was scarcely suitable for a Benedictine monastery which St Peter's, as a cell of Gloucester, had become and arrangements were set in place between Bishop Robert and Gloucester Abbey to amalgamate St Peter's with St Guthlac's on the new site. Nothing remains of the early St Peter's church, for the late-12th- or early-13th-century chancel is the earliest part of the present building. On the south, the tower and south chapel were added in the latter part of the 13th century, whilst the nave was rebuilt about 1300 along with the north and south aisles. The two ranges of choir stalls, in the south chancel, dating to 1430-50, are said to have been brought from St Guthlac's after the Dissolution of the monasteries, and the misericords show carved roses.[20]

With the relocation of St Guthlac's, the buildings and the old cemetery on Castle Green were abandoned. The site could then be developed as a proper bailey to the castle, although still containing a chapel, dedicated to St Martin, to serve the expanded castle, which function it served until the dismantling of the castle in the aftermath of the Civil War in the 17th century.

All Saints church was built within the market-place just outside what was once the North Gate that led into the Saxon city. It certainly existed by 1214, but may have been built earlier.[21] The church consists of a nave and chancel with a south aisle and south chapel facing onto High Street. There is a north aisle and north chapel with the tower at the north-western corner. The present building is essentially of late 13th to early 14th century date, but internally there is some evidence of an earlier 13th-century church incorporated in the side walls of the chancel including parts of a large pier with arches springing all four ways.[22] The roof of the south aisle gallery is of king-post construction with carved spandrels including one of a rather rude male figure.

All Saints' relationship with St Martin's, in the part of the city south of the Wye, is not fully understood, for sometimes St Martin's is described as a chapel of All Saints and sometimes All

Saints as a chapel of St Martin's. St Martin's seems to have had a priest called Gozo in the 1130s so the church existed when the area was burnt in 1138. Perhaps this event, and the subsequent lack of defences of this area, was the impetus for a new foundation within the defended city.[23] (St Martin's church was destroyed during the 1645 siege by the Scottish army in the Civil War and a new church was built in 1840-5, to a design by Robert W. Jearrad, well to the south of the original site.)

Gradually more churches and religious foundations were added to the town plan. Although some may be earlier than the earliest documentary evidence, this expansion seems largely to date from the Angevin period in the mid-12th century. Within the area of the old Saxon town, St Nicholas is first recorded by 1155.[24] The church stood in the middle of the road at the intersection of King Street and Bridge Street (Fig. 12.2). It consisted of a nave, a side aisle towards the north, a chancel, and a tower with six bells. Before the Dissolution, there were two chantries in honour of the Virgin Mary.

It may have been by design, carried out by a number of agencies over many years, that the limits of the town, the outer edges of the suburbs outside the walls, came to be defined by religious foundations. To the south-east lay the church of St Owen's which was probably built soon after the Conquest and was extensively repaired in 1390.[25] It appears that the road branched into two at the west end of the building, to re-unite at the east, leaving the church isolated in the middle of the road, though this is not shown on Speed's map of 1610. (The church was at least partially demolished by the Royalist defenders of the city during the siege by the Scottish army during the Civil War as its tower, just some 50 yards outside the city wall, was otherwise available for use by the assailants.)

Further along St Owen Street lay St Giles, near the junction with the Ledbury road. When the existing chapel, built in 1682, was demolished in 1927 to allow the road to be widened, the site was excavated and the circular foundations of a 12th-century chapel were exposed, some 26 feet in internal diameter with walls 6 feet thick (Fig. 6.14). There were indications of an apsidal chancel to the east with walls 4½ feet thick.[26] Alfred Watkins writes that 'the date of the architecture of the round church and the earliest bits of the almshouse, make it highly probable that they were both built by the Knights Templar, whose round churches were copies of that of the Holy Sepulchre at Jerusalem.' If built by them, they had abandoned it by 1246 as it was where the Dominicans first attempted to settle, amidst hostility from the city clergy, until granted their permanent site on the Wide Marsh in 1319. In 1321 it became, for a few years, the cell of the anchorite Alice, 'daughter of Roger de Atforton', and then became part of St Giles' hospital or almshouses. The round chapel survived until at least 1610, for it is shown as such on Speed's plan of the city (see Fig. 4.1), but was rebuilt in 1682.[27]

Fig. 6.14 Alfred Watkins' photograph of the circular foundation of St Giles' church being excavated in 1927.

The newly placed St Guthlac's Priory marked the edge of the Bye Gate suburb and defined the town to the north-east. To the north, the Knights Hospitaller had their house and chapel on the edge of the Wide Marsh (see also chapter 11). To the west, the bounds of the suburb may have been defined by a foundation which has also been associated with a dedication to St Giles. This may have had some connection with a local leper hospital, also dedicated to St Giles, which was founded by 1250 and of which the burgesses of Hereford were patrons but for which there is very little evidence.[28]

South of the Wye, in St Martin's parish were two more chapels – St Candida's and St Eligius'. Very little is known of these but it is possible that they were located on the roads to the south-east and south-west from a junction at Blackmarston and marked the edge of the town in these directions. In the early 16th century a hermit by the name of James Robyns collected alms for the repair of St Candida's, and also for the repair of the adjacent public roads, the chapel therefore presumably serving travellers.[29]

For a town of its importance, Hereford possessed curiously few houses of religious orders. The Benedictine Priory of St Guthlac (as it had become) remained a cell of St Peter's Abbey, Gloucester, until the Dissolution. To this were added just two houses of Friars.

By 1228, within two years of the death of St Francis, a house of the Grey Friars had been founded by Sir William Pembrugge with the support of Bishop Hugh Foliot. (Hugh Foliot, bishop between 1219 and 1234, was a relative of two previous Foliot bishops: Gilbert, bishop between 1148 and 1163, and Robert, bishop between 1174 and 1186.) Initially the friars would have used an existing building; the date at which they moved onto their riverside property to the west of the city walls and began to raise their purpose-built friary with its church is unknown. The friary soon possessed an important collection of books, some of which survive in the cathedral library's collection (see p.91). Bishop Swinfield seems to have preferred the hospitality of the Franciscans to his own palace.[30]

It is not known how many Grey Friars were at Hereford at any time. Some ordinations are recorded: on 14 June 1337 John Prath and Richard de la Forde were ordained sub-deacons, William Pount deacon and Tomas de Sancto Colano priest. Roger Holyn became an acolyte in 1340 and Maurice de Stanford a sub-deacon in 1342.[31] There were 14 friars at Hereford when the monastery was dissolved in 1538 (see also pp.170-1).[32]

Unlike the Franciscans, the Dominicans or Black Friars had a hard time settling in Hereford. A 1250 bull of Innocent IV actually prohibited their settlement in the city on the grounds that it already had 'a great college' of the Franciscans, several hospitals for the poor and a great quantity of needy folk, meaning that there were no alms to spare.[33] In 1255 Pope Alexander IV confirmed the prohibition of Innocent IV, but five years later he changed his mind and instead the Dean and Chapter were warned not to interfere with the friars.[34] Some citizens appear to have made their own arrangements with the friars. The late 13th century 'Red Book' of the bishop of Hereford records that Margeria Kayes, who rented a house and garden of the bishop's in Bye Street (Commercial Street), was sub-letting to the friars.[35] In 1319 the Dominicans relocated from their original site in the Portfields to that on Widemarsh Street, adjacent to the Hospitallers, where the ruins of the monastery still stand (see also pp.171-4).[36]

A house of nuns in Broad Street has left almost no trace in the records and none on the ground.

7   Hereford as a Centre of Medieval Learning and Art

This chapter considers the evidence for Hereford as a centre of scientific learning in the late 11th and through the 12th century, science then including astrology. This period started under Bishop Robert de Losigna and his successor Gerard and continued at least through to the bishopric of William de Vere between 1186 and 1198. With cartography being one of Hereford's interests, consideration of the Mappa Mundi is included in this chapter, as is the creation and extension of the chained library. The chapter ends with a look at the role that the cathedral played, under its bishop patrons, in creating the Herefordshire School of Sculpture and early Gothic architecture, as another aspect of the city's cultural activity.

Cathedrals as centres of learning

'The Twelfth-Century Renaissance' is a term that conveys the ferment of new thinking that arose in Europe between 1050 and 1250. The eager search for knowledge by Christian scholars led to the translation and discussion of Arab and Jewish writings. Although this was a Europe-wide phenomenon, it expressed itself as a series of regional advances in learning,[1] with links between different centres made through church or personal contacts. Hereford had a significant role in this Renaissance.

Before the rise of the universities in England, the cathedral schools were the principal centres of higher education. In those that were monastic the enterprise was chiefly that of handing on an existing tradition of learning, but in the secular cathedral schools (i.e. non-monastic, like Hereford) there was much more scope for wide-ranging and speculative learning to flourish. Well-known scholars in a particular field would naturally attract like-minded people to gather in the same place, so different areas of study flourished more in one school than another; thus York and Lincoln became renowned for theology[2] and Hereford for natural science.[3]

Although remote and relatively poor, Hereford Cathedral was an important centre of learning, and unique in the formal emphasis and encouragement it gave to its canons, with the mid-13th century statutes allowing study leave for those considered suitably learned.[4] By that time half of the cathedral's canons were styled *magister* (master), indicating a high level of scholarly achievement.

The beginnings of a tradition

The roots of Hereford's scholarly tradition can perhaps be traced to the arrival in 1079 of Bishop Robert de Losigna.[5] He had been trained in one of Europe's leading cathedral schools (in Liège,[6] a school that specialized in mathematics) and brought with him a new vision of what a cathedral could and should be, all very much in line with the Norman desire to sweep aside Saxon ecclesiastical structures. He was skilled in the liberal arts, notably as a mathematician (in an age when numbers were believed to have some occult power and virtue), an astronomer, and a chronographer; he introduced the *Chronicon* of Marianus Scotus into England,[7] writing an introduction to that Irishman's ideas. It may be that Robert gave the Bishop of Worcester a copy of the *Chronicon*; it would account for the use monks at Worcester made of it in their own works.[8] He is also believed to be one of the people who introduced the abacus into England.[9] Astronomy being inseparable from astrology at this time, he looked to the stars for guidance, and so did not set out for the dedication ceremony at Lincoln Cathedral in 1095 because the stars foretold that it would not take place – and it didn't: the Bishop of Lincoln died on the eve of the ceremony!

Bishop Robert is believed to have been in contact with another Lotharingian, Walcher, at Malvern Priory. Walcher observed the eclipse of the moon in Malvern in 1092 and fixed it accurately by means of an Arab astrolabe. He may have acquired this in England, because he observed an eclipse in Italy the previous year and says he didn't even have a clock to determine the exact time. Walcher's experiment in the use of the astrolabe is the earliest recorded in the West,[10] and the instrument he used was, we know (because he names its parts by their Arab names), of a type that had been devised in Toledo[11] (a city which will be mentioned again). Walcher's new method, the 'eclipse method', of calculating astronomical time was clearly at the very heart of the new learning acquired from the Arabs and first brought to England – indeed to the Marches – before its general adoption in the West. It is a method that continued in use until the 16th century.[12]

Walcher was also the first translator of the works of the Andalusian Petrus Alfonsi.[13] Alfonsi, who had lived and worked in Toledo, was a physician, astronomer and philosopher. His stay in England in the reign of Henry I is full of mystery; he certainly acted as the king's physician, but he also emerges as the first teacher of Arabic astronomy in England. Walcher and Alfonsi were friends,[14] and Walcher learnt a huge amount about mathematics and astronomy from him. Alfonsi demonstrated a great breadth of spirit, because in what he wrote about science he addressed himself to other learned men, Christians, Jews and Moslems alike. This was a completely new stance in Western scholarship. For him, and for others he associated with, it's clear that the pursuit of knowledge and truth transcended faith boundaries.[15]

Robert's successor at Hereford, Gerard (bishop 1096-1100), built upon the same tradition. He owned a Hebrew Psalter and encouraged clergy to study Hebrew[16] at a time when the understanding of that language outside Jewish communities was virtually non-existent. He also studied astrology. Perhaps he was more acceptable in Hereford than in York (to which he was swiftly promoted) because he was suspected by the cathedral chapter there of being a necromancer on account of the fact that he would spend part of every afternoon reading a book of astrology (the *Mathesis* of Julius Firmicus). One day, feeling unwell in the garden, he sent his servants away so he could sleep; they later found him dead with the book of astrology under his pillow. The canons at York were so suspicious of the un-Christian practices of their archbishop that they refused him burial in York Minster, and 'would hardly suffer a lowly clod of earth to be thrown on him outside the gates'.[17] This story perhaps confirms our understanding that different cathedral communities specialized in different interests, so that the astronomy and astrology, which were considered unexceptional in Hereford, were a cause for scandal in York, where pure theology was the focus.

The tradition developed

Sicily and Spain were the principal sources of Arabic learning in Europe. Although the Crusades are sometimes cited in this connection it has to be said that (unsurprisingly) very few scholars took part in them, and the intellectual life of the militarized settlement in the Holy Land was no more than that of a Frankish colony.[18] Scholars such as Adelard of Bath and Michael Scot went to Sicily early in the 12th century; in the next generation dependence on the Arabic learning of Spain, learning acquired by long periods of residence and study there (usually in the enlightened multi-faith city of Toledo), becomes apparent. For Hereford this means Roger of Hereford and Alfred of Shareshill (sometimes called Alfred the Englishman, or of Sarashel); it may well mean others whose names and work are now lost to us.

Roger of Hereford (fl.1176-1198) was a later 12th-century astronomer and mathematician whose name is found in various treatises that incorporate Islamic science. In 1178 he adapted the astronomical tables that existed for Toledo and Marseilles to the meridian of the city of Hereford, using the Christian calendar 'because the years of the Arabs and their months are difficult to our people who are not accustomed to them'.[19] Roger also tells us that the time of the eclipse of 12 September 1178 was observed in three cities – Hereford, Marseilles and Toledo – and that their longitudes in relation to Arin, the mythological world centre of Arab cosmology, were determined in that way.[20]

His chief work, the *Compotus* (1176), criticizes the work of Latin computists compared to that of the Hebrews and Chaldeans; Robert Grosseteste seems to have been very familiar with tables set out in it.[21] (Interestingly, it is dedicated to Gilbert; that is probably Gilbert Foliot, who had been bishop of Hereford but was by then bishop of London.[22]) One of his works opens with the very Islamic words 'In the name of God the pious and merciful, here opens the book of the division of astronomy and its four parts composed by the famous astrologer Roger of Hereford.'[23] It seems to be a translation of an Arabic original, suggesting that Roger – like many of his contemporaries – had acquired a facility for Arabic. That again points to time spent studying in Toledo. For all that, it's hard to identify Roger. He appears as Roger of Hereford, but also as Roger the Young, or Puer, or Infans.[24] He must have been something of a boy prodigy because in the preface to the *Compotus* he describes himself as 'a young man who seems presumptuous in rehandling so many writings of the ancients'.[25]

One of Roger's contemporaries was Alfred of Shareshill (fl.*c*.1197–*c*.1222). When Alfred translated one Arabic work he dedicated it to '*magistro Rogero de Herfordia*'.[26] His biographical details are even more obscure than Roger's. He is known to have stayed in Spain, and was a famous man in his time. Robert Grosseteste (1175-1253) the philosopher, scientist, theologian and bishop of Lincoln, who received his early education in Hereford, mentions him.[27] That he is associated with two Hereford figures – Roger of Hereford and Robert Grosseteste – suggests a strong Hereford connection.[28] Three medieval manuscripts bear the rare inscription 'Alured', and are thought to have been his; by happy accident one has ended up in Hereford cathedral library.[29] Alfred's work marks a critical turning point in the intellectual development of medieval England. He goes beyond the mathematical and astronomical preoccupations of people like Roger and his Hereford predecessors, and brings one into the philosophical teaching of early 13th-century Oxford. In his writings there are a large number of quotes from Aristotle (unlike any other Latin author of his time[30]) and this comes, quite clearly, from his knowledge of the Arab Aristotelians. He draws freely on the notions of both Arab philosophers and the works of

Aristotle, including Aristotle's *Ethics* (which his Hereford friend Robert Grosseteste was to translate into Latin from the Greek), and the earliest use of genuine works of the Islamic commentator Avicenna in England seems to be his.[31] Roger Bacon gave him praise and credit as a translator,[32] and one of the pieces of evidence we have that Alfred had spent time in Spain is his occasional retention in Latin of a Spanish word that had found its way into an Arabic text he translated.[33]

A further development
Gerald of Wales (*c*.1146-*c*.1223), topographer, ethnographer, hagiographer, royal clerk, ecclesiastical polemicist, and a canon of Hereford from about 1193, may have arrived in response to a poem of invitation from another canon, Simon de Freisne, assuring him that 'all the liberal arts are studied,' and that Gerald would 'receive due honour as a scholar from men of like interests'.[34] Gerald's presence opens up another area of interest: cartography. Long before the Mappa Mundi was introduced to Hereford (*c*.1300) Freisne said that 'not only astronomy and astrology, but also geomancy' were prized; by *geomantia* he meant divination by means of lines and figures, or by geographical features. Hereford seems to have been a place notable for a great deal of cartographic interest. In a *Letter to the Hereford Chapter*[35] sent shortly before his death (which may in fact have been in Hereford) Gerald promises to send a map of Wales to accompany his Welsh *Description* and *Journey*. Sadly, that map no longer exists. He also appears to refer to another book, containing two separate works about Ireland, his *Topography* and *Conquest*. That very book still exists, though nowadays it is in the National Library of Ireland[36] (having been lost by the cathedral, later recovered, and then lost again).[37] A map is a vital part of the book, inserted between the two works; this is perhaps how he intended the cathedral to bind the map of Wales, between the *Description* and *Journey*. That he spends time explaining this in a letter that is basically just a list of his works suggests how important cartography was to him and to them. It is another sign of the special expertise in natural science that was maintained at Hereford. Ultimately, though, Gerald had been tempted away by Lincoln, where theology was the focus. He wrote to the chancellor there that 'You have said that we ought to write theological works and that this would be more becoming to our maturity'.[38]

The ascendancy of the universities
Hereford's moment as an important centre of learning was relatively short-lived. That great thinker Robert Grosseteste placed himself firmly in the Oxford orbit once his Hereford training[39] was ended, and the senior clergy here were increasingly formed by and looked to Oxford and Paris. Fresh interests and new ideas were capturing the minds of those who gradually turned away from cathedral communities to the greater freedom of universities for learning and intellectual enlightenment, while the expulsion of English students from Paris following the murder of Thomas Becket in 1170 swelled Oxford's ranks with masters trained in the latest knowledge, making it even more attractive. We have to note too that when riots led some scholars and their students to withdraw from Oxford in 1209 it was to join scholars in Cambridge, and to study in Reading.[40] No one seems to have come to Hereford.

Hereford continued to be a place of scholarship and higher learning throughout the Middle Ages, supplying Oxford with several chancellors;[41] but that higher learning was acquired in universities and brought back here; Hereford was now enlightened from outside, rather than itself being a source of enlightenment.

The Hereford Mappa Mundi[42]

In 1684, Thomas Dingley, a much travelled antiquarian who lived for some time in Dilwyn, Herefordshire, recorded seeing in the Lady Chapel of Hereford Cathedral 'an Map of the World drawn on Vellum by a Monk Kept in a frame with gilded and painted Letters and figures'. This is the earliest record we have of the famous medieval *mappa mundi* now displayed in the cathedral's dedicated exhibition space. Modern scholarship of the map and scientific analysis of its original wooden frame have led academics to conclude that the map was made sometime between 1290 and 1310, and probably in Herefordshire. Theories about who made it and what it was used for, however, remain as yet unproven. There is a name at the bottom of the map, Richard of Holdingham or Sleaford, but the true identity of this man, and the role he played in the map's production, has not yet been unequivocally confirmed; moreover, Dingley's claim that the map was made by a monk is probably unfounded. Study of the handwriting and artwork has concluded that a number of different craftsmen were involved in the map's production. Two artists were responsible for the images, a scribe copied out the texts, and an illuminator added the red and gold display lettering.

There is evidence, however, that Dingley's description of the map's decorated and gilded frame was accurate. Nearly a hundred years later, in the 1770s, Richard Gough noted seeing the map in the Lady Chapel and, just a few years later, John Carter made a sketch of the map in the same place. This is the first visual record we have of it. The sketch shows the map at the centre of a lavishly decorated triptych whose painted panels depicted the Virgin Mary on one side, and an angel holding a banner bearing the words 'Ave Maria' on the other. In other words, in John Carter's drawing the map forms the central panel of a triptych depicting the annunciation. Sadly, the side panels disappeared long ago, but it must have looked truly stunning; impressive enough for Gough to write that it had once been the cathedral's altar piece. There is no evidence to support this, however, and many scholars have questioned the truth of Gough's claim. One alternative theory is that it was commissioned to help promote the pilgrimage industry at Hereford Cathedral. Many people find this idea convincing, and indeed, the most likely date range for the map's construction does coincide with the efforts of Bishop Swinfield (d.1317) to encourage pilgrims to visit the shrine of his predecessor, Thomas Cantilupe (1218-82). After Cantilupe's death, miracles were reported at his shrine, which, under Swinfield's bishopric, became a popular destination for pilgrims, bringing wealth as well as reputation to the cathedral. Perhaps the opportunity to see a prestigious map of the world in a gilded and painted frame might have been one of the attractions that brought so many pilgrims to Hereford.

The first viewers of the map, whether pilgrims or not, would probably have been awe-struck. For them, the opportunity to see God's creation in all its diversity would almost certainly have seemed, simply, amazing. The world is drawn into a circle. East is at the top, a convention followed by many Western Christian world maps of the Middle Ages, and The Garden of Eden is shown at the most easterly point. At the centre of the map is Jerusalem, represented by a symbolic, circular diagram. Three continents, Asia, Europe and Africa, occupy the whole of the map's circle. Asia spreads out across the top half of the map, Europe covers roughly the bottom left-hand quarter, and Africa occupies the bottom right-hand quarter. The Mediterranean Sea, home to a mermaid and many different shapes and sizes of fish, reaches inwards and upwards from the bottom of the map towards the centre. This waterway spreads out to a very roughly

Fig. 7.1 The Hereford Mappa Mundi. (© Hereford Cathedral Library)

defined 'T' shape. Its 'arms' reach left and right across the centre of the map, merging with the Black Sea on the left (the north) and via the Nile delta on the right (the south). The world's ocean circles the outer edges of the continents. This ocean is full of peripheral islands, the largest of which are the British Isles. Squashed between the shores of mainland Europe and the outer circumference of the map, the British Isles are strangely disfigured, but their size in comparison with the rest of Europe is, none the less, significantly large. Perhaps this disproportionate importance given to the British Isles is not surprising considering the map was made in England!

Within the circle of the map, drawings and texts locate sites of Classical and Biblical history that at first seem a strangely eclectic mix. There are pictures and texts referring to Bible stories, for example Adam and Eve's expulsion from Paradise, Noah's Ark, and Moses; alongside these, there are also references to Classical mythology. Jason's Golden Fleece lies stretched out beside the Black Sea, and on the island of Crete there is a detailed diagram of the labyrinth built by Daedalus. There are also allusions to Alexander the Great and his campaigns, and mention of medieval saints. For instance, St Augustine, the early medieval bishop of Hippo whose writings were so influential to Western medieval Christianity, is pictured in North Africa, while the monasteries of St Anthony are depicted in the desert. Moreover, the map includes important places marking events in the life of Christ. Jerusalem has already been noted as the centre of the map, but Bethlehem, too, has a place and, significantly, an image of the crucifixion rises above the circular diagram of Jerusalem, like a cross mounted on an orb.

As well as Classical, Biblical and historical sites, the map locates many exotic peoples. Some are strange and physically deformed, like the 'Blemmyes' with no head and with eyes in their chest, or the 'Cynocephales' with the heads of dogs. Some others are morally or culturally depraved, like the 'Griste', who make their clothes from the skins of their enemies, or the 'People of the Scythians', who use human skulls as drinking cups. And the many beasts of the medieval world should not remain unmentioned. Among them, a unicorn, an elephant and a rhinoceros all have a place on the map, as well as the man-eating 'manticore' and the serpentine 'basilisk'.

Closer to home, the countries of Europe are crowded with images of medieval towns, cities, and places of pilgrimage. Some show interesting detail, like Lincoln with its hill and Santiago de Compostela with what looks like a large bell. Some others, like Paris and Rome are represented with grand towers and city walls. Compared to these, Hereford on the map is small and lacking in any recognisable feature. Moreover, today, the drawing of Hereford appears particularly indistinct and almost rubbed out. Perhaps, as often suggested, this is due to the pointing fingers of many Herefordians over the centuries.

An image of the Day of Judgement, or Doomsday, spans the circle of the world like an arch. It is reminiscent of the sort of Doomsday images that once decorated the chancel arches of medieval churches. In some churches today the faded images of these medieval wall paintings can still be made out, but in most places time has dulled the terrifying messages their once vivid colours must have conveyed to their audiences. The drawing on the map, following conventional Doom paintings, shows Christ enthroned, holding up his hands to reveal the wounds of the crucifixion. On either side of him, as if to demonstrate the horror of his cruel death, angels display instruments of the passion: nails, a spear, the crown of thorns and the cross. Seated at the feet of Christ, the Virgin Mary pleads for the souls of humanity. To his right the redeemed rise up out of their coffins and are welcomed into Heaven, and to his left the damned are stripped of all worldly possessions and dragged in chains towards the mouth of Hell. As in many other Doom images, Hell is depicted as the yawning mouth of a large dragon-like beast.

In a medieval church, a Doom painting on the archway between the nave and the chancel marked the boundary between the congregation and the most sacred part of the church. It stood at the threshold between the profane and the holy, the worldly and the spiritual. In a similar way, the Doomsday image of the Hereford map must have provided a graphic reminder to its medieval viewers of the judgement that stands between this world and the heavenly kingdom.

Until further evidence is discovered it can only be conjectured whether the map was made as an object to amaze pilgrims, as an altar piece, or for some other reason. But whatever its original purpose, the Hereford Mappa Mundi is certainly an extraordinary and intriguing survival of the cathedral's medieval past.

Fig. 7.2 Paris as depicted on the Mappa Mundi. The lines defacing Paris might perhaps reflect anti-French feeling during one of the many conflicts with France. (© Hereford Cathedral Library)

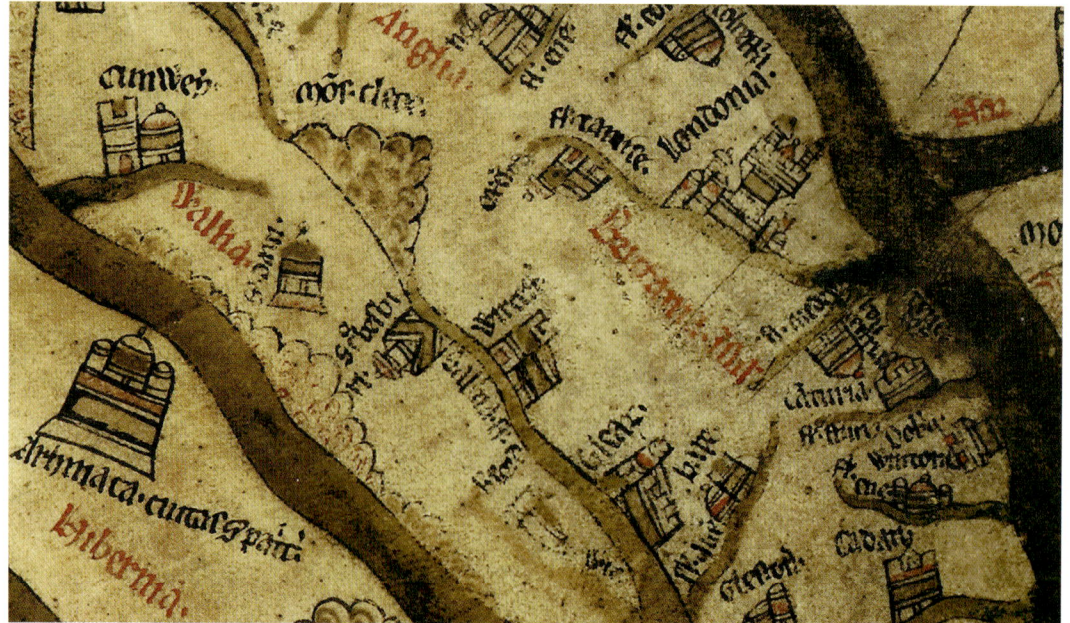

Fig. 7.3 Part of the British Isles as depicted on the Mappa Mundi. The almost rubbed out Hereford is centrally placed near the bottom, with Worcester above it on the banks of the Severn. The Clee Hill is depicted further up the Severn. (© Hereford Cathedral Library)

The cathedral library and other ecclesiastical libraries

The oldest library in Hereford is that of the cathedral. There is little evidence for a pre-Conquest library, but the oldest book in the collection today, the Hereford Gospels of *c*.800 (Fig. 7.5, overleaf), made in western England or Wales, contains within it two Old English documents which prove that it was at the cathedral in the first half of the 11th century, before the building was severely damaged in 1055.[43] A mid-11th-century, finely-illustrated Gospel lectionary (confusingly sometimes also referred to as the Hereford Gospels), now in Pembroke College, Cambridge,[44] contains a description of the boundaries of the diocese of Hereford as determined by Bishop Athelstan, and may also have been kept at the cathedral in the 11th century.

The first bishop to be appointed post-Conquest, Robert de Losinga, bishop from 1079 to 1095, was a scholarly and energetic prelate, interested in mathematics, and one of the few people in England to understand how to use an abacus. He was particularly concerned, as were several of his contemporaries, with computing the precise date of the Nativity.[45] These mathematical interests are not evident in the surviving library, but Charles Burnett has traced a continuous interest at Hereford in mathematics and related subjects from this time forward to at least the end of the 12th century.[46] Three books survive in the library from Bishop Robert's time which may have been made for him: one of the two earliest surviving copies of Archbishop Lanfranc's *Collectio*[47] and two manuscripts, written by the same scribe, which reflect concerns for historical chronology.[48]

During the 12th century the cathedral library developed much the same way as other cathedral and monastic libraries in England,[49] acquiring copies of the works of the Fathers of the Church, glossed books of the Bible and a few volumes of contemporary theology. Hereford had a series of highly educated bishops and many of the canons were also well-educated,[50] so that by the end of the 12th century the cathedral was renowned as a centre of learning, where all seven liberal arts,

Fig. 7.4 The Lord speaking to Hosea, illuminated initial from a copy thought to have been copied and bound locally of the Minor Prophets with the Gloss, mid 12th century, P.IV.3, f. 3. Stylistic links have been noted with the sculptures in Kilpeck church of the same date. (Photograph by Gordon Taylor, © Hereford Cathedral Library)

Fig. 7.5 The Hereford Gospels. Initial decorated page at the beginning of St John's Gospel. (Photograph by Gordon Taylor, © Hereford Cathedral Library)

including astronomy, were taught.[51] As noted earlier in this chapter, the astronomer Roger of Hereford (fl.1176-98), who in 1178 adapted a version of the Toledan astronomical tables made by Raimond of Marseilles to the use of Hereford, had links with Alfred of Shareshill, a key figure in the introduction of Arabic scientific learning into England,[52] but nothing survives in the library to bear witness to this scholarship. Rather the library was an up-to-date working collection concerned with religious teaching and Biblical exegesis. Today it includes an internationally significant collection of about one hundred 12th-century books, up to half of which have always been at the cathedral. Many are in their original bindings and at least 37 were made locally, with recognisable styles of decoration and binding techniques, although there is no evidence for a cathedral scriptorium, a facility unlikely to have been possessed by a secular cathedral with mostly non-residentiary canons.[53] The most important book to survive from the 13th century is the *Hereford Breviary*, which dates from between 1262 and 1268 and is significant as both the earliest surviving source for the pre-Reformation Use of Hereford and the only one to be noted (i.e. with music).[54]

During the medieval period three other religious foundations in Hereford had libraries, or at least collections of books.[55] Thirteen books are known to survive from the Benedictine priory of St Guthlac, seven of which are in the cathedral library today,[56] along with three of the four known surviving books from the Dominican Friary.[57] Around 30 books which belonged to the Hereford Franciscans survive, of which 11 or 12 are still at Hereford, and pressmarks on them suggest that their library could have contained as many as 300 volumes.[58]

The cathedral library developed in the later medieval period mainly through gifts and bequests. The earliest of these was that of Ralph Foliot, Archdeacon of Hereford (d.*c*.1198), who bequeathed 20 books, of which 12 or 13 can be identified in the collection today, a significant survival from a private library at this date. Further important bequests came from Richard Rudhale, Archdeacon of Hereford (d.1476), Canon Owen Lloyd (d.1478), Bishop Charles Booth (d.1535) and Sir John Prise (d.1555).[59] The bequest of the last-named, a scholar and bibliophile as well as a top administrator closely involved in the Dissolution of the monasteries, included 30 manuscript books acquired for his own library from dissolved foundations.

The Dean and Chapter do not appear to have spent much on new books in the 16th century. Only 46 printed books acquired before 1580 survive today, all of them gifts or bequests. A commission of inquiry into the cathedral's administration appointed by Queen Elizabeth in 1582 found the library to be filthy and neglected. In 1583 new statutes were drawn up in response to these criticisms, which laid down that one of the residentiary canons should hold the position of Master of the Library, that the books should be chained, and that books should be purchased with the fees paid by canons and prebendaries on their installations. In 1590 the library was moved into the then redundant Lady Chapel.[60]

The College of Vicars Choral had its own library, first referred to in 1582.[61] The records of the dean's visitation of 1588 noted that it consisted of 'ould books therein safely kept, but to little proffit of anye', as most were in Latin.[62] Today around 600 volumes survive, with a higher proportion of secular books and books in English than the cathedral library.[63]

The Chained Library at Hereford Cathedral

Construction of the chained library started towards the end of 1611, under the instruction of Thomas Thornton, Precentor and Master of the Library. Thornton, also a canon of Christ Church, Oxford, and Vice-Chancellor of Oxford University on two occasions, modelled the library on that funded by Sir Thomas Bodley at Oxford University, which opened in 1602, with books standing upright on shelves. Thornton was adamant that Hereford's library should be of 'good & well seasoned oke ... equal for substance, proportion, & workmanship, to the deskes & seates in the publike librarie of the universitie of Oxon'.[64]

Thomas Thornton bequeathed 35 books, and his contemporary Miles Smith, Bishop of Gloucester, one of the translators of the Authorised (King James) Version of the Bible, also made an important bequest. Later in the 17th century, under Bishop Herbert Croft, the library was augmented through the seizure of over 300 books from the headquarters of the illegal Jesuit province of St Francis Xavier, at the Cwm near Monmouth, during the anti-Catholic hysteria surrounding the 'Popish Plot' of 1678.[65]

During the 18th century books were added steadily, mainly by purchase, and in 1745 James Rawlinson was employed to produce a catalogue of the books,[66] but in 1778 the books were found by Michael Reynolds, engaged to update the catalogue, to be in an 'irregular and confused disposition'.[67] Meanwhile a second chained library had been formed in Hereford owing to the bequest of Dr William Brewster (1665-1715) to the parish of All Saints of 327 volumes mainly of theology and history from his own library.[68]

In 1841 the chained library in the cathedral was dismantled to enable the restoration of the Lady Chapel. The books were at first stored in the upper rooms of the college cloister, then, in 1855, one of the vicars choral, Francis Tebbs Havergal reassembled (but incorrectly) some of the presses in the muniment room over the north choir aisle. In 1897 the west walk of the medieval cloister was rebuilt with a room above it to house part of the chained library. This became known as the Dean Leigh Library after the then dean, James Wentworth Leigh. Acquisition continued apace, partly through the gifts of Caroline, Lady Saye and Sele, the sister of Dean Leigh, and, in 1925, Paul Henry Foley from the Foley library at Stoke Edith Hall.

In 1930 Canon Burnett Hillman Streeter worked out how the library was likely to have been arranged in the 17th century and it was reassembled, one half in the muniment room and the other in the upper Dean Leigh Library. The New Library Building, designed to house the whole chained library in one place, alongside the Mappa Mundi and with a reading room with a lending and reference library, was opened in 1996.[69]

Fig. 7.6 Part of the chained library today. (Photograph by Gordon Taylor, © Hereford Cathedral Library)

Hereford Cathedral: the Romanesque and Early Gothic Sculpture

Construction of Hereford Cathedral was commenced by Bishop Reinhelm, 1107-15, or possibly slightly earlier (see chapter 6) and the church was consecrated by Bishop Robert de Béthune between 1141 and 1148.[70] Work was disrupted during the Anarchy but by then the sculptural workshop was well established and satellites already existed.[71] The Romanesque sculpture of Hereford Cathedral has not received the attention it deserves, probably because much of it was replaced in the Cottinghams' restoration of the 1840s.[72] Yet comparison of the surviving 12th-century originals with the Cottinghams' copies shows that the reproductions are faithful.[73] The point is vividly illustrated in the twin capitals of the inner order on the north side of the east arch of the presbytery. Figure 7.7 shows the Cottinghams' capitals whilst Figures 7.8 and 7.9 illustrate the 12th-century originals which sit on brackets immediately east of the arch: David and the Lion, and a flying angel holding a cross. Similar model-copy relationships are evident in the other capitals of the presbytery east arch, as well as between original capitals from the crossing and eastern bays of the nave now preserved in the passage to the Vicars Choral, and the Cottinghams' replacements. It follows that the Cottinghams' work may be used to interpret the Romanesque work.

Fig. 7.7 The Cottinghams' restored inner north capitals of the east presbytery arch from the south-east. (© Malcolm Thurlby)

Fig. 7.8 (left) 12th-century original of David and the Lion. (© Malcolm Thurlby)
Fig. 7.9 (right) 12th-century original of the flying angel, (© Malcolm Thurlby)

The east arch of the presbytery has five orders along the lines of the multi-ordered west portal of the Bishop's Chapel built by Bishop Robert de Losigna (Fig. 6.1), 1079-95, and ultimately Imperial models like the inside of the nave west portal of Speyer Cathedral.[74] What is novel about the cathedral arch is the rich decoration with angle-roll mouldings, chip-carving and flat lozenge chevron, and scalloped, foliage, figured and historiated capitals. Historiated capitals are used in Normandy before 1066 and appear in England after the Conquest in Westminster Hall.[75] Along with the crossing capitals at Southwell Minster, commenced between 1108 and 1114,[76] the Hereford Cathedral historiated capitals are amongst the earliest in England. In addition to the capitals already introduced, subjects include the Harrowing of Hell (Fig. 7.10), an Annunciation (?), Milfrid presenting a cross to the cathedral (?), God the Father and God the Son (Fig. 7.11), and a large angle mask issuing foliage from the mouth.[77] God the Father and God the Son and David and the Lion both occur in illuminated psalters as illustrations to Psalm 110, and may derive from such a source. Aspects of the capitals belong to an Anglo-Saxon tradition. The iconography and style of the Harrowing of Hell (Fig. 7.10) belong to the same tradition as the Tiberius Psalter, and the carved slab in St Augustine's abbey (later cathedral), Bristol.[78] The flying angel with raised lower legs and fluttering draperies (Fig. 7.9) evolves from the tradition of the pre-Conquest angels above the chancel arch at St Laurence's at Bradford-on-Avon (Fig. 7.12), or in painted form in the dedication miniature in the Winchester New Minster charter and above the chancel arch at Nether Wallop (Hampshire).[79] The

Fig. 7.10 Capital from the presbytery east arch depicting the Harrowing of Hell. (© Malcolm Thurlby)

Fig. 7.11 Capital from the presbytery east arch depicting God the Father and God the Son. (© Malcolm Thurlby)

Fig. 7.12 Detail of flying angel from St Laurence's, Bradford-on-Avon (Wilts). (© Malcolm Thurlby)

pose of Milfrid(?) presenting a cross to Hereford Cathedral is similar to that of Joachim in the annunciation to Joachim in the late pre-Conquest Hereford Troper.[80] If the interpretation of Milfrid presenting a cross to Hereford Cathedral is correct, reference to Anglo-Saxon sources for the Hereford capitals goes beyond fashion to recall a significant period in the history of the cathedral. About 830, Milfrid had erected a stone church at Hereford in honour of St Ethelbert which he enriched with silken vestments and admirable ornaments.[81]

Other aspects of the presbytery east arch capitals presage the work of the Herefordshire School of Romanesque Sculpture. For instance, the head of the flying angel with huge bulbous eyes is repeated on the tympanum of the south doorway at Rowlestone. Similarly, the frontal pose with widely-spread knees of the God Father/Son figures at Hereford (Fig. 7.11) is adapted for the devil on the lintel of the north doorway at St Andrew, Bredwardine, and on grander scale, in the Herefordshire School of Sculpture on the Christ in Majesty/Ascension tympana of Rowlestone, Shobdon, and St Giles Hospital, Hereford.[82] At Rowlestone the octopartite chip-carved decoration on the second order of the arch of the south doorway is a larger version of that on the abaci of the east presbytery arch at Hereford Cathedral.

Fig. 7.13 *Detail of gallery bay in the presbytery.*
(© Malcolm Thurlby)

Fig. 7.14 *Chancel arch at St Mary's, Kempley (Glos).*
(© Malcolm Thurlby)

The main arcade and gallery arches of the presbytery of the cathedral introduce further variations in roll mouldings and chevron, and the chip-carved ornamentation in the tympana of the gallery arches is a three-dimensional version of the painted ornament above the chancel arch at Kempley (Gloucestershire) (Figs 7.13 and 7.14). The Kempley chancel arch itself retains much of its original polychrome, which may indicate the appearance of the Hereford Cathedral chevron and other ornament with its 12th-century colour.

Further variation in chevron design is witnessed on the crossing arches of Hereford Cathedral with a hyphenated lozenge pattern, an early example of a form that reached popularity later in the 12th century and is seen at the cathedral in the vestibule of the Lady Chapel built for Bishop William de Vere (1186-98) (Figs 7.15 and 7.16). Then, in the inside arches of the clerestorey windows in the south transept and the nave arcade arches, lozenge chevron proliferates and is accompanied by various forms of frontal chevron. Analogous delight in patterned variety is evidenced in the crossing capitals, in the foliage, interlace and medallions of the three easternmost capitals of the nave arcades, and even in the scalloped capitals further west in the nave arcades.[83] Variety was the spice of life when it came to the design of the Hereford nave capitals, an aesthetic shared with Romanesque throughout Europe.[84] Yet changes in form can also have an iconographic significance; the elaborately carved capitals of the eastern piers probably coincide with the location of the nave altar whilst the scalloped capitals mark the area for the congregation.[85]

The sculpture of Hereford Cathedral was an important source for the Herefordshire School of Sculpture of which the best-known product is the church of St Mary and St David, Kilpeck,[86] which was given to the great Benedictine abbey church of St Peter at Gloucester in 1134.[87] Kilpeck incorporates so many features from Hereford Cathedral that there can be little doubt that at least one of the craftsmen was recruited from the cathedral. The shafted responds of the Kilpeck apse vault, the scalloped capitals and chevron of the vault ribs are all paralleled at Hereford. Similar analogues are seen on the Kilpeck south doorway, including beak-spur bases, the interlacing foliage on the inner right shaft, the mask issuing foliage from its mouth on the right capital, the chip-carved saltire crosses on the abaci, the foliage on the tympanum, and the beaded medallions with mask ties and animal inhabitants.[88] The egg-shaped heads with bulbous eyes of the figures on the jambs of the Kilpeck chancel arch relate to the flying angel on the cathedral east presbytery arch capital, while some male human-head corbels with nasolabial folds on the Kilpeck corbel table are paralleled on the capitals in the east niche of the cathedral south transept.[89] The stranded interlacing foliage with binding straps on the panel behind the projecting head at the south-west angle of the Kilpeck nave is close to that on a Hereford Cathedral nave capital.[90] The inhabited beaded medallions with mask ties as on the second capital of the north nave arcade at Hereford Cathedral are popular in the Herefordshire School, as at Brinsop, Leominster, Rowlestone, Shobdon and on the Stottesdon (Shropshire) font.[91] Likewise, figures with egg-shaped heads and bulging eyes are one of the hallmarks of the School, as at Fownhope, Leominster Priory, Rowlestone, Shobdon and on the Castle Frome, Eardisley and Orleton fonts.[92] On the tympanum of the north doorway of St Giles, Aston, the profile of the beasts with heads turned *en face* relates closely to the lion on the David and the Lion capital at Hereford Cathedral.[93] The interlace on the frieze of the fonts at Chaddesley Corbett (Worcestershire), Castle Frome and Eardisley is a two-strand version of a three-strand design on an abacus of a Hereford Cathedral south nave arcade capital, whilst the angular interlace on a north nave arcade capital at Hereford Cathedral is repeated on the stems of the Chaddesley Corbett and Eardisley fonts.[94] On the tympanum of the north doorway at Ribbesford (Worcestershire) the pose of archer with head jutting forward is akin to Milfrid on the presentation of the cross capital on the presbytery east arch at Hereford Cathedral.[95] The foliage on a loose capital preserved in Monmouth Priory church is allied to the tympanum of the south doorway at Kilpeck and concomitantly to Hereford Cathedral, and the Monmouth-Hereford link is substantiated with reference to the stepped pattern on a string course on the north side of the west front of Monmouth Priory which is paralleled on a Hereford Cathedral nave capital and a string course above south nave aisle vault.[96] In addition to the work of the Herefordshire School sculptors at Leominster Priory, the central west tower there reflects the

Romanesque arrangement of Hereford Cathedral, and it is likely that the nave of Leominster was originally designed for a high groin vault as in the Romanesque presbytery of Hereford Cathedral.[97]

Aside from works of the Herefordshire School of Sculpture, many aspects of the Romanesque decoration of Hereford Cathedral are reflected in other 12th-century work in Herefordshire and further afield. The position and certain details of the presbytery east arch at Llandaff Cathedral, commenced in 1120, depend on Hereford Cathedral.[98] A window of the tower of Longtown castle is decorated with the same beaded paterae as reused in the east clerestorey passage of the south transept at Hereford Cathedral, and the east arch and south windows of the presbytery of Llandaff Cathedral.[99] In Herefordshire, details of the south doorway of St Andrew, Hampton Bishop; St Peter, Peterchurch; St Mary, Middleton-on-the-Hill; St Michael, Moccas;[100] St Philip and St James, Tarrington; St Anna, Thornbury; St Michael, Upper Sapey; all reflect motifs used at Hereford Cathedral, as do decorative details at St Michael, Bulley (Gloucestershire).

The sculpture of the so-called Dymock or Bromyard School is also an offshoot of Hereford Cathedral.[101] The form of the foliage in the Tree of Life tympana at Dymock, Kempley and Newnham (all Gloucestershire) is based on Hereford Cathedral north presbytery arcade capitals.[102] The mask capitals on the chancel arch at Pauntley (Gloucestershire) derive from those on the east arches of the presbytery nave aisles at the cathedral.[103] Raised semi-circles on the abaci of the chancel arch capitals at Pauntley repeat those on the string course above the east presbytery arch at the cathedral. At the former minster church of St Peter, Bromyard, aspects of the capitals of the three Romanesque doorways may be associated with the cathedral, and some of the foliage relates closely to the capitals at Upper Sapey. It is also tempting to see the modern chip-carved tympana of the Bromyard doorways as accurate replacements of the originals and further to associate them with the richly carved tympana in the presbytery gallery arches in the cathedral.

The Hereford Cathedral font (Fig. 6.5) with standing figures under an elaborate arcade on the bowl is not a product of the Hereford Cathedral workshop or Herefordshire School of Sculpture but is closely related to the fonts at St Michael, Mitcheldean (lower section only), St Peter, Newnham-on-Severn, and St Peter, Rendcomb (all Gloucestershire).[104] None of these has 'support' demi-lions at the base as at Hereford, a feature often associated with Italian church furnishings and German fonts, and also found on the plain tub font at Sutton St Michael (Herefordshire).[105] The various decorated shafts on the cathedral font are paralleled in the east triforium of the south transept of Pershore Abbey where certain capitals are also associated with Hereford Cathedral.[106] The demi-figures on the west capitals of the west crossing arch at Pershore relate to those on a group of lead fonts in Gloucestershire on which the variety of architectural motifs is akin to the cathedral font and affiliates.[107] It should also be noted that the anthemion frieze at the bottom of the Gloucestershire stone fonts relates to the Llandaff Cathedral presbytery east arch capitals on which the cable rolls on the abaci repeats a favourite motif at Hereford Cathedral. Moreover, the idea of association with metalwork should be seen in connection with the Dormington door knocker,[108] and the art of church treasures represented at Hereford in the Deposition ivory in the Victoria and Albert Museum,[109] and the initial to Hosea V in Hereford Cathedral Library P IV iii (Fig. 7.5),[110] which were probably

Fig. 7.15 Detail of the east crossing arch. (© Malcolm Thurlby)

made at Hereford Cathedral and are closely related to the Herefordshire School.[111]

Hereford Cathedral is also rich in Gothic sculpture, some of which is relatively little explored. Here there is only space to introduce aspects of the early Gothic sculpture. Bishop William de Vere (1186-98) commenced the rebuilding of the Romanesque east end with a retrochoir and eastern transepts – the latter was rebuilt later in the 13th century.[112] Of this work there remains a central bay immediately to the east of the presbytery east arch and one bay further east which forms the vestibule of the Lady Chapel. The opening between the Lady Chapel vestibule and the south-east transept (Fig. 7.16) has hyphenated lozenge chevron in the arch which is a more elaborate version of the type initially used on the crossing arches of the cathedral (Fig. 7.15). The

Fig. 7.16 Detail of the opening between the Lady Chapel vestibule and the south-east transept from the south. (© Malcolm Thurlby)

Fig. 7.17 The demi-figure holding a knife and a bunch of grapes in stiff-leaf foliage on the northern capital at the junction of the vestibule and the Lady Chapel. (© Malcolm Thurlby)

mouldings of the outer order and the abaci of the vestibule arch are significantly deeper than their Romanesque counterparts in the cathedral, and are characteristic of early Gothic taste. There is an even greater change in the form of the capitals from the scalloped, and relatively flat foliage and patterned forms to a slim, chalice shape with bunches of foliage known as stiff leaf that grow from the core of the capital. The details, including the nibbed shafts of the outer order and the stepped triple shafts of the inner order, are characteristic of the so-called West Country School of Masons identified by Sir Harold Brakspear.[113] Glastonbury Abbey Lady Chapel and great church (commenced 1184 and 1185 respectively) provide close parallels for the Hereford vestibule details, whilst the northern capital at the junction of the vestibule and Lady Chapel with a demi-figure holding a knife and a bunch of grapes in stiff-leaf foliage (Fig. 7.17) is closely related to figures on high-vault corbels in the transepts of Wells Cathedral probably executed before 1184.

The rib-vaulted Lady Chapel is three bays long with paired lancet windows in the north and south walls in each bay and five stepped lancets in the rebuilt east wall. The date of construction is not documented but there is consensus that work commenced about 1220. The interior articulation is rich with multi-ordered pointed arches carried on stiff-leaf capitals and framed with labels terminating on human-head stops (Fig. 7.18). Parallels for the capitals and the fillets on repetitive roll mouldings in the arches occur in the choir arcades of Pershore Abbey (*c*.1220-40) and the north nave arcade at Llanidloes (Powys) from Abbey Cwmhir.

Fig. 7.18 Detail of the interior of the north window to the Lady Chapel. (© Malcolm Thurlby)

Richard Morris has associated the piercing of the walls above the windows with the Lady Chapel at Winchester Cathedral and ultimately with precious metal shrines.[114]

There followed the remodelling of the cathedral presbytery, specifically the replacement of the former Romanesque groin vault and clerestorey with the present rib vault and clerestorey in which particular attention should be given to the figured and stiff-leaf capitals and the vault bosses.

In conclusion, Hereford Cathedral is the hub for Romanesque sculpture and architecture in Herefordshire. It was an important training ground for sculptors of the Herefordshire School, the Dymock/Bromyard School, and for the decorative repertoire used on most 12th-century churches in Herefordshire. In the cathedral, the early Gothic details are most worthy of visitors' attention. For this, and for much of the Romanesque sculpture, examination through binoculars will enhance your enjoyment.

8   Trade and Commerce in the Middle Ages

Although the new market-place and fresh impetus to trade provided by the arrival of burgage holders from Normandy does not appear to have given an immediate economic stimulus to the city, as is shown in chapter 3, gradually trade grew. This was in part due to the city's extensive hinterland, covering all of what is now Herefordshire as well as areas beyond, notably into south Wales as Norman penetration westwards continued.

The Customs of Hereford and the Jewish Community

As castle-boroughs proliferated in Wales in the 11th and 12th centuries, the liberal customs borrowed from the small Norman town of Breteuil and used in Hereford became the model for many an emergent mercantile community clustered around the foot of pristine castles, and over time became referred to as the 'laws and customs which are in Hereford and Breteuil'. In 1284, with some justifiable pride, John Gaunther, capital bailiff of Hereford, having been consulted by certain burgesses of Cardiff about the nature of these customs, assured them that the king wished to share the laws of Hereford with other urban communities because Hereford was 'the principal city of all the market towns from the sea to the limits of the Severn'. Copies were freely available but a small fee was to be paid to 'our common clerk for his writing and pains'.[1]

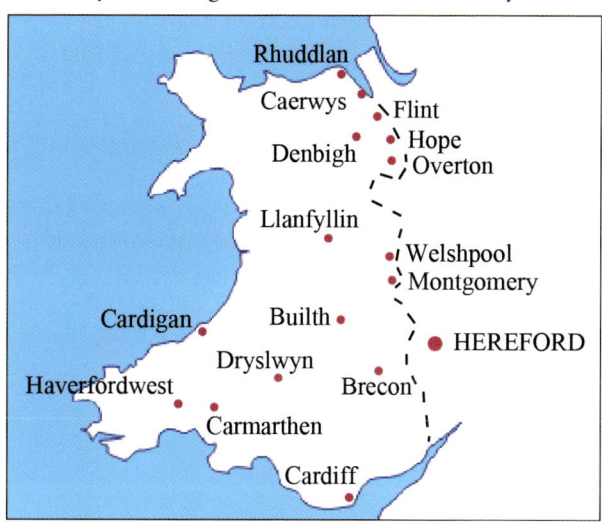

Fig. 8.1 A map showing the boroughs formed in Wales that took their laws from those of Hereford, which itself used those of Breteuil. Other boroughs were subsequently established which in turn used the laws of Cardiff, Carmarthen, Montgomery, Denbigh and Rhuddlan.
(From an original map produced by Joe Hillaby and Reg Boulton and now in the hands of the Mayor of Breteuil)

Just as the Hereford moneyers serviced the king's need for ready cash (as seen in chapters 2 and 3), so the Jewish community in Hereford could provide his barons with loans and, with the king's protection and use of his courts, recover these debts with interest, which in turn paid for the gifts, relief and tallage (taxes) they gave to the king. To pay their debts, landowners sold off or mortgaged their estates, thus facilitating a burgeoning land market, which in turn created mobility among the knightly and mercantile classes. Although the Jews were relatively slow to arrive in Hereford, they found it and its extensive hinterland very rewarding. Within 15 years of their arrival in 1179, the Hereford Jewry ranked 14th out of the 21 in a league table based upon payments made towards Richard I's ransom. In John's reign the Hereford Jews, domiciled in Maylord Street, were legally recognised as a 'community' and in the tallage of 1221, 13 individuals can be identified, headed in wealth by Hamo, who paid ten times more tax than anyone else. The Jews were unable to purchase land for their own use, but they lived well, displayed largesse and, no doubt, purchased consumer durables and specialist food from their Christian neighbours, so contributing to the general prosperity of Hereford in the early Middle Ages (see also p.170).[2]

The City and its Liberty
Hereford was a well-governed city, ruled in the name of the king by its capital bailiff and his two assistants. In addition, from the early 12th century the community of burgesses acted together and apparently met as a council in the porch of St Peter's church.[3] During the 13th century a system of wards was formally established and courts were held in rotation throughout the year, even in the remotest part of the Liberty (see below). This extensive, but simple, system of government helped to unify the city, gradually eroding the importance of the fees (noted in chapter 3), the differences between the English and French settlers and the distinction between king's tenants and those of the Church – the bishop and the Dean and Chapter.[4]

Perhaps uniquely, the city of Hereford embraced an extensive hinterland – its 'Liberty' – which extended to 3,000 acres on all sides of the walled and gated inner enclave. This may have been an endowment given by the Mercian kings to the newly founded cathedral in the 8th century, but by the 12th century it was legally regarded as an extension of the royal city and thus under the control of his bailiffs.[5]

However, much of the land in the Liberty remained in the hands of the Church and included some of the most productive soils in the region. This was managed from the *grangia* at *mora canonicum* (Canon Moor), now lost under the site of a cider factory, to the north-west of the city centre. The reeve's accounts for 1272 indicate that 360 loads of *mixtilio* (a mixture of rye and wheat for bread) was supplied to the 17 resident canons living around the Cathedral Close, and the vicars (who sang the cathedral services) received a further 23 loads, delivered to the canons' bakehouse. The corn was ground by the two water mills the chapter owned at Eign. The accounts also mention cattle, pigs and horses, which grazed on the rough pasture of the Widemarsh Moor.[6]

With heavy demands for hay and fodder for draught animals, the common pasture of Widemarsh, which extended to c.250 acres, was an essential ingredient in the community's economy. As it straddled the Eign-Widemarsh brook system, it also provided an early grass-crop from its flooded water-meadows. Prominent amongst those institutions who exploited this resource were St Guthlac's and the cathedral, but the citizen community, as it grew more confident, was not slow in asserting its rights. Moreover, there was increasing friction between the institutions, richer merchants and the lesser citizens in need of pasture for a nag or milch-cow and, in desperate times, a source of fuel – peat and hedge timber – for their fires. Like similar urban commons adjoining Worcester (Pitchcroft) and Chester (the Rode), there were occasional 'stirs', which in later centuries, when the common had been partially enclosed, led to open revolt (see chapter 12).[7]

Closer to the urban area, to the north-east were the Portfields, also managed as arable by the cathedral, with little evidence in the 13th century that it was cultivated by the town dwellers. Nearer to the River Wye, to the west and south-east of the city were two 'bartons' – *beretun* (barley-farm). In the post-Conquest period the Bartons were regarded as prebendal estates but St Guthlac's also retained an interest in Bartonsham, below the castle, which also enjoyed the *hamme* (water-meadow), occupying a loop made by the Wye. The early hay crop here was clearly valuable for reviving draught animals in the late winter. Aerial photography and LIDAR evidence suggest that it was managed as a formal water meadow.[8]

More extensive meadows, some still within the Liberty, existed to the north of the city, where the River Lugg meandered quietly to its confluence with the Frome and Wye. Here the Crown had a strong interest, since much of the meadowland was administered from the royal manor of Lugwardine, and Domesday records that the king's tenants in the city came and cut the hay-crop. Similarly, via the manors of Tupsley and Hampton Bishop the bishop had a stake, and the Dean and Chapter carefully defended their holding close to Aylestone Hill at Walney. Out of this complex situation a system of common management emerged, which survives today.[9] Above the meadows on Eign Hill there was '*le Wineyerd*' of the Dean and Chapter said in 1400 to be between the Wye and the road to Mordiford (i.e. Old Eign Hill). In 1341 a further vineyard is mentioned near to Widemarsh. The climate in the 13th century made vineyards a possibility, but conditions had declined by the late 14th century, suggesting that these references refer to vineyards long redundant but not forgotten.[10]

Finally, beyond the Wye Bridge there were further meadows. A substantial section of this, within the Rowe Ditch, was attached to the castle and known as the 'King's Garden or Orchard'; when the royal interest in the castle waned, it passed to St Guthlac's. Beyond this enclosure was the royal forest of Haye or Haywood, which provided the city with timber and stone for major building projects.[11]

Hereford's diverse hinterland, much of it within the Liberty, was a major resource for the population of the expanding city in the early Middle Ages. No doubt it did not supply all their needs but even in the era of national crisis in the 14th century caused by famine and then plague, there is no mention in contemporary records of any food shortage.

The Citizens

It has been suggested that on the eve of the Black Death Hereford had a population of 3,000 and, based upon the returns of the 1334 Lay Subsidy, ranked 14th among the major provincial towns of England, ahead of Gloucester but below Shrewsbury, which had a thriving trade in wool and hides.[12] The names of members of the trading community appear in various records and from these it is possible to draw a few tentative generalisations.[13]

By the early 13th century there is still some evidence of a distinct French community in Hereford. Latinised Christian names – Henry, Richard, William etc. – had been universally adopted, but occasionally there are toponyms that suggest Continental origins such as 'Thurgryn', 'St Albano', 'Franceis', 'de Limoges', 'de Paris', 'Hamlyn' and, particularly interesting in the late 12th century, 'Walter de Cormeliis', who leased Scutt Mill at Eign. Cormeilles, in Normandy, where there was an abbey, was patronised by William fitz Osbern, and owned property in Herefordshire.

Measured by remoteness the next group of surnames are those from places in England but fairly distant from Hereford. These include Oxford, London, Chippenham and Lexington (possibly Laxton in Nottinghamshire). Of interest is the apparent lack of surnames implying immigration from Wales – Walter de Brecon in *c*.1230 is unique. Toponyms deriving from counties adjoining Herefordshire are more frequent and include Wenlock, Greet, Washbourne, Evesham, Worcester, Dudley and Gloucester. Most of the citizenry, however, perhaps 70%, is from Herefordshire and much of it very close to the city.

Thus, in the early Middle Ages, the growth in the urban population of Hereford predominantly came from the town's hinterland, presumably comprising men who had escaped from the bonds of feudalism. From the evidence of the later bishops' registers, grants of manumission were fairly frequent, suggesting that where the Church was a landowner, it was not too difficult to raise the money necessary to purchase freedom and, perhaps, set off to the land of opportunity – Hereford.

Trades and Crafts

Surnames frequently make use of trade or craft descriptions. These suggest that in the early Middle Ages there does not seem to have been a dominant trade, but rather that Hereford was simply a successful service centre for its region, which at this time included much of south Wales.

The presence of a large Jewish community, two friaries and many hospitals, which depended upon charity, implies that Hereford was well patronised by the elite in local society, as well as by well-to-do visitors from the king downwards. The royal castle acted as a catalyst in this respect, especially during the early 13th century when it became the base for diplomatic and military initiatives in Wales. Many of the craftsmen involved in enhancing the castle in this period were, no doubt, temporarily domiciled in the city, while the corn market was fixed at the foot of its great gate in Castle Street. The elite visitors presumably sustained the activities of William the Goldsmith, who invested in Eign Mill in *c*.1220. Mercers – general traders – were often among the top rank of shopkeepers. There was John son of Rudolph in Wroughthall *c*.1230 and Thomas, who had premises near the Bishop's Palace. Equally, the spicers, Bartholomew (late 13th century) who had a shop in High Town near St Peter's and his namesake, Thomas (early 14th century), well placed in the Butchery, presumably sold their wares to those with a discriminating palate, such as Bishop Swinfield, who used saffron to make his food more interesting.[14] The bailiffs' receipts for 1276 suggest that Hereford was also well-served by vintners, as the chief means of rewarding its noble and knightly patrons was to give them a gift of a sextary of wine (2 or 4 gallons).[15]

Bishop Swinfield's household accounts for 1289-90 throw further light on the city's medieval commerce.[16] Whilst at Sugwas early in 1290 he ordered 136 gallons of wine from the Hereford vintners together with vegetables from the city and possibly the fish that accompanied them. A little later he bought a huge tablecloth from a Hereford mercer; it was 14½ yards long, easily sufficient to accommodate 40 guests. Plates and dishes, also from Hereford, cost £23 14s 3d and were therefore presumably made of silver. (On an earlier occasion in Colwall, Swinfield's cook had ordered plates and dishes from Worcester, but these were much more modestly priced at 2s 1d.) The bishop rarely used his palace in Hereford but when he passed through the city he always gave alms, and on one occasion tipped the young street sweeper who cleared the pavement as he progressed.

Also serving the elite were specialist craftsmen like the glazier John le Werour and, later, Philip, who were employed installing windows in churches and castles. Similarly, Ade *pictoris* was noticed in 1203 working upon the 'king's house' in the castle and William the Painter (mid-13th century) was also presumably a limner – colouring monuments and embellishing churches – rather than house painting.[17] The building trade was represented by masons who also worked on castles and churches beyond the city; carpenters, on the other hand, must have tended to live in the countryside, near their timber resources, as they do not figure in the city records.[18] Masons, either from the city or living near the quarries, would have built the cellars constructed of stone found beneath several buildings in the centre of Hereford, which generally date from the 14th or 15th centuries.[19] Later in the 14th and 15th centuries several outsiders were involved in work on the cathedral, suggesting that Hereford could no longer sustain a viable community of top-flight building craftsmen.[20]

Travellers who passed through Hereford on their way to more distant destinations were no doubt thankful to find smiths and wheelwrights clustered in the suburbs. On the south side of the city beyond Wyebridge, where the road forked for Ross and Abergavenny, Thomas and Philip the Smiths were to be found, whilst in 1321 Reginald the Smith had the site of his workshop in Widemarsh Street Without transferred to the Black Friars who were expanding their precinct. Nearby, there were Hugh and Roger the Wheelwrights and their neighbour, Arnold, a lime burner, providing an important product for the masons, but one too noxious to be welcomed inside the city. Dyeing was another polluting trade. Thus, William the Dyer (early 14th century) was found outside the walls in Bruton Street, where he could use the city ditch, which ran down via Castle Mill to the Wye, to dispose of his noisome liquors. This was bound to upset the bishop, who had fishing rights in the city ditches.[21] It seems likely that Samson *pistore* (late 12th century) and Walter the *piscator* of Rotherwas (early 14th century) caught their fish in the Wye.

Markets and Fairs
Markets and fairs stimulated trade and meant the city authorities benefitted from the receipts for stallage. The tenants of the king held their fair on the feast of St Denys (9 October) and the two days following, a date presumably chosen by the French burgesses as the saint had a particular following in France. A royal charter confirmed the fair in 1227 and a stallage account survives from 1319 when 4s 6d was collected for putting up temporary standings. The account was kept by Thomas Tope, the bailiff of the toll-house (tolsey) – one of the first references to this building, which eventually appeared in High Town.[22]

The fair of St Denys appears to have been a rather minor event compared with the St Ethelbert fair, held by the bishop, in May. This too was a three-day fair when first granted by Henry I in 1121 but was extended by four more days in *c*.1150 and eventually, in the 13th century, to nine days. The bishop's fair was probably designed to attract pilgrims as well as traders and, for the Church, was a much more significant means of earning income than the citizens' fair. Hence the multitude of restrictions that developed around the event, which were basically designed to stifle commercial activity in the rest of the city and funnel profits for nine days into the hands of the Church.[23] Moreover, the bishop was far more successful in getting the support of the king. In 1262 Henry III ordered that no business or trading was to take place within five leagues (15 miles) of the city during the time of the fair, thus, closing down all normal commercial activities. The bishop's stallholders also had access to free timber from the royal forest of Haye 'to make shops, booths, hurdles and other things during the fair'.[24]

Naturally, the king's tenants resented this enforced monopoly and found many ways of undermining the bishop's warrant, whilst the bishop was quick to close any loopholes. By the mid-13th century the city bailiffs were expected to hand over the keys of the city gates to the bishop's men so that they could control access into Hereford and presumably pocket tolls. Even the control of the city's trading courts – the assize of bread and ale – were handed over to the bishop's officials, who also controlled the pillory and ducking stool. A royal grant of 1265, following Roger Mortimer's attack on the city the previous year (see p.55), invites the burgesses and barons of England to come and enjoy 'as good customs as in any fair in England'.[25] However, the watchfulness and energy displayed by bishops Cantilupe, Swinfield and Orleton was not sustained by their successors and in the bleak times of the 14th century, the citizens seem to have wrested the initiative.

The Later Middle Ages: regional context, relative decline and Royal patronage

With population growth stalling in the late 13th century, severe weather conditions resulting in a famine between 1314 and 1321 and the economy sliding into depression, Hereford's pre-eminence as a regional service centre began to be threatened.[26] Many of the new towns in Wales – like Cardiff, Abergavenny and Newport – were now well established, while the bishop of Hereford had set up flourishing boroughs at Bromyard, Ledbury and Ross, which ringed the eastern edge of the county and reduced Hereford's influence in the richest part of its shire. From the early 14th century many of those who found their way to Hereford were subsistence migrants from the highlands of Wales, who began to replace merchants as the most frequent travellers to cross the Wye Bridge.[27]

Just over 25 years after the end of the famine came the Black Death (see p.174). In 1349 there were 120 deaths in the parish of St Peter's, which, it has been suggested, had a population of something in the region of 700 souls. A second major outbreak in 1361 might have killed as many people as the first one. Extrapolating on the figures for St Peter's, the total population of the city has been estimated at around 3,000

Fig. 8.2 Alfred Watkins' photograph of the White Cross when it still stood on the western side of the road. It is thought to have been built by Bishop Charlton about 1362 to mark a market-place established on waste ground outside the western limits of the city because people were too afraid to go into the town due to plague. It was restored in 1864 and again in 1992.

at the start of the Black Death, which compares with a figure of 2,754 based upon the Poll Tax payments of 1377. If the figures for St Peter's are both accurate and typical for Hereford, then a decline in population of some 17% is slight when England's dropped by around 50% by the end of the 14th century, albeit that other outbreaks of plague are occasionally recorded locally until the early 15th century,[28] and it has been suggested that the decline in Hereford was as high as 43% (see chapter 11). During the archaeological excavation carried out before the construction of the new building to house the Mappa Mundi and Hereford Cathedral Library in 1993, three mass grave pits were found containing the remains of at least 300 people buried in a hurry. Recent radio-carbon dating has confirmed that the most likely cause of death was the plague suffered in the epidemics of 1349 and 1361-2.

The Wye Bridge was beginning to show some signs of wear in the late 14th century, and in 1383 the bailiffs were granted the right to collect 'pontage' (tolls) on all articles carried over the bridge for its repair. Nearly 60 items are mentioned in this list but it was probably a standardised record and therefore not very useful in measuring the real trade. The tolls continued for a decade. The king also granted 30 oaks and 40 perches of stone out of the Haye towards the repairs. Earlier, in 1369, Lugg Bridge, controlling the eastern access to the city, which had been 'damaged by default of the burgesses', was repaired.[29]

In 1394 King Richard II further guaranteed the citizens freedom from arrest when they were travelling through Wales with their merchandise or procuring fish and other victuals. Finally, in 1399 the city received a new charter and in consideration for £100 the citizens had complete judicial control of the city and could pocket any fines levied by their courts.[30]

Market encroachment and the development of Rows

Fitz Osbern gave Hereford a massive market-place, which originally extended from Eign Gate in the west, across High Town, to Bye Street Gate in the east. Thus the two churches of All Saints and St Peter started life as isolated landmarks in this continental-style piazza. On market and fair days they were surrounded by *seldae* (stalls),[31] some temporary, some more permanent with covenants that, in the event of fire, they had to be rebuilt. In 1258 one stall was said to have a loft,

Fig. 8.3 Butcher's Row and High Town from the east painted c.1816 (artist unknown). Butcher's Row backed onto Cooken Row and both came into existence in the 13th century. On this picture, painted just before their demolition, the Rows backed onto the Market Hall which was completed in 1576. (© Herefordshire Museums Service, ref: 3212)

Fig. 8.4 Butchers' Row by David Cox (1783-1859)
Cox was a romantic painter so Butchers' Row – with the Old House in the centre – looks decidedly picturesque. Apart from those in the foreground, none of the buildings look particularly ancient, suggesting that they were regularly rebuilt. This watercolour was completed in 1815, by which time the building to the right of the Old House had already been demolished.
(© Herefordshire Museums Service, ref: 2746)

suggesting even greater permanency, and by the early 14th century a stall in High Town, said to be in the Butchery, near St Peter's, carried a rent of 5s. Clearly, this had become a permanent structure, indistinguishable – apart from the absence of a garden or yard – from the shops on the old burgage plots around it. Indeed, it is likely that the burgage holders elsewhere in the city held stalls to capture customers flowing through the great market-place.

By the middle of the 14th century the once open market-place was encumbered from end to end by these quasi-temporary structures, some of which began to form into Rows. Next to the Butchery, near St Peter's, was *Cokenrewe*, first mentioned in 1347-8; beyond it, towards All Saints, were the 'King's fishboordes' – occupied in 1372 by a fishmonger from Glamorgan. Butchers, cooks and fishmongers were ubiquitous Row-dwellers throughout Europe since, of course, they sold perishable goods.

Other Rows included *middlerewe*, first mentioned in the late 13th century and located between *guldefordestret* (Eign Street) and *beaufalestrat* (Bewell Street) in 1428-29. Middle Row seems to have had a mixed trading character but with leather workers predominating, hence a later reference to *corveseresrewe* (1386-87), but elsewhere it is called *merceriérewe*, thus identified with the general traders settled there. The buildings on the east side of Commercial Street (Bye Street), which form a wedge-shaped block flanking the north side of St Peter's church, also occupied an extensive area of market colonisation. There are several late medieval cellars here but an earlier and more permanent colonisation of this area presumably took place before it becomes well documented in the late 13th and early 14th centuries.

The decline in stallage fees collected at the fair of St Denys between 1284 and 1319 suggests that the numbers of temporary stalls were declining, and it is probable that the formation of these permanent Rows threatened the smaller itinerant country trader who had no desire to set up shop in Hereford. In the late 13th century John le Gaunter urged the bailiffs to demolish buildings in 'a place where there is common access', and action was taken in 1270 to remove a shop belonging to John Tirri 'harmful to the market of Hereford'. In exchange he was given some property in Widemarsh Street.[32] Today, the narrowing of the thoroughfares approaching the market-place, e.g. Widemarsh Street, Church Street and Bewell Street, suggests that traders here pushed their stalls and shop fronts forward over the centuries, to compete for attention from potential customers. The problem was not solved until the commissioners of the Lamp Act (1774) declared war on picturesque irregularity and superimposed measured uniformity.

New sources of income: Pilgrims

The canonisation of St Thomas Cantilupe in 1320 brought a new source of income to the city (see also pp.165-8). The process was managed around the two crisis points of the early 14th century – the famine between 1314 and 1321 and the first outbreak of the plague in 1349. Adam Orleton, bishop from 1317 to 1344, was both an excellent administrator and a churchman of international significance. He clinched the canonisation, long delayed by the papacy, erected a temporary tomb, persuaded the pope to issue a 40 day indulgence and cajoled the king – Edward II (not his favourite person) – to attend the translation of the saint's body to its gilded tomb in 1321. In October 1349, at the climax of the plague, Cantilupe was moved to his permanent home in the Lady Chapel, where there was space to allow for the circulation of the crowds of bewildered and disorientated survivors of the worst disaster for many centuries. (See also p.174).[33]

Penelope Morgan noticed that the peak of popularity coincided with the period of greatest rebuilding at the cathedral, culminating in the erection of the central and west towers between 1295 and 1315. At this time the Cathedral Close was turned into a 'centre of feverish activity with a small army of masons, stonecutters, carpenters and other craftsmen'. She estimated that over 60% of the sums involved in paying for the work came from pilgrims. However, the peak was soon to pass and in 1336 the pope reduced the opportunist tax that had been levied on the wax sold to pilgrims, because their number had dropped so dramatically. By the late 14th century the sale of wax candles was only producing a few pounds per year. The community of Hereford must have missed them, for they came from all classes – rich and poor – and those who came from some distance would need to buy the necessities of life and find accommodation, contributing to the well-being of the city.[34]

The City as a Wool-mart

After the Black Death, the price of labour rose and corn prices declined as result of a shrinking population. A new class of post-feudal farmers, who now enjoyed favourable leases on the lands of the Church and aristocracy, turned to sheep and cattle as the most profitable way to farm the under-fertilized ground, exhausted in the days of high farming in the mid-13th century. Wool and leather provided a new basis for prosperity for many English towns.[35]

There are references to the cloth industry in Hereford in the 13th century but only in the 14th did it become a staple industry. The sale of wool had, however, already become another issue which created acrimony between the ecclesiastical establishment and the citizens. In 1241 Bishop Peter d'Aquablanca complained to Henry III that during the time of St Ethelbert's Fair the citizens continued to sell wool and skins to foreign merchants behind closed doors, thus avoiding the tolls levied by the bishop's bailiffs.[36] A few years later, in 1270, the monks of Dore Abbey made an agreement with two merchants from Douai in Flanders, who were to buy wool from traders in Hereford who would wrap it and have it ready for collection. It might have been as a result of this trade that the monks owned a portfolio of properties in the city, including a substantial house in Bridge Street (1334) which had stone chambers – for security? – and a garden where saffron was grown, presumably for its yellow dye.[37]

A key element in the production of cloth was fulling, which cleansed and shrunk the cloth before it was sold to a dealer. This had become a mechanised process and required capital investment, which the Church was keen to support. The Dean and Chapter owned a bank of mills across the Wye at Bartonsham. These had originally been leased to the monastery of St Guthlac but were repossessed in 1355 when the flagging institution found it could no longer pay the rent.[38] At this date there were only two mills operational and there is a set of accounts for 1395/6 showing that the fulling mill operated at least 48 times during that year, producing an income of 30s 2d, and that the other mill operated as a corn mill grinding wheat and other grains.[39] Lugg Mill to the north-east of the city, over Aylestone Hill, also operated as a fulling mill for the bishop but in 1404 it was said to have been 'wasted for many years'. The alternative means of fulling was 'walking' and William Boure was described as a 'walker' in 1398. He lived next to a convenient watercourse – the 'Smallporse', a tributary of the Widemarsh Brook in Widemarsh Street.[40]

In the later Middle Ages it seems that every major landowner and farmer had a flock of sheep. When Simon de Brugge of Hampton Bishop made his will in 1385, top of his bequests to his wife, Isabella, was 'all my sheep and entire crop on the farm'.[41] In 1291 Dore Abbey had 3,000 sheep on its lands. Hardy sheep, grazed on high pasture, produced the best wool and Dore sent its wool to Windsor for royal use and supplied both Flemish and Florentine merchants.[42] Henry Catchpole, capital bailiff of Hereford, was said in 1355 to have been the ring-leader in a consortium of wool merchants that tried to defraud a Venetian merchant who was trading out of Bristol. In 1393 he gave his house, later the Booth Hall, on the south side of High Town, to the burgess community as a place to hold sessions, as the shire hall in the castle bailey was ruinous. However, Catchpole's house was also used for other purposes – by the mercers as a guildhall and as a mart for wool.[43] Tree ring dating suggests that it was substantially rebuilt in the late 15th century.[44] Most of Hereford's cloth was probably sold on as weavers and dyers are rarely mentioned in the records, though tailors are. One, Maurice Taylor, a tailor and clerk, was falsely accused in 1452 of stealing various garments from a fellow tailor including a quantity of green cloth, which may have been a local speciality.[45]

The Cathedral and the City

Disputes between the royal bailiffs and the Church authorities over the markets and fairs continued into the late Middle Ages, with the advantage clearly falling to the former. In 1389 the Dean and Chapter petitioned Richard II to secure the enclosure of the cemetery. The royal response, taking its cue from the petitioners, paints a lurid picture of thieving, immorality, disorder, secret burials and feral pigs digging up recent burials. Moreover, the stealing of goods and jewels from the shrine of St Thomas and the threats to Church officials by 'wild and untamed persons' is cited to support the strengthening of gates and locking them at night after curfew.[46] All this drama was designed to curtail the everyday usage of the Close by the wider community of citizens. Indeed, as an ancient thoroughfare it is likely that the Close was still used as an informal market-place, closely connected with the corn market in Castle Street, which is referred to during this period.[47] The reaction of the citizens was to tear down the new gate which led from Church Street (*cabochlone*) into the Close. In 1434 Bishop Spofford complained to the Dean and Chapter about the 'unseemly trading' which made the Close more like the king's highway (*regie strate*) than a holy place dedicated to God. He urged the Dean and Chapter to remove all trading and use lock and key to stop anyone entering the cemetery.[48]

The resolution of this dispute seems to have been the restoration of the *status quo*, since right was clearly on the side of the citizens and probably dated from before the use of the Close as a cemetery, which only commenced in the mid-12th century.[49] Moreover the bishop's desire for a 'holy place' was undermined by the loss of Church Street as an extension of the ecclesiastical landscape. In 1321 Bishop Orleton commented on the ruinous canonical houses around the Close. This was at a time when there were still 12-15 resident canons and before the Black Death when the numbers dropped to eight or nine, and by the 15th century to six or seven.[50] As a result of this decline the royal bailiffs began to take steps to integrate Church Street into the commercial community. This was not unattractive to the Dean and Chapter who were keen to augment their rent-roll notwithstanding the bishop's sensibilities. In 1378 the citizens received by Letters Patent permission for Thomas Worthyn, a layman, to build shops in front of a ruined canonical house.[51] A further rebuilding lease was granted in 1381 for a new hall (*aula*) with room attached and, in 1393, five further shops. More explicit details of the process of change is given in a lease of 1397 when the cathedral carpenter, John Menysere, was granted permission to repair the hall he occupied 'and other houses adjacent' and, with the consent of the Dean and Chapter, to sub-let the property.[52] A further three shops follow in 1404 next to the tenement of Thomas Chippenham, five times capital bailiff of the city between 1390 and 1420. It is possible that this was Chippenham's home, who like many subsequent well-to-do citizens found the uncluttered townscape near the Cathedral Close particularly convivial for domestic life.[53] Thus, by the early 15th century Church Street was integrated into the royal city and access to the Close via the *scherio cimiteri* ('the cemetery stile or scallions') was made permanent. The mention of scallions – steps – suggests that the level of the ground around the cathedral had gradually risen as a result of the number of burials.

Hereford and the Wars of Roses

Between 1450 and 1475 Hereford played a key role in advancing the Yorkist cause. Richard, Duke of York (1411-60) was the heir to the Mortimer lordships, which extended from Ludlow through mid-Wales to Carmarthenshire. As a descendent of Edward III he saw himself as the natural protector (and successor) of the declining and hitherto childless Henry VI, but his intentions were frustrated by a group of ambitious courtiers and the king's wife Margaret of Anjou. Richard was a northerner and outsider, but Hereford at the heart of the Mortimer territories was within easy striking distance of London and the Midlands.

On returning in 1450 from Ireland, where he had served for a year as Lieutenant, governing the country, Richard came to Hereford to raise money by mortgaging some of his properties in south Wales. Keeping an eye on him was Reginald Boulers, abbot of Gloucester who became bishop of Hereford in 1451. One of Richard's first acts was to imprison him in Ludlow Castle. Boulers was quickly released but thereafter he rarely came to Hereford and was soon looking for another more comfortable bishopric at Coventry.

Richard also orchestrated a number of demonstrations in English towns to emphasise the poor government of Henry VI and his favourite Edward Beaufort, Duke of Somerset. The most successful and long lasting was in Hereford where Richard's principal lieutenant, Walter Devereux of Weobley, skilfully exploited the resentment of the lesser tradesmen – known as the 'Welshmen', because many of them were recent immigrants – against the substantial burgesses, the councilmen. This began during mayor making in 1448 when the 'Welshmen' invaded St Peter's church and left a trail of damage, which Devereux paid for following an appeal to the king. Similar demonstrations occurred again in 1450 and 1452, when Devereux fitted out 32 Hereford tradesmen in his livery as a private army. This brought a commission of oyer and terminer, which accused Devereux of waging war against the king. The Yorkists took control of the city gates but Richard's campaign, encouraging the lower orders to rebel, brought general disapproval and he was forced to come to terms with Somerset.

A further crisis developed in 1456 when Jasper Tudor, with the consent of the king, took Carmarthen Castle, which belonged to Richard. Devereux, assisted by Sir William Herbert of Raglan, gathered a force in Hereford and having purged the city of its Lancastrian mayor – presumably John Chippenham – hanged six citizens and emptied the city prisons, recaptured Carmarthen and went north to take Aberystwyth Castle. Jasper was imprisoned and the victors seized the royal seal for south Wales and gave themselves permission to hold royal sessions to deal with their enemies. King Henry and Margaret, accompanied by a large force, equipped with 26 new guns called 'serpentines' – suitable for knocking down gates and town walls – marched from Kenilworth to Hereford and spent the whole of April taming the city and its region. Devereux was imprisoned until 1458; Herbert was pardoned and Richard went into exile.

The next four years represented the low point of the Yorkist cause but following Warwick's victory over the Lancastrian forces at Northampton in July 1460, Richard returned and made a royal progress down the Welsh Border, via Hereford. In December he was killed at the Battle of Wakefield and it was his charismatic son Edward, Earl of March, who raised an army of local troops – a veritable roll call of the Herefordshire gentry – led by the tireless Walter Devereux and Lord Herbert's son Richard, which destroyed Jasper Tudor's Welsh and

> Breton army at Mortimer's Cross on 2 February 1461. Owen Tudor, Jasper's father, who had married Catherine of France, the widow of Henry V, was captured and taken into Hereford.
>
> A local – improbable – legend tells that it was at the forerunner of the Green Dragon Hotel in Broad Street that Edward stayed with his prisoner after the battle. What is without doubt is that Owen was beheaded in the market-place (High Town). Owen was called 'the handsomest man in England', which might have inspired what followed. After his head had been placed on the market cross, a madwoman combed his hair and washed the blood from his face. She also lit more than a hundred candles, placing them around the cross. Owen's body was afterwards buried in a chapel at the Greyfriars.
>
> Edward was soon king and acknowledging his debt to Herefordshire he made a royal progress to the city in September 1461. Twelve years later in 1473 he sent his son Edward and a number of counsellors to the city to establish what became the Council in the Marches of Wales but presumably because of the ruinous condition of the castle, by the end of the year they had moved to Ludlow. Edward and his queen came again in 1475 when, no doubt, they were received by Bishop Thomas Mylling who as abbot of Westminster had protected Elizabeth and her infant son during Edward's enforced exile. Young Edward was Mylling's godson and he was frequently at Ludlow assisting the prince in the government of Wales and the Marches.

The Leather Trades and the decline in prosperity

During the 15th century the number of leather workers in the city seems to suggest a movement away from wool-trading as a staple activity and perhaps a general decline in the prosperity of Hereford. General leather workers and shoemakers – corvisors – were to be found in many parts of the urban area, such as beyond Wye Bridge (1477) and Widemarsh Street (1398), but they also gathered in their own quarter in High Street called *corveseresrewe* – first mentioned in 1386/7. Also working in leather were saddlers and glovers (Maylord Street, 1463) and two tanners working the raw material in Widemarsh Street Without.[54] Leather strapping was also an important element in contemporary armour and from a case brought before the mayor's court in 1407/8 it seems that a substantial amount of armour was then being made in the city as well as later in the reign of Henry VII.[55] Smiths were present in the city in all periods and a forge is referred to in Union Street in 1368. William Anglice, the smith, died in 1433 and seems to have been fairly well off as he bought a place of burial in the cathedral churchyard. His son Thomas took over his business.[56]

Manufacturing and marketing of wool and leather was probably shifting to the countryside, free of the regulations imposed by city-based trade guilds.[57] By 1503 there were at least 22 trade companies in the city, listed as participants in the Corpus Christi pageant. The guilds probably had their origins much earlier in the Middle Ages but little is known about them until the 15th century when they began to enforce restrictive practices. In 1497 it was ordered that every tradesman who practised his craft within the city and its Liberty was to pay a 22s fee to join a trade guild.[58] Such restrictions were designed to preserve the monopoly of the craft or trade but ultimately it had a damaging effect on the prosperity of the city as traders set up in the countryside and the less regulated small towns. In terms of the cloth industry Hereford's loss was Ledbury's gain, for prosperous clothiers are found there in the 16th century.[59] Early in the same century the Coningsbys of Hampton Court set up a woollen mill at Hope-under-Dinmore and, in mysterious circumstances, the fulling mills on the Wye below Hereford, belonging to the Dean and Chapter, were destroyed.[60]

A glimpse into the state of Hereford in the late 15th and early 16th centuries is provided by a rental of the property belonging to St Guthlac's Priory running from 1436 to 1559.[61] The priory, a cell of Gloucester Abbey, had been on its last legs since the late 14th century and found difficulty in recruiting monks, having suffered at least twice from the plague. It was virtually bankrupt and yet it had a large portfolio of property in and around Hereford. Like many institutions in this era it was having difficulty collecting rent, which seemed to be fixed at a nominal rate. George Scudamore of Holme Lacy, for example, held about 100 acres of freehold land by knight's service at one or two pence per acre, when the average in England was more like six pence per acre. Customary tenants paid a little more but during the century covered by the rental, which was steeply inflationary towards the end, the rents remained virtually static. There were nominally about 100 tenements held by the priory in the city, some of which, as time went on, were either lost or could not be identified. There was a tendency for these to become garden ground or remain empty, being referred to as 'void ground' or 'being now decayed' – yards, orchards and 'myskyns' (dung heaps) proliferated. Hereford was in decline and although there were still prosperous citizens to be found, they lived cheek by jowl with poverty and degradation. It come as no surprise to find that a few years later, in the reign of Henry VIII, Hereford appears on a government list of English towns 'in need of re-edification'.

9   THE MEDIEVAL BUILDINGS OF HEREFORD

WITH THE LOSS of income and business as the importance of Hereford Castle declined and the new towns in Wales secured their own economic hinterlands, Hereford's economy started to stagnate. Taxation records show the city's national ranking slipping from 13th place in 1334 to 19th in 1377. It was still at 19th place in 1523-7, but by the end of the 16th century there is evidence that the suburbs were losing population. Henry VIII's closing of two fulling mills and two corn mills would have contributed to a decline in prosperity and perhaps also to a shift in the production of cloth away from Hereford to the smaller towns and the countryside. Nevertheless, the city authorities deemed that trade warranted the construction of a new three-storey timber-framed Market Hall in High Town, whilst several cellars appear to have been built in stone in the 15th century (see below). It would seem most likely, therefore, to have been the Civil War that seriously damaged Hereford's economy, for it does not feature amongst the top 42 provincial towns listed in the 1662 Hearth Tax returns.

The lack of economic stimulus during the 1600s and early 1700s, which lasted until there was a drift of population to the towns in the Georgian period, meant that Hereford remained a settlement comprised largely of timber-framed buildings well into the 1700s. Only then, with the cost of coal to fire brick kilns becoming cheaper, due first to the improvement in the Wye Navigation in the late 1690s and then the construction of the Hay tramroad, did building in brick become the norm (see chapter 12). Even then, many of the existing timber-framed buildings were only partially replaced, often being simply faced in the new brickwork.

The use of stone
The exceptions to this rule were the ecclesiastical buildings, which were largely built of stone apart from the College of Vicars Choral, which consisted of a timber-framed first floor over a stone-built ground floor. Hereford does not have an available supply of building stone close at hand and that used to build the cathedral and the churches of All Saints and St Peter's largely came from quarries at Capler near How Caple some 9 miles away. With the river often not at a level suitable for transport upstream of the quarries, most of the stone had to be brought to the city by cart. (The sources of stone used for the city walls in the 13th and 14th centuries are less certain, with some use of Old Red Sandstone but possibly also a mixture of stone from glacial deposits in the Wye and Lugg Valleys.[1])

Stone was also used to create a number of cellars, including the Saxon one found during the excavation in advance of construction of the building to house the Mappa Mundi and cathedral library (see p.26). A thorough investigation of the medieval cellars and undercrofts of the buildings in the city centre has never been possible, in part because of their use as storage areas by the shops above and also due to difficulties in access. From what is known, it appears that the earliest cellars under the existing shops date from the 13th century, again supporting the views of William of Malmesbury concerning the poor state of Hereford in about 1125 (see p.32).

One of the cellars that has been investigated, on the north side of Eign Gate, shows it to have contained a rear room which had recesses with low ceilings, suggesting that they were designed to hold storage vessels or possibly barrels, allowing the building to be used as a cellar tavern, with the room at the front for customers. The building would have been substantial, for its frontage was over 30 feet (equivalent to two 'normal' burgage plots). The thickness of the wall dividing the front and back chambers and the presence in it of a fireplace (with the implication of a stack rising above) suggests that the building would have been divided between a commercial frontage range – probably (as now) a row of shops – and a hall range immediately to the rear – an arrangement paralleled widely in other towns and elsewhere in Hereford.

The above cellar was built of ashlar, as is the case with others investigated in High Town and St Peter's Street. There cellars were accessed by steps leading directly down from the street and were given at least some light through light-wells, whilst several had barrel-receptive recesses suggesting use as cellar taverns. Of the five that have been investigated, all appear to have been built in the 15th century, probably in the latter part, pointing to a period of rebuilding that is now only represented above-ground by the Booth Hall.

Fig. 9.1 *The cellar bar at The Pippin, 3 Widemarsh Street, in the latter part of the 20th century with, inset, a boss from the neighbouring cellar*

The design of buildings

In contrast to the narrow plans evident in High Town, the undercrofts that survive beneath the rear of 2-5 Widemarsh Street are indicative of an extremely wide mercantile plot in single ownership in the 15th century. The principal building, in this case fairly certainly a very substantial hall and cross-wing, was laid out across the rear of the plot whilst the frontage was densely sub-divided into commercial tenancies. The high-quality workmanship throughout and the decorative panels and possible merchants' marks set into the vault demonstrate that at least the main cellar was a space that was designed to be seen and to impress (Fig. 9.1). Its use may well have been purely mercantile, for the selling of whatever goods its 15th-century owners dealt in, but its eventual use was as a tavern, a use that continued into the 20th century as The Pippin.

The narrowest plots or burgages were those facing onto High Town – the Anglo-Norman market-place. As with many early market-places from which burgage plots radiated, the oldest surviving buildings were constructed in the 16th or 17th centuries with their main rooms arranged at right-angles to the street. It is likely that these buildings followed the plan of their forerunners, which would match what is found in other towns. The front ground-floor room would have been the shop from which, when open, a horizontal plank or board would have extended the display space out into the street. Above the shop were the main rooms of the house. Behind the shop would be the open hall (floored over with rooms at first-floor level from about 1550 onwards) whilst service and storage rooms would lie to the rear, these rooms being dimly lit from a side passage.

As seen in the layout of the building above the cellars in Eign Gate and that at 2-5 Widemarsh Street, the other medieval floor plan saw the hall built parallel to the street, across the width of a plot and set back behind a commercial frontage. Such buildings did not survive well after the Middle Ages, becoming sub-divided, generally on the line of the frontage tenancies. Some very wealthy inhabitants were able to build such 'wide' houses with no commercial frontage, such as the early 17th-century Farmers' Club, just within Widemarsh Gate, built for a family of recurrent mayoral office-holders. Another example was 50a St Owen Street, built in the late 16th century just inside the city gate, where three rooms formed the frontage.

In all probability Hereford's main trading streets would have been fronted by two-storey structures from the early 13th century. By the beginning of the 15th century, buildings with three-storey frontages are more likely to have been present on the main streets and those with two-storey frontages on secondary ones.

After about 1550 building styles changed in Hereford, following trends elsewhere. As noted above, the open hall was converted to a ground-floor hall with rooms at first-floor level, requiring more hearths and chimney stacks. Additional storeys required stair towers so as to reach the upper rooms. Within buildings, rooms that had once been interconnected were often, by the end of the 17th century, reached via a corridor.

Lofts, floored attics and dormer gables to light spaces at attic level were all new features of city buildings from the early 17th century, and must have irrevocably changed the city skyline. The Old House of 1621, for example, has attics in the dormer gables with a cockloft (a small upper loft) above.

Timber-framed Buildings
No timber buildings survive from the first three or four centuries of the beginning of Hereford as a town, the only evidence being from archaeological excavations. These show that the earliest type of structure – a timber building reliant on the load-bearing capacity and rigidity of earth-fast posts set in post-holes – began to be superseded in the 10th to 12th centuries by more complex self-supporting framed structures based on horizontal sill beams. There then followed a widespread transition to stone foundation walls or plinths that carried properly braced timber frames; such masonry footings were relatively damp-proof and the superstructures they carried could survive for very long periods. According to the archaeology, this transition took place in the mid to late 13th century.

Most of the medieval framing is box-framed with varieties of square panelling, the panels being typically quite large and the stave supports for the wattle-and-daub infills quite substantial and almost structural. Close studding is known to have been used in the city towards the end of the medieval period. It was not a structural necessity – it was a display of wealth, the lavish use of timber implying that money was no object in a new building. The largest scale use of this technique in Hereford survives in the cloister walk of the College of the Vicars Choral.

Hereford was clearly not a town with flamboyantly decorative timber-framing to rival the likes of Ludlow or Shrewsbury. The fanciest domestic timber-framed façade surviving from the medieval period was at 3 High Street, with a single-bay frontage, jetties at three levels, carved brackets with masked heads, boxed oriel five-light windows with ovolo-moulded frame and quatrefoil-pattern studding: this is now marooned at first-floor level in the 1960s' building that now houses New Look. Easily overlooked and rarely cleaned, it is better known locally as the building that, whilst the Littlewood's store was built, was moved off its site on rollers, left in High Town for a while and then moved back again, rather than for the exemplary quality of its carpentry.

Ceramic ridge tiles first appear in Hereford's archaeological record in the mid-13th century, but more commonly after the end of that century; flat ceramic roof tiles do not appear until the 16th.[2] The absence of flat tiles before that date may suggest (in the absence of stone tiles in contemporary archaeological contexts) that organic roofing materials were commonly used, either thatch (cereal straw) or wooden shingles. Stone tiles eventually appear as waste material in 16th-century and later deposits, but it is difficult to estimate how long they had been commonly in use prior to that.

Internal Decoration
Before 1500, most of the internal decoration that survives is limited to moulded and shaped timbers, most notably still evident in the Bishop's Palace, but elsewhere too, such as 20 Church Street, 50a Commercial Street, the surviving rear part of 41a Bridge Street and the Booth Hall.

Documentary evidence for medieval decoration and furnishings in a middle-class domestic setting is scanty, but perhaps the earliest evidence there is for furnishings concerns John Viall, one of the cathedral canons at Harley Court, who left in his will of November 1526 one bed with a tapestry coverlet ('a coverynge after Carpet makinge'), and to Master William Edwards, who was to have the house after him, 'all my hanging of my house'. It looks as though these hangings were made to fit the house and so it made sense for his successor to inherit them.[3]

After 1500 and up to c.1700, most surviving internal decoration takes the form of plasterwork, sometimes original to the building, sometimes added. Most of this is fairly naïve, perhaps provincial or even rustic, but enthusiastic. Amongst the finest plasterwork in the city is that in one of the first-floor chambers of 24-5 Church Street known as the Mayor's Parlour. The decoration probably dates from the rebuilding of the house prior to 1627 by James Lawrence, who leased the property from the Vicars Choral. This is probably the James Lawrence who was Mayor of Hereford at the time; he was also a J.P. and may have adapted the building as an office in which to conduct his legal affairs.

There is a surprising lack of surviving high-quality woodwork in the city after 1500 – with no really grand 16th- or 17th-century staircases or elaborately wainscoted rooms, although contemporary inventories show that they were a feature of the wealthier houses in Hereford.

Wall Paintings[4]

A few buildings in the city are host to wall paintings, a form of decoration used in wealthier homes largely in the period 1570-1625. They were a development from painted cloths which had been used as a cheaper form of wall hangings than tapestries, and before the hanging of paintings on walls became common practice. The wall paintings were sometimes simply decorative friezes, sometimes more complicated patterns that incorporated both the timbers and panels of a wall within a timber-framed building. Some of the panels might include the family's heraldry (after all, such decoration was usually in the rooms to which the owner would invite guests whom they wanted to impress), religious or moralising texts, architectural patterns, geometric designs or, as in many of the examples in Hereford, human figures. These might aim to show the house owners in a particular light, or refer to biblical or classical stories.

The Black Lion in Bridge Street was built between 1550 and 1575 and altered in the first quarter of the 17th century. A series of paintings in a first-floor chamber show the breaking of the Ten Commandments. The paintings have text beneath and are separated from each other by ornamental bands. The labour-intensive design indicates that this was the house of a well-off merchant or inn-keeper.

In the ground-floor parlour of The Old House is the painting of a figure (Fig. 9.2) and some text which are original. The building is also home to wall paintings moved here from other buildings. Two Old Testament scenes – of Joseph interpreting the pharaoh's dream (Fig. 9.3) and of Joseph presenting Jacob to the pharaoh (Fig. 9.4) – painted c.1600-25, were moved from 5 (formerly

Fig. 9.3 Joseph interpreting the pharaoh's dream   *Fig. 9.2 Figure at The Old House*

3-4) Widemarsh Street and probably came from a first-floor chamber. The other is a figure of Euterpe (Fig. 9.5), one of the nine muses who was subsequently assigned the role of the muse of music, and is shown playing the flute, a common depiction. This is probably of a later date than most wall paintings, possibly *c.*1677.

By the end of the 17th century interior decoration was becoming more sophisticated, plasterwork more restrained, and colour coordination more important. At 24-5 Commercial Street John Rawlins had a blue room, a green room and a red room in his house when he died. A green room features in Richard Andrews' inventory at 10-11 High Town, whilst at the King's Head, by the old North Gate to the Saxon town, the room-names – the Flower de Luce, the Mitre, the Sun, the Rose, the Half Moon and so on – presumably reflected the distinctive decorative schemes to be seen in each.

Fig. 9.4 *Joseph presenting Jacob to the pharaoh*   Fig. 9.5 *Euterpe*

Some Individual Buildings

In considering some examples of the city's buildings, a number have been selected in what is sometimes termed 'the cathedral city' – north and east of the Close, around Church Street and Castle Street – and others in the 'commercial city', centred on High Town. The former is essentially devoid of retail functions and largely still comprises medieval and Georgian architecture; the latter the rest of the intra-mural city where commercial functions predominate.

The Cathedral City

As the new stone cathedral rose in the first half of the 1100s, the surrounding area had also to accommodate dwellings for the bishop, the dean and the residentiary canons or prebendaries (known as such as each was supported by the tithes of a living – a prebend – in the diocese). Canons have been described as 'the elite of the medieval church'. 'Able and established clerics, they were highly educated with successful careers in the service of the church or crown by the time they became canons. Possession of a canonry was a highly desirable reward and mark of status, much sought after by ambitious clerks.'[5] Since the canons were not chosen for their musical ability and in any case were often absent, either living at their prebend or away on cathedral business, vicars choral (vicar means substitute) were appointed to sing the services. The vicars choral also had to be housed. Other buildings included the canons' bakehouse, barns for the produce provided by the prebends and a school.

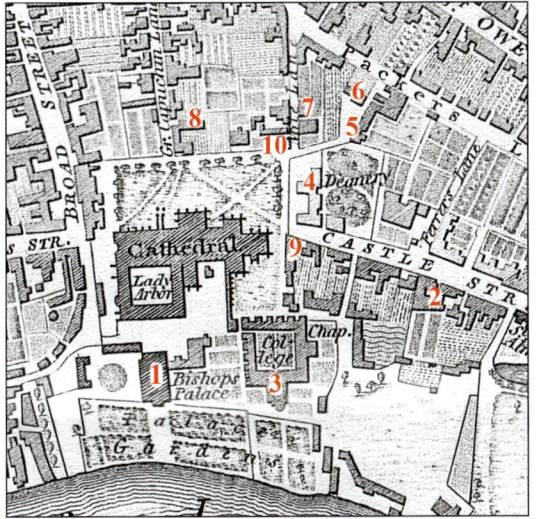

Fig. 9.6 Brayley's map of 1806 with the location of the buildings in the Cathedral City mentioned in this section numbered in red. Note that St John Street was then called Mile Lane (it was Mill Lane on Taylor's map of 1757) and also Milk Lane, and Church Street was called Great Capuchin Lane.

1. The Bishop's Palace

At the time that the new Norman cathedral was being built it is likely that the bishop was living somewhere to its south, near where Bishop Robert de Losinga built a chapel of two storeys dedicated to St Katherine and St Mary Magdalene (see p.61).

The present palace was probably begun by William de Vere (bishop 1186-98) about a hundred years after Losinga built his chapel. De Vere is known to have been a great builder, familiar with current architectural fashion (he supervised Henry II's building project at Waltham Abbey) and far from being an archaic anachronism, the design and construction of the palace were in the forefront of current technology. The initial building took the form of an aisled hall, some 32m long by 17m wide, with masonry gable ends and aisle walls but with a timber-framed arcade and a clerestorey. It had four bays with a stone porch in the west wall and a narrow chamber-block of three floors over a basement built at right-angles against the south gable wall. This building would have been a fine example of a timber-framed lordly hall, with a central fireplace open to the roof. It reflected the most up-to-date styles of the Angevin court and is one of the grandest 12th-century timber buildings to survive in England.

The building has undergone major transformations over the centuries, with large scale re-organisations by Bishop Bisse (1712-21) and Bishops Huntingford and Musgrave in the first half of the 19th century, during which the hall was truncated and turned into a two-storey entrance hall. Within this hall six of the original posts survive, representing three bays, and the

Fig. 9.7 Roof timbers of the Bishop's Palace aisled hall showing decoration on the arched braces. (Photograph by Gordon Taylor, © Hereford Cathedral Library)

Fig. 9.8 The vignette from Isaac Taylor's map depicting the Bishop's Palace with the cathedral behind as seen from across the river. On the left is the old three-storey chamber block with its several chimneys. On the right is the external chamber block joined by a covered passage to the main hall. The relationship is shown on Taylor's 1757 map (see p.x).

arches connecting these posts can be seen in the attics (Fig. 9.7). The posts supported the side aisles of the hall and extended above the arches to allow a clerestorey.[6] The timber may have come from the Forest of Dean where Bishop Robert Foliot, de Vere's predecessor, is known to have left felled and sawn timber when he died.

At some stage a much larger chamber block was built to the east of the hall and attached to it by a covered passage. This block was destroyed in one of the 19th-century rebuildings but can be seen on 18th- and 19th-century maps of the area and is portrayed in the vignette

Fig. 9.9 The west elevation of the hall before work began in the 1840s.
(Herefordshire Records and Archive Centre)

accompanying Isaac Taylor's map (Fig. 9.8). Until recently understanding of this structure and the rest of the palace was based on archaeology and the surveys of the building, now in the Bodleian Library, by the architect, Philip Hardwick, who was responsible for the 1840 modernisation and repair work.[7] Recently, however, instructions issued to the builders regarding the dismantling of the chamber block have come to light at Herefordshire Archives.[8] Care was to be taken during the work, and the stained glass, the Norman entrance door, and all 'Reliques or Curiousities' were to be retained, whilst the dismantling of the entrance porch was singled out to be done with 'very great care'.

Any remains of the chamber block are now under the lawn to the east of the Bishop's Palace.

2. College of the Vicars Choral, 29 Castle Street

In 1395 the vicars choral were incorporated into a college by Richard II as *Collegium vicariorum in choro ecclesie Herefordensis* and it is usually assumed that No.29 Castle Street, the college's first home, dates from the incorporation.[9] However, a licence from the Chapter in 1336 had already granted a 'habitation' in Castle Street to the vicars choral[10] and a charter of 1375 describes how an old blind vicar choral, Roger de Clehungre, assigned property in Hungery Street (now St Owen Street) in exchange for a room called the *cysterne chaumbre* in the communal house of the vicars in Castle Street and a promise that he should receive meals in their common hall for life.

This may imply that the Vicars Choral building was already in place before 1395. It is at least possible that old blind Roger heard that his erstwhile colleagues were getting the benefit of a new building and took action to secure his own position there. If this speculation is correct the ancient structure embedded in 29 Castle Street is the hall where Roger ate with his brethren and can be dated to *c*.1375.

The 10m long and 6.7m wide hall, which lies behind the present Georgian façade, is built of old red sandstone at right angles to the street and has a fine timber roof with cusped wind braces. Two tall narrow windows survive on either side of the building and the matching doorways (now blocked) to the screens passage remain at the north end of the hall. Little is known about the layout of the rest of the building although clues can be gleaned from later documents.

As far as the vicars choral were concerned, however, the new building was not an unqualified success. The vicars complained that some of their number could not attend the midnight service because of the distance from the cathedral and the danger from 'evil-doers'. In 1472 a site for a new building was therefore agreed, nearer the cathedral and east of the garden of the Bishop's Palace.[11]

The later history of 29 Castle Street is of some interest. In 1578 Catherine Darnell took a lease of the 'Old College' and two houses to its west. Mrs Darnell was to 'well and sufficiently and townlike build a forefront upon the old building from the hall doore or porch of the said college unto a back yate [gate] upon the East side' within the following seven years.[12] It appears the service wing had been demolished and she was required to replace it with a proper urban façade. The entrance porch was presumably on the west side of the hall and the new frontage extended from this to the 'back yate', possibly the exit at the other end of the screens passage.

Nearly 100 years later in 1670 another deed, made to Nicholas Phippotts, described the site as 'divided into three dwellings' and having a gatehouse and outbuildings. There were dovehouses next to the river, probably at the end of Quay Street, on one side while a lane led to the castle and waste ground called the castle ditch on the other (St Ethelbert Street). It seems likely that the Old College occupied this large block.

A reference in a 1720s probate inventory to an 'Inner Court' and another to the 'Benches round the room' suggests that the built-in medieval benches round the hall still survived and that the 'inner court' may represent the cloister of the mediaeval establishment, perhaps shown on Isaac Taylor's map of 1757 (Fig. 9.6, above the figure 2 in red).[13]

3. The new College in the Close[14]

The site chosen in 1472 for the new (and present) college previously housed two of the canons, Canon Wolston and Canon Greene. Canon Wolston's house may have burnt down some time previously, but the great hall of Canon Greene's high status house had been used by the bishop for transacting business as recently as 1466. It seems that Greene's hall formed the basis for the new college hall and that the cloister adjoined it to the north.

The cloister, sandwiched between the cathedral and the castle motte, was built of old red sandstone, like its predecessor, with an open arcade to the courtyard. It contained 27 two-roomed units. The upper floor of each of these units, a two-bay hall, projected over the cloister walk, the lower smaller room being divided from the walk by a timber-framed wall of close studding. Each room was provided with a fireplace (Fig. 9.10). In contrast to the front walls of

Fig. 9.10 The College of Vicars Choral built at the end of the 1400s, as seen from the north-west. (Photograph by Gordon Taylor, © Hereford Cathedral Library)

the lodging, the partition walls between them were constructed of wide panelled timber frames with wattle and daub infill, while within each lodging the bays in the upper hall were divided by an arch-braced truss with a trefoil pattern formed by cusping. The timber corbels supporting the principal rafters were decorated with shields.

The north, west and east ranges of the cloister were similar in length but the south range was considerably shorter, resulting in an irregularly-shaped structure. It has been suggested that this was due to late changes in the design during the three-year building programme, when it was decided to replace one two-storey lodging on the east side with a chapel and library over, and to provide an extra lodging in the northern range. In recognition of the vicars' original complaint, a covered passage was added between the north-eastern corner of the cloister and the south-east transept of the cathedral, allowing the vicars to reach the cathedral unmolested.

The custos (warden) occupied one of the lodgings in the north range and there was also a kitchen where a cook concocted the meals that the vicars ate communally in their hall. Thomas Dingley, writing in the 1680s, described this hall as 'very fair and square … looking into their Garden and towards the River Wye'.

There have been considerable changes to the building over the centuries. The reduction in the number of vicars choral in the post-Reformation period led to over half of the lodgings being disused and others amalgamated to make larger houses. At the end of the 17th century the medieval hall, the remains of Canon Greene's house, was rebuilt and it was further extended before the Three Choirs Festival in 1783. A disastrous fire in 1828 was the cause of the south-west end of the southern range – which had previously been the preserve of the butler and other servants – being rebuilt in brick.

The canonical houses
Apart from the canonical houses that were incorporated into the new Vicars Choral College, there are a group of dwellings along the northern side of the Close that housed the canons or prebendaries who served the cathedral. They include Nos.1 and 2 The Close (The Precentor's House and The Archdeacon's House) and 20 Church Street at the rear of No.2. To the north of the Old Deanery (on the east side of the Close) is a small lane called Harley Court that leads eastwards to Harley Court itself (now two houses). To the north of this lane, on the corner with St John Street, is Harley House, and No.3 St John Street is on the opposite side.

4. The Deanery
The Deanery was rebuilt in the mid-19th century with financial help from Queen Adelaide[15] and is now part of the Cathedral School. Its garden had occupied a large plot on the north-west corner of Castle Street since the 13th century. The grounds of the Deanery probably stretched for some distance along the north side of Castle Street.

5. Harley Court
Harley Court (as it was known from the 19th century) was, unusually for a canonical residence, administered by the Dean and Chapter rather than the bishop.[16] The house was granted to Master John Gatesby in 1406 in consideration of the repairs he had carried out.[17] This house, described in 1263/4, as 'in the corner near the Dean's houses', was later often described as in Milk Lane (later St John Street).

In the 16th century Harley Court was occupied by a number of canons. John Wardroper, who died in 1515, was granted the property in 1512 and was followed by Canon John Viall. Viall's lease, made in 1515, contained a clause requiring him to repair the house and to supply materials except for 'the large timber' which would be provided by the Dean and Chapter.[18]

The next known lease was granted in 1524 to Master William Edwards, who was one of Wardroper's executors, but John Viall was still the occupant. It seems likely that when Viall died in 1525, Edwards, by now a canon, moved back into the property and remained there until he resigned his prebend in 1528, for Viall left him all the hangings in the house (as noted above). John Viall's will also indicates that he had a parlour, with a room over it, and at least two beds well provided with linen. He had a servant and a butler, and Alice 'of the kechyn' was presumably his cook.

The house was retained as a canon's house until the early 17th century when it was leased to Herbert Westfaling, the son of the then bishop of Hereford (1585-1602). It was probably in the 1740s that the present brick façade was added, and the two large semi-detached Georgian houses alongside were built almost anew. In more recent times No.5 was split into two houses, the southern part being the home of Alfred Watkins in the early 20th century.

The southern part of Harley Court includes a cellar with the remains of a 14th-century timber-framed hall above. The remainder of the building is of later date. The roof was drawn by W.W. Robinson in 1884 (Fig. 9.11). It consists of four arch-braced principals, besides the end ones, two having tie beams. One row of purlins divide the roof into two panels, the rafters being strengthened and decorated with handsome cusped wind-braces. Watkins states that 'the timber-framed house to which it is now attached is about 150 years later in date with a huge central chimney stack, but its Elizabethan style is, like the earlier hall, completely disguised by the whole being faced with bricks in early Georgian days, the pretty doorways ... the neatly panelled doors, and the simple staircase belonging to that period'.[19]

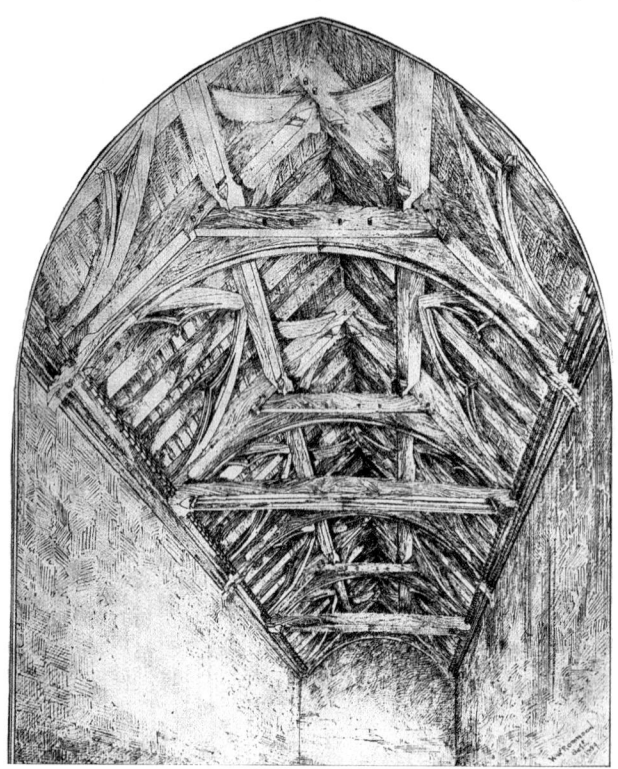

Fig. 9.11 The roof of Harley Court from a drawing by W.W. Robinson in 1884, when the house was being restored. It is of likely early 15th-century date and as such would probably form part of the repairs carried out in 1406.

6. Harley House

Harley House, on the north side of Harley Court Lane, is of three storeys with cellars and attics; the walls are of stone with some brick and the roofs are tiled. The walls of the cellars and the narrow south-western block are probably medieval, the upper part of this block being partly rebuilt in the 16th century. In the 17th century the south-east wing and the north stable wing were added. The former was refaced in ashlar in 1739, with stone said to be derived from the destroyed chapter-house. In the 1930s the Royal Commission noted that 'In the garden are numerous worked and moulded stones of 12th to 15th century date'.[20]

7. No.3 St John Street

The north-west wing was built late in the 14th or early in the 15th century and has a roof of five bays with simple hammer-beam trusses, and the cross-wing at its east end was added or rebuilt in the 16th century and then extended to the south in the 17th-century; the staircase wing is also of this date, but the staircase is modern although incorporating some 17th-century material. On the east front are two 16th-century windows, with four-centred lights in square heads.[21]

8. 20 Church Street

In 1328 the bishop decided that the Dean and Chapter were oversupplied with houses for the canons and that two empty houses on small plots at the cathedral end of Cabache Lane (now Church Street), should be replaced by one larger more suitable house.[22]

Fig. 9.12 Church Street runs northwards on the edge of this photograph taken from the cathedral tower. The roof and upper floors of No.2 The Close are in the foreground with 20 Church Street behind it. (© Derek Foxton Archives)

Fig. 9.13 The crown post roof at 20 Church Street.

By 1397, the house was in need of repair and modernisation. In the manner of the time the building was leased to John Carpenter (also Menysere),[23] who, within four years, was required to repair the existing house together with others on both sides of the road.[24] In addition he was to modernise the house by adding a chamber of two bays. This was probably the cross wing at the east end which was demolished and rebuilt in brick in 1723. Menysere was forbidden to sell stone, tiles or timber from the site, but he was granted a 40-year lease which allowed him to recoup his outlay on the building by letting the property to secular tenants.

In 1428 the house was let to David Leche, citizen of Hereford; it lay between Master John Stanway's canonical house to the south (probably the site of No.2 The Close) and the lane to John Radenor's house to the north, and extended from Cabache Lane on the west to Master John Berewe's garden (probably No.1 The Close) on the east, and included a row of shops along the frontage. In 1440 it was once again occupied by a canon, Canon Ashby.[25] The access to 20 Church Street was then by a narrow lane from the Close between nos.1 & 2.

The property consisted of a medieval two-storey, three-bay timber building with a crown post roof, believed to be an unique example in Hereford and rare in the county (Fig. 9.13). There was a large room on each floor, the upper floor forming a high status space, open to the roof, reached by decorative doorways and lit by large windows. The lower floor was also well lit, but with plainer decoration. Doorways at the west end of the upper walls demonstrate that this was only part of a much larger house and a later inventory, that of Robert Crowley or Crawley, sheds light on the accommodation in the mid 16th century.

Robert Crowley was a prominent Protestant writer and printer. He fell foul of the authorities during the reign of the Catholic Mary Tudor and fled to the Continent, where he lived in Frankfurt. On Mary's death he returned to England and, in 1560, was made first a canon and then archdeacon of Hereford Cathedral, although he retained a parish in London.

Despite being a popular preacher and writer, Crowley's uncompromising adherence to Protestant doctrine caused him problems. He refused to wear vestments when preaching on the grounds that they were 'popish', and he also created a disturbance over the robing of the choir at his London church. For this he was deprived of his living and imprisoned in 1566. The following year he resigned his archdeaconry at Hereford and spent the rest of his life in London, where he died in 1588.

His inventory of 20 Church Street was obviously written in haste and may reflect the pressure he was under to leave. Unlike a probate inventory, which sets a value on furnishings, this merely lists his own property. We can picture him hurrying round the house with paper, quill and inkhorn, scribbling down the items that would need to be loaded on to the carrier's wagon for the journey to London.[26]

In the parlour, probably the upper hall, he noted table, chair, form and fire irons. His own room merely contained bed and bedding as did an inner chamber, both perhaps in the cross wing. He had pewter and linen in the buttery, an iron 'stooffe' (stove – possibly from his continental travels) in the lower hall and andirons in the kitchen, which probably lay between the hall and the street. There were more beds and bedding upstairs in the great chamber next to Cabache Lane and his 'chamber of boks' contained over 200 volumes of all sizes.

The early 18th century saw the demolition of the east wing and the building was repaired again in 1747.[27] In the 19th century it became the home of three successive organists, the last being Dr George Robertson Sinclair, a friend of Sir Edward Elgar, whose bulldog Dan was immortalised in Variation 11 of Elgar's Enigma Variations.[28] By the 20th century it was in a 'bad state' and was sold by the Church Commissioners in 1930.

The following buildings also formed part of the Cathedral City.

9. The Canons' Bakehouse

The grain provided from the tithes of the canons' livings was not only used for the support of the canons but also supplied the charitable giving of the cathedral. The bakehouse was in existence by the early 13th century and stood on the south corner of Castle Street and the Close, now occupied by the Cathedral School. There was also a communal oven and a chapter brewhouse.[29]

10. The Cathedral Barn[30]

The barn, now used as a school centre for the cathedral, stands at the north-eastern corner of the Close. Archaeological excavations have shown that it stood on top of the remains of a massive wall, assumed to be a boundary wall for the Close (see p.75). This wall was probably in use until the 16th or early 17th century; the barn must have been later in date.

To help resolve its dating, the barn was surveyed in detail in 1987 and it was suggested that 'the building was probably of 13th-century origin with a later phase of development in the 15th century.'[31] These conclusions were reinforced in 1996 when samples of the main timbers were taken for dendrochronological dating. The earliest samples provided a felling range of 1253-88, whilst samples from the later period gave a precise felling date of 1491.[32]

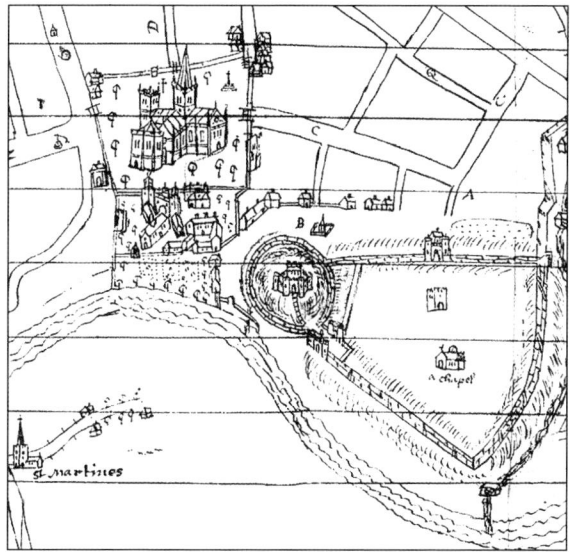

Fig. 9.14 An extract from Speed's 1606 sketch of Hereford (in preparation for his map of 1610) which clearly shows the Cathedral Close's precinct wall. (Merton College Library D.3.30, no.7, reproduced courtesy of the Warden and Fellows of Merton College Oxford)

The tree-ring dates were incompatible with the presence of the stone precinct wall and this was well brought out in a short report for a visit by the Society for the Protection of Ancient Buildings (SPAB) in 2010 entitled 'A sixteenth-century re-cycled prefab'.[33] This was not just an eye-catching title, for all timber-framed buildings are first laid out in framing-yards where the joints are carefully made and marked with numbers. When all the parts of the frame have been completed, the timbers are taken to the construction site and the building can then be quickly erected. The reverse is, of course, true. When a building of this nature is taken down, the individual timbers are then available for re-use, either as a reconstruction of the whole or part of the original building, or for use as individual timbers, often cut and in new positions. This is what happened at the barn site, the timbers belonging to a building that originally stood on another site.

Fig. 9.15 *The roof of 1492 which was reused in the Cathedral Barn*

Fig. 9.16 *The Cathedral Barn as reconstructed from its two separate buildings*

There were sufficient remains of this earlier building within the barn to reconstruct a reasonably accurate picture of what had been a medieval structure, probably aisled and of four bays, the eastern bay being shorter that the rest. The parts that were removed to the barn included seven of the ten aisle posts and substantial parts of the two arcade plates that joined them together. The roof of the hall having been badly weathered by time, that of a second timber-framed building, somewhat the same size as the barn, was re-used in the construction of the new building.

Part of the 16th-century timber south wall and the lower part of the end gables were rebuilt in stone in the late 17th century, while the wattle and daub infill was probably replaced in brick in the 18th century.

The open nature of the building suggests that the 16th- or 17th-century builders had intended it as a barn, possibly for space for grain storage much needed by the canons (known to have been an issue at that period), and so living up to its name that has been passed down over the centuries.[34] Extensive repairs carried out in 1879 show that the barn had been used for some time as a coach house and stables by the occupants of No.1 The Close.[35]

The Cathedral School

The cathedral is known to have had a school since the 12th century, but its original location is in some doubt.[36] In 1406 one of the canons was granted the property between the house of the Dean of Hereford, the canonical house of Henry Buyton (probably Harley House) and the highway called Olde Scole Street. This would place the earlier school in the region of Harley Court (see also p.177).

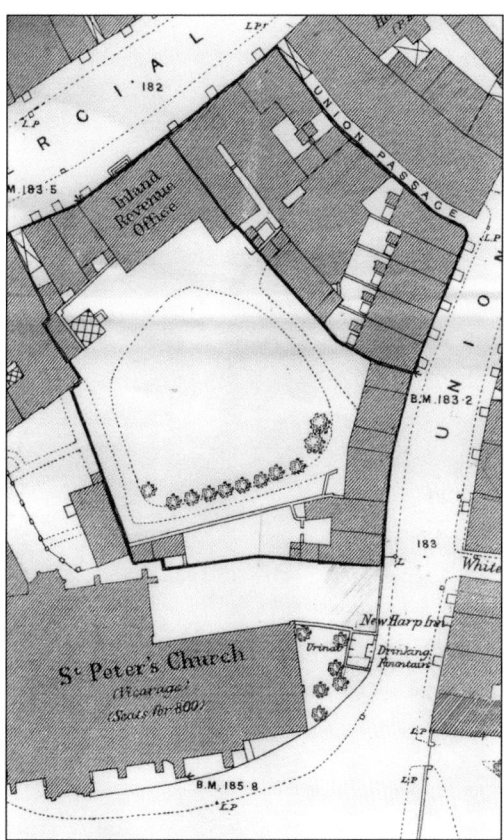

Fig. 9.17 The original plot to the north of St Peter's church outlined in black. This might have originally served to house the church's canons.

The Commercial City

At much the same time as the Norman cathedral was being built and the castle was spreading its bulk across the river frontage, William fitz Osbern was laying out a huge market-place to the north of the Saxon boundary ditch. A great triangular space was formed at the junction of the roads leading from the north, east and west.

Into this triangle Walter de Lacy built St Peter's church, a collegiate church where the services were led by a group of secular canons. It has been suggested that the plot immediately to the north of the church, whose shape and size is unlike any of the established building plots in the area (see Fig. 9.17), housed the canons who served the church.[37]

There are a number of buildings with mediaeval origins which are associated with this part of the market-place. Some of these are still standing, if only in part; others are known from maps and paintings. They comprise the Old House – the last remaining vestige of the buildings in the Market Rows, the 15th-century Booth Hall, the adjoining Blue Boar, and, to the north of St Peter's church, No.50a Commercial Street. At the end of the Rows stood the fine timbered Market Hall, completed in 1576.

The Old House

According to the shield above the central gable, the Old House was built in 1621. All the images of the building depict it as a butcher's shop and the arms of the London Butcher's Company are displayed above the porch. It was not the final house in the row, for another house was built, probably about the same date, to the east of it.

Fig. 9.18 Some of the decorated bargeboards on the north-east elevation of the Old House.

Fig. 9.19 The north-west and south-west elevations of the Old House.

The building is the best-preserved example of a timber-framed building in Hereford. The north-east elevation has a partly original bay window supported on scrolled brackets on the ground floor, three similar bay windows on the first floor, and the projecting top storey has a moulded bressumer with pendants representing bunches of grapes. Above are bargeboards carved with scrolls, birds and other decoration (Fig. 9.18). The south-west main front is broadly similar but also includes the partly restored porch. Inside, the ground-floor room to the north-west has original moulded ceiling-beams and panelling, whilst the room to the south-east has a plaster ceiling. There would originally have been no windows in the north-west and south-east walls as these would formed part of the longer row of buildings.

The occupants of the Old House in 1664 were Mary Jones, almost certainly the widow of the butcher John Jones, and Griffith Greenway, who probably ran the shop for her as Mary must have been in her 80s.[38] It was probably for John Jones that the house was built in 1621. Mary had a turbulent past. In 1625 she was indicted for being 'a comon sould, a drunckard and disturber of her neighbors, and one that is a comon curser swearer and blasphemer of gods name to the disquiett of his majesties subjects and disturbance of his highnes peace within the same Citty'.[39] In 1661, by then a widow, she had been fined for allowing her pigs to roam the streets.[40] She must have died in late 1664 or early 1665, for that year Richard Vincent is listed in the Hearth Tax returns, paying for the four hearths in the building.

After the clearance of the rest of the Rows, the house was bought by Alfred Gurney and, in 1882, it was sold to the Worcester City and County Bank which later became part of Lloyds Bank. The bank restored the house, making alterations as they did so, including removing the panelling from the 'dining room' to the bank premises on the ground floor. The bank moved to larger premises in 1927 and the following year donated the Old House to the city, whereupon further restoration was carried out. This included installing two fireplaces taken from other buildings: that in the main room being moved from Holmer Hall, and that in the smaller room from 9 Eign Street. The original first-floor ceiling structure is more complete than that on the ground floor, and this floor also retains its original fireplace and elaborately carved Jacobean over-mantel.

Two of the painted panels are original to the house, the others were moved here from other buildings in Hereford (see pp.119-20).

Fig. 9.20 Location plan for the buildings mentioned in the Commercial City.

The Booth Hall[41]

A record in the Hereford Corporation Archives of a grant made by Henry Cachepole on 28 September 1392 of the tenement called 'Bothealle' to three people is the first reference to this building and also indicates that it was used by the Merchants Guild. This was presumably an earlier building than the current structure, for tree-ring dating has shown that the timbers of the present building were cut down somewhere between 1454 and 1492.

On 2 February 1393 there is a further entry which reads:

> Licence from the King to the Mayor and citizens of Hereford, because they have no house, as they say, within the Castle or City of Hereford in which the justice of assize or peace, or the pleas of the City, can be held, to acquire in mortmain a messuage worth sixty shillings annually which belongs to [the three owners mentioned in the earlier record] and is held of the Crown in free burgage by the annual service of 18 pence.

As a Tolsey, which sometimes served as the Guildhall, was built in High Town in 1490, it is not known whether the city authorities used the Booth Hall for the purpose of justice for any length of time after they had acquired it.

In the 16th century the walls were repaired with wattle and daub, plastering was carried out and a side window was mended. There are several records in the Town Council archives concerning repairs to the building during the 16th century, when it was described as having 'fallen into ruin and decay.'[42] Towards the end of the 16th century the town council were augmenting their income by leasing out at least part of the property. However, in 1581 a petition from George Elyott, freeman, complained that the lessee Margaret Partridge 'will neither permit or suffer freemen to have their chambers at the Booth Hall according to the ancient custom, neither does she repair the chambers'. She also refused freemen access to visit their imprisoned colleagues in the premises which adjoined the Booth Hall. These were used to house freemen who had committed offences, instead of the less salubrious gatehouse in Bye Street (see p.48). Imprisoned freemen were also allowed the privilege of going to church, suitably accompanied, and also to go out to dine. However, in 1616, the earliest entry in the minute book of the Mercers Company records a levy of 6s 8d on the admission of new members towards the reparation of the chamber for the meeting of the said Fellowship, and in 1686 a further minute has a mention of the house or place called the 'Booth Hall'.

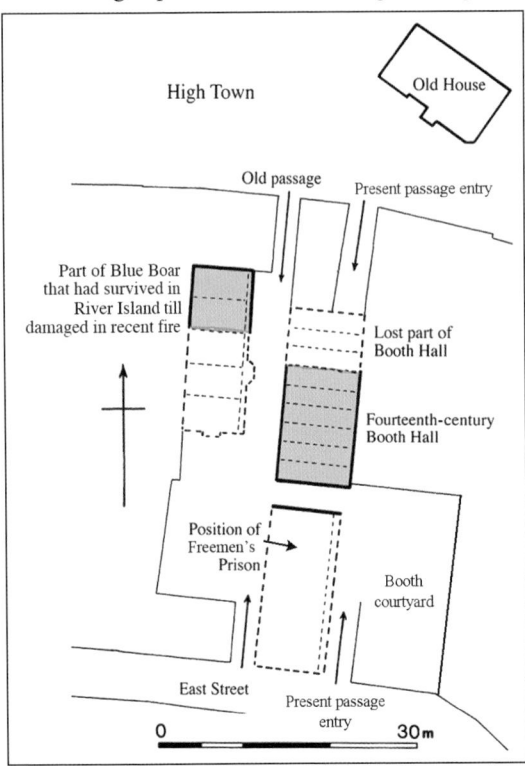

Fig. 9.21 Plan showing the layout of the Booth Hall, Blue Boar and Freemen's Prison.

In 1665, when the mayor and citizens granted the lease to a tanner, William Bowen, they expressly excluded the freemen's chambers.[43] Alfred Watkins, writing in 1934, states that the freemen's chambers were part of the neighbouring Blue Boar, but it seems more likely that they occupied the area between the Booth Hall and Packers Lane (East Street), part of which became the Booth Hall Inn at a later stage (Fig. 9.21).[44] It is known that the hall had a gallery at least in the 17th century, for James Carwardine was killed when he fell from it in 1625.[45]

It is uncertain when the Booth Hall actually became an inn, but it must have been before 1686 when Thomas Parry declared that 'Hee was att the Cockpitt at Peter Seabornes house called the Booth Hall seeing a cockfitting'.[46] However, there is evidence for an earlier date, for one Francis Goodier was indicted for selling ale without a licence in 1624.[47] The property was let to John Cule, who was also landlord of the Ship Inn in Butchers Row and who

Fig. 9.22 A sketch of the restored Booth Hall after the fall of a chimneystack revealed its existence in 1919.

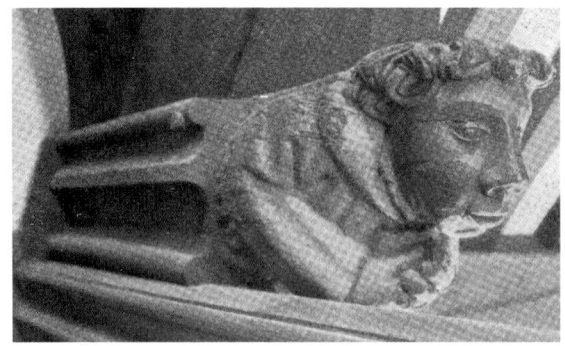

Fig. 9.23 One of the carvings in the restored Booth Hall.

paid the Hearth Tax on eight hearths for the Booth Hall in 1665.[48] There was access from High Town to Packers Lane (East Street) actually through the hall, a source of irritation to some landlords. Elizabeth Thorpe, using this 'common passage through the Boothall' as a short cut to her house in Milk Lane in 1690/91, was met by the publican who called her 'Bitch' and threw a bucket of water over her![49] Other landlords were themselves the cause of irritation. Philip Stephens kept a 'Boghouse' sufficiently close to the passage as to cause 'a great annoyance to passengers'.[50] Surviving leases show that various members of the Gwillim or Willim family were licensees during much of the 18th century. In the early part of the 19th century the Booth Hall had a notable landlord. This was Thomas Winter Spring (1795-1851). He was a barefist fighter and achieved fame in 1821 as the 'Champion of All England). After his illustrious career, Tom Spring took over the Booth Hall Inn in 1824. In 1827 Spring sold the Inn, the new owner and landlord being William Probert.

In 1876, a writer in the *Hereford Times* recollected that, in his youth:

> many times hearing of a ghost that was said to have haunted it, and that it was positively laid by a visitation of dignitaries of the Cathedral and other clergymen and pious people and sundry laymen, several of whom were somewhat of the wag genus. I have heard the late facetious 'Tom Cooke' describe the event, but I have now forgotten the particulars.

For many years the historic Hall was not the main part of the inn – this was the 19th-century range of buildings that extended from the Hall through to East Street and included an impressive Assembly Room that stretched through the present first and second floors. At this time the historic Booth Hall was partitioned into several small rooms with a ceiling concealing the elaborate timber framing.

The ceiling was only rediscovered in 1919 when a chimneystack fell, exposing the magnificent medieval roof timbers. The building is some 45 feet long and consists of six bays which could then be seen to have alternate tie-beam and hammer-beam trusses. The hammer-beams include figures of angels facing downwards, whilst cusped wind-braces form arches and quatrefoils in the roof. It was built as a first-floor hall and although the whole of the original ground floor is now completely lost it may well have consisted of an open area with the upper floor supported on pillars. Indeed, the Booth Hall Passage, which was a much wider driving way in the 18th century, goes directly underneath the Hall.

Several bays to the north were lost many years ago, for it was in 1783 that the front of the property was completely rebuilt by George Willim 'in a handsome and ornamental manner'. In 1850 the front of the site, now designated 16 and 17 High Town, 'formerly part of the Boothall Inn', was sold to Thomas Evans, who employed the architect Thomas Nicholson and builder Richard Pritchard, to carry out further work in 'good workmanship and substantial

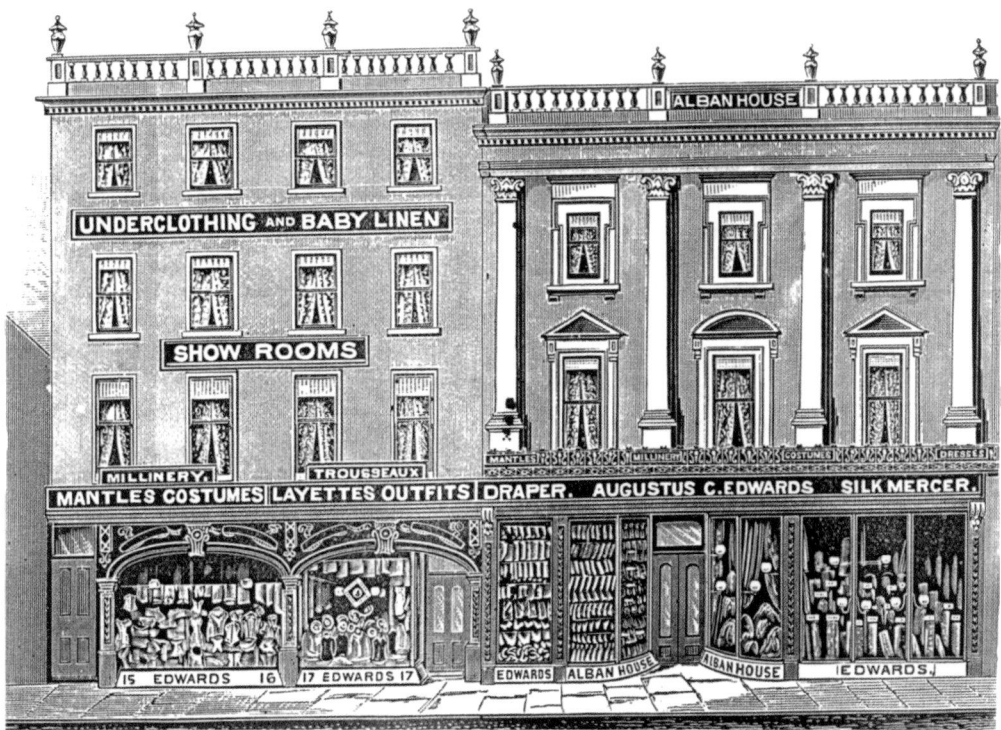

Fig. 9.24 Nos.16, 17 & 18 High Town as the premises of Augustus Edwards in the 1890s, indicating how well the medieval cores of the buildings were concealed.

manner'. The contract stipulated that old materials should be reused. By 1875, No.18 had been bought by Augustus Charles Edwards and by the 1890s the three properties 16, 17 and 18 had been united as one impressive shop (Fig. 9.24).[51] Much of the front building was destroyed in a fire in 2010 and the passage that led from High Town to the Booth Hall Inn is closed at present.

The carpentry and decoration of the 15th-century Booth Hall, with its spectacular hammer-beam roof, make it one of Hereford's finest secular buildings.

The Blue Boar
This was apparently the property next door to the Booth Hall (Fig. 9.20) which appears in the records of the Vicars Choral in 1536, although it cannot be traced after the 16th century.[52] It also appears in the Hereford Great Black Book (in which deeds were enrolled and many items affecting the Town Council were recorded) as adjoining the Booth Hall. It was then held by Matilda Bromwich, widow, almost certainly the widow of Richard Bromwich.

The Bromwich family were prosperous and prominent citizens. Thomas Bromwich was Mayor of Hereford in 1478.[53] Even so, he was indicted along with his neighbours for tipping the dung from his stables into part of Packers Lane that belonged to the Vicars Choral. Robert Bromwich, probably his son, was mayor in 1499. A third Robert, perhaps a grandson, had inherited the property by 1563.[54]

In the 17th century the building (then No.18 High Town) was turned into an inn, the fate of many large houses when they went out of fashion. Known as the Golden Fleece in 1620, it then belonged to Thomas Curtis, whose wife held a licence to sell ale. In 1704 St Peter's parish poor rate[55] records that the building next to the Booth Hall belonged to an innkeeper called William Bullock. Bullock left an inventory on his death which records that he had a large property with a very well-appointed kitchen, a dining room, three chambers overlooking the street (two with hearths), two back rooms and a heated parlour.[56]

Between 1725 and 1732 Edward Drew is recorded as the occupant and called the inn the Blue Boar. In 1737 David Daniel was the owner of 'the Blue Boar formerly the Golden Fleece'.[57]

By 1803 the property had been divided into two tenements.[58] In 1835 these were used by a drapery business but in the 1870s they were bought up by Augustus Charles Edwards and subsequently rebuilt as one unified shop front as Alban House (Fig. 9.24) (see also the Booth Hall).[59] It was also badly damaged in the recent fire of 2010.

From an examination of its timberwork, the building appears to have originally been part of a very grand merchant's house, the date of which is uncertain. Some of the mouldings and the 'close-studded' floor construction suggest a date in the middle of the 16th century, but the windows photographed by Alfred Watkins in 1933 in the part that was demolished suggest a date towards the end of the century. Although similar features had been observed in the neighbouring building, 16 High Town, destroyed in the fire of 2010, they have not been discovered elsewhere in Hereford and are not standard in the wider region.

As with 20 Church Street, it would seem Hereford's merchants and builders often went for individuality of design.

50a Commercial Street

50a Commercial Street is instructive in that the historic building remains show that the 'townscape grain', whether surviving or as recorded by the Ordnance Survey in the late 19th century, cannot always be taken to represent what was there in the Middle Ages.

Here there is a surviving medieval open hall, originally 5m long and 6.3m wide, at the rear of the property. Structurally of two bays, intermediate trusses in the roof structure give the impression of four narrower bays (see Figs. 9.25 & 9.26). The hall is at right-angles to the frontage (which has been rebuilt) and so suggests another 'right-angle type/narrow-plan' tenement as elsewhere in High Town. However, the documentary evidence seems to tell a different story. First, the hall appears to have been part of a very large block of property belonging to the Hyde family. A detailed inventory of 1567, when John Hyde leased the property to Richard Seaborne, includes a long list of rooms including a 'grete Chamber', a 'Chymney Chamber,' a 'myddell Chamber', a 'Steyer Chamber', a 'Chamber by the Courte', a 'halle', a 'grete parlor', a 'lytle parlor', a 'grete Kechyn', a 'lytle Kechin', a 'larder howse', a 'Chamber over the larder howse' and a 'Bulting howse'. It looks as though a number of the rooms were built round a courtyard which contained the service rooms and was overlooked by the hall and parlours. As built the hall may therefore have been part of a much wider plot than now appears to be the case, possibly including numbers 49 and 50 as well as 50a. Post-medieval sub-division of the properties here was intensive: even the remains of the open hall were split longitudinally, and the roof sawn through to do it.

The inventory of 1567 included a list of the furnishings, as these were part of the lease. This was necessary because the heavy beds, tables, panelling and glass were regarded as fixtures but, like carpets and fitted kitchens today, could, in theory, be removed by unscrupulous tenants. The list included bedsteads with testers in the five chambers, and tables with frames or trestles and built-in forms in the hall and little and great parlours. It may be significant that there were no tables in the chambers, suggesting that the parlours and hall were on the ground floor where the table supports would be dug into the flooring. There were hangings in all the chambers and in the great chamber hangings of 'newe worke', while the hall and little parlour had both hangings and wainscot. There is no indication as to whether these hangings were of tapestry or the ubiquitous painted cloths of the time. The faint traces of painted plaster still visible in the upper part of the hall may have covered the parts the hangings did not reach, or they may be

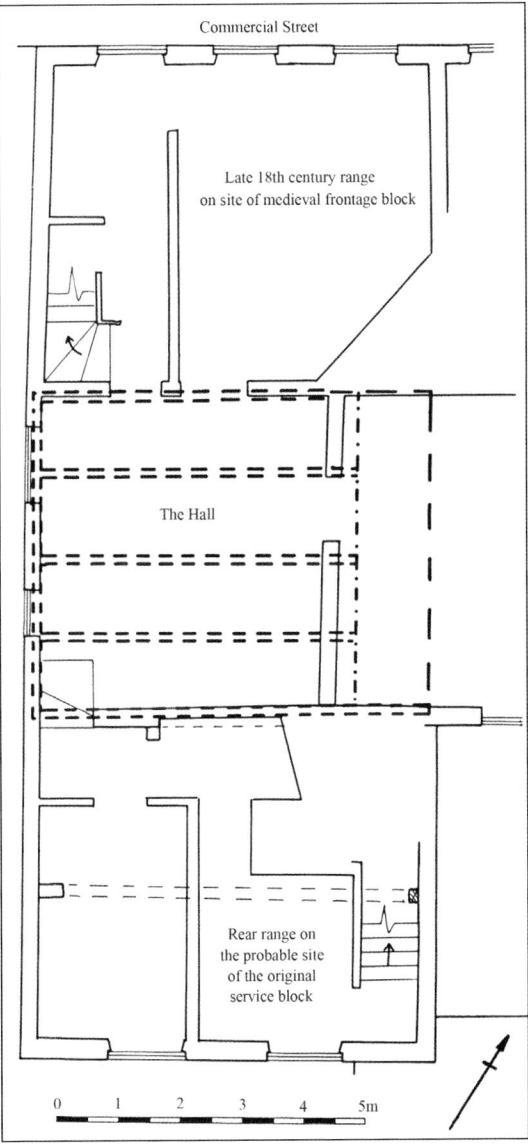

Fig. 9.25 (above) The roof of the richly decorated medieval open hall in what is now the central part of 50a Commercial Street, showing the intermediate roof trusses indicated by dotted lines on the plan to the left.

Fig. 9.26 (left) The plan of 50a Commercial Street.

later decoration. Evidence from elsewhere suggests that such a large amount of panelling was unusual at this date and indicative of a high-status dwelling. The final line of the inventory refers to the glass and lattice of the 'hole howse'.

The house as it was sold in 1567 was already more than 150 years old and had recently undergone modernisation as evidenced by the chimney chamber and the glass (still regarded as moveable) in the windows. Many of the fittings itemised in the inventory are described as 'new' and the kitchens are well fitted out with dresser and shelves. The modernisation may have seen the focus of the house shift from the hall to the great parlour, for it was here, in the inventory, that the 'great table' was to be found, whilst in the hall was a 'large table' with forms and trestles.

Nothing is known about the 16th-century Hyde family, although it can be deduced that this was once the family home, later split between the two brothers, Thomas inheriting the back property and John the front.

The original building was clearly that of a medieval merchant with a small but richly decorated open hall. The block at the front of the property on Commercial Street was rebuilt in the early to mid-18th century, and had probably been rebuilt once before that.

Fig. 9.27 The east elevation of the Market Hall as envisaged by John Clayton in 1846.

Fig. 9.28 Some timbers from the demolished Market Hall were used to build a summer house at Holmer Park, as seen above in a recent photograph. (Photograph by David Whitehead)

Fig. 9.29 The Market Hall as it was prior to the remodelling, but painted some years later by W.C. Hughes in 1860. (© Herefordshire Museum Service, ref: 1989-24)

The Market Hall

The most ornate carpentered building in the whole city was undoubtedly the Market Hall, thought to have taken three years to build, which was completed in 1576. There is evidence to indicate that its predecessor was not on this site, but at what was described as 'St Peter's Cross'. There is no record of who designed the new Market Hall, but in view of the date of construction the legend that it was John Abel (1577-1674) cannot possibly be true. A half-timbered building of three storeys, it was erected towards the western end of High Town. Supported on 27 pillars arranged in three rows, the first floor was used for magistrates' chambers and courts as well as for meetings, and the second provided chambers for 14 craft guilds. The open space between the pillars was used as a market-place. The town council met in the Tolsey, at the other end of High Town, a building of stone from which the market itself was administered and tolls collected. The Market Hall clearly had its dark corners where revellers and others could congregate, for in 1628 it was recorded that there was 'A void place under the west end of the Market Stairs ... defiled by disorderly people'.[60] The following year it was noted that 'Boards which had been put up by the Mayor to prevent a common nuisance pulled down'.[61] It seems it wasn't always well maintained, for by 1638 it was already noted to 'be decaying'.

The remodelling of the building in 1770 is covered on page 212.

Fig. 9.30 A photograph by Alfred Watkins of the Oak Sitting Room in the Green Dragon Hotel. This illustrates further how pieces from earlier buildings have been recycled when other buildings have been refurbished. The panelling, frieze and plaster ceiling date from 1600, whilst the oak lintel above the fireplace is 14th-century. All were reclaimed from houses on the site when the hotel was enlarged in 1931-2.

10 THE CIVIL WAR[1]

CHARLES I came to the throne in 1625. The then 'balance' between Crown and Parliament, was that the king called a Parliament when he needed to raise money, at which Parliament would present a number of petitions and proposals to the king for consideration. A period of bartering would then ensue, the king giving more ground the greater the tax revenue he required. Charles, however, was a firm believer in the 'divine right of kings' and soon he and Parliament were at loggerheads and with agreement not being reached, Parliament was dissolved and Charles embarked on a long period of personal rule. His need for finance remained, of course, and one of the ways he could raise it was through ship money, a tax for which he did not need Parliamentary approval. Supposed to be used only in emergencies for coastal defence, Charles sought to use it to raise money on an almost annual basis. The first occasion it was levied in Herefordshire it was largely collected, but each subsequent levying saw greater non-compliance and levels of anger. A further cause of friction was religion (see pp.180-2). In addition, Charles married a Catholic, Henrietta Maria, daughter of Henry IV of France. She brought many of her Catholic friends with her to the English Court and this caused considerable ill feeling amongst the staunch English Protestants.

In due course Charles's financial needs were such that he had to recall Parliament in 1640. The first was dissolved by a frustrated king after just a few weeks, but in October he had to recall it again. What became known as The Long Parliament was summoned in October, but by this time grievances across the country were such that Parliament sought extensive concessions from the king. In March William Laud, Archbishop of Canterbury, was imprisoned for High Treason and in the summer rumours of papist plots, a Catholic invasion, and then Catholic atrocities in Ulster abounded. Parliament pressed ahead with Puritan reform of the Church. In January 1642 Charles, fearing for his family's safety, left London, establishing his Court in York in March. Fears of an armed confrontation between Crown and Parliament were now openly expressed and each side tried to gain control of the counties' trained soldiers and their ammunition stores. The Herefordshire magazine was held in St Owen's Gate and in 1626, at the beginning of Charles' reign, it contained 1,206 pounds of powder, 926 of match, and 3,928 of lead – apparently a normal amount for that size of magazine. Parliamentarian support was mainly in the richer eastern and south-eastern counties, including London, while the Royalists depended on Wales, the south-west, the midlands, and much of the north. Hereford was very much a Royalist stronghold in terms of the gentry, although several of the principal families supported the Parliamentary interests. However, the commitment of the general population to the Royalist cause was to prove much less wholehearted. In July 1642 the gentry were busy laying claim to the magazine and preparing to raise troops. To the wider population it came as no great shock when they heard that the king had raised his standard at Nottingham and called on all loyal citizens to support him.

Hereford, in the middle of the 17th century, was still largely enclosed within its medieval walls. All six gates were standing, although they had not been used for defensive purposes for many years. The royal castle had been allowed to fall into total disrepair and many of its buildings were in ruins. At the beginning of the Civil War Hereford was described by George Hyde, an adviser to Charles I and subsequently created the Earl of Clarendon, as:

> a town very well affected, and reasonably well fortified, having a strong stone wall about it, and some cannon, and there being in it some soldiers of good reputation, many gentlemen of honour and quality, and three or four hundred soldiers, besides the inhabitants well armed.

Command of the Parliamentarian army was given to the Earl of Essex, who rapidly took Northampton then, appreciating that the king had moved from Nottingham towards Shrewsbury, countered by moving towards Worcester. News reached Essex that a convoy of gold and silver plate, sent by Oxford's colleges as a contribution to the Royalist war effort, was also nearing Worcester, and he sent a detachment to capture it. In turn, Prince Rupert sent cavalry to ensure the convoy's safety and the two forces met outside Worcester at Powick Bridge, where the Parliamentarian force was scattered. Shortly afterwards Essex occupied Worcester and then sent Henry, Earl of Stamford, to take Hereford – a city which, he had been told, had neither governor nor garrison. Not surprisingly, the city was totally unprepared when the Parliamentary force appeared outside the walls on 30 September 1642.

One of the soldiers in Stamford's force was Nehemiah Wharton, an apprentice who had been sent by his master with a pocketful of money and a scriptural blessing 'to live and die with the Earl of Essex'. Wharton wrote several letters to his master, including one from Hereford in which he said:

> After we had marched ten miles we came to Bromyard, the wether wet, and the way very fowle: here we got a little refreshment, and from hence marched ten miles further to Hereford, but [it was] very late before we got thither, and by reason of the raine and snow, and extremity of cold, one of our soldiers died by the way; and it is wonderfull wee did not all perish, for the cowardly Cavalleers were within few miles of us.
> In this poore condition comminge to Hereford, the gates were shut against us, and for two houres we stood in dirt and water up to the middle legge, for in the city were all malignants, save three, which were Roundheads. ... [They had been told that if we were let in] we would plunder their houses murder their children, burne their Bibles, and utterly ruinate all.[2]

After some parleying, the mayor, one William Price, let them in, the Roundheads thus occupying the city with hardly any resistance. Price was a tradesman with London connections who had a leaning towards the Puritans and did his best to help the Parliamentarian troops in Hereford. The following day Wharton had a walk around the city, and described it as:

well scituate, and seated upon the river Y, environed with a strong wall, better than any I have seene before; with five gates, and a stronge stone bridge of six arches over the river, surpassing Worcester. In the city there is the statelyest market place in the kingdome, built with columns after the manner of the Exchange [the old market hall in High Town]. The Minster in every way exceeded that of Worcester, but the city in circuit not so large. The inhabitants are totally ignorant in the waies of God, and much addicted to drunkenness and other vices, but principally unto swearinge, so that the children that have scarce learned to speake doe universally sweare stoutlye. Many here speake Welsh.

Sabbath day, about the time of morninge prayer, we went to the Minster, when the pipes played and the puppets sange so sweetely, that some of our soildiers could not forbeare dauncinge in the holy quire; whereat the Baalists were sore displeased.

One of the most fascinating accounts of the Civil War period is from the account book of Joyce Jeffries[3] who, just before the war, had built a house just outside the Widemarsh Gate – where the multi-storey car park now stands – costing the then enormous sum of £500. She lived in the city until 1642 when she sought refuge with friends in the countryside. She had other properties in Widemarsh Street, all apparently outside the gate, and all let out to tenants. When she heard that the Earl of Stamford was about to arrive, she moved to Garnons, north-west of the city. She made a bad choice of refuge for she wrote:

On Tewsday morning, October 4, captain Hamon [Hammond] and his barbarous company plundered Mr. Geereses house at Garnons, both them and me of much Goods, toke a way my 2 bay coache mares and som money, and much Linen; and Elyza Acton's clothes.

She must have kept in touch with her servants in Hereford, for she arranged for provisions to be bought for four soldiers who were quartered in her house.

Stamford had written in a dispatch 'So long as I can find any Means of Subsistence, I shall remain here', but failed to raise any significant credit in Hereford, and had to obtain supplies on the issue of promissory notes for payment at a later date, a system known as 'free quarter'. Essex had withdrawn to London and Stamford, hearing that the royal forces had occupied Worcester and that they had a base some 7 or 8 miles from the city (probably at the Mynde in Much Dewchurch), appreciated that he was almost surrounded by Royalists. With no money, he had no choice but to retreat and on 14 December 1642, having held Hereford for some ten weeks, he left the city for Gloucester.

A Royalist detachment under Sir Richard Lawdey immediately moved in and started looking for traitors. A report read:

Hereford was sold by that perfidious mayor, Price, who was Mayor of this City when the Earl of Stamford was there. He even desired his Lordship to name his new baby 'Parliament', but this was declined because it had not then been resolved whether 'Parliament' were a Christian name.

Price came in for some harsh treatment. His house and shop were plundered, he was called a rebel and traitor, and threats were made to hang him at his front door.

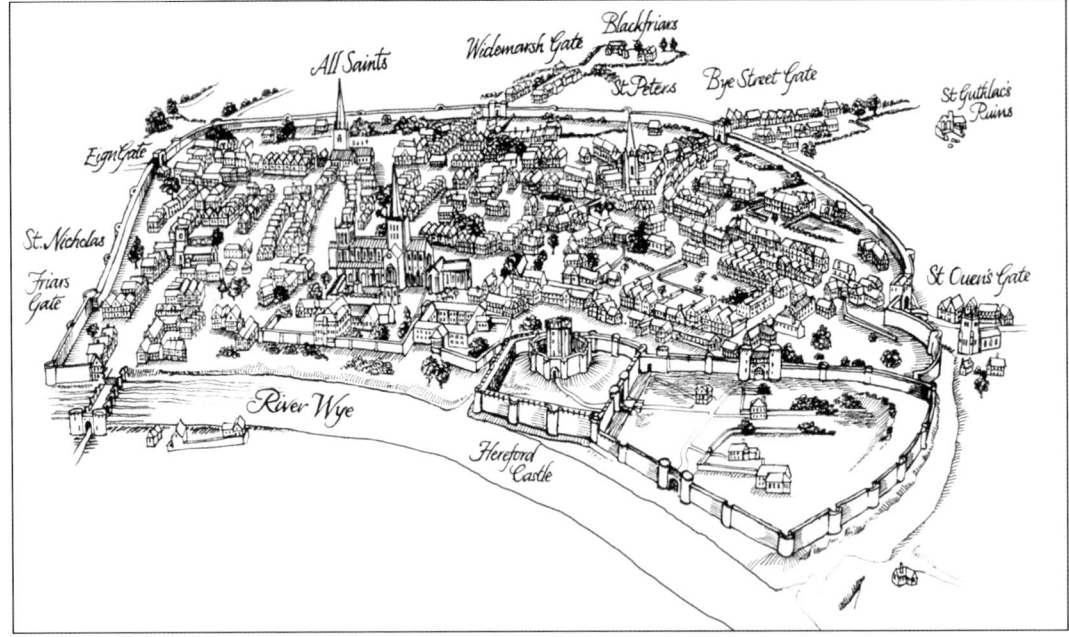

Fig. 10.1 A drawing showing how Hereford would have looked at the time of the Civil War

Colonel Fitzwilliam Coningsby of Hampton Court, a cousin of Joyce Jeffries, had been appointed by the king as sheriff of the county and later as one of the commissioners of array. On 20 December he became 'Gouvernor of the Cittee and garrison of Hereford as touching the Militia'. His town house was in part of the old Blackfriars monastery in Widemarsh Street – he was thus a near neighbour of his cousin. Coningsby had a similar problem to Stamford – a lack of money to pay the garrison – but he probably had more local help. Joyce Jeffries, for instance, sent him £50 and 'a fatt bullock worth £6 [as] a present'.

The city should have used the peace that followed to repair its defences and restore the castle to the strong point it had once been. The city ditch needed cleaning out to ensure that it held a good depth of water; the city gates needed repair to withstand the cannons of any attacker; and drawbridges were needed to replace fixed bridges and prevent a direct attack on the gates. The river frontage was open to approach by boat and needed additional defensive works, particularly along the edge of the castle. But the most important requirement was one which could not be taken easily – the demolition of all buildings outside the gates which could be used to conceal anyone attacking the city. Little was done. The winter of 1642 was a quiet time throughout the country although some effort was made to consolidate positions and stake claims to adjoining areas. Early in 1643 the king sent Sir Richard Cave to secure Monmouthshire and south Wales and to attempt to unite the local Royalist forces. He liaised with Lord Herbert, who was based at his home – Raglan Castle – and was responsible for all the troops in the area, and apparently had some success. Eventually, on 15 April 1643, Herbert and Cave arrived in Hereford together with the latter's small force of 80 horse and 100 dragoons. Although by this time Sir William Waller and his Parliamentarian troops were close to Ross, Lord Herbert departed from Hereford, leaving Cave effectively as governor of the city and in charge of the Royalist forces, though there was to be confusion between his role and that of Coningsby.

Cave was very concerned about the lack of preparations in the event of a siege. His advice for improvements to the defences gives a graphic picture of the state of the city:

> ... first 'that the breast-work should be made on the bank of the river, upon both sides of the bridge, and that the way under the castle, being upon the same bank, very plain and as open as a highway, would be likeways strengthened with a good worke and turnepike, to hinder any entrance by land under the castle, or by water in boats';
> secondly 'that a breast-work should be cast up to defend the entrance into the castle by the mill, as plain and open a place as the other, only there is a small ascent';
> thirdly 'that deep trenches, with any moveable bridges, until drawbridges could be provided, should be digged and made within every open gate';
> fourthly 'that Byster's Gate should be dammed up';
> fifthly 'that some old houses in severall places on the wall, should be taken downe'.

Cave determined to do what he could to strengthen the city defences, but with the split Royalist command he only had some 80 men under his direct control. He therefore sought the help of the citizens by having the Common Bell rung, which was only used in emergencies and was meant to summon the inhabitants. Thus

> the mayor was sent for to summon the citizens, to come in with all the materials they could bring, to cast up breast-works to strengthen the weakest parts of the Town. But upon the next morning, not withstanding the ringing of the common bell (which is the strictest summons that can be given to the Citizens, and upon which they are bound by oath to appear), so few came that nothing was done that whole day.

Even the imminent threat of plundering had little effect and the only work carried out was the 'damming' of Byster's Gate. Thus, by April 1643, when Sir William Waller approached Hereford with some 2,500 men, the city was just as indefensible as it had been when Stamford left the previous December. Widemarsh Gate and the nearby Eign Gate were still defended by no more than 'a little iron chaine, knee-high, on the outside'.

Sir Richard Cave could only discover some five barrels of powder in the city – far too little for an effective defence against Sir William Waller and his army. They were approaching from Ross and, early in the morning of Tuesday 25 April, Cave went to the castle where 'it beginning to be light, the enemies whole forces were discovered to be within less than a mile of the towne'. This suggests that the Great Tower of the castle still stood to provide the vantage point. Cave, by drum and trumpet, attempted to get his troops from their lodgings to their posts, but meanwhile the Parliamentary army approached nearer and nearer 'both in the ditches and under the hedges, and in the suburbes about the town, beganne to shoot on all parts'.

The attackers started to use boats to ferry their musketeers across the river but they were beaten back. However, Waller was to succeed in taking the city with the loss of only one man. Mr Corbett, a minister from Gloucester, was with Sir William Waller's army and wrote:

> ... to help forward the capture of the City, Colonel Massie drew up two sakers [cannons with a 3.5 inch bore and 9 feet long, firing a 6 lb. shot] in a straight line against Wide Marsh gate, not without extreme hazard of being shot from the walls, and himself gave fire, and the first cannon-shot entered the gate and took an officer's head from his shoul-

ders and slew some besides. More shots were made, each of which scoured the street and so alarmed the enemy that they presently sounded a parley which was entertained by Sir W. Waller.

By this time the only alternatives available to the Royalists were a desperate sally or an honourable treaty. The latter was agreed, and, while some of the horse and dragoons marched away to safety, Cave went to Widemarsh Gate to treat. The initial terms were unacceptable, with Cave declaring that 'wee ought every man to dye in the place rather then yield to such conditions'. Negotiations continued during which process the Royalist troops gradually left rather than surrender. Eventually a treaty was signed and the Roundheads entered the town, confining the gentry to their lodgings for eventual transfer to Bristol.

Sir Richard Cave managed to escape from his lodgings, helped by an alderman's son, 'over the towne wall, and through the mote, which was not over my bootes'. He rejoined the king at Oxford where he was put under arrest and charged with 'dishonourably giving up the city of Hereford, after it had been entrusted to his care'. He attempted to justify his actions and to lay the blame for the poor showing of Hereford on the general lack of co-operation from its residents. His defence was perhaps a little doubtful – Waller discovered some 40 barrels of powder in the city which Cave could not explain away! However, he was eventually completely exonerated at his court martial. Cave was to die at the Battle of Naseby.

In Hereford, although he raised some £3,000 from the citizens by agreeing that his troops would not plunder the city, Waller had the same problems as Stamford had had, and could not hold the city. Within a fortnight of the surrender he left, taking his prisoners to Bristol where they were all liberated on 30 June 1643 when that city surrendered to Prince Rupert. One exception to this was Viscount Scudamore, who had been Chief Steward of Hereford. For some time before the war started he had been busy amassing a vast collection of weapons at his house at Holme Lacy so as to arm his followers. He was commanded to appear before Parliament and eventually was held captive for some three years before purchasing his release for the sum of £2,690. Scudamore is perhaps best remembered for his research on grafting and planting apple orchards, and was responsible for developing a much improved variety of cider apple known as the redstreak and thus, in some way, for the future prosperity of the county.

When Bristol surrendered to the Parliamentarians and the Herefordshire Royalists were released, they returned to Hereford looking to gain revenge. There was only one area of the county where Parliamentary rule was accepted – a few villages in the extreme north-western corner. All were within the protection of Robert Harley's castle at Brampton Bryan. Sir Robert was in London attending to his Parliamentary activities, leaving his wife, Brilliana, with the custody of the castle. The conquest of this stronghold was an object dear to the heart of all Herefordshire Royalists. So, in July 1643, Sir William Vavasour, then Governor of Hereford, with some 600 men laid siege to the castle, a siege that continued for a month. In August, Lady Brilliana wrote to her son: 'Now, my dear Ned, the gentlemen of this county have brought an army against me. Sir William Vavasor has left Mr. Lingen with the soldiers. The Lord in his mercy preserve me.'[4]

A few days later her prayers were answered. Lingen, on hearing that a Royalist army had been defeated at Higham outside Gloucester, with the loss of some troops raised to defend Hereford, withdrew on 6 September. During the siege the church and the whole village had been burnt, but at the castle a troop of 600 men had been successfully repelled for a full six weeks by a small band of Puritan ministers, retainers and domestic servants led by an old soldier from the German wars called Hackluit. Lady Brilliana had been ill for several years and the siege must have been the final blow to her delicate health. On 9 October she wrote to her son saying 'I have taken a very great cold, which has made me very ill these 2 or 3 days'. She died a day later within the walls of the house she had so well defended.

Brampton Bryan Castle survived a little longer, but it was again besieged in March 1644. Cannon were brought against it and eventually the defenders had to surrender. An account at the time describes the walls as being 'battered even with the ground leaving little else but the cellars'. The direct loss to Sir Robert Harley in terms of buildings and furnishings was £6,650 including a study of books and invaluable historical documents valued at £200.

Waller had left Hereford in early May 1643, and the city was to remain in the hands of the Royalists for over two years. In April 1644, Colonel Massey, with 400 foot and a regiment of horse, took up quarters at Ledbury and made a reconnaissance as far as Hereford. They made every effort to provoke the defenders by setting fire to a house in the suburbs, but no-one ventured outside the walls. On their way back to Ledbury, the Parliamentarian troops came across John Pralph, the 80-year-old vicar of Tarrington, who was walking the 8 miles home from Hereford. Normally his age would have secured him respect and protected him from aggression, but it was not to be, for he was given the usual challenge 'Who are you for'? The standard answer was the safe one – 'for the King and Parliament', but the old gentleman had spirit (or perhaps he was confused, for to an old man all troops may have looked the same) as he replied 'for God and the King'. He was immediately shot through the head and killed. The Tarrington Parish register for May 1644 records his burial with the comment that 'He was murdered by some of the Parliament Soldiers near the Well at Stoke Edith'.

Late in 1643, Parliament had managed to secure the services of a Scottish army by promises of pay and the acceptance of Scottish Presbyterianism. This army, under the control of Alexander Leslie, first Earl of Leven, entered England early in 1644 and, joining with a Parliamentarian army under the overall command of the Earl of Manchester, brought the Royalists under Prince Rupert to battle at Marston Moor in early July. In a confused battle where advantage swung successively from one side to the other, it was eventually Cromwell's steady control of one wing of the Parliamentarian cavalry and his tactical eye which brought an overwhelming victory for Parliament.

Before the final outcome was known, elements of fleeing Parliamentarian forces spread news of a Royalist victory. When the rumours reached Hereford on 8 July, Royalist sentiments came to the fore when two shillings and six pence was paid 'for ringing the bells [at All Saints church] at the Scots overthrow in the North'. The bells must have been rapidly muted when the full extent of the losses was appreciated, for this battle had resulted in the death of over 4,000 Royalists and the loss to the king of much of the north of England.

In another change of command that often bedevilled the Royalist war effort, Colonel Barnabas Scudamore was appointed Governor of Hereford on 10 September. In this instance, however, a good choice was made and he soon carried out a careful survey of his forces, finding 466 men in arms lodged in houses throughout the city, the weekly cost being £53 4s.

In the rest of the country, after his success at Marston Moor, Cromwell came to the fore, and managed to persuade Parliament that the various Parliamentary armies should be amalgamated under a single command. The result was the New Model Army under the command of Sir Thomas Fairfax – an efficient, fully mobile army under the control of proficient and dedicated officers. Its first test was in June 1645, when the Royalist army, again under the leadership of Prince Rupert, met Fairfax at the Battle of Naseby in Northamptonshire. The New Model Army with Cromwell at the head of the cavalry proved victorious. The king decided to retreat westwards and passed through Kidderminster, Bewdley and Bromyard on the way to his destination, Hereford, where he arrived on Thursday 19 June. He stayed in the city for almost a fortnight. But the Scottish army under Leven was now following on his heels.

Hereford had been taken twice by Parliamentarian forces and Scudamore was determined that it would not happen again. By this time the city was under military rule and it is apparent that he carried out much of the work that had been recommended by Sir Richard Cave in advance of Sir William Waller's attack. He must have strengthened all the gates, presumably with new timber doors, and replaced fixed bridges with drawbridges. He also carried out some repair work at the castle, but his main effort was to clear the areas outside the gates of all buildings and other features within or behind which attackers could hide.

Sir Henry Slingsby, a noted Royalist officer, remarked on the changes at Widemarsh:

> There we found all places about the town made Level where before there had been fair houses and goodly Orchards. I went to see the house where I was formerly Quartered, & found it pull'd down, & the Gentlewoman that had lived in it dead upon grief to see the ruins of her house.

Mrs Jeffries must have been made of sterner stuff for she just entered in her accounts for May 1645:

> Received from Maud Prichet half a years rent for her house in Widmarsh Street being the last that ever she paid, for she removed, and my houses were pulled down. Young Mr Holmes, the mercer in Hereford, bought my great new house' [which had cost her £500] for £50.

The Scots army, which consisted of 8,000 foot and 4,000 horse, was described in one report as being:

> not so civilised as we could wish, but they are good soldiers and hardy men, and are usually clad in a light plaid or speckled stuff; and in this attire they usually march. They have darts, and bows and arrowes, and great knives; and (which is a wonder for none are very religious) they all hate bishops, papists, and caviliers [sic], and they threaten to pull them all to pieces, one limb from another.

The Scots army intended 'to make a line from Chester to Shrewsbury, and from Shrewsbury to Hereford as good as that ancient Trench called Offa's Dyke' and by 20 July they were on the county border at Tenbury. The Royalist base at Canon Frome stood in their way and had to be taken before any attempt could be made on Hereford. It was held by a resolute officer, one Colonel Barnold, who, on being invited to surrender, told Leven that he would defend the moated site as long as he had a drop of blood in his body – and proceeded to do so. There were only about 120 men in the garrison and the Scots army made short work of the attack. About half of the defenders were killed during the action and 30, who attempted to flee, were put to the sword. The rest were only saved by the approach of Lord Callender, who had a reputation as a merciful commander.

The army continued, with the Earl of Leven complaining to Parliament about the state of the roads in Herefordshire, which he described as being the worst that the Scots army had encountered, such that his army could only accomplish 8 miles in a day between Bromyard and Ledbury. From Ledbury, the army advanced towards Hereford in two brigades, 12 miles apart, arriving in front of the city on 31 July with some nine siege pieces including three great brass guns.

Scudamore's efforts were now to pay dividends. Hereford had ample provisions; the fortifications had been strengthened, the castle had been repaired, the gates had been stopped up and drawbridges put in place and made to work. Ammunition had also been obtained and, most importantly of all, the areas around the gates had been cleared of all possible obstacles. Hereford was as prepared for a siege as it could be. The city then had a population of some 4,500, with some 1,500 soldiers and townsmen carrying arms.

The Scots horse reached the city at 10am on Wednesday 30 July and Scudamore recorded that he welcomed them with cannon fire. On the following day the Scottish foot appeared in front of the walls and the city was surrounded. Leven demanded total surrender, but Scudamore wrote:

> I am not to give up the King's Garrison upon any Summons or Letter, neither shall it be in the power of the Mayor or others to condescend to any such Proposition. I was set here by the King's Command, and shall not quit it but by special order from His Majesty or the Prince.

Fig. 10.2 Model in the Old House showing the Wye Bridge, its gate at the southern end, and the advantageous position that any attackers could have gained by using the tower of St Martin's church

By 1 August the Scots had started to dig in and prepare their huts in the Bartonsham meadows, where they built an embankment that is still visible today on the meadow side of Park Street. The defenders had to abandon the St Martin's suburb and the Scots made use of the old earthwork, Rowe Ditch, that crosses Bishop's Meadow. They probably filled in the ditch on the south side and thus reversed it as a defensive feature. On Monday, cannonades were fired from the castle across the river at regular intervals. During one of several sallies made over Wye Bridge, one side of St Martin's church tower was demolished. According to the defenders, this tower would otherwise have 'much annoyed us at the Bridge and Palace'. On Wednesday 6 August Scudamore wrote 'They raised their Batteries at Wye-bridge and played hot upon the Gate for two days together, and battered it so much that it was rendered useless.' The response was to stop the bridge up with Wool-sacks and Timber, and, 'for our greater assurance we then broke an Arch, and raised a very strong Work behind it'.

By Wednesday 13 August preparations were being made for a full assault on the city. This included the construction of a temporary bridge across the Wye, probably at Putson. On Friday the 'great assault' began with an attack on Friars' Gate using four cannon against the walls. It continued on Saturday but with a total lack of success. On the 17th there was a notable sally at St Owen's Gate where prisoners were taken, with the loss of only one man. Scudamore recorded that 'little boys strived which should first carry Torches and Faggots to fire their works'. The Scots retaliated during the following days by destroying St Owen's church which stood just outside the gate.

Between Wednesday 20 and Tuesday 26 August there was a week of continual rain that dampened the ardour of both sides. The Scots were attempting to dig mines underneath the wall, but the defenders stole out at night and

> ... fired their Works, securing their retreat under the protection of our Musketeers upon the wall, and what our fire could not resolve (though it burnt fair and suffocated some of their Miners) our water did, breaking in upon them and drowning that which the fire had not consumed.

Fig. 10.3 A coloured engraving which clearly shows the arch (third from the left) that was rebuilt having been broken to prevent the Scots reaching the city across it.

From the Leaguer before Hereford

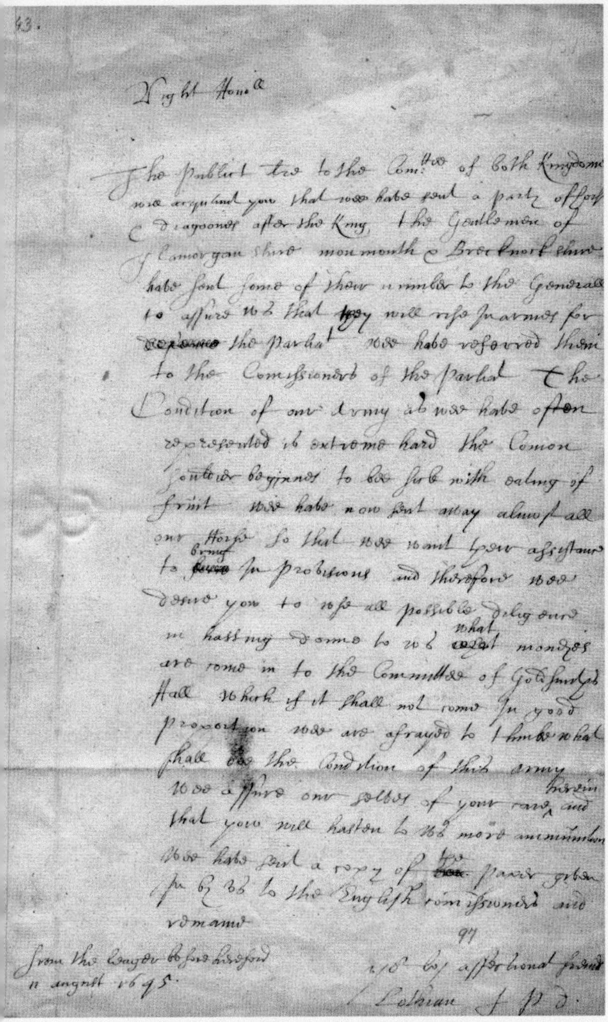

Wight House

The ———— true to the Comttee of both Kingdoms so we aquaint you that wee have sent a party of foot and dragoones after the King. The Gentlemen of Glamorganshire, Monmouth & Brecknockshire have sent some of their number to the Generall to assure him that they will rise in armes for the Parliat. We have referred them to the Comissioners of the Parliat. The condition of our army as we have often represented is extreme hard. The *** & bayonets do bee sick with oatmeal & fruit. We have now sent away almost all our Horse so that wee need your assistance to _____ for provisions and therefore wood desire you to use all possible diligence in hasting my desire to ___ what moneys are come in to the Committee of Goldsmiths Hall. Which if it shall not come in good pros___ we are afrayed to think what shall bee the Condition of this army We assure our *** of your _____ herein and that you will hasten to _____ more ammunition We have sent a copy of the paper _____ _____by ___ to the English Commissioners and remain

from the leager before Hereford   yours affectionataly
11 august 1645   Lothian

*** some archaic word meaning common soldier

Fig. 10.4 A letter sent by William Kerr, 3rd Earl of Lothian, on 11 August 1645, with a transcription alongside. It records the despatch of Sir David Leslie with 4,000 horse who had been sent by Parliament to Newark after the king. Charles in fact was making his way down the country, arriving in Hereford on 4 September. The letter is obviously written to someone in authority who is capable of influencing the restocking of the Scots army with money and ammunition. The location of Wight House is not known.

Firing and flooding their mine workings must have been successful and Scudamore described:

> the valor of our common Soldiers and Townsmen, who hazarded themselves by making up of breaches till the Cannon played between their legs; and even the Women (such was their gallantry) ventured where the Musket bullets did go. What frequent alarms we gave them! By fire-balls, lights upon our Steeple, by Dogs, Cats, and outworn Horses, having lighted Matches tied about them and turned out upon their works; whereby we put the enemy in such distraction, that sometimes they charged one another. This recreation we had in the midst of our besieging: and one morning, instead of beating Reveille, we bad a cry of Hounds, in pursuit after the train of a Fox about the Walls of the City.

By the end of August the Scots had prepared ladders and hurdles for scaling the walls and were attacking Bye Street Gate, and the half-moon tower next to St Owen's Gate, with their cannon. It was then that they received news of the king's potential arrival at the head of an army. Their cavalry already having been sent north, the Scots were in no position to be caught between the two Royalist forces and withdrew, initially to Fownhope. In the words of Scudamore 'this Scottish mist began to disperse, and the next morning vanished out of sight'.

It was not just the city that had suffered during the siege. The Scots army needed food and although the army included commissioners appointed by Parliament whose responsibility it was to requisition the necessary supplies, this was unsuccessful and the Scots had to take the remedy into their own hands. During the Civil War there had been suffering throughout the country, but it was asserted that no other county was 'more systematically plundered than that of Hereford'. A later account gives an indication of the extent of the losses in the surrounding villages. At Mordiford the cost was £490; at Holmer £531; at Hampton Bishop £511 18s 4d and at Dinedor £484 7s 8d. Bearing in mind the size of these villages and that the wages of the Scots army varied from 4s a day for a Major down to 6d per day for a common soldier, the extent of loss must have been extreme.

The defence of Hereford had been a serious business during the siege and all the citizens had been expected to support the cause. Once the siege was over a hunt took place to root out all those who supported the Parliamentary cause. Many disappeared, but their wives and children were turned out of their homes and some of their houses were burnt. One such case involved a Mrs Hyde who was arrested for giving away the time and place of a sally. Apparently she was a widow with a small son and said that she did it for money. This was not considered an adequate excuse and a little later she was hanged.

Fig. 10.5 The coat of arms of Hereford city after its augmentation by King Charles

Fig. 10.6 This early 20th-century window in Hereford Cathedral by the London firm of Powell and Sons shows the visit of King Charles I to the city in September 1645. It includes the principal persons who were in Hereford during the Civil War at the time: King Charles, Prince Maurice, Dean Croft (inaccurately dressed as a bishop, a post he did not hold until after the Restoration in 1660), Barnabas Scudamore, the Mayor (William Carter), the town clerk (James Clarks) and John Scudamore (chief steward). Notice the Market Hall in the background.

On Thursday 4 September the king arrived in Hereford again. Sir Henry Slingsby, accompanying the monarch, remarked that the castle resembled that at York 'for it hath a round tower mount'd upon a hill; like Clifford Tower, and ye mills near it, with some little works about'. Church bells rang out and Charles showed his appreciation by granting Barnabas Scudamore a knighthood immediately on his arrival. However, this was virtually the last success for Charles. He stayed for several days and on 16 September honoured the city as a whole by an augmentation to its coat of arms: the three lions of Richard I are now adorned with a border of ten saltires on a blue background, representing the ten Scottish regiments that took part in the siege (Fig. 10.5). The new motto *'Invictae Fidelitatis Praemium'* translates as 'The reward for faithfulness unconquered'. The lion on top of the coat of arms represents the Defender of the Faith, whilst the gold-barred peer's helm is otherwise only found in the coat of arms of one other municipality – the City of London.

Shortly afterwards, Sir Barnabas Scudamore attempted to retake Castle Frome, where there was still a Parliamentary garrison. He decided on a direct assault and arranged for the king's carpenter, John Abel, who had been of considerable assistance during the siege, to make a machine called the Great Sow – a tower with bullet-proof sides that was sufficiently high to scale the walls of Canon Frome. With great effort it was towed by oxen from Hereford almost to Canon Frome where it was left whilst the troops went into Ledbury for a well-earned drink.

Unfortunately, the defenders at Canon Frome, realising what was happening, came out, dealt with the small guard on the Great Sow and towed it into Castle Frome before it could be used!

The final assault on Hereford was undertaken by Colonel Birch. By this time Hereford was one of the last strongholds to hold out for the king as his fortunes continued to wane. One of the main actors in this final scene was Sir John Bridges, who had a grudge against Barnabas Scudamore. Sir John, who lived at Wilton Castle near Ross, had had nothing to do with the Civil War having spent much time campaigning in Ireland. When he returned to recruit more troops, he was asked to allow his house to be occupied as a royal garrison, but refused. For this Scudamore and his fellow Royalist, Sir Henry Lingen, decided he should be punished. Tradition has it that a body of soldiers set the house on fire on a Sunday, whilst the family was at church. This led to Bridges seeking refuge in Gloucester, where he became a firm supporter of the Parliamentarian cause.

Colonel Sir Thomas Morgan, governor of Gloucester, met with Bridges and planned the taking of Hereford. Whilst these two men were the organisers, they needed someone to carry out the work. They decided on John Birch, whose commercial enterprises in Bristol had fallen into decline due to the disruption caused by the Civil War. Like many others in a similar situation he had little choice but to take up arms and eventually found himself governor of Bath and Bristol. The three men were aided by Alderne and Howarth, two discontented Royalist captains with whom Bridges was in touch, who were prepared to sell whatever information they had about the defences of Hereford to the Parliamentarian forces.

Birch was given the power to promise a sum of money, not exceeding £3,000, and went into Herefordshire in disguise to meet the two traitors. They met near Ledbury and the basic outline of a plan was established, a plan put into effect in the middle of winter. Birch started his stratagem by marching his troops from Ledbury towards Hereford through the night of 15 December. When he was some four miles from the city he turned them back and returned to Ledbury, letting it be known that he had abandoned his ideas on advancing on the city. This information rapidly became public knowledge in Hereford, allowing the garrison to relax.

However, at nine o'clock on the following night – 16 December – Birch gathered his troops together again and began once more to make his way towards Hereford. Roe, Birch's secretary, recorded in his diary:

> And thus marched you almost to Heriford ... without speaking one word, still expecting to be engaged; which thoughts kept the souldiers warme that terrible night of frost and snowe. ... When you had marched soe far, the officers cam to you wondring they heard of noe enimy; to which you replyed, they are retreated. ... Whereupon they every one returned to his place, marching on speedily, but soe silently that a dog scarced barked all the night, though wee marched through three or four villages [probably Tarrington, Stoke Edith and Dormington]; but in deed that was not strange, for if a dog had bin without doores that night hee would have been starved to death.

Meanwhile Birch rode rapidly to Canon Frome, where he had previously made some arrangements. He had hired seven men, dressed up as labourers, together with a constable, and gave him a forged warrant to allow them to work in the city. Roe commented that the men were given 'their pickaxes and shovells, bound up for them very black rie bread and cheese in course table napkins, soe that to see them goe a man would have ventred his life they had been country labourers indeed'. Roe continued:

> Whereupon, being marched neere the cittee. you laid your maine body in a hollowe ground which you ffound as you were advised fitt for your turne [thought to be Scots Hole on Old Eign Hill]; thence drew 150 firelocks into that old priory which lay just by the roade leading to Bysters gate. ... Thus the severall parties lay close in the snowe twoe full howers, noe man soe much as stirring, hope keepeing them warme.

The old priory outside Byster's Gate was the one dedicated to St Guthlac. The attackers, hiding in the ruins of the priory, heard the 'Morning prayer-bell ring out, and Travalley [*reveille*] was beaten in the city'. There was even an accidental discharge of one of the raider's muskets, which must have sounded loud in the crisp air of the frozen dawn but failed to alarm the garrison. Eventually eight o'clock arrived and:

> At last the gate was opeined; (upon the first letting-downe of the draw-bridge, three men came out of the city, not discerning anybody) and within a quarter of an hower after few souldiers you could see about it; and you [Colonel Birch] supposed as it proved, that that terrible cold morneing of ffrost and snowe had sent them to a fire. Whereupon you gave notice to the constable, whoe in respect of his cold, which made him and his six men goe as if they were almost starved, and alsoe by reason of their broad hatts, great breeches, spades, pickaxes, and bundles of bread and cheese they might well have decieved a wise man and vigilent comander. Thus went hee on peaceably to the gate; which when hee came close unto, and goeing to show the officers and souldiers that were with the centry his warrant to bring those men to worke that day.

A pamphlet published shortly after the events went into more detail:

> Whilst they were looking upon it [the warrant], the six men came near with their pick-axes and shovels, and so soon as they were on top of the bridge, the constable killed the sentinel with his edge bill, and the six labourers killed two more. Then Colonel Hammond, who stood on the hill, gave the signal by holding up his hat to the 150 firelocks that were in the priory, who rushed out and made their way over the bridge and held it for the horse to enter. Captain Temple led the horse, and first entered, and did special service, for he presently made his way to the main guard (situated at North side of the castle) where his horse was shot under him, and he fought so stoutly that his sword was broken to the very hilt. One of the troopers was killed, and two others; which was all the loss. The commanders both of horse and foot did excellent service, and came on so gallantly, although they had lain all night in the snow, that they quickly seized all the guard, insomuch that at last many of the enemy passed through the Market-place up to their chambers, and thence discharged their muskets and pistols upon our men (many of the malignant townsfolks did the like out of their windows) which so enraged our men that they slew eight on the streets, but when the enemy saw our men come in great numbers they cried out for quarter. By this means the soldiers fell to plunder and rifle, took what they could catch, from which the governer of Gloucester could by no means restrain them, for they accounted all their own

in regard they entered the city by onslaught, and had so much opposition. So every man got what he could, and by twelve of the night they had taken most of the prisoners, only some hid themselves and were not discovered.

Not all was lost by the Royalists for Roe noted that 'the governer Barronet Scudamore with some ffiftie others escapeing over the River Wye on the ice, which that night was ffrozen soe hard that they were able to goe over'. Scudamore went to Worcester where he was imprisoned, but rather than wait for a possible court-martial he published his defence in advance. In it he stated that there had been treachery afoot in the city during that cold night – treachery at the hands of a Lieutenant Ballard, who drew off the guard leaving just four soldiers to their fate, and Lieutenant Cooper, who let down the drawbridge against all instructions and called on the enemy. There can be little doubt that these two officers, as well as Captains Alderne and Howarth, were well paid for their services.

The rapid loss of Hereford, as compared with the unsuccessful six week siege by the Scots army, was received with great enthusiasm in the House of Commons. Colonel Morgan's secretary, who brought the first account to Parliament, was immediately voted £30. The 'constable', Berrow, received a gratuity of £100 and an annual pension of £50. The rapid defeat of Hereford was in part due to treachery, in part to good planning based on internal knowledge, and in part

Fig. 10.7 The cathedral's Chapter House depicted in the early 1800s by Thomas Hearne, showing its state of decay some 150 years after its roof had been stripped of lead for use in the castle.
(© Herefordshire Museum Service)

due to the weather. Although called 'A New Tricke to take Townes', the method can lay little claim to originality – such stratagems are as old as the Trojan horse.

Birch was appointed Governor of Hereford and carried out further repairs to the castle to ensure weather-proof protection for his garrison, using lead from the cathedral Chapter House, a building deemed redundant by the new regime (Fig. 10.7). Timber, presumably extracted from the estates of local Royalists, was delivered to the castle in May 1646, and in August Birch acquired the castle for himself, though he seems to have used the Bishop's Palace as his residence. The city, however, rapidly fell into a desperate state – the streets were foul with dung, there were filthy beggars everywhere, law and order had more or less completely broken down, and throughout the city and county the roads and bridges were all in need of repair. John Birch's response was to declare martial law on 15 January 1646. Slowly, the citizens grew used to being under military government and accepted that normal life had to continue.

Fig. 10.8 Roundel on the west face of the cathedral depicting Herbert Croft being confronted by armed Parliamentary soldiers. (Photograph by Gordon Taylor, © Hereford Cathedral Library)

It was during the Royalist occupation of the city that the dean had died and Herbert Croft was appointed in his place. When the city was captured by the Parliamentarians, he ran a considerable risk of imprisonment or worse because of his outspoken denunciations of the troops and their ways. He is depicted on a roundel on the west face of the cathedral (Fig. 10.8) because:

> ... soon after the taking of Hereford, this excellent Doctor, preaching at the cathedral there, inveighed boldly and sharply against sacrilege; at which some of the officers then present (so little doth a guilty conscience need an accuser) began to mutter among themselves, and a guard of musqueteers in the church were preparing their pieces and asked whether they should fire at him, but Colonel Birch the governer prevented them.

Fig. 10.9 John Birch as depicted on his memorial in Weobley church

In April 1649, an Act was passed that abolished deans and chapters, and allowed their lands to be sold.

Fig. 10.10 Goodrich Castle

At this time the cathedral canons were also removed from their houses around the Close, and the 'singing vicars' lost their homes in the College of the Vicars Choral. The low prices that the properties brought could possibly have been by arrangement, but may well have reflected the rather doubtful security of tenure. Thus when the College was sold, it only raised £220. The potential value may have been lessened either because of the 'homeless poor' – the vagrants and beggars – who were still occupying the building or because the buildings had suffered some damage during the siege.

The citizens of Hereford were well aware that there was still a Royalist stronghold only a few miles away at Goodrich Castle with Sir Henry Lingen in charge (Figs. 10.10 & 10.11). On 9 March 1646, Birch was successful in burning the stables at Goodrich but Lingen apparently replaced them with little trouble. A few days later, when Birch was away at Stow, Lingen decided to make one more daring attempt on Hereford – the type of escapade that is still seen as being typical of the flamboyance of the Royalist forces.

Birch had left some 700 foot and 50 horse to garrison Hereford, but Lingen arrived at noon, with a mere 30 horsemen. He charged the gate at the southern end of the city and slew four of the guards. He would probably have entered had there been assistance from within, but support was not forthcoming and so he returned to Goodrich Castle where he continued to be a thorn in Birch's side for over four months. Goodrich Castle, in the southern part of Herefordshire, had been designed as a 14th-century military stronghold, but was ill equipped to survive against the artillery of the 17th century. However, its walls were thick and strong and it would not succumb easily. Henry Lingen was certainly the man to hold it in the king's name for as long as was possible.

Fig. 10.11 Sir Henry Lingen

Birch was equally determined to remove this irritation, and proceeded to lay siege to Goodrich with the intention of staying there until the defenders surrendered, for they had little or no chance of reprieve. The offensive started with the use of cannon and attempts at mining underneath the walls. When it had been under way for a little while, Birch wrote a letter to the Speaker of the House of Commons on 18 June 1646 'from the leaguer in front of the castle' and said:

> I am approached within reach of their stones which they throw abundantly and am now almost ready to play upon them with a mortar piece, which I have cast here; carrying a shell of about two hundred-weight; I have planted my battery, and am going on with my mines.

It was this new mortar piece, possibly cast at Old Forge not far from the castle, that eventually became known as 'Roaring Meg' (Fig. 10.12).[5] Cast on its surface, although now so faint than it can hardly be seen, are the numbers and letters '16 Co. Jo. B. 46'. This can only mean Colonel John Birch, 1646. Described as being little more that a 'toss-pot', it was nevertheless capable of doing a tremendous amount of damage with its 13¼ inch shot. Birch recorded six weeks later that 'I had very much torne the Castle with my mortar piece, that no whole rooms was left in it'. Birch's great mine, 'of ten yards through solid rock' running underneath the Ladies' Tower was opposed by a countermine, but a battering from Roaring Meg so damaged the tower that it fell, blocking the countermine, and opening the interior of the castle to the attacking forces.

Lingen was forced to surrender and Goodrich Castle fell to the Roundheads on 31 July 1646, the last survivor of the Royal strongholds in the loyal County of Hereford. In true Royalist spirit, the defenders are reputed to have marched out to a lively tune, now lost, called 'Sir Harry Lingen's Fancy'.

After its service at Goodrich, Roaring Meg, then the largest mortar piece in England, was first used in the siege of Raglan Castle and was then brought to Hereford by Birch. For many years it languished, upside down, as a corner post at the corner of Bridge Street and Gwynne Street until, in 1839, it was decided to move it to the terrace on Castle Green, although the move didn't take place till 1846. Early in the 20th century it was placed on top of Hogg's Mount (Fig. 10.12), the north-eastern corner of the castle defences, where it had two other guns as company. Some time later it was moved from Castle Green to Churchill Gardens Museum

Fig. 10.12 Roaring Meg on Hogg's Mount with a shell. (Photograph by Alfred Watkins)

and, when that closed, it was moved again and is now fully restored and stands proudly in the courtyard of Goodrich Castle.

Following a widespread revolt in March 1647 by the unpaid Parliamentary army, fanned by extremist groups like the Levellers, Parliament proposed that Hereford should be 'disgarrisoned' and Birch's regiment sent to Ireland. Significantly, the 'new works' at the castle were to be demolished, although the castle itself – presumably the great tower – was to be manned by Colonel Samuel Moore with a reduced detachment of 160 men. Dislodging Birch's men was far from easy and within their 'new works' they were a threat to both Parliament and the local community. Birch initially supported his men but by March 1647 he was MP for Leominster and happy to bring his military career to an end. He sold the castle in April 1647 to Sir Robert Harley, the leading figure on the Parliamentary Committee for Herefordshire, and five other members of the committee for £600. These men pledged that they would eventually 'employ the castle and lands … for the public use, benefit and advantage of the county of Hereford and the inhabitants thereof'. Harley and his fellow committee members, basically the moderate and middling gentry of the county, hoped this would be the first step in getting rid of the troublesome garrison. The soldiers, however, who had still not been paid, mutinied and when Birch came to Hereford in July to mediate, they seized him and his brother, plus the £200 they had found within his coffer in the tower. He was eventually released and the House of Commons voted £7,500 to pay the arrears demanded by the soldiers, whereupon they disbanded and went home.

In December 1652 Parliament had the castle surveyed, providing the first detailed view of its condition since Leland's visit over a century before. The 'tower on the mount' was noted, below which stood a dwelling house called the Governor's Lodge – presumably Castle Cliffe House – which had three rooms above ground and three below. There were two buildings on Castle Green. One was probably the 12th-century church of St Martin, which had been used by the guard and for quartering soldiers. The Green itself was enclosed by the ruins of an old wall 'with diverse fortifications built upon it' – perhaps the ramparts erected by the Parliamentary garrison. In the north wall stood the 'old ruinous gatehouse', also covered with lead from the Chapter House.

The Interregnum

The Civil War destroyed the social and political consensus that had existed in Hereford from the reign of Elizabeth. The depredations of Royalist and Parliamentary armies – constant demands for subsidies and military rule – undermined the old hierarchies and created factions, based upon religious and ideological differences. After the Scottish siege, when the city was full of foot-loose cavaliers, one account commented that violence and looting was commonplace, church services had been abandoned, Catholics openly celebrated masses, lands given for charity were sold; there was no schooling for the young, no baptisms, no regulation of alehouses, and apprentices were left to lay-a-bed. Naturally, the author's sympathies were decidedly Puritan and in favour of 'godly rule', sobriety and social discipline.

This was 1646, giving the Puritans of Hereford 14 years to impose their mores with the help of the Commonwealth government, which established its military rule within the city, with a governor and garrison stationed in the refurbished castle. County government via the part-time justices was suspended and replaced by a committee appointed by Parliament, which confiscated land and levied fines on Royalist 'delinquents'. Most of the gentry families in the county were in this category, together with several notable citizens of Hereford.

Fortunately, for Herefordshire the sequestration commissioner appointed by Parliament to undertake this task was a Shropshire man, Silas Taylor, who was also an antiquarian and, as John Aubrey, his friend, reported was soon 'beloved by the king's party' in the shire. Together with Edward Harley of Brampton Bryan, his patron, and latterly a reluctant Cromwellian, along with some other erstwhile Parliamentarians, the excesses of military and Puritan rule were moderated. On one occasion in 1652, Taylor, who Aubrey said was 'very musical', organised a music meeting in Hereford, conducted by his friend, composer Matthew Locke, who was a notorious papist. The Royalist gentry were invited to the concert, which upset the garrison commander, Captain Wroth Rogers, who kept his men to arms all night. Locke unnerved the authorities again two years later, when he accompanied Thomas Walton, a Catholic and convicted murderer, to his execution. Locke was arrested and accused of consorting with the Jesuits, but with arguments too subtle for his interrogators, he was released. The moderating spirit of Silas Taylor and his gentry-collaborators enabled Hereford to make the transition from the 'general crisis of the 17th century' to an age of stability moderated by the landed elites who asserted their political and cultural dominance.

The Fate of the Castle

The order to demolish the great tower was made by the Second Protectorate Parliament, called the 'Rump', which was restored to power in May 1659. The work took place in April 1660 – a month before Charles II re-entered London. Some of the stone was sold to the Dean and Chapter to build a dining hall for the Vicars Choral and the city bought the rest to erect a Tolsey at the east end of High Town.

As some of the six purchasers of the castle died, the city authorities assumed greater responsibility for the site, responsibility that was not formally acknowledged by the Harley family till 1748. Over time the authorities dismantled all the other buildings in the bailey with the exception of the 'Governour's Lodge' and the castle gatehouse. The latter, on the north side of Castle Green, was refurbished and used for a while to store the county records before it too was demolished. By 1682, the governor's lodge had been converted to become a workhouse and for many years it was used as a House of Correction or Bridewell. It still survives as a private house called Castle Cliffe. From 1724 the city authorities gave permission to 'all persons to take gravel from the mount there till the same be levelled'. Presumably the mount was quickly removed, for within a decade the council was reserving the right to dig gravel for its own use. The castle hill was finally levelled by the late 1780s: in 1801 it was stated that 'it has not been reduced or levelled more than 12 or 15 years'.

Lord James Beauclerk, the grandson of Nell Gwynne and Charles II, bishop of Hereford in the mid 1700s, provided the patronage for the establishment of the walks on the 'castle green' and is reputed to have laid out the 'admirable and attractive promenade' in 1746. In 1752 the Society of Tempers was formed to take over the management of the green from the city authorities and run it as an open public space.

The visible traces of the Civil War are slight. There is the Rowe Ditch embankment across Bishop's Meadow, possibly used in attacks against the castle. Even less apparent is the slight earthwork that joins two parts of the Wye behind the Park Street gardens at Bartonsham, which could have formed the landward defence for the Scots leaguer. Then there is the enigmatic Scots Hole, adjoining Old Eign Hill, once the main road from Hereford to Mordiford Bridge. Was it used by the Scots? Enough stretches of the city wall remain to give an indication of the extent of the walled city, but all the gates were demolished towards the end of the 18th century to 'allow the free circulation of air in the city'.

11   Faith and Religion

AT ALL TIMES the cathedral was not only a place of worship, but also a destination for pilgrims. In the 11th to 15th centuries people believed fervently in the saints as divinely blessed intermediaries and examples to follow, and relics were valued as tangible means of contact with this select company. The hoarding of them by cathedrals, monasteries and churches became common throughout the Christian world, and Hereford was no exception. Many of Hereford's most treasured relics had been lost in the raid of 1055, including those of St Ethelbert, so it was a great acquisition when Philip de Fauconberg, a canon of Hereford, was able to present the cathedral with what he declared to be one of St Ethelbert's teeth.

Pilgrimages were big business, and the offerings of pilgrims were an important source of funds for the cathedral. Thus, when the opportunity came to obtain a second saint in the shape of Thomas Cantilupe, bishop of Hereford from 1275 to 1282, it was seized upon. During his episcopate Cantilupe was devout enough to endure the discomforts of a hair shirt, which was considered a mark of piety and penitence, but he nevertheless had a somewhat abrasive character, and was very firm and unyielding. He especially opposed anything that he considered an infringement of his episcopal rights. He fell out with the earl of Gloucester concerning hunting rights on Malvern Chase, and even managed to rile his own chapter; at one time there were two rival deans, each appointing his own sub-dean.

Miracles at Cantilupe's tomb were reported from April 1287 onwards, the first concerning Edith, the wife of 'Robert the ironmonger' of Hereford, who was cured of strange and aggressive behaviour, including excessively vicious attacks on her mother and her husband, reviling her neighbours and blaspheming against God. Nearly 500 miracles were recorded between then and 1312. The cures included cripples who rose from their stretchers and walked; the disappearance of a growth on a man's neck which he claimed had troubled him for ten years; the healing of injuries sustained by Sir Milo Pychard, a well-known knight of the shire, in a tournament; and blind people receiving their sight. Initially, most of the pilgrims came from within about 20 miles of the cathedral, but they travelled from increasingly distant towns and villages as news spread about the cures. Irish sailors, it seems, gained a special love for St Thomas.

With the addition of Cantilupe's shrine, even before he was canonised, the cathedral fabric roll showed an income of £178 from pilgrims in 1290/91, when it has been suggested as many as 1,200 pilgrims passed through Worcester on their way to Hereford.[1] It was common to see several litters on the floor of the cathedral nave with invalids in them who had paid a penny or more to be carried from nearby villages. Some would have been transported by wheelbarrow. A list of offerings drawn up on 29 August 1307 by papal commissioners sent to the cathedral, just 21 years after the first miracles were reported at Cantilupe's curative shrine, and midway between his death and his canonisation, included, among a much larger number of items, the following:

> 170 silver ships (the shrine was associated with many ships being saved at sea)
> 41 wax ships
> 129 silver images of whole bodies or of human limbs
> 436 whole wax images of men
> 1,200 wax images of limbs and other parts of the body
> 77 figures of horses, animals and birds
> 95 silk and linen children's shifts
> 108 walking-sticks for cripples
> 10 large square candles
> 38 cloths of silk and gold
> 450 gold rings
> 70 silver rings
> 65 gold brooches and pins
> 31 silver brooches and pins
> divers precious stones lances, spears, swords and knives.[2]

This inventory did not take account of oblations of coins, which were probably far more common than images. The precious metal votives were eventually melted down, and the candles

Fig. 11.1 (above) The Cantilupe Shrine in the 1830s
Fig 11.2 (right) The Shrine in the new millennium

were used by the cathedral for practical and liturgical purposes, but some of the wax images were preserved at the shrine. By a somewhat circuitous logic, the very existence of such objects was used as proof of Cantilupe's sanctity and miraculous powers.

The commissioners who drew up the list of offerings also investigated the claimed miracles at the shrine. They interviewed people who asserted that such miracles had taken place, asking what words were used by those who prayed for the miracle, and whether any herbs, stones or other natural or medicinal preparations or incantations had been used. Each witness had to say whether they had known the subject before as well as after the miracle. There were questions about the illness involved, whether the healing was complete and how long it took for the cure to be fully accomplished. Details were also gathered as to what year, month, day and place, and in whose presence, the wonderful event itself occurred. After their enquiries it appears that the commissioners were satisfied that such miracles, or at least an acceptable proportion of them, were authentic.

After the canonisation of Cantilupe in 1320, 38 years after his death, the cathedral conducted a campaign to promote the popularity of his shrine, and it was a lengthy process. Several bishops offered indulgences for visitors; and collectors toured England armed with royal and archiepiscopal letters of commendation and schedules indicating the spiritual rewards on offer. The signs are that a substantial amount of money reached Hereford as a result of the enterprise. The canonisation provided a focus for a cult that persisted throughout the Middle Ages although, unlike the cult of Thomas à Becket, which was on a European-wide scale, that of Cantilupe rested largely on his local reputation and his grasp on the popular imagination was more tenuous. Nevertheless, he attracted thousands of pilgrims, initially mainly women, though by the 14th century evenly divided between the sexes, who congregated in the north transept, praying at his tomb, making offerings and some undergoing miraculous cures. The fall in the value of offerings at his shrine in the last two decades of the 13th century – in 1383-4 they were under £3, and in 1386-7 under £2 – shows the decline in the popularity of his cult. Although the income had recovered by 1478-9, when it stood at £23, it fell to around £10 a year under Henry VIII.

Fig. 11.3 Carving of a pilgrim (about 1 foot tall) on the outer band of carvings above the eastern springing arch in the inner north porch of the cathedral. The majority of the carvings on the arch are believed to relate to Cantilupe and his cult.
(Photograph by Gordon Taylor, © Hereford Cathedral Library)

The effect of the Crusades on Hereford

Despite the intense parochialism of most of the inhabitants of medieval Herefordshire, they were not entirely insulated from what went on beyond their own small world. Even international events and movements occasionally impinged upon them, especially when they were as momentous, far-reaching, full of actual and supposed acts of chivalry, and protracted as the crusades. Support for each crusade was initially largely dependent on the level of commitment and enthusiasm displayed by the current king, but by the end of the 12th century the crusades had gripped the public imagination and were generally applauded. It was considered thoroughly appropriate for Bishop Swinfield (1283-1316) to remind abbots and priors not to proceed against any monk who decided to join a crusade. No one who was marked with a cross on his garments to signify that he was a crusader was to face legal proceedings, and the bishop threatened any head of a religious house with excommunication if he took such action.

One of the long-term results of the crusades was the founding of Christian military Orders. Of these, the Hospitallers were of special significance for Herefordshire. They probably originated in the mid-11th century, and by 1100 they had a hospital at Jerusalem. Their purpose was to provide hospitality to pilgrims and crusaders, and to this was added the care of the sick. They were organised as a band of military brothers. The core group was a guard of carefully selected knights to protect pilgrims, and this soon developed into a regular army.

The Order was established in England in about 1144, with its headquarters in London. One of the Order's most important commanderies or preceptories was situated at Dinmore, a few miles north of Hereford. It was founded some time prior to 1170, and among the distinguished Preceptors who had charge of it, two, Sir Thomas Docwra and Sir John Weston, became Grand Priors. Attached to the commandery of Dinmore, and the only property in the City of Hereford belonging to the Order, was a small lordship, or tenure of land, granted to the Hospitallers by Richard I in 1190 in exchange for military and other services. It lay alongside what was to become the site of the Blackfriars Monastery and was used as a cell or branch attached to the main house at Dinmore, functioning as a hospital for poor and infirm old men. Among the many privileges of the Order was that of sanctuary for felons who fled to their houses.

The Knights Templar were a similar company of elite noblemen. The Order was founded when Hugh de Payens, a knight of Champagne, and eight companions, bound themselves in 1118 by a solemn vow to protect pilgrims from bandits on the public roads of the Holy Land. At the peak of its influence in the 12th century the Order had about 50 regional organisations in Britain. One of these, and the next largest house of a military Order in the county after Dinmore, was based at the preceptory of the Templars at Garway. Other churches of the order included one at Harewood, near Ross-on-Wye. There was also a preceptory at Upleadon that passed into the hands of the Hospitallers when the Templars were disbanded in 1312. The round church dedicated to St Giles to the east of the city (see p.79) is presumed to have been built by the Templars, though why they subsequently abandoned it is not known.

The Jewish Community

The crusades brought Christendom into a direct and intimate relationship with the Jews in an unprecedented manner, and this had repercussions locally. The attitude of the Church in Herefordshire to its Jewish neighbours underwent great and sometimes dramatic changes, in part as a result of international trends and events, but was generally and more often hostile rather than friendly.

One incident during the episcopate of Bishop Richard Swinfield illustrates the contrast between the generally amiable relations between Jews and Christians, albeit with occasional conflict and animosity, and the frequently very dogmatic, aggressive and dismissive stance taken officially by the Church. In the late 13th century there were numerous Jews in Hereford, a number of whom were very wealthy (see p.102). Bishop Swinfield was offended that there was typically a familiar and quite relaxed social interrelationship between them and Christians, and unambiguously pointed out how perilous and harmful was any form of such fraternisation. He conceded that Christian charity obliged Christians to be friendly towards Jews, yet it was the fault of the Jews themselves that they were condemned to perpetual servitude, and he felt that Jews did not hold back in pouring contempt and insults on Christians. In August 1286 there was a Jewish marriage in the city, and despite the prohibition of the bishop (Swinfield objected to the rites and felt that the ceremony disparaged the Christian faith), a number of Christian neighbours attended. His injunction having been disregarded, Swinfield ordered the offenders to be publicly denounced on Sundays and at mass on feast days until they repented of their evil ways and did penance for their misdoings. Any who were found to have done the Jews honour were to be excommunicated unless they made satisfaction within eight days.

Hereford's Friaries

Francis of Assisi (1181/2-1226) received the approval of Pope Innocent III for a simple rule for his band of 12 devotees in the second decade of the 13th century. He called them Friars Minor, and he defined them as 'a company of people differing in humility and in poverty from all who had gone before, and content to possess Christ alone'. He may be regarded as the first of the friars, and he exemplifies what was entailed in such a calling. His small, pioneering group of followers soon expanded rapidly. They were later given the name Grey Friars to distinguish them from the Friars Preachers, or Black Friars, founded about the same time by Dominic. The Franciscans and the Dominicans accounted for virtually all of the many friars to be found throughout Herefordshire and indeed the whole of medieval England.

A Franciscan friary was founded in Hereford, on low-lying ground to the west of the city, in about 1228 (see p.80). Access to the city was via Friars' Gate at the western end of St Nicholas Street. The friary appears to have been prosperous throughout its life, and the Franciscan friars appear to have enjoyed good relations with at least some of the

Fig. 11.4 The effigy of Sir Richard Pembridge on his tomb in the nave of Hereford Cathedral. A member of the family that had supported the founding of the Franciscan friary in Hereford, Sir Richard fought alongside the Black Prince at Poitiers in 1356 and was created a Knight of the Garter.

bishops, with Bishop Swinfield being entertained by them in 1289. The friary also benefited from the early patronage of Sir William Pembrugge / Pembridge and others, with burials of members of the Chandos, Cornwall and Pembridge families being made in the church. The highest ranking burial was that of Owen Tudor, who was beheaded after the Battle of Mortimers Cross in 1461 (see pp.112-3). His grave was in a chapel or chantry on the northern side of the friary church. At the Dissolution there were 14 friars in residence.

After the Dissolution part of the site was rented out to John Younge for 21 years. This included a hall called the 'Hostrye' with adjoining rooms, a garden to its west and another area of land between a friary orchard and the city wall. The rest of the friary premises, which were leased to Walter Nott, consisted of a great hall with four rooms (which were apparently beneath the rooms rented to John Younge), a kitchen with its adjoining garden, a bakehouse and stable with a piece of land between the two, a house called 'The Gardener's' and a water course. Some of the buildings survived into the 17th century and two large buildings surrounded by a wall are shown on Speed's map of 1610 (Fig. 4.1). The buildings must have been demolished by 1724 when William Stukeley mentions a gatehouse and other masonry, no longer visible, but remembered by persons still living. Taylor's map of 1757 shows the site as an open field. Much of the site is now buried under Greyfriars Avenue and its associated buildings.

It was the arrival of the Dominicans in the city that introduced tension, friction and endless quarrels. They were granted a site in the Portfield outside St Owen's Gate in 1246 on which to build their friary and church. From the outset they were opposed by the local clergy. Throughout the episcopate of Peter d'Aquablanca (1240-68), the bishop and his chapter, together with the Hereford Franciscans, fought to prevent the Dominicans erecting their friary. This entailed long drawn-out litigation at the papal curia. Opposition was not confined to verbal attacks. In 1253 the Dominican house at Hereford was invaded; the inmates were expelled and detained in a field while their friary was utterly destroyed. This was not an isolated example of physical aggression against the Order and its members. Hostility continued until 1270, when the friars received letters of protection from the king.

The Dominicans moved from the Portfield site in about 1319 when Edward II granted them lands and tenements on which to build a new friary, land which adjoined grounds given to them by Sir John Daniel and the bishop of Hereford immediately behind the house of the Knights of St John on Widemarsh Street. By 1351, after further acquisition of land, the priory precinct was probably delineated by the present-day Widemarsh Street on the west, Coningsby Street on the south, and the Tan Brook to the north. Canal Road may well have formed their eastern boundary.[3]

The precinct was walled, with a main gateway onto Widemarsh Street as shown on Speed's map of 1610 (Fig. 4.1). The various construction dates for their buildings are unknown, but as the priory reached the height of its prosperity in Richard II's reign (1377-99), when three successive priors occupied the post of Royal Confessor, it can be assumed that most of the building work was then complete. In 1351 the friars were given exemption from episcopal jurisdiction and as a result several high status burials took place in the friary church, including those of the earl of Pembroke in 1376 (by when the church must have been complete), the bishop of Chester in 1394, and William de Beauchamp in 1408. Nevertheless, the friary had been burnt down three times by 1424 when the friars received a grant of indulgences towards the repair of the buildings. At the root of the antagonism was money. As wandering, often popular, preachers

Fig. 11.5 The preaching cross at Blackfriars in the late 1700s by Edward Dayes. This is the only surviving example in England of a friars' preaching cross, and it was located in the friars' cemetery. It stands on high steps, is hexagonal, with an openwork panelled parapet and a stone roof bearing a tall cross-shaft and cross that did not allow the preacher much space in which to stand or move about. (© Herefordshire Museum Service, ref: 5633)

they frequently diverted revenue that the cathedral could otherwise have received. They attracted offerings from the people, gifts and benefactions, and income from lands they occupied in the form of rents and tithes previously due to the cathedral chapter. They also threatened the cathedral's monopoly on burials and the receipt of funerary and mortuary offerings.

The priory was suppressed on 25 August 1538 when its inhabitants included a prior and seven friars (11 brethren were recorded in addition to the prior in 1352). The priory's debts of £52 14s 3d were paid off by the selling of £15 worth of jewels with the balance coming from the sale of fruit, saffron, wood and corn held in store, and the profits from a cider mill.

The site eventually passed to Sir Thomas Coningsby of Hampton Court, and by 1614 he had founded the almshouses known as Coningsby Hospital nearby (Fig. 11.7), using materials from the ruins of the priory church. During this process the workmen discovered a flight of steps leading down to a vault in which were lead coffins; these were re-buried in the hospital chapel.

Fig. 11.6 The remains of the Blackfriars' refectory and Friar's house dating from 1322, as depicted in 1859. (© Herefordshire Museum Service)

Fig. 11.7 Coningsby Hospital as depicted in 1859. (© Herefordshire Museum Service)

It seems certain that it was Coningsby who rebuilt the west cloistral range to be his town house and the architectural style of the inserted domestic features such as windows and doorways would seem to support the premise that this took place at the start of the 17th century. The carved initials 'TPC' (Thomas and Philippa Coningsby) occur frequently in the hospital buildings and also on the first-floor fireplace in the ruins. The house was approached by a gatehouse on Widemarsh Street which still survives immediately to the south of the hospital. By the 1680s the house had clearly been in ruins for some time. This may well have been a result of damage, deliberate or otherwise, during the Civil War, as Fitzwilliam Coningsby, then High Sheriff of Herefordshire, was a noted Royalist.

The Black Death
For the people of Herefordshire the crusades may often have appeared remote and irrelevant. Their lives were hardly disturbed by the suffering entailed, or touched by the glory that was occasionally achieved. Of far greater significance in their intensely localised life was the plague, known as the Black Death, that ravaged England in 1348 and in the following years. The disease had a devastating and traumatic effect in Herefordshire.[4] Its cause was then unknown, but it is now thought that the horrific scourge was borne by rats and entered the country in a ship that landed at Melcombe Regis in Dorset. Within a fortnight it was in Bristol, then Gloucester, and probably in Hereford soon after that. Death rates in the period 1348-50 seem to have ranged from 38% in the diocese of York to 48% in Exeter, Norwich and Winchester; in Hereford it was 43%.[5] Bishop Trilleck attempted to keep the plague at bay by arranging for the shrine of the then recently canonised St Thomas de Cantilupe to be carried in procession through the city. The bishop also prohibited theatrical plays in churches, possibly as a precaution against the spread of infection. The Church's ability to respond was of course hampered by deaths caused by the plague amongst the clergy. St Peter's in Hereford had three vicars between 1348 and 1350, probably due to the plague. Subsequent outbreaks, although not nearly as severe as the first, also carried off members of the clergy, the one in 1361 seeming to have killed about half as many as that of 1348-9. After the 1361 plague had abated, Bishop Lewis de Charlton built a white cross, decorated with his coat of arms, about a mile west of Hereford. It was located on an angle of the road where it branches off in two directions, one to Stretford Bridge and Pembridge and the other to Hay and Breconshire, and marked the site where farm produce had been brought when the people had been afraid to approach the city because of the ravages of infection.

The Later Middle Ages
At the end of the 13th century the people of Hereford were raised on Christian beliefs and practices from birth to death. Miracle plays were performed in public areas, while fraternities or guilds for religious and social purposes effectively complemented and reinforced the work of the parish churches.

The institutional Church, ruled by the pope, was regarded as the only haven of salvation, and the fount of all spiritual wisdom. Church and society were identified as one and the authority of the pope was reckoned as incontestable. It was accepted without question by all but a dissident minority that he was the final and unquestioned judge on Earth in spiritual matters. This attitude prevailed despite some tension and disquiet at having to make payments to meet papal taxation demands.

Nonetheless, by the early 15th century the very foundations of the Church, and more particularly of the papacy as the head of the Church, had been severely shaken. The reputation of the papacy was grossly tarnished as a result of the papal exile at Avignon from 1309 to 1377 (which also aligned papal policy with that of France, to the annoyance of England), and far more so by the Great Schism from 1378 to 1417 when there were two popes. The bitter division was manifested at every level as each of the popes established their own ecclesiastical structures and spheres of influence.

Herefordshire also had to endure its own particular traumas. It had hardly recovered from the suffering caused by the Black Death when it was rocked in the early years of the 15th century by the Welsh rising under Owain Glyn Dwr. In the meantime the county had become one of the main centres of the Lollards.

The Lollards

John Wyclif (*c.*1330-1384) was a leading theologian of his generation and came to accept the Bible as the supreme authority for his own and the Church's teaching and practice. In doing so he rejected the doctrine of transubstantiation – the belief that the elements of bread and wine were changed into the body and blood of Christ by the liturgical acts of the priest in the mass. This struck at the very heart of medieval Catholicism because the mass and the theology surrounding it were at the centre of the Church's life.

His insistence that what the Bible taught should inform all aspects of doctrine and conduct had other consequences. He blamed all the ills of the Church and of society on an unwillingness to submit to the precepts of Scripture, and he called for a radical reformation of the Church. Such views were dynamite, and he was fortunate to die peacefully at Lutterworth, rather than agonisingly at the stake.

The essence of what Wyclif had come to believe was perpetuated and promulgated by a band of enthusiasts called Lollards. They were always a scattered and persecuted minority, with small pockets found in certain parts of the country; and Herefordshire was one of these focal points, especially in the 35 years after Wyclif's death.

In Oxford, where Wyclif taught and where his influence was strongest, four Wyclifites had made their presence felt by 1384: Nicholas Hereford, John Aston, Philip Repington and John Purvey. Of these, Hereford, Aston and Purvey had some links with Herefordshire or at least with the West Midlands. Despite his name, it is not known if Hereford was born in the city. He was a priest who continued as an active Lollard in the Nottingham area after he left Oxford, but he was reconciled to the Church in 1391. He thereafter led a life of blameless orthodoxy and piety, including service as the chancellor of Hereford Cathedral, in which capacity he was a zealous persecutor of heretics. Aston was also a priest. He was from the Worcester diocese, and he preached and evangelised in that region. He recanted, but then reverted to his former views and died as a Lollard in 1388. Purvey was Wyclif's amanuensis, and he remained an active Lollard, preaching around the Bristol area and in Herefordshire.

The most remarkable of the early Lollard preachers, however, was William Swynderby. He was especially effective in attracting and winning over to his cause craftsmen, artisans and small tradesmen of the type who had provided the core supporters for the Peasants' Revolt, the events of which had not touched the city. He moved to Worcestershire and joined Hereford, Aston and Purvey in a vigorous promotion of Lollardy there and in the Welsh Marches. Swynderby had a number of assistants, the most prominent of whom were Walter Brut and Stephen Bell, both of them active in Herefordshire. Brut was summoned to appear before Bishop Trefnant in 1393, in preparation for which he submitted written answers to accusations of heresy. The very erudite court before which he was arraigned sat for three days, on the last of which Brut meekly submitted to correction, but in words that were so ambiguous that they hardly amounted to a recantation. Swynderby was particularly reluctant to appear before the bishop. When asked to do so in Bodenham church in June 1390, he only concurred when he had obtained a safe conduct, apparently in the form of a written promise that he would not be detained. In the following year he sent a servant instead of attending himself when cited to appear before the bishop in July, did not attend just over three weeks later when next ordered to come before the bishop, and did not respond when summoned to appear at different venues on two other occasions in the next month. On 2 September he was formally excommunicated.

It is impossible to gauge the extent of Lollardy in the county. There is no evidence to show that the dispersed groups of Lollards in various parts of Herefordshire coalesced or even attempted to communicate with each other. The sect was especially assailed by Bishops Trefnant and Mascall in the years from 1389 to 1417, but this did not prevent its proliferation within the diocese. The most common offence committed by the 'heretics' was the possession of the Bible in English, reflecting one of the main aims of the Lollards, which was to place an English translation of the Bible into the hands of every person able to read.

Bishops, the diocesan staff and the diocese
The bishops who had to deal with Lollardy were still as powerful as ever, and their general lifestyle was little changed in this late medieval period. They expected, and almost invariably received, due respect, deference and obedience. In 1449, the bishop 'placed under an interdict the churches of All Saints and St Peter's for not ringing the bells on his arrival, in accordance with the laudable right and custom. Next day, Sunday, however, on the humble submission of the clerks of the said parishes, and in the presence of the dean, on their acknowledging that the bells ought to have been rung, he graciously removed the interdict.'[6]

In like vein, in 1486 a Hereford rector, who had failed to appear at the bishop's triennial visitation, was also immediately disciplined. Such lordly demeanour was thought appropriate for the bishop despite the fact that Hereford was one of the smallest and poorest dioceses in the country. The drastic reduction in the revenue from pilgrimages, and the absence of significant income from wool production, or other sources, meant that the diocese was not able to afford the levels of staff found in other sees.

At the end of the Middle Ages the chapter of the cathedral was assuming a higher profile within the life of the diocese. The six or seven resident canons, together with the dean, had gained a reputation for being a strong-willed body of men. By the 15th century two-thirds of them had a university education, and it was unusual to find non-graduate canons after 1450. It is evident that they were practical about the academic discipline they chose, with 45% having studied either civil or canon law. Theologians were relatively few and far between. The overwhelming majority of the graduates studied at Oxford, which reflects its strong links with the west of England, where most of the canons were born and bred.

Pluralism was accepted as the norm for the canons, and even taken as a measure of success. Most of them had acquired several posts and the payments attached to them by the time they had become canons. These ranged from parish churches to prebends in other cathedrals or collegiate churches.

The Reformation

There is no evidence to indicate that the Church in Herefordshire was in an irretrievably degenerate condition in 1520.[7] It was to a great extent undertaking its required liturgical, administrative and organisational tasks, and it was maintaining traditional forms of diocesan and parochial life. It was satisfactory in that it was keeping the ecclesiastical ship afloat.

Nevertheless, there are signs that it had become tired and listless. It had lost its vitality, its sense of mission, and its evangelistic and pastoral cutting edge and had largely been reduced to the routine performance of outward acts prescribed by custom and current convention. Stress was given to church attendance and the power of relics, and reliance was placed on outward religious rituals and modes of conduct such as the purchase of indulgences, the prayers of cantarists, and pilgrimages, but even these had generally become so stereotyped that they had lost their vital spiritual content and meaning. In a nutshell, the Church in Herefordshire had become somewhat ossified.

The life of Hereford Cathedral was not immediately or greatly affected when Henry VIII introduced his Reformation by Act of Parliament in the 1530s, and when the English Church broke its 1,300 year relationship with the pope.[9] The destruction of Cantilupe's shrine, whereby at a stroke the cathedral was deprived of one of its main attractions as a place of pilgrimage, was

---

Hereford Cathedral School[8]

The school probably had its origin in the 12th century, at a time when Hereford was a centre of learning (see Chapter 7). In its early days the school was overseen by the Chancellor of the cathedral, who was responsible for appointing the headmaster. As such the school had 'an equivocal status … [being] neither fully part of the cathedral body, nor altogether detached from it'. Statutes dating from the mid 13th century indicate that there were in fact two schools, one a grammar school and one a song school, the latter supervised by the Succentor. For the grammar school, a key ingredient was to teach the reading, writing and speaking of Latin. The Reformation appears to have left the school relatively untouched and still under the overall control of the Chancellor, though no doubt what was sung in the song school underwent a change. In addition, fee-paying for attendance at the school was abolished as a result of a royal injunction in 1547. Endowments from the late 16th century onwards were to provide the basis for funding the school in subsequent years.

The cathedral school remained stoutly Royalist throughout the Civil War, with the boys actively engaged in defending the city against the Parliamentary forces. In the course of the military operations its life was inevitably and seriously disrupted, and its buildings were damaged. It made great efforts to rectify some of the harm done, and new regulations were introduced in 1665, after the Restoration, in order to ensure its effective management. It was only in 1893 that the school was formally established as its own entity, outside control of the cathedral, and only in 1853 that the name 'Hereford Cathedral School' was used for all purposes, the school having been known as Hereford Grammar School, Hereford Free School and Hereford Collegiate School, amongst other names, over the course of time.

significant, but even this was not of great and lasting importance because pilgrimages themselves were soon undermined by the Reformation movement in England during the following half century. Of more fundamental and, as it proved, lasting effect, however, was the way that the new Catholicism – without the previous acknowledged headship of the pope and the assumption by the king of that role – started to change the whole ethos of the medieval Church.

The Dissolution of the monasteries between 1536 and 1539 did not generate widespread and popular rejoicing. Whatever the state of any of the eight or so monasteries and three nunneries that still existed in Herefordshire, they often provided alms for the poor, upon which a number of destitute people had come to rely for their sustenance. Hospitals belonging to religious houses likewise offered a valuable and much appreciated service to the needy. These institutions were familiar to all the people and had been around for a long time. Their removal was a quite traumatic matter.

It was during the decades after Henry's death in 1547 that the cathedral felt the full force of the wind of change as Protestantism replaced Catholicism under Edward VI (1547-53) and Elizabeth. From October 1545 an English litany displaced the Latin processions on Sundays and feast days, and from 1547 it was sung kneeling in the choir, without procession. The removal of images and altars from the cathedral is recorded in 1550, and the new service of Holy Communion was introduced in November 1552. The services in the vernacular from the Book of Common Prayer made the Latin breviary, missal and antiphonal redundant. During the reign of Mary the Latin rite was temporarily restored, as were altars for masses, but with the accession of Elizabeth the new Protestant order was once more adopted, and this time permanently.

The tension within the highly conservative chapter generated by the process of Protestantisation was especially great because for much of the Reformation period the diocese was in the hands of bishops who favoured such a trend. The dean and canons were decidedly unenthusiastic, and indeed hostile, when the ultra-Protestant Edward Foxe was appointed as bishop in 1535. They were further aggrieved when, after the death of Foxe in 1538, they found that his replacement, John Skippe, was perhaps even more pronounced in his support for the Reformation. He had cooperated with his predecessor, Foxe, in the publication of the *Institution of a Christian Man* in 1537, and he was intimately involved in writing the *King's Book* in 1543. These two works incorporated a mixture of Catholic and Protestant doctrines, but they were important landmarks in the promotion of Protestantism. Skippe was a close associate of Thomas Cranmer and probably helped in

Fig. 11.8 Bishop John Skippe

drawing up the first Prayer Book of 1549, although when it was completed he was dissatisfied because it was not sufficiently Protestant in tone and content from his point of view.

The cathedral also felt the impact of the short reign of Mary Tudor (1553-8). Bishop John Harley, the chaplain to the Duke of Northumberland, was deprived, and was replaced by the reliably conservative Robert Parfew (also known as Purfoy or Wharton), a former Cluniac monk who was translated from St Asaph. In 1554 married clergy were removed from the cathedral staff, in compliance with articles issued by Edmund Bonner, Bishop of London, and those deprived included the precentor, John Barlow, and three prebendaries, Thomas Carpenter, Edward Welsh and Rowland Taylor. Another married priest was inhibited from performing the sacraments, and action was taken against married clergy who served in cathedral benefices rather than in the cathedral itself, which included proceedings against some former monks.

Most of the members of the Hereford chapter were delighted with the signs of restored Catholicism, but they were further alarmed when it became clear that the rule of Mary was but an interlude in the implementation of the Reformation. The still predominantly conservative cathedral clerical staff were dismayed when Queen Elizabeth appointed the ex-Dominican friar John Story as bishop in 1585. He was a known and enthusiastic Protestant, whereas all the residentiary canons bar one were still devoted to the ancient faith. The new bishop received an unenthusiastic, not to say unfriendly, welcome, and he was equally unhappy with the cathedral chapter, which he described as 'a nursery of blasphemy, pride, superstition and ignorance'. The canons made his life almost intolerable.

It was the cumulative effect of the new Books of Common Prayer, as formulated in 1549 and 1552, and the package of measures in the first five years or so after Elizabeth's accession in 1558, known as the Elizabethan Settlement, that achieved the distinctive Elizabethan Protestant *via media* and finally started to produce radical changes. The new liturgies in English, incorporating some distinctively Protestant doctrinal points, would have had a particularly powerful impact on local communities. The new formularies were a wonder of conciseness and simplification, and couched in language of almost unparalleled beauty. Such changes would have been a shock to everyone, for all were required to attend services; no options were on offer.

The latter part of Elizabeth's reign saw the first signs of organised dissent by those who thought that the Church of England had not travelled far enough along the road of reform. It was then that the first Presbyterians appeared, and there were indications of the imminent emergence of what soon became the Independents and Baptists. During the Elizabethan era, however, such dissenting individuals and groups were largely confined to Cambridge, London and a few other areas, mainly in the south and east of England. There is no evidence of them, at least in any corporate and organised form, in Herefordshire before the 17th century.

Meanwhile, the majority of Catholics gradually conformed to the Church of England. Few people, and certainly only a very small number of those from among the poor and the members of the lower social and economic groups, were able or willing to withstand the social pressures militating against non-conformity, and to face the dangers implicit in resistance to government decrees. Nevertheless, a sizeable minority of Catholics resolutely held on to the beliefs and practices of their forebears, and by the late 16th century a number of Catholics practised clandestine baptisms, marriages and funerals, sometimes in the darkness of the night, and there were prosecutions for such practices in various parts of Herefordshire.

The intensity of the persecution increased throughout England with the arrival of priests trained at Douai college in France along with Jesuits. Both papal agencies had a clear message: conformity to the Church of England in any way was unacceptable. These priests were the storm troopers of the Catholic Church, and they suffered for what they were doing. In Herefordshire the outstanding Catholic martyr was Roger Cadwallador, a native of Stretton Sugwas, just to the west of Hereford. He was ordained priest in 1593 after studying in Rheims and Valladolid. In the same year he returned to England and for 16 years he undertook a dangerous ministry mainly in Herefordshire before being captured in 1610, condemned to death and executed. Cadwallador was not the only Catholic priest in the county to be put to death.

The road to Civil War
When Elizabeth died on 24 March 1603 a dynasty died with her; but a new sovereign and a new dynasty came to power without opposition. To anyone living in Hereford in 1603, as for those anywhere else in England, the swings of the religious pendulum during the previous seven decades must have seemed inexplicable, bewilderingly and thoroughly disorientating. Catholicism was out as the faith of the nation, and Protestantism was in. A single, virtually unopposed tradition was out, and a national Church, together with the glimmerings of organised dissent, was in. A largely passive laity was out, and a more literate, questioning laity, with far less regard for authority, was in. Almost total theological conformity was out, and a medley of theological views was in.

The 16th-century Reformation had set in motion religious forces that could not be stopped, and now led to conflict within Protestantism itself. One group, the high churchmen, notably in the cathedral and among the upper strata of society, were essentially Arminian in doctrine, stressing the free will of men and women in every aspect of the Christian life. They placed immense emphasis on the organised, formal Church, the episcopate and the priesthood. They gloried in elaborate ritual, vestments and a sense of the mysterious in worship. They strove to introduce church decorations, such as stained glass and elaborate wood carvings, which would heighten the sense of religious awe and impart a greater awareness of the presence of God in worship. The more extreme adherents of this tradition, such as the main protagonist, Archbishop William Laud, were very well disposed towards the pope and Catholicism, and they were ardent Royalists.

The other group comprised the Puritans, who tended to stress predestination, emphasised the priesthood of all believers, and were thoroughly anti-Catholic. They especially valued plain worship, and they placed great value on godly behaviour in individuals, in the family and in the body of true believers – the Church. They dismissed all the pomp and ceremonial of the high churchmen as vain and unnecessary trappings, a diversion and a distraction for those who sincerely sought to worship God. The Puritans were convinced that the high church Arminians were spearheading an attempt to reintroduce Catholic beliefs and practices into England by the back door, under cover of the established Church.

Recent historical work has rightly drawn attention to the danger of distorting the picture by making the contrast between these two groups too stark. Nonetheless, the differences were real and came to a climax with the Civil War, and then with the Restoration in 1660. The most significant long-term outcome of the religious history of this period, and yet another product of this confrontation, was the emergence of new denominations, most notably the Quakers, and the consolidation of the Presbyterians, Independents, or Congregationalists, as they were later called, and the Baptists.

Herefordshire was very much sucked into the national maelstrom of these violent years. At an early stage in the rapid emergence of high churchmanship in the country, the Laudian policies were implemented in the cathedral, albeit in a somewhat piecemeal and hesitant fashion. They included the stipulation that every member of the cathedral clergy should wear a surplice and hood at services where the presiding priests were obliged to make obeisance to the dean as well as to the altar when entering the choir. The bishop was given great reverence and an exalted status. When he was present, it was obligatory to light two candles at his throne. He alone was accorded the highly significant power of interpreting doubtful points of doctrine or practice, although an appeal from the diocese to the archbishop was recognised. Matthew Wren, who was briefly bishop in 1635, was entrusted by Charles I, on the advice of Archbishop Laud, to draw up a new body of statutes for the cathedral, based on high church principles, and Laud was happy to sign these the following year.

All of this changed when the Puritans took control of Parliament. Bishop George Coke (1636-46), protested about some of the Puritan government measures in the 1640s, and he, together with eight other bishops, was imprisoned in the Tower of London for 18 weeks for his impertinence.

Fig. 11.9 Bishop George Coke's tomb in Hereford Cathedral

From 1645 the Puritan Directory for Public Worship was legally substituted for the Prayer Book, and in the next year the Long Parliament legislated to provide 'preaching ministers' for the city and county. The Vicars Choral were expelled from their college and the chambers used to lodge poor homeless people, cathedral clergy were ejected from their houses and choral services came to an end. Episcopacy was abolished in October 1646, and three cathedral preachers were appointed. The pendulum was very clearly swinging in a Puritan direction, and even the conservatively inclined Church in Hereford found it difficult if not impossible to maintain former liturgical practices. The cathedral became a meeting house that resounded to the sound of unaccompanied psalm-singing and the preaching of sermons; ministers preached each morning between 7 and 8 o'clock. They also delivered the customary weekly so-called lecture on Tuesdays and must have been quite impressive, for they even won the respect of Dean Croft. They certainly had novelty value, and must have been a curiosity in an age when sermons were very unusual, or when provided were often of poor quality.

The Restoration

A Puritan minister, Edmund Quarrell, was arrested by the city magistrates for referring to Charles II as the 'son of a papist whore'. He was discharged after finding two friends to stand security at £100 each. The investigation showed that this outburst was a reaction to one of his neighbours, Anne Clarke, who admitted praying for the return of the king, and the people of Herefordshire in general were extravagant in their manifestations of joy at the return of Charles II. Most of them looked for security and stability and thought that the means to that end were the strengthening of the established, national Church, and intolerance of any form of dissenting belief or practice.[10] Many people in Hereford were therefore glad when a strong line was taken against Roman Catholics and Dissenters. During the period from the Restoration to the passage of the Toleration Act in 1689, every Roman Catholic or recusant, every Anabaptist – that is all people who rejected child baptism and thought that the rite should be restricted to adult believers – and every Quaker in the county, was excommunicated. Churchwardens were required to report any they knew who fell within such categories. Compulsory attendance at church was enforced on all holy days.

With the Restoration also came evidence for the retention and continuance of ingrained folklore, or 'popular religion' as a part of what was considered the accepted pattern of life. The character and form of such beliefs and behaviour had changed but little over countless years. The issuing of curses continued, and belief in witchcraft was widespread. In 1662 Philip Benny, a citizen of Hereford, asserted that Mary Hodges indulged in witchcraft in her house; and he told how, every night, she took the andirons out of the chimney, placed them across one another and fell down on her knees using prayers attributed to witches. She then made water in a dish and threw it on the andirons and went out into the garden. Such conduct was not generally regarded as curious or unbelievable. Many people treated it with great seriousness, and were prepared to attribute it to malevolent magic, but the enlightened justices simply bound her over for good behaviour in the future.

Although conservatism was the predominant mood at the time of the Restoration, the spirit of Dissent was very much alive in the county.[11] In Hereford, George Primrose, educated in Scotland and France and much admired by Bishop Croft, carried his congregation with him when he was sacked as a cathedral lecturer in 1660. He became a clandestine preacher but with

Thomas Traherne

Thomas Traherne (1637-74) was born in All Saints parish to a family of shoemakers said to have come from Ledbury. He was a child during the Civil War and witnessed three sieges of the city. Traherne mentions the meanness of his surroundings as a child, yet was well educated at the Cathedral School and Brasenose College, Oxford. He graduated in 1656 and was presented to Credenhill rectory where he spent most of the rest of his life and was quick to conform to the restored Church of England. Known for his poems and religious writings, only some of his work was thought to have survived at his death. Some resurfaced after a sale of papers stored in an attic in Ledbury in the 1800s, whilst two manuscript books bought for a few pence from a market barrow in London in 1896 were recognized to be his work. In 1910 more of his notebooks and poems were found in the British Museum and in 1967 a bound manuscript, later recognized as his, was pulled smouldering from a rubbish tip in Wigan. As recently as 1997 the manuscript of a long poem was found uncatalogued in the Folger Library, Washington DC; and in the same year five more treatises were identified in the Lambeth Palace library. His best-known work is *Centuries of Meditations*, in which he reflects on Christian life and ministry, philosophy, happiness, desire and childhood. Images conjured by this work form the basis of recent stained glass windows in the Audley Chapel in the cathedral (see p.267).

the passing of the Declaration of Indulgence in 1687 he returned to Hereford and gathered around him the 'Independents' who, in *c.*1700, settled at Eignbrook, just outside the west gate of the city, where a meeting house was built in 1707.

The experiences of other non-conformists, as they became known, were less satisfactory and like the Catholics, they endured a period of persecution, as a consequence of the infamous series of anti-disssenting parliamentary Acts of the 1660s collectively known as the Clarendon Code. Those who refused to attend Anglican services found themselves fined, while, in 1670, Thomas Felton, having publicly reviled the Book of Common Prayer was sent for trial. The city magistrates and their constables regularly visited 'conventicles' and imposed fines on those they found there – surviving records show that 59 fines were imposed in 1669 and 47 in 1686.

When the storm subsided to a great extent in 1689, with the passing of the Act of Toleration, it became apparent that Dissent was far from having been obliterated. Licences for meeting places had already been granted to the Baptist, Edward Price, in July 1672, to Thomas Seaborne and Samuel Smith Snr, described as Presbyterians ejected from the Episcopal Church in 1660, and to the Presbyterians, Francis Griffiths and John Wilde. In each case the venue approved was the house of the person named. Representatives of the Baptist community in Hereford attended the Assembly in London in 1690 and in the early 18th century they shared a pastor with the flourishing Baptist congregation in Leominster. It was not until 1838, however, that a purpose-built chapel was erected in Bye Street (Commercial Road), on the site of the present Italianate building.

Another strand of non-conformity made its first appearance in Hereford in September 1655 when a northern 'Seeker', John Camm, arrived with his companion John Audland to nurture a nascent group of 'Friends'. In time a meeting house was constructed in Friar Street, beyond the city walls, but, in 1676 it was despoiled by townspeople. Less than a decade later, six Quakers were arrested at the house of James Exton and each fined 5 shillings. Within a few years the meeting house was repaired but vandalised yet again, suggesting that the quietism of the second generation of Friends had not yet allayed the fears of the citizens of Hereford who still regarded the 'Seekers' as allies of the infamous 'Ranters'. Eventually the community obtained official recognition and protection following the Toleration Act of 1689, which acknowledged the presence of a meeting house in Friar Street, which soon became known as Quakers' Lane. A further 'design' to pull it down in 1715 was thwarted by the authorities and in 1806 the present meeting house was constructed in King Street.

But all voices of religion soon faced testing times as a result of scientific advances, the consequence of philosophical trends that stressed that man is the measure of all things, or a combination of both these powerful forces in the 'Age of Reason'. Perhaps as a result there is little evidence of growth or vibrancy among any of the old dissenting bodies in Hereford from the early 18th century to the Victorian era.

In the latter half of the 17th century Herefordshire Roman Catholics, meanwhile, not only continued to practise their faith, but may even have increased in number, though they still faced persecution.[12] The Bishop of Hereford, Herbert Croft, who himself had been educated at Douai and whose father had joined the English Benedictines in his old age, was urged on by Parliament to be more energetic in hounding the Catholics.

Harassment of Roman Catholics persisted in the 18th century. They were not allowed to hold Church property, nor to celebrate mass publicly, so their services were held in secret. In Hereford it seems that a garret in a private house in Church Street was used for this purpose. Franciscan friars moved from town to town seeking to say mass and to supply the spiritual needs of the people; but they were dressed as ordinary gentlemen in order to avoid detection.

St John Kemble

For more than half a century, from 1624 onwards, Father Kemble ministered to a scattered flock of recusants in Herefordshire from his base at Pembridge Castle, the home of relatives. When he was apprehended in his 80th year, it was largely the result of an upsurge of popular anti-Catholic passion throughout the country aroused by Titus Oates, who maliciously propagated what he knew to be a false tale of a proposed papal plot against king, Parliament and the Church, and thereby caused widespread panic. Kemble was arrested at Pembridge Castle in December 1678 by John Scudamore and committed to Hereford gaol. From there he was taken to London for examination, though Oates refused to implicate him in the fictitious plot. He was returned to Hereford where, at the Summer Assizes on 4 August 1679, he was indicted for saying mass and, although there was not a shred of evidence to show that he was guilty of any treason, he was condemned to death. During his last days he and the governor of the prison used to smoke their pipes together in unalloyed friendship. In the evening of 22 August 1679, after sharing a farewell cup and pipe with his guards, he was dragged on a hurdle to Widemarsh Common. Here, after half-an-hour of hanging on the gibbet before a silent crowd he was cut down and decapitated, and probably drawn and quartered as well. The expression, to share a Kemble cup, meaning a sad farewell, was to pass into Herefordian dialect. He was buried at Welsh Newton. Kemble was beatified in 1929 and canonised by Pope Paul VI in 1970.

The Roman Catholic church of St Francis Xavier

The church, designed by the architect Charles Day, for which the foundation stone was laid in 1829, opened for worship in August 1839. It is a tall yellow building on the east side of Broad Street. The two tall columns at the front of the church in Doric Greek fashion appear to be too narrow for the double doors that lead into the building. It was said to resemble the Treasury of the Athenians at Delphi, Greece, but Pugin described it as 'a pagan temple' and 'a Catholic concern hall'.[13] One of St John Kemble's hands is preserved in a shrine inside the church.

Fig. 11.10 St John Kemble's hand in its reliquary

The Church of England

Within just a few months of the restoration of the monarchy Dean (later Bishop) Croft and his protégé, George (later Dean) Benson had restored the canonical community. Surveys of lost estates were carried out, an income stream re-established and more slowly the 'beauty and holiness' of the fabric of the cathedral was restored. Both Croft and Benson were conscious of the role of the cathedral in the city. Thus, preaching was flagged up for those who might miss the group of independent preachers, appointed by Parliament to continue the cathedral ministry, who had been summarily dismissed in 1660 (of whom George Primrose had been one). Extra vicars were also appointed to the churches in and around the city and since 'polite' activities were increasingly encouraged, the paths through the Close were gravelled and trees were planted to make it a pleasant place to promenade. A new and expensive organ, paid for by public subscription in 1686, was installed which prepared the way for future music meetings. Moreover, the considerable work necessary for the reparation of 'puritan vandalism' at the cathedral – as the Anglicans saw it – provided much employment for building craftsmen. Many Georgian masons and carpenters established dynasties on the back of regular contracts at the cathedral. Thereafter, apart from endemic trouble from naughty boys who kicked balls and threw stones at the windows of the church from the Close and the predations of Elizabeth Barlow, who stole several brasses in 1722, the restored cathedral settled comfortably back into the religious and social life of the city.

The city records show, however, that the old routines of regular church attendance, associated with the rites of passage and civil ceremonies, were difficult to re-establish. The young were a particular problem, being found gaming and sporting on the Lord's Day and yet ignored by the parish constables. In 1715 a list of unlawful games was published which included such activities such as skittles, tennis pins, rooley pooley, thimbles and shooting pigeons. Memories of Ranters and Seekers came back to haunt the magistrates when in Easter week 1706 a sturdy beggar parodied Christ riding into Jerusalem, sitting on an ass with a long coat and a large periwig 'to the great scandal of the Christian religion'. He was bound over to appear at the next sessions.

Yet, for the bishops, life in Herefordshire in the 18th century and early 19th century was almost totally devoid of incident or any notable achievement (excepting the collapse of the west front of the cathedral; see p.204). They could devote themselves principally to local affairs of no great consequence.

There was some sense of animation when disputes arose between the bishop and the city. The old problem of the bishop's jurisdiction at the Fair of St Ethelbert caused slight friction. For more than 600 years the fairs had attracted many visitors to the city, and had been a source of revenue for the cathedral. In 1275 the bishop received £20 from the event, which compared very favourably with the £7 accruing to him from the equivalent event in Ledbury in 1234. Control over this important activity in the life of the city was understandably cherished by the bishop and regarded with envy by the city fathers. There was also the exemption of the cathedral chapter from municipal taxes, which was periodically questioned by local civic leaders. For these and other reasons there was inevitably some, albeit momentary and fleeting, aggravation, and this occasionally somewhat agitated the canons in their otherwise serene and undisturbed lives. Then there were the times when the civic authorities made a claim on the bishop and cathedral to contribute to the repair of the Wye Bridge, asserting that their refusal to make such a payment deterred others from contributing. Stirred up by these periodic challenges, the canons no doubt aroused themselves to take up the cudgel in their own defence. Overall, however, it was all rather soporific and reminiscent of Trollope's Barchester.

Fig. 11.11 A window designed by Arthur Davies and made by the Bromsgrove Guild which was installed in the Stanbury Chapel in Hereford Cathedral in 1923. It shows the west front before its collapse, and also the central tower when it had a spire. Bishop John Stanbury is shown arriving at Hereford for his enthronement. (Stanbury in fact walked barefoot from St Guthlac's Priory.)

12   Georgian Hereford[1]

Georgian society – and Georgian Hereford – can only be understood by reference to the recent political history of England. Tudor paternalism had modulated in the early 17th century into Stuart absolutism, imitating the political systems of Spain and France. But without the ideological foundations of Catholicism, the country divided and Charles I was defeated by that part led by Parliament – an institution absent on the Continent. However, the Civil War released the 'hydra-headed monster' of lower class radicalism represented by the Levellers, Diggers and a multitude of religious sects. With the Royalists on one side and the radicals on the other, the victorious army, led by Oliver Cromwell, established military rule. The experience of this during the Interregnum created a new consensus among the political elites to return in 1660 to the monarchy, moderated by 'free' parliaments. They took a great risk and it is only with hindsight that the Restoration can be regarded as a turning point.

As the court records of Hereford Council show, between 1660 and 1688 the city lived in a constant state of turbulence as old and new scores were settled in public and thwarted aspirants for one cause or another gathered in the back rooms of the city's inns to organise political advance or counter-revolution. Catholics and dissenters quickly abandoned radicalism but they continued to be regarded with suspicion throughout the 18th century. Hereford's Common Council was eager to pacify the government and collaborate with the county gentry who became the guarantors of the new regime, along with the restored Anglican Church. Many historians have noticed that after the 'General Crisis' of the 17th century the European aristocracy reasserted their control over political, social and cultural life and, as will be shown, Hereford was a willing participant in this process and recovered its status as a regional capital by serving the needs of the expanding landed elite.[2]

Governing the City

The royal borough of Hereford was fully incorporated by Queen Elizabeth's charter of 1597. The corporate body of the city was made up of a mayor, aldermen and a common council of 31 members. The council was an oligarchy and recruited its own members. Only freemen were politically enfranchised. Charles II confirmed this charter in 1682, but at the same time robbed the city of its independence by reserving for the Crown the right to approve membership of the council. Whether Charles and his brother James II exploited this power is unknown, but in 1697 the council took the initiative to secure the restoration of Elizabeth's charter, without the offending codicil. This was an expensive process and put the council in debt to Lord Coningsby, who acted as the council's agent, for £300.[3] Indeed, in the late 17th century

Fig. 12.1 The opening of Elizabeth I's charter for Hereford City

the council became increasingly dependent upon the nobility and gentry of the county. This is reflected in the parliamentary candidates who represented the city. Bridstock Harford II, M.P. for Hereford from 1679-81, was the last citizen to represent the city for nearly 40 years – and he was descended from the Harford family of Bosbury. Instead it was members of prominent landowning families, such as Paul and Thomas Foley, Henry Cornewall, James Brydges and Timothy Geers, who used the city as a springboard for their political careers.[4]

Moreover, the city increased its dependency upon the gentry by grants of freedom, e.g. to Lord Coningsby (1695) – also chief steward of the city; Samuel Pytts of Kyre (1698); Henry Gorge of Eye (1700); and Lord Arthur Somerset of Badminton (1701). Thus, any tendency towards dissent or radicalism could be monitored, but this informal supervision was far outweighed in the eyes of the city's council by the advantages brought by connection with the county elite. In exchange for freedom, the city expected favours – often unspecified in the order books. For example, Lord Coningsby, Paul Foley and James Brydges (Lord Chandos) were effective advocates in Parliament of the Wye navigation. As Speaker of the House of Commons Foley was especially useful, and when he was attacked in 'libellous verses' in 1696 the council were quick to come to his defence. From at least the late 17th century the local gentry met regularly in London at the Herefordshire Club held in the Blue Post in Chancery Lane, enabling these 'backwoodsmen', (mainly Whigs in the late 17th century), to meet and discuss local issues and put pressure upon the government. The connection with the Foleys continued and in 1761 the family paid for a new fire engine. Additionally, the city's noble patrons could be called upon to subsidise a 'free bush' – the official junketings that punctuated the civic year. If Lords Coningsby, Chandos and Scudamore were invited to these bonding occasions – as in 1729 – they supplied copious wine from their cellars and venison and guinea fowl from their parks.[5] Equally useful were the charitable activities carried out by these men. Lord Chandos, for example, augmented the Scudamore Charity (see below) by £100. As one of the trustees of the charity, he fought an indecisive duel on Castle Green in 1701 having been accused of corruption by James Morgan, one of the city's M.Ps.[6] An entry in the Common Council minute book suggests that the council too had its worries about the management of the charity. Thomas Foley, Paul's son, gave £50 to be invested for the poor when he became M.P. in 1701.

The Freemen
Because of the nefarious activities of Esther Garstone, who in 1830 was convicted of larceny for selling precious documents for waste paper, not all the minute books of the council survive from the 18th century. There are also no account books which might compensate for this loss. Nevertheless, it is possible to construct vignettes for particular periods, for example, the late 17th and early 18th centuries, and paint a broader thematic picture elsewhere.

The city was ruled by its freemen – some of whom as we have seen were outsiders – but for the majority of citizens, freedom of the city gave the right to trade within the walls. However, the regular markets and fairs also enabled foreigners to enjoy this privilege – albeit briefly. In 1700 the town clerk was seeking precedents to punish traders who were resident in the city but not free. Paying a toll at the city gates was presumably regarded as an entry fee. However, toll collecting was declining – most neighbouring towns gave free access – and it had a detrimental effect on trade in general. Hence in 1726 the council filed a bill with the Exchequer to force payment and allow the council to prosecute non-payers, but soon after, tolls were discontinued and the city gates began to be demolished.[7]

The late Stuart and early Georgian council had a problem recruiting new councillors as many of the indigenous traders refused to accept the burdens of office. The issue seems to have related to the informal expenses required from an office holder. First of all he was expected to contribute to the regular feasts – the free-bushes – but also there was a strict dress-code for formal occasions. These included attending the mayor to church and the cathedral on Sundays, other Christian celebrations and significant national occasions such as coronations. For non-attendance or not wearing the proper gown freemen were fined £1. When William Matthews refused to purchase a gown and still attended mayor-making in 1701 he was forcibly removed by the sergeant-at-arms. In this year the matter came to a head when John Ravenhill refused to become a freeman and, in addition, ignored the £20 fine, saying that he refused 'to impoverish his children'. This caused consternation; the charter was consulted, discussions took place but in the end it was decided that any councillor who swore on oath that his personal estate was under £500 was not liable to a fine if he turned down high office. Thereafter being elected to the Common Council or promoted to alderman ceased to be burdensome and was regarded as an honour. Disputes over freedom fines and holding office faded from the order books.[8]

Finances and Land
Freedom fines were an important part of the city's income but since the reign of Richard II it had also been able to accumulate property. One of the most important benefactors was Richard Phillips, a draper and six times mayor in the early 16th century. In 1535 he gave property with an annual value of 40 marks to the city in order that the heavy tolls on the city gates that inhibited trade could be reduced, though as noted above this was not achieved until the mid-18th century.[9] Other lands in the hands of the council were given for specific charitable purposes, especially to give small short-term loans to traders to meet temporary difficulties. For example, in 1695 James Trehearne, a glover, was given £6 of canon Dr Gardener's gift – derived from

20 acres of meadow at Kenchester and a messuage at the Weir – to apprentice his son James to another glover, William Baker. Hereford had also accumulated a considerable portfolio of lands that supported almshouses, these being used to house the 'deserving' poor, mainly freemen. Very heavy demands were made upon the council's charities in the years immediately after 1660 when several old Royalist veterans appealed to the city for support with finely composed stories of their wounds gained in support of the king's cause.[10] The largest charity in the city was that set up by Viscount Scudamore in 1669, which invested £400 to buy stock to establish a woollen manufactory where the poor would be employed. Something similar had been established by Bishop Scory in 1595 but all trace of this had disappeared by 1701, when an inquiry showed that the investments had vanished during the Civil War. Unfortunately, the woollen industry had become mechanised and had moved to the Cotswold valleys and Yorkshire dales, so several attempts to fulfil the terms of the Scudamore Charity failed. In 1774 the trustees tried to divert the money to pay for the paving and lighting of the streets – a cause very warmly supported by polite society – but this was clearly contrary to the aims of the donor. Efforts were still being made to employ the money when the Charity Commissioners arrived in Hereford in 1836 and the investments stood at over £5,000. In 1852 it was used to endow the Hereford Scudamore National School, which still exists under local authority control.[11]

Fig. 12.2 The Georgian period was to see a transformation in the appearance of Hereford. The church of St Nicholas, which had stood at the junction of King Street and Bridge Street, was damaged during the Civil War. It was restored in 1718 and is shown in this picture by R.F. Perling from Friars' Gate alongside Georgian period buildings on the left. The church was taken down in the early 1840s, after a new church was built on a plot which is now just outside the inner ring road. (© Herefordshire Museum Service, ref: 1978-378)

In 1698 an Act of Parliament was sought to build a workhouse. This was a separate institution from the Bridewell on Castle Green, which was managed by the county justices, and the new city workhouse was set up in Byster's Gate. This presumably proved unsatisfactory and a new Act of Parliament was proposed in 1730, but in 1768 Byster's was still in use. Beggars and vagrants upset the sensibilities of respectable townspeople as they could also be disruptive; a riot mentioned in 1705 was probably linked with the problem. In times of great need, for example in the winter of 1771-2, the council bought coal and distributed it to the poor, but these were needy householders and not beggars or itinerant labourers.[12]

The council owned several areas of common land around the city, including Cuckold's Green and Eign Hill in Tupsley, Broad Green in Lower Bullingham, King's Acre and Widemarsh. The council fought a constant battle against squatting and illegal exploitation that sometimes surrendered to the inevitable and accepted a small rent from a successful settler. The barbican of the castle was also similarly threatened until 1725 when a new wharf was constructed here to exploit the new Wye Navigation. Widemarsh caused the greatest tension. This had been considerably reduced from the 200 acres that existed in the late Middle Ages to somewhere around 160 acres in the Georgian period. For the poor it provided an opportunity for free grazing, squatting, fuel and clay for bricks and tiles. For the council it provided a source of income derived from the grazing rights bought by the freemen of the city, which was traditionally used to pave and cleanse the streets, pay a wage to the bellman of St Peter's who regulated the market and occasionally, as in 1694, pay for a large project like reconstructing the Lugg Bridge causeway.[13]

The council was not opposed to regulated enclosure on Widemarsh but it had to be on its terms. James Wall, for example, paid 4s yearly for a house he had lately erected in 1696 and in 1701 John Tomkins was allowed a rent rebate for hedging a piece of 'waste ground out of old Widemarsh'. However, when John Apperley was found digging clay in 1662 he was fined, but he seems to have regularised his holding and in the event it was his hedge that caused riots in 1698. Initially, the rioters were bound over for good behaviour but subsequently several rioters were pursued in the Kings Bench. Further riots took place in 1699 when it was John Lewis's garden that was broken open by the rioters who were clearly opposed to further enclosure. Other prosecutions followed and the council ordered the felling of illegal trees that had grown on the waste 'before their houses and lands', i.e. the recently enclosed holdings. During the mid-18th century there seems to have been less pressure on Widemarsh and the owners of Moor House, a private estate in the midst of the common, which until the Reformation had been held by Llanthony Priory and now belonged to the Cooks and Haworths, began nibbling away at their surroundings. In 1775 what was left of the common was enclosed and as a new money-making venture the council established a race course, providing the county gentry with a focus for their principal hobby and, no doubt, some entertainment for the lower classes.[14]

Population and Topography

As mentioned in chapter 8, in the early 14th century Hereford ranked 14th after London in the league table of English cities and the population in the Poll Tax of 1377 has been estimated at 2,754 souls. By the early 16th century Hereford's ranking had slipped to 19th and by the late 17th century, the city is not even present in a league table of 23 English towns, which contained Worcester at 13th and Shrewsbury at 14th. Gloucester is also absent. In an earlier list

based simply on hearth tax returns, Hereford is missing from an extended list of 42 towns. The hearth tax for Hereford in 1665 refers to 364 households, which using a generous multiplier of four brings the population to 1,456. This is clearly an underestimate and does not take into account those who were too poor to be assessed or had no hearths – like servants and lodgers. Furthermore, it only accounts for those living within the walled city. In 1757 Isaac Taylor put the population within the walls at 3,878, with 1,714 outside, whilst in 1801 the first census gave the population within and without as 6,828. Whatever the limitations of the enumeration, the general trend is significantly upwards and is made more remarkable considering that Hereford had no staple industry in this period and was remote from the areas of dynamic growth like the Midlands.[15]

Samuel and Nathaniel Buck's *NE Prospect of the City of Hereford* (1732) (Fig. 12.3) depicts a medieval town dominated by its churches, around which are clustered many high gabled buildings, including the lantern-tip of the Market Hall (14). St Owen's Gate is visible along with its straggling suburb, ending with the chapel of St Giles (2), which had been there since the late 13th century. The suburbs outside Byster's Gate and Widemarsh Gate appear to have been rebuilt since the Scottish siege. The latter terminates with the Coningsby Hospital (20) and the isolated tower of the Blackfriars, whilst the most notable feature in the former is the tall house of Mr Price, set back from the road, on the site of St Guthlac's Priory. Both suburbs appear to be very well planted with trees and much softened by vegetation; planted, no doubt, in the gardens frequently leased to gentlemen of the city.

Within this pre-lapsarian landscape, not very far removed from the 15th-century scenes of Burgundian towns found in the *Book of Hours*, there were signs of change, which can be detected on the Buck *Prospect*. Trows laden with goods are moving to and fro on the river serving Hereford's quays, hidden behind the bulk of Castle Green. Within the city one or two

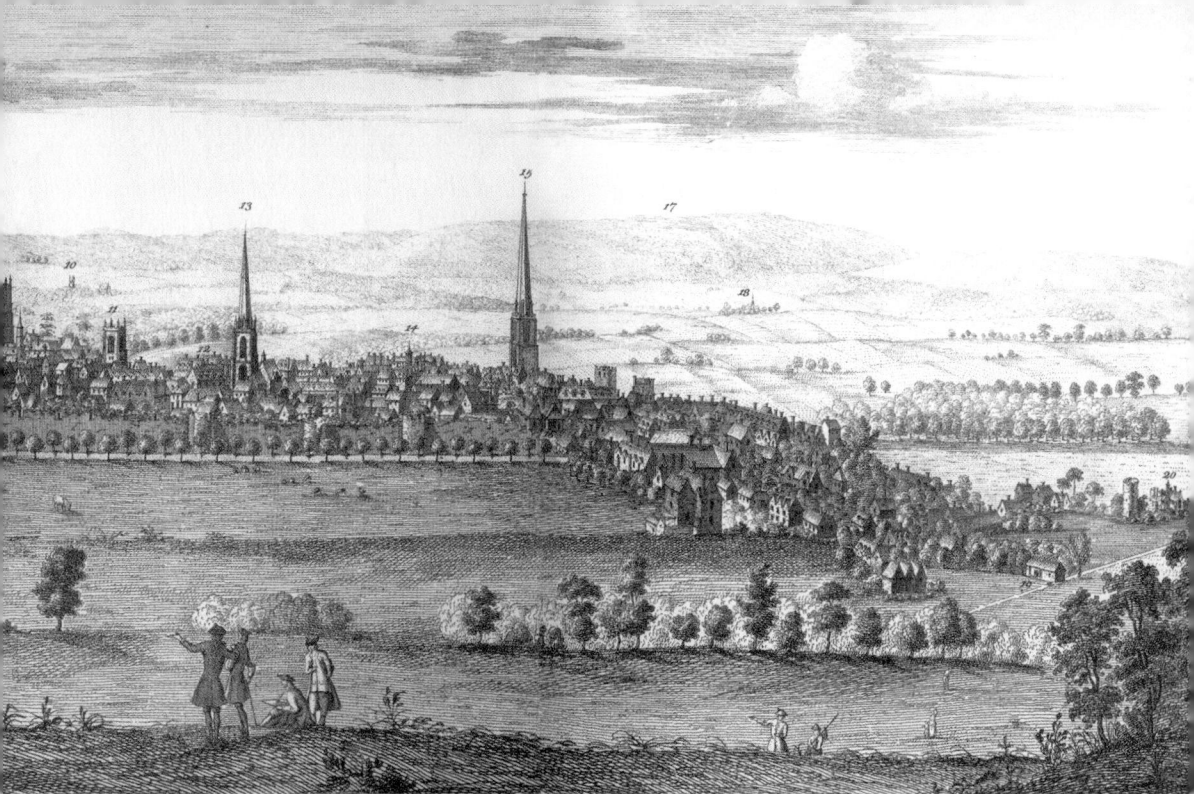

Fig. 12.3 Samuel and Nathaniel Buck's North-East Prospect of the City of Hereford (1732). The artist, Samuel, is sitting a little way above the modern Bodenham Road, a view now blocked by the railway embankment and the County Hospital. In the background the major landscape features are named – Garway Hill (1), St Michael's Mount (the Skirrid) (4), the Sugar Loaf (6) and between the last two, the Lodge (5) at Haywood. Nathaniel, Samuel's brother and his business manager, no doubt anticipated selling a copy of the finished panorama to Mr Wellington, the owner of the house.

houses have the square double pile profile of classically inspired brick houses with low, pitched roofs. The city wall is in decay and decked with ivy, its crumbling state providing a picturesque backdrop to the Sally Walk, so named after the pollarded willows which flourished in the city ditch. Buck marks the trees as a well-ordered row of lollipops, as one might expect. Beyond, the Portfields appear to be entirely dedicated to pasture, providing grazing for the townsmen's horses. This is also where the busy tradesmen take their recreation. Three of them have come to visit the artist sketching on the south-westerly slopes of Aylestone Hill, pointing out the beauties of Hereford or perhaps the landmarks beyond. Approaching this group are other figures, including a woman and child and a traveller, holding a staff. They are coming up from Bye Street where Buck notices another symbol of the modern city, the Leather Mill (19), sited on the Widemarsh Brook; into which the noxious contents of its vats were probably dumped.

The contrast between the ancient and modern city is well reflected in the views of Celia Fiennes, who came to Hereford in 1696, and Daniel Defoe, who visited in 1725. The former was taken by the traditional character of the townscape and described it as 'a pretty little town of timber buildings, the streets are well-pitched and handsome'. Defoe, on the other hand, was less interested in its medieval character and was looking for signs of progress, so he found the town 'mean built and very dirty'.[16]

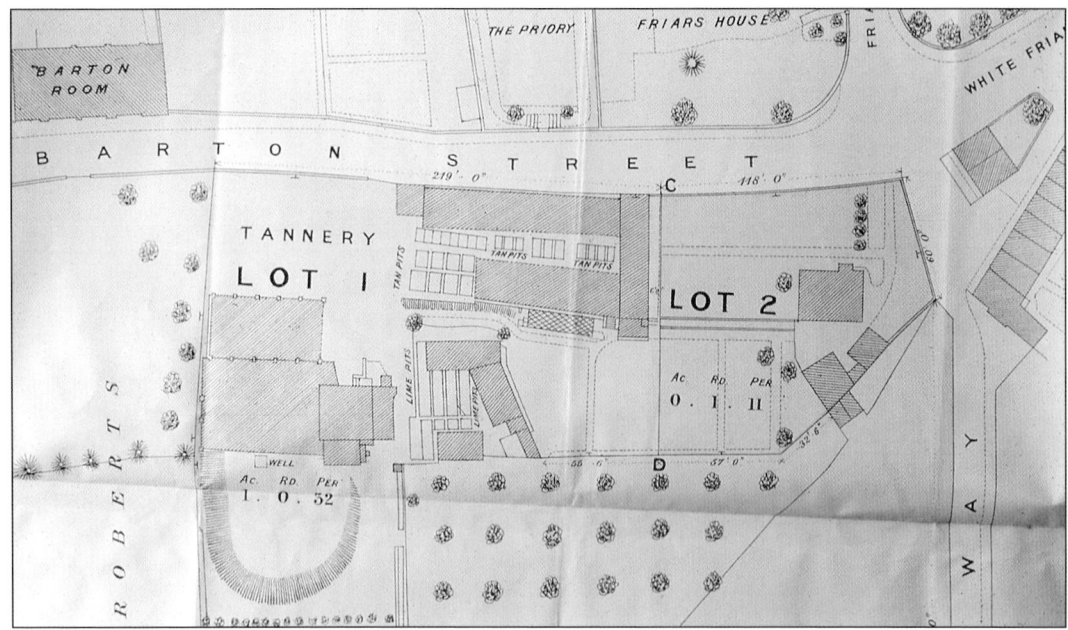

Fig. 12.4 Plan of Hatton's tannery on Barton Street. Tanners existed in Hereford in the late Middle Ages, usually establishing their businesses on the Widemarsh Brook, where it passed, with tributaries, through the northern suburbs of the city. Their presence is reflected in the name Tan Brook for the stretch of stream between Widemarsh Street and Bye Street, close to the spot where Buck marks his Leather Mill (19) on his panorama. In the late Georgian period these mills were taken over by the Hatton family, who eventually established themselves on the site of the Greyfriars in Barton Road. This plan shows the tannery there when it was finally sold by Charles Hatton in 1906. The failure in the 18th century to establish a viable gloving industry ultimately drove the tanners away.

Gloving – 'too poor a trade'

Buck in the legend beneath his *Prospect* notices that there was 'an extraordinary market on Fridays for cattle', one of the key products of Herefordshire in the early modern era, with its well-managed water meadows for fattening. John Duncumb in 1804 mentions the Michaelmas Fair in Hereford when cattle '5 or 6 years old, in a thriving condition are sold to graziers from Buckinghamshire and other adjacent counties where they are prepared for the markets of the Metropolis'. No doubt, the hides of some inferior cattle, worn-out oxen and redundant milch cows found their way to the Leather Mill at Monkmoor, which survived until the 20th century. There was another long-lived tannery outside Friars' Gate, referred to in 1705 as belonging to William Weave, which finally stopped working in 1905 (Fig. 12.4). In the late 17th century the tanners of the city marketed their wares from a standing under the market house, where the finished leather was sold for the glove trade.[17]

Thomas Baskerville commented on his visit to Hereford in 1673 that 'here they make very good gloves' but in 1746 Samuel Simpson also noted that 'the manufacture for which (Hereford) is anything famous, is gloves, and that is too poor a trade to make a place of that bigness flourish'. Gloving was a cottage industry and thus, extended into the surrounding countryside, with the principal traders living in the city. The artist James Wathen (1751-1828) was a glove merchant and left his widowed mother in his counting house in Eign Street whilst he collected the finished gloves from his out-workers. Occasionally he visited Bristol where he sold the gloves and this itinerant existence provided much of the subject matter for his sketches.[18] In 1796 John Price believed gloving, 'formerly a large trade … is now upon the decline', whilst Duncumb was a little more optimistic. stating that it 'is still carried on with success but not on a large scale'. In Worcester, by contrast, the master glovers brought the finishing processes into the city, large manufactories were established, steam-power harnessed and by the early 19th century 30,000 workers in the villages around the city were dependent upon the trade. In Hereford, from the evidence of the freeman's certificates and the council minute books, gloving reached its peak in the mid-18th century. Rather significantly Hereford's glovers are often found seeking relief from charity funds and placing their children in different trades.[19]

Textiles

Duncumb recites a litany of failed projects to exploit woollen products for the benefit of the underemployed workers. Notwithstanding the efforts of Bishop Beauclerk, the mayor and corporation only one entrepreneur was attracted to Hereford in 1772 to establish a woollen manufactory, financed by Lord Scudamore's charity. The brave candidate was a clothier from Gloucestershire who instructed a number of inhabitants in the spinning of wool, but for no apparent reason the scheme failed and £300 was lost. At about the same time another 'ingenious and skilful mechanic of the city', George Bradford, set up a carpet manufactory in the city and produced 'many carpets of excellent quality', still wearing well in 1804. They were woven with the finest wool Herefordshire could provide but the project failed, according to Duncumb, because of a 'want of public encouragement'.[20] Bradford seems to have been an iron-founder and provided the city with its first iron weighing machine set up in St Peter's Square in 1771. A further abortive project is noticed in the *Hereford Guide* (1806), which reported that a flannel manufactory had been established in King Street with help from the Scudamore Charity and was employing 20-30 hands. However, by the 1826 edition of the *Guide* this enterprise goes unnoticed. Price blamed the failure of these projects on the 'uncertain state of the River Wye', which made the price of coal uncertain and water carriage, in and out of the city, especially in the summer, 'entirely stopped'.[21]

Notwithstanding the failure of these enterprises, the woollen trade is still well represented among the freedom certificates in the early 18th century. Another textile that makes a brief appearance in the city is flax. Several mature flax dressers paid for their freedom in the 1690s but such was the combustible nature of this dried material that the council placed restrictions upon its production within the walls. As offenders against this regulation were fined £5 for each offence, no further flax dressers are mentioned. There are one or two weavers in the late 17th century but the trade is rarely mentioned in the 18th century. Since Harper's Charity was set up in 1633 specifically to help indigent textile workers, it suggests that the trade was already in decline in the Stuart era. Dyers also flourished in the latter part of the 17th century and Thomas Baskerville noticed in 1673 that 'about the town much saffron is planted'. It was grown by Joyce Jeffries, close to Widemarsh Street, between 1638 and 1642. The flowers of saffron provided yellow colouring for food but also a yellow dye for textiles. On the banks of the Wye, close to the bridge there was a 'blewhouse' in 1672, which again sounds like a dyer's establishment. But dyers like weavers disappear in the mid-Georgian period.[22]

A Place of Great Resort

So with the failure of its staple industries, how can Hereford's flourishing state in the Georgian era be explained? The answer is simple: the city regained its position – diminished since the early Middle Ages – as the service centre of its region.

Between 1660 and 1800, the number of town dwellers in England rose from 8% of the population to 20%. In many cities, including Hereford, the burgeoning population, it seems, simply filled those spaces created by late medieval contraction. However, there was one major difference, noticed by Adam Smith: Georgian towns, in contrast to their medieval and contemporary continental towns, embraced with commitment the market economy which brought with it civility and humanity, as well as continuous expansion and profit.[23]

First of all there were many trades, like bakers and butchers, who recycled the products of the countryside for the citizens of Hereford. With the Wye becoming more navigable in the late 17th century Hereford became a centre for malting, drawing barley from the city's hinterland and exploiting cheaper coal as a fuel. A malt house in Bewell Street, offered for sale in 1779, was said to be capable of making 7,000 bushels of malt. In 1780 the 'stack of corn-mills' close to Eign quay, belonging to John Lacock, maltster, were said to be 'remarkably well situated for Bristol or country trade'.[24] Whereas the city's mercers and tailors dominated the clothing trade in the 16th and 17th centuries, in the 18th they were replaced by more specialist traders such as upholsterers, collar makers and milliners. Similarly, while blacksmiths and farriers were still located on the main roads approaching the city, they lost their monopoly for metal working to ironmongers, cutlers and tinmen – the latter working with soft metals.[25]

Specialist and luxury trades also start to appear: a writing master in 1695; painters Matthew and William Fisher who were made freemen in 1734 and spent a great deal of their time painting and gilding 'mitres, crooks, knobs, candlesticks and dials' around the cathedral; clockmakers also started to make an appearance. Thomas Banister was made free in 1698 on condition that he repaired one of the city's clocks. There were also surveyors and mapmakers. In the late 1780s James Cranston of Kings Acre became a prolific enclosure surveyor but he also ran a nursery and with the assistance of Uvedale Price of Foxley set himself up as a cheaper alternative to Humphry Repton, laying out the grounds of the gentry as far afield as Leicestershire and Westmoreland. Many of the new tradesmen depended upon the growing middling and genteel clientele who saw the city as a centre for specialist and luxury crafts.[26]

The city also had its vintners or, as the century progressed, wine merchants. The landlord of the Boothall, George Willim, rebuilt the inn in 1783 and henceforward described himself as a wine merchant. Benjamin Maddy, also described as a wine merchant, expanded his business in 1792 by building a 'brewhouse' in a 'substantial, handsome and uniform manner' in Bewell Street.[27] Unlike cider, gin is not a beverage that one would readily associate with Hereford, but one of the few distilleries outside London was established in East Street by William and John Pulling in 1813. A large range of underground vaults was constructed not only to deal with the products of the stills but also to bottle and store spirits, champagne, port, sherry, claret and most other wines, whilst on the opposite side of the street there was the bond, consisting of a three-storeyed red brick building. This contained the blending vats for whiskies and other spirits and a bottling department and stores, all under the eye of excise officials. Pullings were eventually taken over by Tanners of Shrewsbury, equally venerable independent wine merchants dating from 1842 and still trading in Hereford today.

Fig. 12.5 The Pack Horse Inn by George Reynolds Gill (1827-1904). Originally a tavern, and so allowed to sell wine as well as ale, the inn was run for many years by the Kerry family. When Byster's Gate and its associated prison were demolished, the inn became in essence the focal point of this entrance to the city. In 1848 it was demolished and rebuilt as The Kerry Arms Hotel. (© Herefordshire Museum Service, ref: 1978-462)

Other elite tradesmen included Thomas Mayo, goldsmith, who leased property from St Giles' hospital in 1762; and stationers and book sellers, beginning in the early 17th century with William Cooper, who held a considerable portfolio of property in the city, and Roger Williams, whose stock of 162 books was seized for a debt in 1695. The collection included works on theology, history plus a number of texts for use in schools. Better known was John Allen who came from London in 1779 and opened a shop in the Butchers' Row but was soon in trouble with the Improvement Commissioners for his projecting bow window, which he was asked to remove within 20 days.[28]

In the late 17th century the inns of the city were centres of political and religious dissent, facilitating clandestine meeting places for both Jacobites and supporters of the Good Old Cause. In 1688 the Glorious Revolution polarised opinion and opened old wounds. Whilst some congratulated William III for 'preserving the ancient customs from the jaws of popery and slavery', Nathaniel Priest was found drinking the health of King James and further scandalised those near him by offering to toast the pope, who he regarded as both a 'prince and a gentleman'. Three years later a riot took place at the Catherine Wheel in High Town where a gathering of Jacobite gentlemen, who met regularly to 'read private news and drink healths' was broken up by a cohort of soldiers. The landlady, Bridget Andrews, and her maid servant, who took turns to guard the conspirators, joined in the debacle and the inn was closed.[29]

Remarkably, a century later some of the inns of the city were hosting political meetings for neo-Jacobins, talking up the rights of man and looking forward to another English Revolution. In 1797 John Thelwall, the 'Jacobin Fox', regarded by Pitt's Tory government as the most dangerous man in England, had taken refuge, by changing his career to that of an upland farmer, and was living at Llyswen, near Brecon. He made several visits to Hereford where he used John

Fig. 12.6 The Black Swan in Widemarsh Street was a principal inn of Georgian Hereford. Built in the late 17th century, it was one of the earliest brick buildings in the city. In 1973 it lay neglected and the building was condemned at a public inquiry, but it was still standing five years later. A campaign was launched by the infant Civic Trust to save it, but before this could be achieved, new owners demolished the building one Sunday morning in October 1978. (Photograph courtesy of David Whitehead)

Fig. 12.7 The Swan and Falcon, later the City Arms, in Broad Street, painted by James Wathen. This is a puzzling picture since the building that exists now has none of the baroque flourishes shown here. It is probable that this was a design produced by Thomas Symonds and when he died in 1791 a new design was produced by William Parker, architect of the Infirmary, where he succeeded Symonds in similar circumstances. Wathen was very interested in before and after stories and probably sketched the earlier plan.

Allen's library and read the national newspapers. Government spies also noticed in 1798 that he visited the Crown and Sceptre in Widemarsh Street, where there was a Jacobin debating society.[30] Most inns in the city, however, were much more respectable, increasingly becoming centres of trade and commerce, places where dealers in cattle and corn, and much else, could meet local producers and strike bargains. When Thomas Baskerville visited Hereford in 1673 he was very impressed by the Black Swan, just below the Crown and Sceptre in Widemarsh Street. The landlord, Mr Jones, was 'an honest and ingenious man ... whose wife is a distiller of incomparable strong waters'. Baskerville drunk 'the brave red streak cyder' here and beer for breakfast of 2, 3, 4, or five year's age 'kept in lusty great vessels'. He also tried roasted kid and found it a very delicate meat. The Green Draggon (*sic*) makes an early appearance in 1710 in the possession of Thomas Addis, whose profession had previously been noted as a cordwainer (shoemaker). A new venue for the respectable citizens in the late 18th century was Woodcock's Coffee House in St John Street, which was in trouble with the Improvement Commissioners in 1787 because of its projecting porch.[31]

The proliferation of professional services in the Georgian town underpins the development of the polite society as these men, located within the city, principally served the needs of the county. Doctors of medicine like Bridstock Harford (1607-95) began to make a regular appearance in the 17th century. He was a man of Parliamentary sympathies, who was warden and rebuilder of William's hospital in St Owen Street, near where he lived. His grandson (1654-1713) also practised as a doctor in Hereford and was mayor of the city in 1697. The presence of medical professionals in the city seems to have been an innovation, for in 1610 two sisters suffering from 'several disease, wherewith they are grieved' found it necessary to call upon the services of Humphrey Walden a 'chirurgion' of Bromsgrove. From the mid-18th century the city was served by several members of the Cam family. John Cam, a physician, was on the staff of the Infirmary in 1779 and his descendants continued to practise in Hereford throughout the 19th century from Wargrave House in St Owen Street. Surgeons appear to be more numerous than doctors in 18th-century Hereford with nine being licensed by the bishop between 1683 and 1801. Doctors and surgeons were also often associated with apothecaries.[32]

Fig. 12.8 A fine lithograph of the City and County Bank in High Town. The bank, run by F. Hoskyns Matthews and Co. (whose bank had gone bankrupt in 1827) was supported by Lubbock and Co., London. The bank failed in 1863.

During most of the 1700s credit was arranged on a private basis. James Wathen, for example, lent money to the architect and builder, William Parker, whose investments in the Hereford Theatre found him teetering on the edge of bankruptcy. This was in the 1790s, by which date Bodenham's Bank had been founded, to join the two others already in existence. Lawyers, barristers and solicitors were also thriving and several like Thomas Bird, who was land agent for John Scudamore of Kentchurch in the late 18th century, were frequently consulted by the squirearchy. A cursory glance at the classified advertisements in the *Hereford Journal* shows that many of them also operated as estate agents.[33]

Elegant Improvements

The hearth tax of 1665 indicates that many county families had houses in the city, and this accounts for the many mansions assessed at between five and eleven hearths. Moreover, surviving architectural features, such as fine plasterwork, wall paintings etc within 17th and 18th century structures, noticed by the Royal Commission on Historical Monuments in the early 1930s, suggests that there were many high-status domestic dwellings in the city – some of them dated from before *c.*1700. Taken by wards the hearth tax figures are as follows: Bye Street, 16; Wye Bridge, 7; Eign, 15; St Owen's 15 and Widemarsh 9. Elite interest in the city intensified in the 18th century and the calendar of charity property, managed by the council, also indicates substantial investment by the county community in urban property.[34]

In 1660 Hereford was a timber-framed city and its inhabitants still lived in fear of fire, which regularly devoured other pre-industrial towns like Warwick and Honiton. Hereford council took this threat very seriously, campaigning especially against wooden chimneys or 'fimbrills' and insisting on stone or brick for stacks. It obviously had some success since brick of Malvernian origin has been detected in the chimney of No.14 Church Street, a house said to have been built in *c.*1595. Other measures included the prohibition of flax and hemp dressing

Fig. 12.9 James Wathen's painting of St Martin's Street in June 1798 shows how the suburbs appeared even then, and how much of the city would have appeared before the Georgian 'refurbishment'. Soon after this sketch, the street received a fine classical terrace.

Fig. 12.10 *Even in the centre of the city parts were left untouched during the Georgian era. This house in Bewell Street was photographed perhaps by Alfred Watkins in the early 20th century when it was condemned as a slum.*

within the city walls and providing, in various places 'buckets, hooks and other instruments necessary for preventing the danger of fire'. Surprisingly, there were no regulations about the use of thatch, as existed in Worcester, where clay tiles were insisted upon. A fire is recorded in 1685 when the Dean and Chapter gave £5 to the city authorities to relieve those affected by several recent fires in the city. A further measure taken to prevent the spread of fire was the purchase of a fire engine – first mentioned in 1705 when it was 'out of repair'.[35]

The simplest way of escaping from the constant threat of fire was to build houses in brick and clad their roofs in clay or stone tiles. Brick had been occasionally used for country house building in Herefordshire in the 16th and 17th centuries – Hellens (*c.*1550), Kinnersley Castle (*c.*1590), and Gatley Park (*c.*1630) – where timber, necessary to fuel brick kilns, was readily available. When small numbers of bricks were required – for chimneys and paving – these were imported from beyond the Malverns, where fuel was available in the relict royal chase and pottery makers occasionally diversified into brick-making. At this period timber was too precious a resource to be used in large-scale production of brick. Coal was the obvious alternative fuel, but although the Welsh coal fields quadrupled their production in the early 17th century, it was expensive to carry such a heavy material by road. In the 16th century some coal was sold in the market place in Hereford but it was mainly purchased by smiths.[36]

The solution came with the creation of the Wye Navigation in the late 17th century and the expansion of the Forest of Dean coalfield. However, coal on its own burnt too strongly, producing twisted and cracked bricks, and needed to be mixed with ash or clay to dampen the combustion. This made brick production economically viable but very polluting albeit some cities like Worcester and Stafford were already producing bricks by this method.[37]

In 1663-4 an elderly veteran of the Civil War, Henry Traunter, who lived in a cottage on the site of the royal castle, requested relief from the city authorities and was described as a 'brickmaker'. Maybe he used the trickle of coal that reached Hereford following the first Navigation Act of 1662 to make a few bricks. Brick and tile making also seems to have been taking place at this time close to Widemarsh Common, as John Apperley was presented at the sessions in 1662 for digging clay on Widemarsh, and a year earlier another 'tyler', John Tringham was similarly presented for making a pool at Burcott Row, to the north of the common. He later owned property in Whitecross Road, where Price's almshouses of 1665 were constructed out of early bricks. Moreover, Moor House, which sits on the common, also has the appearance of an early

Fig. 12.11 Nash's Warehouse, one of the earliest brick buildings in the city, which appears to have been reroofed in 1732 when two craftsmen carved the date and their initials on a tie-beam. In the 1980s, after a long campaign by the Civic Trust, it was converted into smart cottages and is an object lesson in how to deal with the nooks and crannies of a historic town.

Fig. 12.12 (above) Decorative plasterwork in 29 Castle Street dating from the late 17th century.

(Photographs this page courtesy of David Whitehead)

Fig. 12.13 (left) A fine Early Georgian staircase in Bewell House, the balusters sunk in a new partition. The ramped handrail on the left, terminating with a lion's paw, is probably Regency.

brick house of the late 17th century, suggesting that the Haworths of the Moor took advantage of the local industry that developed on their doorstep. One of the earliest brick buildings in the city sits just below Wyebridge in St Martin's parish. This is traditionally known as Nash's Warehouse but has recently been converted to domestic use. The coarse texture of the brick fabric – much twisting and cracking – used in this building suggests an inexperienced brick-maker, unfamiliar with coal as a fuel.[38]

Four years after the passing of the Wye Navigation Act of 1695, Sir Standish Hartstrong, a High Court judge and Radnorshire landowner, was given permission to make a clamp of bricks on Aylestone Hill. According to Duncumb he built a house 'nearly opposite the south door of St Peter's church' – probably the building now occupied by Tanners, the wine merchant. This concession seems to have opened the floodgates for brick-making for in the following year the council prohibited the making of brick at Aylestone and 'elsewhere on the waste of the city' unless permission had been given by the mayor and corporation. Those who had made brick on Aylestone illegally were expected to pay the council £6 for every 1,000 bricks and fill up the brick pits, said to be 6 feet broad and adjoining the highway. The authorities seem to have had difficulty in imposing these restrictions and later in the year Sir Standish and Mr William Matthews were granted further permissions to make brick as long as they repaired the damage. Little more is heard about brick-making on Aylestone Hill, for the time being, but occasionally prohibitions were imposed elsewhere.[39] For example in 1770 Edward Black was prevented from

Fig. 12.14 Broad Street and All Saints church sketched in James Wathen's distinctive 'leaning' style. By the late 18th century brick architecture was beginning to dominate Hereford's streets, albeit many interiors survive from an earlier period. The bollards reflect the growing gentility of the town; pedestrians loitering and shopping needed protection from the animals and wheeled traffic.

burning a clamp of bricks at Scutt Mill, adjoining the road to Ledbury. Eventually, brick-making found its permanent home on Aylestone Hill and when two million bricks were required by John Nash in 1793-4 to build the new county gaol in Bye Street Without, the brick maker rented land there at £21 per annum. Three brick yards – one described as 'old' – are marked on the tithe maps of 1839-46, on the slopes of Aylestone, below Venn's Lane and Folly Lane.[40]

Thus, over time, Hereford's streets were lined with 'neat' and fire-proof houses (though often enclosing at least elements of the earlier timber-framed house), displaying the symmetry which comes with building with a rectangular medium, but also complementing the classical taste that held sway in the Georgian era. It also reflects once again the 'Grand Manner' of the European elites who espoused the *gravitas* and *dignitas* of Greece and Rome. This is well represented in St Owen Street, which seems to have been favoured by the gentry. Apart from the house of Sir Standish, Barroll House, named after a family domiciled at Byford, is probably the best house in the street and dates from 1700. Further up is Chandos House, built by James Brydges, 1st Duke of Chandos in c.1720, but now altered. He moved here after failing to get permission to build an even grander house on Castle Green.[41] Other documented gentry residences, built in brick, include 29 Castle Street and the Mansion House in Widemarsh Street, both with excellent plasterwork and built, respectively, by members of the Geers family of Garnons and Dr William Brewster of Eardisland. Building in brick was promoted enthusiastically by the Improvement Commission set up by the Lamp Act in 1774 and today it is still possible to identify 'commissioners' classicism' – plain and unfussy – in many corners of the city, for example the fine stuccoed terrace in St Ethelbert Street.[42]

It comes as no surprise to find that by the mid 18th century, building craftsmen dominated the freeman's registers and like many other Georgian county capitals, Hereford became a centre for craftsmanship, which engaged with the surrounding countryside providing new country houses, farm buildings and church monuments. Prominent among these purveyors of good taste was Thomas Symonds, a monumental mason with a yard in the north-west corner of the Cathedral Close who made the transition from artisan to 'architect', using his drawing skills as a stone cutter to provide well-executed plans and perspectives for country houses. Symonds was also an artist and the first native professional surveyor of the fabric for Hereford Cathedral, but because he was unable to prevent the fall of the west end on the afternoon of Easter Monday 1786 – which had been pending since the building of two towers in the 14th century which were constructed on inadequate foundations – he was sacked by an ungrateful Dean and Chapter.[43] The *Hereford Journal* of the time reported that '… the ruins, though aweful, afford a pleasing view, especially to behold the statues of kings and bishops resting one upon the other'. James Butler was appointed bishop in February 1788, and with him came the architect James Wyatt, who had done much work on Oxford colleges. The repair work finally started in September with a modest estimate of £6,500, indicating that Wyatt hoped to mend, rather than repair. However, a further collapse of part of the nave roof in February 1790, killing at least two workmen and injuring others, meant that the repairs had to be more radical. In the event, the western bay of the Romanesque cathedral was abandoned and a totally new front built one bay back in the Gothic of the period. The total cost of the work up to the end of 1796, when the cathedral reopened, was in excess of £16,650.[44]

Hereford council, and to a lesser degree the emergent shire council, set a good example for the inhabitants of Hereford by maintaining and restoring, and sometimes demolishing and

Fig. 12.15 The fallen west front of Hereford Cathedral in the late 1780s by Edward Abbot (1737-1791). Note the Music Room on the right. James Wyatt was appointed to undertake the reconstruction of the medieval cathedral.
(© Herefordshire Museum Service, ref: 6932)

rebuilding, the public buildings under their control. Moreover, both institutions were eager to support public buildings and facilities promoted for charitable and social purposes by the wider community. One of the largest burdens placed on the post-medieval council was the maintenance of the city walls, its gates and the Wye Bridge. After a brief period of renewed interest in the walls, after the Restoration they were left to decay and generally regarded by both the authorities and the public as a convenient source of building material. However, the Georgian council began to realise that they were losing an important resource and started to police the walls insisting upon consent and/or payment before stone could be removed. The gates were also important for siphoning outsiders into the town, but to ease the burden of maintenance each one was leased and domesticated, placing their maintenance in private hands. The downside of this measure was that the passage through the gate became obstructed, so that at St Owen's Gate in 1707 the authorities stepped in and removed 'a house of office'. The first gate to be completely removed was Friars' Gate in 1782, pulled down by the Improvement Commissioners. The other gates followed quickly, with Widemarsh being the last in 1799. The commissioners showed no nostalgia and were unaware that visitors to the city, like Viscount Torrington in 1784, who noted in his diary that the walls and gates gave 'an air of antiquity', saw them as a positive attribute. But such a view was restricted to visitors and antiquarians; most of the population applauded the decision, which made the city streets more open and airy – and healthy, they thought.[45]

Wye Bridge and Lugg Bridge were both maintained by the city council, either from special taxes or the income from Widemarsh. Roads and bridges beyond the city were also of concern and in 1726 the council petitioned parliament to bring in a bill for the repair of highways 'from Hereford to the sea'. Their wish was fulfilled by the creation of turnpike trusts controlling the main thoroughfares out of the city. In 1759 representatives of the council and the gentlemen of Breconshire met to discuss the improvement of the road between Hereford and Hay, and a new toll-bridge at Bredwardine was suggested. An Act was obtained, helped by loans totalling £200 from the council, to be repaid out of the tolls, and the new bridge was opened in 1764. The Great Flood of 1795 damaged Wye Bridge and the architect, John Nash, ever the opportunist, provided a plan for reparations. He was already engaged to rebuild bridges at Bewdley and Stanford-on-Teme, both casualties of the same storm. The exact nature of the work on Hereford's bridge is not recorded but the final accounts were approved in January 1798. Later, the widening of Wye Bridge in 1826 was undertaken by the famous local bridge engineer John Gethin.[46]

Fig. 12.16 Hereford Cathedral and Wye Bridge by John Powell (1780-1833). Tourist boats seem to be operating from upstream of the bridge, whilst the masts of barges can be seen on the downstream side above the bridge's parapets. (© Herefordshire Museum Service, ref: 5785)

Hereford's River Trade

In 1695 the second Rivers Wye and Lugg Navigation Act aimed to create a navigable Wye, which had not materialised with the passing of the previous Act in 1662. Financing was transferred to the county, the 'mills with their weirs and fishing weirs were to be removed and the shallow places deepened' and provision was made 'for the building of warehouses or storehouses' on the site of Hereford Castle.[47] Between 1696 and 1700 improvements took place, carried out by William Williams,[48] the first known bargeman at Hereford, followed by Luke Hughes and William Welsh at the start of a period of flourishing river trade in Hereford.[49]

The flat-bottomed boats that served Hereford were termed barges and were 'keel-less, flat-bottomed vessels of great dimensions, drawing but little water. They were fitted with a tall mast, which could be lowered by a small winch carried on the forward decking'. Although the barges carried a single square sail, lack of wind or a breeze blowing in a contrary direction meant that the best means of progress was provided by teams of men known as hauliers. High up the mast was a block through which the tow-rope was run.[50] Between 1791 and 1850, the high point of traffic on the River Wye, a range of barges traded up and downstream from Hereford. Amongst them were the *Mayflower, Eliza, Charles, Hereford Sloop, James, Ann, Charles and Mary, George, Mary and Elizabeth, Wellington* and *Trader*.[51] From 1787 barges were built at Hereford, the first being the *William*, a 43-ton barge built by Richard Lewis at Crompton's Wharf. Many others followed, including the remarkable *Water Witch*, a 'steam vessel' built in 1834 by Captain Radford RN, who founded the Wye Steam Boat Company.[52]

The first known traders to own barges in Hereford were Joseph Trumper, a glover, and Philip Symonds, a mercer, who leased a 'piece of ground formerly inclosed into a garden' at Castle Hill, where the two partners built a wharf in 1725 for their 'Trows, Boats, Barges and other Vessels'.[53] By 1759 William Baker had established himself as a barge owner in Hereford, trading from his buildings, warehouses and dye house yards where he kept his 'Trow and three Barges'.[54] Towards the end of the 18th century other owners included Daniel Pearce with his fleet of four, James Biss, a corn factor and carrier, and Jonathan Crompton in the porter trade.[55] From 1801 George Buckle, from a family of shipbuilders, wine merchants and maltsters owned many vessels,[56] and during its last years in the 1830s and '40s the trade was monopolised by Easton, Swift, Cooke, Pearce, Pulling and Bunning.[57]

The barge masters were often also part owners of their barges and traders.[58] They included John Crumpton based at the Anchor in 1784, Jonathan and Adam Crompton in the 1790s, and, after the opening of the Horse Towing Path in 1809, William Hoskins and Thomas Jones, 'masters' of the first horse-drawn barges in 1811. Then from 1825 Francis Goodman, George Pearce and William Moxley were operating barges for The Liverpool & Bristol Company.[59]

Wharves and Cargoes

The Hereford wharves, timber yards and quays were located along the banks of the Wye at Eign, Putson, the Bishop's Meadow, two at Castle Green, three at Wye Bridge and one at Friars north of Wye Bridge.[60] These riverside sites with their tying up places, coal and timber

Date	Name	Type	Builder	Tons
1787	*William*	Barge	Richard Lewis	43
1790	*Valiant*	Barge	unknown	43
1795	*Molly*	Barge	Richard Lewis	44
1799	*William*	Barge	Thomas Maund	43
1801	*Kitty*	Barge	Thomas Maund	38
1803	*Peggy*	unknown	unknown	23
1812	*Ann*	Barge	George Crompton	32
1812	*George*	Barge	George Crompton	32
1814	*Thomas & Mary*	Barge	Thomas Mann	41
1815	*Rhoda*	Barge	Philip Woore	39
1822	*Hereford*	Sloop	Evan Hopkins	54
1822	*Hereford*	Sloop	John Easton	60
1823	*Pomona*	Snow	Evan Hopkins	108
1824	*Helen*	Snow	John Easton	122
1824	*Herefordshire*	Schooner	Evan Hopkins	90
1825	*Champion*	Snow	John Easton	124
1825	*Mary*	Snow	John Easton	130
1826	*John & Mary*	Trow	John Easton	48
1827	*Paul Pry*	Steam	William Radford	31
1827	*Earl of Hopetown*	Steam	John Easton	140
1828	*Mary & Elizabeth*	Barge	Joseph Thomas	46
1832	*Collinque*	Schooner	John Easton	140
1834	*Water Witch*	Steam	William Radford	24
1837	*Bee*	Trow	Thomas Swift	18

Fig. 12.17 The names of boats built at Hereford (or Bullingham in the case of the Mary & Elizabeth) largely for the Wye trade.

yards, warehouses, boat-building yards and nearby inns would have presented a bustling scene of men loading and unloading barges, stacking timber, making bark ricks, weighing coal, rolling barrels and handling baskets, bags and boxes. From Hereford quantities of timber, bark, lime, cider and grain were exported downstream as far as Bristol, whereas the main import was coal transported from Lydbrook and the Forest of Dean. It had been estimated that Hereford required 3,650 tons of coal per year.[61]

Bells from the churches of St Nicholas and All Saints were freighted from quays in 1718 and 1769 to be recast at Gloucester, and in 1779 hogsheads, gallons of cider, 'tuns of cole' and 'dozens of lime' were delivered by barge for Mr J. Woodhouse. During the 1780s and 1790s the Dean and Chapter were receiving deal, candles and beeswax from Bristol and large amounts of stone from Hay, Coldwell and Brockweir at 12s a ton.[62] James Packwood,

*Fig. 12.18 The Water Witch, built in Hereford in 1834.
It drew just 17 inches of water as launched and 34 inches once fitted out,
a task undertaken in Chepstow. It was originally destined for Liverpool,
and was reported to still be plying a river in South Africa towards the end of the 20th century.*

Thomas Bird and Jonathan Crompton took deliveries of lime in the early 1800s, bricks came from Stourbridge in 1802, slate from Bristol in 1810 and two years later Mr Price at Hereford was dealing in wines, spirits, hurdles and spokes from his wharf.

During the 1820s wines, spirits, cider, bark and slate were transported by Messrs Pulling; chests, bags, hampers, bottles, soap and sugar were carried on the *James* barge; paper came from Brockweir; hoops and corks from Bristol; and many other items including cheese, glasses and iron bars were conveyed on the *Mayflower, Hereford Sloop, Ann, Charles and Mary* and *Eliza* of the Liverpool & Bristol Company. On the return journey oats, wheat, timber, hops, hurdles, hoops, poles and cider went downstream to Wilton, Monmouth, Brockweir, Chepstow and Bristol.[63]

Apart from all the river activity at Hereford there would have been barges sailing past the city without loading or unloading. Some were moored while stocking up with provisions before continuing an easy downstream journey or hiring extra hauliers for a strenuous upstream haul. Barges sailing past Hereford in the early 1720s carried stone from Gloucester and an altar from Bristol destined for Tyberton church. These were 'transported by barge to Stretton Sugwas up the River Wye and hauled to Tyberton'.[64] During the 1770s a few barges made the long journey from the Forest of Dean and past Hereford to deliver coal at Hay and Glasbury, and timber was exported downstream from Glasbury and Whitney and the Canon Bridge 'timber yard' either on barges or as floaters – lengths of timber lashed together to form rafts – to Chepstow. An unexpected arrival at Hereford in 1772 was a crewless barge carrying 15 tons of bark, which had broken from her moorings at Moccas, 'but was prevented from passing under Wye Bridge by her mast'.[65]

Lime – so important to agriculture, building and tanning – was conveyed from the Vention Lime Works at Lydbrook to various places up the Wye as far as Stretton Sugwas at '£1 a barge load'.[66]

The Final Years of Hereford's River Trade

Even though the navigation on the Wye had reduced the price of coal delivered to Hereford, it was still a comparatively expensive commodity. In 1801 there was a proposal to build a tramroad to Hereford from the Forest of Dean, a plan modified in 1802, the new proposal showing a tramroad from Lydbrook to a terminus at Wye Bridge. Although this came to nothing, a proposal of 1825 to construct a tramroad from Hereford to Monmouth Cap, to link with a tramroad that connected with the Brecon and Abergavenny canal at Llanwenarth, was successful. This tramroad was completed on 21 September 1829, horse-drawn trams transporting coal from the south Wales collieries in competition with coal barges from the Forest of Dean. At its peak in the mid 1830s it was transporting rather more than the 6,000 tons of coal to Hereford that had been predicted.

The river trade began to decline, leaving Messrs Pulling & Sons dealing in spirits, cider, bark and slate in the 1840s and Thomas Lewis at Eign Wharf in 1851 competing with coal merchants trading on the Hereford and Gloucester Canal, which had reached Hereford in 1845, only a few years before the railway.[67]

Fig. 12.19 Work-a-day scene below Wye Bridge in c.1800. Before a firm quay was established below the Saracens Head there was room to beach the occasional barge for refitting.
(Watercolour by an unknown artist in a private collection)

Other Public Works

Among the public works planned by the council was a waterworks, to be attached to the Castle mill, which would raise water from the Wye for delivery by pipe to a conduit in St Peter's Square. Specialist engineers were consulted in 1696 but nothing more was heard of the plan. It would not be until the 1850s that a city-wide approach to a clean water supply was instigated.[68]

One of the particular concerns of the council was the management of the market-place in High Town. There were a variety of buildings here, some marked on Taylor's plan of 1757. One of these was the High Cross, which stood at the top of Widemarsh Street and was presumably a medieval structure. It was perhaps defaced during the Civil War, for in 1678 it was restored at a cost of £60 14s 9d out of the receipts from the markets and fairs. A more obscure building was the guard house, which was ordered to be pulled down in 1703 to make space for the apple- and pear-mongers, but reappears as the fire engine house in 1763.[69]

At the junction of High Town with Bye Street stood the Tolsey, another early building where, as its name suggests, market tolls were collected; it also acted as a guildhall and was used for public meetings. In March 1759 a decision was taken to demolish the building, but arguments over what should replace it and how the work should be funded meant that nothing had been done by May 1768 when it was reported that the existing building was beyond repair. The council was now without a permanent home, but in 1772 it expended £100 in repairing the Mansion House in Widemarsh Street, which had been given to the council by the heirs of William Brewster (d.1715). By 1775 this was being referred to as the New Tolsey and was used regularly for public meetings. Eventually, property was also acquired on the opposite side of Widemarsh Street by the council, which operated from here until the present town hall was built in 1902.[70]

Fig. 12.20 Part of Taylor's plan of 1757 with High Town at its centre. The position of the High Cross is marked by the letter A in red.

Fig. 12.21 The Market Hall in Hereford c.1860, by W.C. Hughes. There was little love for the mutilated building in the 19th century and most artists preferred to remember it as it was. Its demolition in 1861 followed upon the changes made in 1770. (© Herefordshire Museum Service, ref: 1989-24)

Adjoining the Tolsey at the centre of High Town stood the Market Hall, which functioned as a shire hall, described by a 17th-century visitor as the 'stateliest in the kingdom, built with columns after the manner of the Exchange' (in London). It was built between 1574 and 1576 in a thoroughly gothic style, without any hint of dawning classicism (Fig. 9.29).[71] Responsibility for upkeep was shared by the council and the county magistrates. A substantial restoration occurred in 1749 when £220 was expended in refenestrating with sash windows. The city council can never have met here as the first floor contained two court rooms and the second floor was divided into compartments for the trading companies of the city, which were now mostly defunct. The stability of the building was of great concern to the city since its retail market sheltered among its 27 columns. Its dire state was brought to the attention of the county magistrates at the Easter Sessions in 1770 by a prominent carpenter/builder, Francis Thomas, who frequently worked in partnership with Thomas Symonds, the mason. Francis reported that a number of the columns had given way, creating lateral tension, which was pulling the building apart. The west end was also slumping, pulling the sash windows out of alignment. As a solution he recommended that the semi-redundant upper floor should be removed and a new roof provided. A second opinion was sought from the architect Thomas Farnolls Pritchard of Shrewsbury, whose country house practice extended into north Herefordshire and who had skills as a structural engineer. He was the architect of the Iron Bridge at Coalbrookdale. Pritchard's report basically confirmed Francis

Fig. 12.22 High Town and High Street by John Varley. The medieval High Cross, which had been restored in 1678, was demolished in 1776. It stood where the trestle-tables stand. Varley excluded the Market Hall since its stuccoed façade would have diminished the picturesque qualities of his sketch. (© Herefordshire Museum Service, ref: 3727)

Thomas's diagnosis, but added the recommendation that, following restoration, the building should be 'rough casted' to weatherproof the walls.

The result was an essentially classical building with only its columns giving any hint of its antiquity (Fig. 12.21). Contemporaries no doubt felt that it was very 'neat' but within a couple of decades observers like John Price in 1796, with an eye for the picturesque, were complaining that 'elegance had been sacrificed to utility ... and beauty deformed'. Ironically, by 1837 views of High Town were being published by the local bookseller, W.H. Vale, with the old Market Hall in its full glory, based upon a sketch by the artist George Robert Lewis.[72]

By the mid-1770s the spirit of improvement was running strongly in Hereford and in August 1776 the High Cross was taken down, together with the stocks and pillory. The council were able to reorganise the market-place, finding a new site for the 'fish boards' in an attempt to resuscitate the ailing fish market. From 1813 the buildings in the centre of High Town, by then known collectively as Butchers' Row, were gradually demolished, a process not completed until 1837. By this date the country market had been reduced to a few informal stands and was eventually accommodated within the Butter Market, designs for which were drawn-up by the architect Henry Hake Seward in 1811-12. As a result of this building High Town had finally been tamed and was now essentially an Italianate piazza, all very convenient for the promenade.[73]

Fig. 12.23 Castle Cliffe, the quay and the cathedral from the Wye, from a painting by F. Jukes (1797). Castle Green is looking rather unkempt but provides a suitable setting for some unlikely ladies and a party of boisterous steers who have escaped from the Bartonsham Meadows. A new pavilion had been erected on the south front of the Bridewell in 1788 but the building was now empty and its unhappy inmates transferred to John Nash's new gaol.

The county magistrates had other responsibilities in the city, which impacted upon public sensibilities. On Castle Green there was the old Bridewell, located in a medieval building on one side of the private promenades maintained by the Society of Tempers whose object was to promote 'the pleasures of conviviality and good fellowship'. This amiable design was inconsistent with the function of the workhouse, albeit located in an ancient building. The Society attempted to tame it by clamping a classical pavilion on its south front (Fig. 12.23) and in 1788 the magistrates also tried to make it more acceptable by asking Thomas Symonds to give it a gothic makeover, whilst extending its accommodation. This was rejected and a further attempt was made to extend the county gaol in St Peter's Square – on the site of the future Shire Hall. The vociferous prison reformers, like John Howard, found this unacceptable and in 1789 the magistrates decided to erect a purpose-built gaol on a new site in Bye Street Without, to be designed by John Nash of Carmarthen who had recently built a new county gaol at Cardigan. The old Bridewell was sold as a private house in 1800, when the new county gaol opened, and the conflict between pleasure and punishment was resolved. A new 'alcove' was built on the south side of Castle Cliffe House. As for Nash's new gaol, its temple-like façade made it a 'feature of the country where it was placed' and a walk to the gaol on execution days provided moral lessons as well as purposeful exercise.[74]

Fig. 12.24 A lithograph of c.1840 celebrating Hereford's new civic centre. The mayoral church of St Peter is now accompanied by Smirke's Greek revival Shire Hall, borrowed from a civilisation with values that were seen to underpin Georgian governance. In contrast the earlier Georgian gothic weighing machine looks like a public convenience. (© Herefordshire Museum Service)

In 1774 the Revd Dr Talbot launched an appeal for funds to build an infirmary. Subscriptions came in slowly whilst the price of the building rose from £3,000 to £6,000 in 1777. Land for its construction on the banks of the Wye downstream from Castle Green was given by the Earl of Oxford and the new building was eventually opened for patients in April 1783. The original plan was provided by Thomas Symonds but was superseded by an extended building, now designed by William Parker, which also included a lunatic asylum. The latter was attached to the south end of the Infirmary and was eventually built by John Nash in 1794. An infirmary was the apogee of charitable achievements for a Georgian town. Not only was it an expression of good taste but it was also prominently displayed, its purpose reflecting well on the moral rectitude of both the citizens and the wider community. Naturally, the public walks on Castle Green were extended past the new building and round the Bartonsham meadows.[75]

The greatest gift of the shire to the city was the new Shire Hall built between 1815 and 1817. In August 1814 a meeting of the magistrates was held, which secured an Act of Parliament in April 1815 and set up a committee of commissioners to run the contract. Already architects had been invited to provide designs for the new building. Among those who submitted plans were Thomas Hardwick and William Atkinson, both involved in projects elsewhere in the

Hereford Turnpike Roads 1726-1868

Acts of Parliament were required to establish Turnpike Trusts which then maintained a designated network of highways through tolls collected from road users. The name is derived from an early method of placing a long pike across a road to stop traffic; when the toll was paid the pike was turned, hence 'turnpike'. Under the terms of the Acts the trustees were empowered to erect gates or turnpikes, receive tolls, choose collectors, appoint surveyors, mortgage tolls, demand statute labour and elect new trustees. The roads were also to be provided with milestones as directed by the Acts.[76]

Although Ledbury had formed a Turnpike Trust in 1721, it was not until 1726 that the Gloucester Trust turnpiked two routes to Hereford, which included the 'great Road from London to South Wales'. Three years later the Hereford Trust was established to improve the main routes into the city, which 'by reason of the deep Soil thereof, the many heavy Carriages and Droves of Cattle ... are become so ruinous and bad, that many Parts thereof are impassable in the Winter Season for Wagons and other Carriages, and also dangerous to Travellers'.[77] Determined to improve the roads, the newly formed trust turnpiked 13 routes spreading like a spider's web from the city, including the administration of the two former Gloucester and Hereford Trust roads to Harewood End and Lea.[78]

The turnpikes and toll houses were situated at crossroads and junctions so as to catch a maximum amount of tolls from travellers, and by 1754 the city was surrounded by turnpike gates. The tolls in the 1850s ranged from one horse not drawing: 1½d; horse drawing with broad wheels: 2d; horse drawing stage wagons with broad wheels: 4d; horse drawing with narrow wheels: 5d; coaches: 6d; droves of cattle: 10d per score.[79]

In 1840 the Hereford Trust had responsibility for 34 main toll-gates, four side-gates and bars, and about 156 miles of road. Six of the toll gates were located at strategic positions on the outskirts of the city: St Owen's, Aylestone Hill, Widemarsh Street, Above Eign, Barton Road and St Martin's Street. In terms of length of road the Hereford Trust was second only in size to the Bristol Trust, which at that time had responsibility for 173 miles. With the arrival of the canal, the opening of the railway and a changing political climate the turnpike system became increasingly obsolete and led to the abolishment of the Hereford Turnpike Trust on 1 November 1868.[80]

Fig. 12.25 The Widemarsh Street toll gate in the early 1850s.

Fig. 12.26 The design for the Shire Hall submitted by Thomas Hardwick displaying mainstream classicism rather than the fashionable Greek revival.

county. However, the scheme was awarded to Robert Smirke, who came highly recommended by Lord Somers of Eastnor, one of the principal magistrates. Not only was Smirke in the midst of building a new castle at Eastnor but through the influence of Lord Somers he was already building a new shire hall at Gloucester, which with its four columns forming a portico was the prototype for Hereford – albeit Hereford got six columns![81]

The Act of Parliament allowed the commissioners to spend £33,000, which included the purchase of a house for the judge in High Town. In confidence Smirke sent a copy of his estimate to Lord Somers, which indicated that the main structure would cost £24,500 but the magistrates also wanted a militia building (£16,000) and a depot of arms (£3,000), which he implied was rather ambitious. Eventually, the depot was accommodated in the basement of the new building. The sum was collected via the usual county rate, levied upon both landowners and tenants. The sheriff of the county, Colonel Matthews of Belmont, who was also a local banker, played a major role in managing the contract, assisted by Benjamin Fallowes, the clerk of the peace, who was paid £1,491 for his services throughout the project. As Smirke ran a busy office he appointed Charles Heather as his clerk of works. Heather was a protégé of John Nash and had recently supervised the building of Garnstone Castle at Weobley. Heather's efficiency at the Shire Hall led to his eventual appointment as county surveyor in 1825.[82]

The work progressed smoothly between 1815 and 1816 and the opening of Smirke's 'superb edifice' at Gloucester, with its 'remarkably elegant portico' was duly recorded in the *Hereford Journal* in August 1816. Lord Somers noticed that the court room had an annoying echo but Smirke assured him that this would not occur at Hereford because of its 'square form'. The following April the *Journal* eulogised on the 'truly beautiful edifice' and describes in detail its internal arrangement – two courts, an assembly hall and miscellaneous offices. Finally, in August 1817 the first assizes were held there and a subscription was commenced for a large portrait of King George. Lord Somers opened the list, but contributions were limited to one guinea, to enable all classes to be included in the subscription. As an honour, Smirke was commissioned to design the frame and supervise the hanging.[83]

In rather gushing terms the *Hereford Journal* thought the new building was a 'splendid ornament to the city' and a symbol of 'the liberality and taste of the county'. Indeed, the 'classic simplicity' of the portico, 'its sweetness of effect and truth of proportion' was a fitting climax to the age of improvement for the city. Nothing as impressive would be built again until the arrival of the Town Hall in 1902 but even then, it could be argued that this could not 'vie with the best productions of antiquity' and was perhaps, a lesser building in design and execution; a reflection too of a more insecure age.

The Urban Renaissance

The subscription lists for the Infirmary and King George's portrait represent a roll call of the gentlefolk of the city and county. In many ways the latter had made a substantial investment in Hereford, both financially and socially and by the end of the 18th century there were many new reasons to come to Hereford, both for business and pleasure. Urban historians have recognised this sense of cultural renewal, which enveloped provincial towns in this period and rather grandly, designated it an 'urban renaissance'.[84] In Hereford it was expressed in the increasing diversity of services provided by the city. Shopping, for example, became a matter of pleasure rather than convenience and the city now boasted hairdressers, milliners (selling oriental silks and cottons), booksellers, furniture makers, nurserymen, toy-men and artists, like the portraitist Thomas Leeming and landscapist, David Cox who also ran an academy in Bye Street. The city also developed a season. In the summer this coincided with the assizes and focussed upon the races and every three years, the Music Meeting. Balls, assemblies and public breakfasts accompanied these events, making them popular as well privileged occasions. For example, the horses and their riders could be inspected by all at the inns in the city and the race course itself became increasingly a fairground. Rehearsals for the Three Choirs concerts were open to the non-subscribing public and the frequency of the performance of Handel's music, sung by celebrity soloists, was clearly a symptom of popular interest. The balls after the concerts were held in the Great Room of Woodcock's Coffee House on the corner of St John Street and East Street. Significantly, Thomas Woodcock, its proprietor, was an accomplished violinist, but one, who according to Lysons, preferred country music to Corelli.[85]

Fig. 12.27 Davies's Bookshop on the corner of High Town and Widemarsh Street: one of the several bookshops that thrived in late Georgian Hereford. Notice that you could get some printing done here and secure fire insurance. Hereford had become a city of commercial diversity.

Fig. 12.28 Woodcock's Coffee House, now used as a hat shop and solicitors, on the corner of Packers Lane and Mill Lane (East Street and St John Street). There are still elements of a mid-Georgian building here with the premises of the Hereford Permanent Library just visible on the right. (Photograph by David Whitehead)

Music remained a staple feature of cultural life during the winter with subscription concerts held in College Hall. In addition there were theatrical entertainments by 'Mr. Kemble's company of comedians'. Initially these performances took place at the city inns or Woodcock's Coffee House but in 1786 the company took up residence at a purpose-built theatre in Broad Street. The *Journal* regarded it 'as handsome a building of its kind as can be seen anywhere'. It was designed and built by William Parker and boasted a pediment adorned with busts intended to represent Shakespeare and Hereford-born William Powell and David Garrick. Parker recouped his outlay via benefit performances on 'Builder's Nights'. The theatre accommodated 5-600 people, with all classes gathering together in the body of the auditorium until galleries were built in 1798. There was much audience participation – some unwelcomed by the management – with intervals of music and dancing, together with visiting spectacles like Dr Katterfeltro's flying cats, powered by electro-magnets.[86] It was initially managed by John Bowles Watson, but when he was declared bankrupt in 1796, the new owner ran the building as a combined hop exchange and theatre.

Conclusion

Such was the vitality of urban life in Hereford in the Georgian era. Slowly but surely the convivial atmosphere of the Georgian city changed in the early 19th century. The Napoleonic Wars and their aftermath, which included threats to the social order in the 1820s, eroded the earlier harmony. The jolly evenings at Woodcock's Coffee House, the social melange of the pit at the theatre and the lively company that could be found at the races, where gentlemen rubbed shoulders with artisans and labourers, was being replaced by a more stratified and more serious society. The new middle classes were drawing away into a private life of good manners, hard work, temperance and evangelicalism and made it their vocation to tame the boisterous, gregarious and liberty-loving spirit that characterised late Georgian society. Artisans and labourers were thus separated from polite society and needed 'reforming' whilst the gentry and aristocracy, who had tolerated harmless high spirits among their inferiors, also turned to more serious matters to sustain their position in society or ended in profligacy and debt. James Wathen (1751-1828), the clothier and artist, noticed the changes in Hereford just before his death. He blamed the 'novel doctrines' of a local clergyman who caused discord among his friends, severing intimacies and dissolving natural ties. Victorian Hereford became a different place where social harmony was much more difficult to find across a wide spectrum of local society and the 'Age of Cant' (to quote an unruly poet, Lord Byron) had dawned. Ironically, this world had been left behind in the 1650s, during the Interregnum mentioned in chapter 10. Hypocrisy and double standards replaced individuality and originality, resulting in life becoming a lot less fun in Victorian Hereford.[87]

13   Victorian Hereford

In 1836 John Wood, a well-known cartographer from Edinburgh, published a map of Hereford city (Fig. 13.1). Comparison with Taylor's map, published in 1757, shows that comparatively little expansion had taken place in the interim. Essentially Hereford was mainly confined with the line of the city walls – by Wood's time the gates and much of the walls had been demolished – with some development along the roads radiating from Hereford. There had been an increase in population: Taylor recorded on his map that the population within the walls was 3,816, and outside the walls but within the Liberty of the city, was 1,776, a total of 5,592. In 1801 the population of the city was recorded as 6,828; in 1811, 7,306; in 1821, 9,090; in 1831, 10,282 and in 1841, 10,921. Hence there was a steady increase, which faltered in the 1830s. Some of the increase in population was catered for by infilling. The few houses on the east side of St Martin's Street, for instance, had been replaced by Norfolk Terrace, with Prospect Terrace round the corner.[1] There were the beginnings of development in what is now Bath Street but had previously been a walk on the outside of the city ditch, and Richmond Place in Moorfields had been built. But the increase in population was mostly accommodated by more people being crowded into the slums that already existed, some of which remained until the 20th century. Industrial development was in its infancy, with the iron foundry in Friar Street (begun in 1834) being marked on the map, and the gas manufactory at Monkmoor in evidence (more or less on the site of what is now Morrison's supermarket). This was incorporated by an Act passed on 28 May 1824 and the streets of the city were first lit by gas-lamps on 3 October 1825. As well as the General Infirmary, built in 1781-3, in the same vicinity was the lunatic asylum, built by subscription in the 1790s and opened in 1798. Initially this had six cells – a name suggestive of how the inmates were treated – but by the time it closed in 1853, there were 20 patients who were transferred to an asylum in Abergavenny.[2]

Despite the infilling, the overall extent of the built-up part of the city was much as it had been nearly 80 years before. By the end of Victoria's reign, the city's population had doubled, reaching 21,382 in 1901, and there was a consequent expansion of the city outside the line of the old city walls, considered in detail below.

Also during this period there were substantial changes in how the city was administered. The Municipal Corporations Act of 1835 did away with the old, self-perpetuating Common Council of the city, and replaced it with three wards (Ledbury, Leominster, and Monmouth), with six elected councillors for each ward. There were also six aldermen, with a mayor as the leading citizen. However there was a conflict between the new town council and the 57

Fig. 13.1 John Wood's Survey of 1836. (© Herefordshire Library Service)

unelected commissioners appointed under the 1774 Paving Act.³ Although under the new law of 1835 the commissioners could have handed over their powers to the new town council, they declined to do so, and the inevitable conflict meant that no substantial improvements were made to the city until the Hereford Improvement Act of 1854 extinguished the powers of the commissioners. To supervise its work, on 15 February 1859 the new town council initially set up six standing committees – for Waterworks; Markets; Police and Gas; Paving and Streets; Gaol and Fire; Watch, Finance and Sanitation. (Down the years the numbers of committees proliferated, reflecting the increasing responsibilities placed on the council.) Under the Act of 1854, Hereford was greatly improved, proper sanitation installed, and by the end of the century the city was a much more salubrious place to live.

The Canal

The first proposal to link Hereford to the canal network came in 1777, with the aim of linking Stourport-on-Severn with Leominster, Hereford and Gloucester, a distance of about 70 miles. However, only part of the ambitious project was ever built, linking Leominster with the Pensax colliery. A more realistic proposition was the construction of a canal between Hereford and Gloucester, for which an Act was passed in 1791, superseded by a revised Act in 1793. The costs proved much more than estimated and the canal, started at the Gloucester end, only reached to

Fig. 13.2 An engraving of the middle arm of the canal basin, a few years after it opened in 1845. To the left is a bark rick, and unprocessed timber is evident, as are the horses which hauled the barges.

the outskirts of Ledbury by the time the money ran out, a section which opened on 29 March 1798. The project effectively became dormant until 1827, when the inexperienced but talented Stephen Ballard was appointed as engineer. In 1829 he made a detailed report on completing the canal but work did not commence for a further ten years. The slow progress continued and it was only in 1844 that an aqueduct over the Lugg Meadows was completed, and in the following year that the last section, including a quarter-mile tunnel under the north-west side of Aylestone Hill was built. Water was admitted through the tunnel on 21 May 1845, allowing canal boats to reach the canal basin in Hereford the following day, marking the completion of one of the last of the major canals to be constructed in Britain.[4] In 1845 Price and Co. of Gloucester established warehouses at Withington and Hereford, from which they supplied guano, timber, slates and salt amongst other goods. Three years later these were taken over by Edward George, their former manager, and he continued to sell timber and slates. Subsequently this became the well-known firm of George and Tudor.

The canal was completed in an age when railway fever had begun, and it was inevitable that its success would be affected by any scheme to add Hereford to the developing railway network. To some extent this was anticipated, and the canal was engineered in such a way that it would be possible to use the route as the basis of a railway, making a takeover by a railway company a possibility.

Fig. 13.3 Map of 1858 showing the canal and its basin, the arrival of the first railways (highlighted in yellow) and the position of the toll gates (marked in red).

The Railways

Hereford was the last cathedral city to be joined to the expanding rail network, but once it gained its first connection, other routes rapidly followed.[5]

Various schemes to connect Hereford to the railway network were suggested from 1836 onwards, but the first two Acts allowing construction of the necessary railways both received royal assent on 2 August 1846. These were for the Shrewsbury and Hereford Railway, and the Newport, Abergavenny and Hereford Railway. The former, in general following the line of the old coach road, was opened for freight to a temporary station at Barrs Court on 30 July 1852, and to all traffic on 6 December 1853. The latter, in part built on the line of the old tramroad,

Fig. 13.4 The approach road to Barrs Court Station in the 1920s. Although the station has been restored in recent years, the canopy over the entrance has now disappeared.

was completed soon after, and the first train from Newport arrived at the also temporary Barton Station – where Sainsbury's now stands – also on 6 December 1853, and the line was opened to traffic on 2 January 1854.[6] The temporary Barton Station was replaced in 1856 by a building designed by John Clayton, a local architect. The termini of the two railways were initially separate, but were joined in January 1854 by about a mile of track, known as the Worcester mile, built by the Worcester and Hereford Railway in collaboration with the Newport, Abergavenny and Hereford Railway, and so enabled a direct north-south route.

Hereford also came within the orbit of the Great Western Railway. A broad-gauge line from Gloucester to Ross and Hereford was promoted by Brunel at a meeting in the Shirehall in 1850, and the Hereford, Ross and Gloucester Railway opened to passengers in 1855, using the newly built station at Barrs Court, so that the station served both standard and broad gauge railways.

The Worcester and Hereford Railway, which joined the Shrewsbury and Hereford Railway at Shelwick Junction, arrived in Hereford in 1861, at which time it was part of the West Midland Railway. It was also served by Barrs Court Station, and in 1862 was subsumed by the Great Western Railway, as was the Hereford, Ross and Gloucester Railway. Finally, there was the Hereford, Hay and Brecon Railway, which was built under an Act of 1859. The section to Eardisley was opened in June 1863, using a very basic station at Moorfields, and the line to Hay was opened a year later, at which time the terminus was moved to Barton Station. The terminus was moved back to the Moorfields Station in 1869 where it remained until 1874, when, after complicated negotiations, the terminus was relocated to Barton Station once more.

In the early 1860s there was a proposal for a loop of track across the south of Hereford, which would complete the encirclement of Hereford by the railways. Subsequently an amended route was promoted by the Great Western Railway and London and North Western Railway, begun in spring 1865 and opened in August 1866. The section between Redhill, where it joined the Abergavenny line, and Rotherwas Junction, where it joined the Gloucester line, was built with two tracks of standard gauge, while from Rotherwas Junction to Barrs Court Station there was a double-track mixed-gauge line. Not that the broad gauge lasted long; the line from Rotherwas to Grange Court, well on the way to Gloucester, was converted to standard gauge in less than a week in August 1869.

There were pressures to make Barrs Court the principal station, and in February 1883 the Great Western Railway and the London and North Western Railway announced plans to make this so. Subsequently the Midland Railway negotiated to join in this scheme, which was completed in 1893, and Barton Station was then demolished, but leaving its substantial engine sheds. As part of the reorganisation, the Widemarsh Loop, cutting off a corner between the Hay line and the Worcester mile, and the Brecon curve, to facilitate access to Barrs Court from the Worcester Mile, were built and opened in January 1893. This left the system in the form it was to take for the next 70 years.

The Turnpike Trust

Inevitably the arrival of the railways affected the Turnpike Trust (see p.216). One consequence was that in the 1850s the turnpike gate at Above Eign – now Whitecross Road – was moved further away from the city, so that Barton Station lay within the ring of turnpike gates. Also the turnpike gate on Widemarsh Street was moved further out, close to the Heart of Oak Inn, although in that case it was because what is now Edgar Street had been built, and offered a way out of the city which bypassed the ring of turnpike gates. But these were but final flourishes as the tide was turning against the use of turnpikes. In 1866 the Act was renewed for a year, and then again in 1867 for another year, but it expired on 1 November 1868 when the roads became toll-free. Within a couple of years most of the six turnpike houses on the outskirts of Hereford were demolished, and the only physical remaining signs are a house in Barton Road, called Turnpike House – not, however, the site of the turnpike gate – and the house at the turnpike gate on Whitecross Road, still named the Toll House and sited just west of the junction with White Horse Street.

The End of the Canal

The canal had a brief period of prosperity when it carried materials for the construction of the railways, but thereafter it suffered a slow period of decline as goods such as coal that would formerly have been carried on the canal were sent by rail instead. In 1861, the canal company opened negotiations with the Great Western Railway (GWR) and the West Midland Railway companies, which were promoting a railway from Ledbury to Gloucester, on the basis that part of the canal would be used for the bed of the railway. An agreement with both companies was made in January 1862 and the GWR took over the canal in October 1870, closing the Ledbury to Over section to traffic in June 1881, when work began on converting it from canal to rail. The section between Hereford and Ledbury was cut off and gradually decayed away.[7]

The Victorian Suburbs

The increase of population in the middle of the 19th century led to overcrowding in the slum areas of the centre of the city, notably Bewell Street, and there was a need for additional housing. In the 19th century the emphasis was on self-help, and attempts were made to improve opportunities for those described as the 'industrious poor'. This line was adopted by the Hereford Freehold Land Society – officially called the 'Hereford City and County Benefit Building Society' – part of a movement which began from political motives. Even after the 1832 Reform Act, the electoral franchise was very limited, but included those who owned property worth 40s p.a. or who lived in property worth £10 p.a. Thus, in 1847, the Freehold Land Society movement was started with the aim of enabling working men to obtain land worth 40s p.a. and thus become able to vote. Although this movement was inspired in the Liberal interest, in Hereford it was supported by influential citizens of all political persuasions. The Hereford Society was set up at a meeting on 9 April 1850, the object being that working men should subscribe fortnightly towards shares in the society, and that the society would buy suitable land at effectively wholesale prices, divide it up into suitable plots worth at least 40s p.a. and pass on

Hereford Freehold Land Society developments
Fig. 13.5 (above) Portfield Street
Fig. 13.6 (top right) Clive Street
Fig. 13.7 (right) Park Street

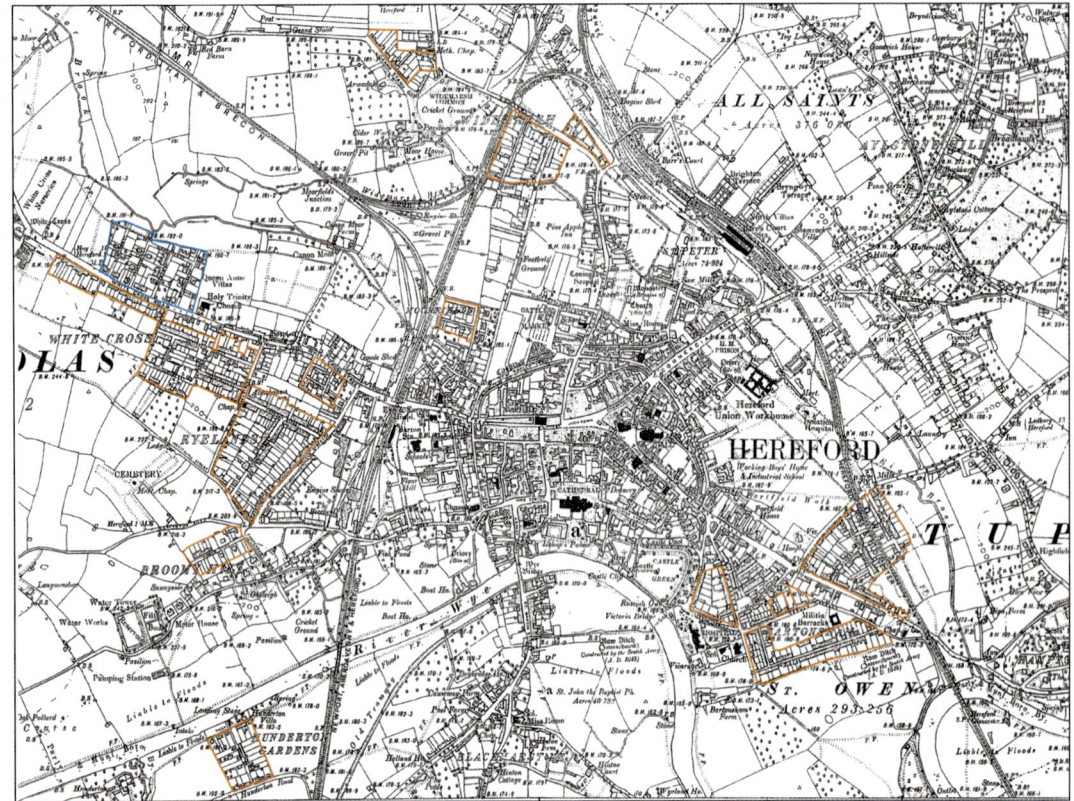

Fig. 13.8 Map of Hereford in 1905, showing the location of the various 19th-century Freehold Land Society developments, those by the Hereford Freehold Land Society outlined in orange, and that by the Conservative Land Society in blue. Not shown is the Hereford Freehold Land Society development at Westfields, comprising Highmore, Westfields and Lyde Streets. This was well away from the centre of population and consequently was only slowly developed.
The fully developed system of railways which surrounded Hereford can be seen on this map, with the exception of the Hereford Curve, which completed the ring of steel and was opened to passenger traffic in August 1866; it lies further to the south.

these allotments at cost to subscribing members.[8] If those members had not subscribed enough, the society would hold a mortgage on the land. The allotments could either be used for gardens or as building plots, and since they were of generous proportions, many allotments had more than one house built upon them.

During the course of the next 50 years, the society bought and allotted estates in most parts of Hereford, including Newtown (1851 and two in 1856), Hunderton (1851), Above Eign (1853), Moorfields Place (1857), Bartonsham (1859/6), Westfields (1862), Whitecross (1862), Lower Portfields (1867), St Giles's (1868), Tower Road, Barton (1867/8), Castle Green 1878), Ryelands Street (1882), and Cornewall Street (1886/7). In each case the estate was only gradually built on by the allottees, the rate depending on the popularity of the particular estate, and while this was going on the estates must have presented a very haphazard appearance. Although most of this housing would normally be described as artisan, some members of the Freehold

Fig. 13.9 (above) Hereford Freehold Land Society development in Cornewall Street
Fig. 13.10 (top right) Conservative Land Society development in Baggallay Street
Fig. 13.11 (right) Conservative Land Society development in Ingestre Street

Land Society subscribed for more than one share and built larger houses, which explains the mix of houses in such as Park Street. The success of the society was emphasised at the annual general meeting which took place on 25 May 1887, when it was stated that to date the various estates developed by the society had provided 880 allotments, each sufficiently large enough for the erection of two houses of moderate size, and that about 8,000 people or two-fifths of the population of Hereford lived in houses erected on the allotments. Although only a relatively small amount of development was subsequently carried out by the society, the impact on Hereford over a period of just over a third of a century was immense. With the developing interest of local government in housing for the poorer members of society, the Freehold Land Society declined after its Cornewall Street development, and only embarked on further projects after the end of the Victorian era.

Nationally there was a Conservative Land Society, whose objects were much the same, but the allotments on whose developments were on a different scale, designed for more affluent citizens. Its only involvement in Hereford was that of its own Moorfields Estate off Whitecross Road, bought late in 1865 and allotted in 1866, although as there were not enough subscribers in Hereford not all the plots were accounted for. Of the five streets of this estate, Ranelagh, Meyrick, Ingestre and Gruneisen were named after influential members of the society, (of whom only Col. Meyrick, from Goodrich Court, was local) while Baggallay Street was named after the local MP.⁹

At the time that the Freehold Land Society began developing the Castle Green estate, development had already begun along St James Road, on the opposite side of Green Street. This road had been constructed a few years previously to provide better access to the Infirmary from Eign Road, at the expense of Dr Lingen, who had made the initial suggestion. At the time that the survey was carried out for the Ordnance Survey (OS) in 1885 a number of plots along this road had already been built upon with larger houses than those on the Freehold Land Society developments, also round the corner into Harold Street, which backs onto St James Road. On the north-west side St James Road backed onto the St Owen's Nursery, occupied by William Grove, who also had a nursery at Tupsley where he lived. This nursery was ripe for development and two roads were laid out, Grenfell Road – named after another local MP – and Grove Road. The earliest date-stones on the houses are from the 1890s. The development was somewhat piecemeal, although the south-east side of Grove Road is occupied by Llanbleddian Terrace, dated 1897, clearly all built at the same time, and hence by a developer.

The most prosperous of Hereford's citizens would not have wished to live on any sort of estate, and during the 19th century large houses were built on the higher ground surrounding Hereford. Broomy Hill was developed from c.1840, the large house Belvedere on the south side being built for William Moore Gibbs, a prosperous local draper. The main development

Fig. 13.12 Victorian housing in Grove Road

Fig. 13.13 An example of a Victorian villa built for the most prosperous of Hereford's Victorian residents in Bodenham Road.

of the upper part of Broomy Hill came after 1863, when the area on the north side of the road was sold in lots, there being then only one house in this section.[10] This may have been stimulated by the development of the Hampton Park estate, from 1862, built on land belonging to the Litley Court estate. Building plots on the estate were advertised in the *Hereford Times* from 29 March 1862, and the first stone on the estate was laid on 9 September 1862.[11] As part of the development the Hampton Park brickworks was set up to supply bricks for the estate.

Aylestone Hill is one of the city's prime residential areas, and Wood's survey (Fig. 13.1) shows a few houses on the south-east side of the slope. There were also a few houses as the road drops away from Hereford. To the west of the turnpike gate at the top of the hill was what was then called Holmer Road (now Venn's Lane) with a few houses, and to the east (now Folly Lane) there was only a house called, not too surprisingly, The Folly. By the time that the area was surveyed in 1885 for the six inch OS map, further development had taken place on, and just off, Aylestone Hill, including such large houses as Overbury Lodge (by 1841), Broadlands (1869), Athelstan Hall (by 1860) and Danesmere.[12]

During the Victorian period, development took place on both sides of Aylestone Hill. The survey by the engineer Timothy Curley (see p.234) shows a short road on the south-east side, which was subsequently cut through as Southbank Road, from which Bodenham Road was cut through in 1885. Elm Road had also been developed by this time. Then, in 1885, Hafod Road, effectively a continuation of Bodenham Road, was laid out, apparently on the line of an earlier roadway, and by 1902 the development was mostly complete.

There was little development on the opposite side of Aylestone Hill. Barrs Court Road was in existence, and the west end was joined to Newtown Road by a bridge over the railway and canal. The first houses in Barrs Court Road were the two pairs of houses called North Villas, which were built in the later 1850s.[13] At about this time, or probably a little later, the long Bryngwyn Terrace was built at right-angles to Barrs Court Road and set back from it, a development that survived well into the 20th century.

Church and Chapel building

With the increase of population, the existing churches – St Nicholas, All Saints and St Peter's, (the parish of St John, recently amalgamated with other parishes, was served by the cathedral) – were inadequate, and an effort was made to make greater provision for the established Church. The mediaeval church of St Nicholas, standing at the top of Bridge Street where it was an obstruction to traffic, was replaced by the existing building by the ring road, built in 1842 to the design of Thomas Duckham; its chancel was enlarged in 1910. South of the river there was no church, that of St Martin's having been destroyed in the Civil War. A new St Martin's was built on a new site, and consecrated in 1845. Another church that had been destroyed was St Owen's, just outside St Owen's Gate, and to provide for this expanding part of the city the new church of St James, Bartonsham, was built in 1868-9 to the design of Thomas Nicholson. Expansion was also taking place in Tupsley, and the church of St Paul's was built in 1864-5. Hereford was expanding in the opposite direction too and a new church of Holy Trinity, Whitecross Road, was built in 1884. In the original designs, by local architect F.R. Kempson, there was provision for a splendid tower and spire, but this has never been built.

Urgent repairs were needed to Hereford Cathedral early in Victoria's reign. In 1841 it was discovered that the central tower was unstable and likely to collapse, and the tower had to

be supported on a massive framework while the four piers were rebuilt under the supervision of Dean Merewether and his architect Lewis Nockalls Cottingham. Other work to the nave and some restoration of the exterior of the Lady Chapel was also carried out, but work ground to a halt in the early 1850s due to lack of money. Restoration began again in 1858, under the architect George Gilbert Scott, and included further underpinning of the nave and choir aisles. The mediaeval stone screen or pulpitum on the west side of the crossing was removed in 1841, leaving an open space, and it was now decided to replace this at the east side by an ornate structure of iron, copper, brass, tinted glass and polished stones. Designed by Scott, it was made in Coventry by the metalworking firm of Francis Skidmore, and was in place by June 1863 when a

Fig. 13.14 A postcard of the early 1900s showing the Skidmore screen in place in Hereford Cathedral with Fig. 13.15 (top) showing a detail from the restored screen now in the Victoria & Albert Museum.

service marked the reopening of the restored cathedral. The screen remained at the cathedral for just over a hundred years but was then condemned as 'out of place and out of date'. It was dismantled in 1967 amidst great local and national outcry and sold to the Herbert Museum, back in Coventry. It was presented to the Victoria and Albert Museum in 1983.

The Roman Catholic church of St Francis Xavier with its Grecian front with two giant Doric columns was built in Broad Street in 1837-39 after restrictions on Roman Catholics were removed (see chapter 11).

In Berrington Street there was the chapel of the Countess of Huntingdon's Connexion, built in 1789-90, and flourishing at the beginning of Victoria's reign. In 1887 the congregation moved to an iron structure at the Crozens in Eign Road, their former premises becoming Messrs Heins showroom for pianos and parlour organs: its later history as a cinema and theatre is covered in chapter 14.

Earlier in foundation was the Congregational chapel at Eignbook (now the United Reformed Church), a congregation founded in the 17th century. This chapel was rebuilt in 1829, and then again in 1872-3, using internal cast-iron columns. Of a slightly later date was the Baptist chapel in Commercial Road, described in 1851 as a 'small neat building.' In 1880-1 it was rebuilt in an Italianate style. In front was an old house where the Eye and Ear Institution (see p.237) was established in 1882, but which was soon demolished to leave the chapel in full view from the main road.

St John's Methodist church, St Owen Street, was built in 1879-80 to replace a Primitive Methodist chapel just outside St Owen's Gate. The latter building was erected in 1838 and is still in existence, latterly having had a chequered existence, seemingly as a workshop, then converted to Hereford's first cinema in 1917, and currently a launderette. A further Primitive Methodist chapel was built in Clifford Street, Whitecross, the foundation stone for which was laid in September 1867 and while the building still remains, it was converted to living accommodation after a new chapel was built in Chandos Street in 1902-03.

A Wesleyan chapel was opened in Bridge Street in 1829, and rebuilt 1867-68, while that in Holmer Road, built in 1878-89, is now a Christadelphian Hall.

The origins of the Barton Hall, the meeting house of the Plymouth Brethren in Barton Road, lay in a theological dispute with Revd John Venn, as a result of which a number of members seceded from his congregation at St Peter's in late 1837 or early 1838. Initially they met in Bridge Street, and in 1840 they purchased a piece of land in Barton Road to be used as a cemetery. A subscription to pay for a Meeting Hall was begun in 1856 and the hall was opened for worship in 1858.

Finally, in 1822 the Quaker congregation moved from their former Meeting House in Quakers' Lane (now Friar Street), to more central premises, accessed via a passageway from the north side of King Street. A former flannel manufactory, the building was converted into a Meeting House in 1821-22.

Public Health

At the beginning of the Victorian period Hereford had no proper sewerage system, and although there were paid scavengers who tried to keep the streets clean, the disposal of human waste was a matter for each householder. The most usual way was for cesspits to be dug in the gardens behind each house/shop, into which the effluent from the privy drained. Since

Hereford is situated on a gravel terrace above the River Wye, the liquid matter would slowly drain away, although the cesspit would eventually fill, and another be dug, to continue the process. Thus the city would have been malodorous, to say the least. There was also another health risk, since most properties relied on wells, dug down into the gravel beds, as their source of water, and the effluent from any cesspit in the vicinity would tend to contaminate the water. All this, and the quantity of the poorer residents who were packed into the slums (or stews), made it remarkable that major epidemics did not take place. In this instance Hereford's remote location was an advantage, and cholera, which was spread by contaminated water, never reached the city.

Although a Public Health Act had been passed in 1842 it was not until 1853 that an enquiry was set up, under Thomas Rammell, to ascertain what needed to be done to provide safe drinking water, establish a decent sewage system and provide for burials as the city churchyards were becoming full. As a result of his report, in November 1853 the town council commissioned the engineer Timothy Curley to survey the city, and to draw up plans and estimates for a cemetery, water works, and a system of drainage. A new cattle market was also to be part of the plan. Prior to the middle of the century, cattle markets were held in the city streets, with consequent fouling of the roadways. Discussions to resolve this had been ongoing since 1844 and a permanent site even proposed in Aubrey Street, but rejected by the town council on various practical grounds. One of Curley's recommendations was for a market site on what is now the Old Market, a site which cost about £2,500 to buy. The provision of clean water supply was the key part of the improvement scheme, and Curley proposed to build this on top of Broomy Hill, to give a suitable pressure of water. There would be a reservoir and filter beds, to which water would be pumped from an intake from the River Wye. Curley's proposals and estimates formed the basis of the 1854 Hereford Improvement Act.[14]

It was decided to obtain tenders for a single contractor to carry out all the work, except for the cemetery, the closing date for which was 3 April 1855. The lowest tender, for £22,000, submitted by Mr William Moxon from Dover, was accepted. The contract was due to be completed by 1 October 1856 – a tight schedule: it is not therefore surprising that it was reported that his plant was already on the way from Dover in anticipation of the contract being awarded.

The waterworks were completed by the summer of 1856, and were opened on 8 July,

Fig. 13.16 One of Hereford's Victorian landmarks – the tower of the Broomy Hill waterworks.

the opening being celebrated with a regatta on the river. For a while there were problems with leakage from the reservoir at Broomy Hill, which meant that for a time the citizens had unfiltered water. The drainage system was completed within the contractual time, but the cattle market was completed marginally late, on 17 October, due to what was described in the *Hereford Journal* of 10 September as 'very bad ballasting'.

The drainage system saw sewage effluent still draining into the Wye and in 1867 the system was extended to drain the expanding Broomy Hill and Whitecross districts. Subsequently it was necessary to take measures to implement the 1874 Rivers Pollution Act and some 81 acres of land at Tupsley were bought to be used as a sewage farm. Too late it was realised that there were practical problems with this site and instead John Parker, appointed city surveyor in 1881, proposed that a sewage treatment plant be installed at Eign, near Park Street. Despite some opposition the plant was opened in May 1890. In 1897 a refuse destructor was erected at the sewage outfall works, designed for burning some 5,000 tons of material each year.

As the city expanded, the water supply needed improvement to maintain supply, with new pumps installed in 1862 and 1881. In 1886 a new water tower was built, designed by local architect G.C. Haddon, and is still a dominant feature on the Hereford skyline (Fig. 13.16). In 1895 a new high pressure pump was installed, still a feature of the Hereford Waterworks Museum.

When the Cattle Market was built, both Blackfriars Street and Edgar Street, the latter previously a pathway leading from Moorfields to Widemarsh Mill were constructed. In 1885 increased accommodation was created for livestock at the market, a sign of the market's success. In 1888 and 1897 further expansion took place.

The Municipal Cemetery

The proper disposal of the dead had been a problem for many years, since, up to 1791, burials could only take place in the Cathedral Close. Subsequently parochial burial grounds were established, but these were inadequate. Rammell's report included recommendations for increased provision. In October 1856, the bishop offered to give eight acres of land, off Breinton Road, for a cemetery on condition that it belonged to the several parishes of the city. This offer was not considered satisfactory as it would exclude the burial of non-Anglicans, and it was decided by the town council to offer £1,200 to buy the land outright. Problems ensued, and no progress was made until 1858, when Bishop Hampden gave one acre for a burial ground for All Saints parish, followed by similar gifts to the parishes of St Nicholas, St Peter's, St Owen's, and St John's in 1859. A United Parishes Burial Board was formed, which supervised the laying out of the cemetery including a chapel that could hold 40 people, a two-bedroomed lodge, walls and roads, from money raised by a parish rate. The new burial ground was consecrated on 28 May 1863.

Hospitals and the Dispensary

Hereford was fortunate in that it had at least some provision for the sick, the General Hospital having been opened in 1783 on a site donated by the Earl of Oxford, overlooking the Wye. At the beginning of Queen Victoria's reign the hospital had just been expanded by the building of two wings, opened in 1834, funded by a bequest of £10,000, made in 1831 by John Morris. The surroundings of the hospital were improved as a consequence of the 1854 Act: the Castle

Fig. 13.17 A postcard of Hereford Infirmary or General Hospital c.1910 exudes the pride felt by the city in the facility.

Mill was closed, the city ditch was culverted, and the mill-pond filled in. In 1863 part of the site of the mill was sold to the hospital authorities and an entrance lodge built. A critical report in 1866 led to improvements in ventilation, lighting and drainage.

Accommodation for female patients was extended in 1882 by the erection of a two-storey building which had a ward for 28 female patients on the upper floor. Partly funded by a donation of £1,000 from Francis Hawkins, chairman of the Board of Management, the building was named after him. At this period there was no separate children's accommodation, and early in 1887 the Board of Management agreed that this was necessary. A public appeal was launched, and a new wing was built as a memorial for the Queen's Jubilee, to which the Hutchinson family contributed £1,050 of the total cost, the block being opened in 1888. As well as a children's ward, there was accommodation for the nursing staff on the upper floor. After the Victoria ward for children was opened, the number of beds available for in-patients increased from 89 to 107. Between 1892 and 1899 about £5,000 was spent on repairs, improvements and extensions.

At the end of the century about 650 patients were admitted annually, and more than 2,500 out-patients received free advice and medicine. All this was provided through annual subscriptions to the hospital, and by donations and fundraising activity

The work of the hospital was supported by that of the Dispensary. Established at a meeting held in May 1835, subscriptions were such that it was opened on 8 September, and the report of its opening in the *Hereford Journal* explained that its object was 'to administer medical advice and assistance, together with needful medicines, to the poor of this city and vicinity, and visit such as reside within one mile of the Town-hall, who are unable to attend'. In its first year 178 patients were treated, a number which had increased to 4,389 in the year 1900-01. Initially held in the house of the medical officers, the Dispensary moved to a building in Commercial Street, where it was held for many years. Capital having been accumulated, mainly from legacies, it was decided to build its own premises, and a site was found in Union Street.

Initially supported by a few private subscribers, the Herefordshire and South Wales Eye and Ear Institution was established in July 1882 in premises in Commercial Road under the honorary surgeon, Mr F.W. Lindsay. The call for its services was so great, however, that it was decided that it should become a charitable institution, and it re-opened as such on 1 January 1884. The premises soon became inadequate and in 1887 funds were raised to build a new hospital in Eign Road, which opened on 20 August 1889. Many of the fittings were the result of donations; for example the encaustic floor tiles were the gift of the Messrs Godwin and Hewitt of the Victoria Tile Works. The queen's permission was sought, and given, for it to be named the Victoria Eye and Ear Hospital. (It became the Victoria Eye Hospital in 1923.)

On 16 December 1891 the hospital was incorporated under the Companies Act, and was governed by a board of management, at that time chaired by Colonel Scobie, a strong supporter of the hospital from the beginning. In 1898 the Common Room was enlarged, and a new ward built over it, the cost being met by an anonymous donation. There was then accommodation for 20 in-patients, and at this time there were about 1,350 out- and in-patients per year. As with the General Hospital, the work was largely funded by annual subscriptions and donations.

In the latter part of the 19th century, the local Health Authority had a duty to take measures to prevent the spread of infectious disease, which occurred rapidly under crowded conditions. For Hereford, the Sanitary Committee temporarily relied on tents off Gorsty Lane, Tupsley, quickly replaced by a 12-bed prefabricated building, erected on the site and opened on 10 May 1893 as an isolation hospital. This hospital was doubled in size in March 1898, and further staff accommodation was provided as well as a porter's lodge.

There was also provision made for isolation accommodation at the General Hospital, where such a block was opened in 1897. This had two wards, each with three beds. Within a short time the ceilings fell down due to defective materials, although no injuries were caused. Because of pressure on accommodation the wards were subsequently closed, one factor in the decision no doubt being that there were facilities for isolation available not far away in Tupsley.

Business

Hereford is surrounded by a ring of market towns, the distance of each being about a day's travel in former times. Those market towns served their immediate locality for the necessities of life, as a centre for farmers to do business and to sell their produce. Hereford was a larger centre, with a greater variety of shops, which could supply more sophisticated demands.

A snapshot of Hereford at the beginning of the Victorian age can be found in Robson's trade directory of 1840. If a new pair of boots were required, there was a choice of 32 boot or shoe makers, who would probably use leather produced locally and prepared by one of four tanners. Clothes could be provided by 16 tailors and drapers, and would vary from better quality clothes to rough working apparel. There were also 17 linen and woollen drapers, who could supply materials for making clothing at home. There was even enough trade to support seven hatters. Food would mostly have been produced locally, with 20 butchers, 23 bakers,

21 grocers and tea dealers, and 6 fruiterers. If you were well enough off, there were four confectioners.

As well as these businesses, there were also the trades which supported life in the city, amongst them 7 ironmongers, 8 builders, 4 bricklayers, 8 carpenters, and 9 saddlers and harness makers. There were a surprising number of professional people: 31 solicitors, 6 auctioneers, 14 surgeons (probably some of whom were of the barber variety), and 2 physicians. To support the latter there were 11 chemists and druggists, although many of the poorer inhabitants would not be able to access these, or indeed the patent medicines which would have been retailed by some of the 8 booksellers and stationers, a surprising but not uncommon combination.

Within the list there is a hint of things to come, for there is one ironfounder included, William Radford, who had started his foundry in Friar Street (listed incorrectly as Friars Lane and previously known as Quakers' Lane). This foundry had a chequered history, and closed a few years later, but other foundries took over.

The picture then is one of relative self-sufficiency, with most necessities being available locally, but some were goods such as cloth and coal being imported.

Although not mentioned in the 1840 directory, there were regular markets held on Wednesday and Saturday each week. In the 1820s there were six fairs, the one starting on 19 May being described as 'a pleasure fair and toys', but livestock was also sold on the first day, and butter, poultry and other produce was sold during its duration at the south end of Broad Street. This pleasure fair, known as St Ethelbert's Fair, was held under the authority of the bishop and was of nine days' duration. Because of the disturbance it caused, mainly in Broad Street, it was reduced to three days by an Act of 1838. By the middle of the century the number of fairs had been increased to eight, but now the only one that now survives is the May fair.

With a regular influx of people into the city for business and pleasure there was a need for places of refreshment and accommodation. In 1840 there were three hotels listed – the City Arms, Green Dragon, and Mitre – all in Broad Street; 43 taverns and public houses; and 12 beer retailers. The most prestigious hotel was the City Arms, so well known that it was often just known as the 'Hotel', followed by the Mitre, almost opposite the Green Dragon. The City Arms had a very large assembly room, which hosted many of the important gatherings in Hereford, but in the 1860s the symmetrical front was spoiled by the north wing being sold off and demolished to build premises for a bank. The Mitre became known for its elaborate cast-iron porch, still a feature of Broad Street, and the Green Dragon was gradually developed and expanded during the course of the 19th century, and is now the only survivor of the three.

By 1851 there were some 68 hotels, inns and taverns, and 19 beer retailers, all this for a population of 12,108. In 1890 there were listed 9 hotels and 98 inns and taverns, the latter including beer houses, for a population of 20,267 in 1891, a slight increase of population to licensed establishment!

Hereford also produced its own iconic retail businesses. In 1832 Messrs Barrett and Smerdon bought an existing draper's business. In 1856 they bought out a competitor in High Town and closed it down. Smerdon died in 1860 and Robert Barrett soon took George Greenland as a partner; he became the sole owner after Barrett died in 1874. Greenland expanded the business during the 1890s and by the time he died in 1901 there were three separate premises in use: 31 & 34 High Town, and the adjoining 1 High Street. The expansion gathered pace in the 20th century under George Greenland's five sons, and resulted in a good part of the south

Fig. 13.18 The Butter Market depicted soon after it opened in October 1860. Damaged by a fire in 1924, it was repaired and reopened in October 1925. The cast-iron columns have now been removed and the roof obscured by a suspended ceiling.

side of High Town being incorporated into the business. For Herefordians of a certain age, a Christmas visit to the grotto at Greenlands is an abiding memory. Alas, all this came to an end in 1968 when the shop closed, and most of the premises on the south side of High Town were demolished, replaced by the building which now houses the Hereford branch of Marks and Spencer.

Another iconic business was that of Augustus Edwards, again the successor of earlier businesses. In 1835 a linen and woollen draper's business was set up in High Town by Pember and Davies, in a premises formerly used by an ironmonger. The partnership was dissolved in 1845 and the following year John Pember set up on his own account, in different premises. He retired in 1866 and his business was taken over by Messrs White and Edwards, and after a few years Augustus C. Edwards was the sole proprietor, making his name not only in drapery but also as a furrier, advertising as 'The Furrier of the West' (Fig. 9.23). The business prospered into the 20th century, under various members of the family, and the firm celebrated its 90th anniversary in 1956. However, it closed without prior notice in 1964. The furrier's business was transferred to part of the newly-built Franklin Barnes House, but the wearing of furs was becoming unfashionable and it too closed after a few years.

For older residents of Hereford the business of Harding Bros., ironmongers, in Commercial Street, was always noteworthy. Having served an apprenticeship with the ironmonger Charles Bennett, in 1856 Richard Morris Harding became a partner in his business in High Town, which lasted a little over a year. He set up on his own in Commercial Square in 1859, moving a few years later to premises in Commercial Street, which backed onto Union Street. He prospered, and in 1876 took over the Hodges iron foundry round the corner in Bath Street. New premises were built in Commercial Street in 1884. Taking his two sons into the business, he retired in 1890, and at the end of the 19th century the business was in a flourishing state, and was expanded as the new century progressed. It was formed into a limited company in 1914, whereafter the involvement of members of the family reduced. In 1964 the firm was amalgamated with a Worcester firm, but closed the following year, the only surviving part of the business being a shop in Union Street, dealing in white goods, which lingered on for a number of years.

Of the main 19th-century retail businesses there are two notable survivors. That of Philip Morris was established in 1845, the proprietor being William Pudge, who set up as furnishing and general ironmonger, brazier and cutler in premises in Widemarsh Street opposite to the entrance to the produce market. From the start the shop was run by Philip Morris, who, in 1848, bought the business from William Pudge and ran it under his own name. In 1902 the business had expanded, and there was a branch at 4 High Street, where gunsmith's work was carried out and cartridges retailed, as well as fishing tackle and bicycles.

The other survivor is the Pritchard family business, opened at 1 Bye Street – now Commercial Street – by William Pritchard in 1836 as a tailor, hatter and hosier. This soon gained an excellent reputation and expanded into premises next door. In 1890 W. Pritchard and Sons advertised that they were hatters, hosiers, glovers, and gentlemen's outfitters, and that they supplied ladies' jackets and riding habits, indicating that they were supplying the top end of the market.

Provision for the Poor
In the 19th century, the poor were not well provided for, particularly the aged poor. Whilst there were a number of almshouses, founded in earlier centuries, the number of places in these

Fig. 13.19 Hereford Workhouse, now part of the County Hospital

were limited – just over 80 for the 11 institutions listed in Lascelles' directory of 1851. These rarely catered for the poorest people, and often had restrictive conditions, so, for instance, the Coningsby Hospital in Widemarsh Street offered accommodation for 11 poor soldiers, sailors, and serving men.

For the majority of the destitute, young and old, the only possibility was the workhouse. Relief of the poor was radically reorganised by the 1834 Poor Law Amendment Act, under which unions of parishes were formed, and a workhouse was built to serve each union. The Hereford Union was established in 1836 to serve a union of some 47 parishes in and around Hereford and its workhouse, with capacity for 300 inmates, was opened in January 1838, when the residents of the parish workhouses of All Saints and St John's were transferred. Supervised by a married couple, who acted as master and matron, the staff included a superintendent of industrial labour who oversaw the inmates' work at picking oakum and stone breaking – hard, repetitive, manual labour. The workhouse system was designed so that the poor would have seen it as a last resort. Men and women were separated, families were broken up, and the regime could be harsh and intolerant, as depicted in Dickens' *Oliver Twist*.

Despite this, the demands on the workhouse were high. The building, initially constructed for 300 paupers, had 319 residents in 1881. At about this period infirmary blocks, one for each sex, were built to the north of the workhouse, and also a chapel erected, although there had been a chaplain appointed to serve the workhouse from the start.

The relief of the poor was the objective of other charitable institutions, and those listed in the 1851 directory include the Infirmary and Dispensary, the Benevolent Society for relieving the Sick Poor, and the Lying-in Charity. On the Victorian principle of self-help, there was the Society for supplying Poor Women with Needlework, and the Society for Aiding the Industrious, of which John Venn was a prime mover.

The Revd John Venn came to Hereford in 1833 as the vicar of St Peter's church, and was active in a number of initiatives which were of benefit to his parishioners and to the city in general. In 1838 he was influential in setting up the Herefordshire Friendly Society, of which the principles and rules were explained at a meeting on 2 August 1838, when it was stated the 'every industrious working man ought to join it as speedily as possible'. After a slow start the Society flourished, and for a number of years in the middle of the century there was even a branch in Leominster. In 1841 Venn helped establish the Society for Aiding the Industrious. This let allotments of land on which to grow vegetables, provided soup in severe weather (from a kitchen behind the Society's premises in Commercial Street), lent small sums at low interest, let out items of

Fig. 13.20 John Venn

Fig. 13.21 The mill building in Bath Street built by The Society for Aiding the Industrious. In more recent years this has been the offices for the Hereford Times, *a business centre and a base for various commercial enterprises.*

comfort to invalids for a small payment, and received and distributed charitable donations. One of the tribulations of the poor was the cost of coal, particularly during the winter, when prices rose sharply. One early scheme promoted by the society was the buying of a stock of coal at summer prices and then selling it at a discount on previous winter prices. Although the scheme was run at a slight loss, it was considered worthwhile, particularly during the long winter of 1846.

The society also developed more grandiose projects. After the repeal of the Corn Laws, a proposal was made by John Venn that the Society could help by providing a corn mill at which the poor could have their corn ground at cost. This was accepted, land was bought in Sally Walk (later, for a short time, Mill Street, now Bath Street) and work began in 1847, the mill being open for business in June 1848. Within ten years the debts incurred to build the mill had been paid off, and by 1876 it was producing an annual profit of £1,000.

This was followed, in 1851, by a proposal for washing baths, to improve the hygiene of the poor, to be built to the rear of the corn mill, convenient because the excess steam from the corn mill could be used to heat the water and the building itself. These baths were opened to the public on 12 April 1852. Most of the land to the rear of the corn mill and baths was bought by the Society in the 1860s (and a further 8 acres was added in 1872). Much of this land was used as allotments, but in 1870 John Venn proposed that part be used to add a swimming bath to the complex behind the corn mill, and that ten cottages should be built. Both of these proposals were accepted, and the swimming pool was opened in November 1871. (It was closed in 1930 when the council opened a new swimming baths in Edgar Street and is now part of the Masonic Lodge.) A road was built alongside, called Venn Road, subsequently Kyrle Street, and the ten cottages were completed in 1872. There was also a stores building, and experimental gardens, which had mixed success. There was even less success with a model farm that was established at this time, and by 1877 the enterprise was wound up, and the ground returned to allotments.

Other changes at this time include the sale of some of the Portfields, further along Bath Street, on which was built the Working Boys' Home, opened in 1877. In 1885 new offices and a new soup kitchen for the Society were built on the opposite side of Bath Street to the corn mill, and the old premises in Commercial Street sold. In the same year the old Society was dissolved, and another incorporated under the same name, taking over the functions of its predecessor, but putting the affairs on a more businesslike footing, and in a better position to meet the challenges of the next century.[15]

The end of Victoria's reign

At the end of the Victorian age the state of Hereford was a marked contrast with its condition at its beginning. It had expanded much, although in a somewhat piecemeal manner, and had the infrastructure to cope with this much expanded city. Aspects such as the workhouse would not meet with modern approval, but nonetheless there was better provision for the poor, and there was the opportunity to gain at least an elementary education, as a number of schools were founded during the course of the Victorian period, and all were gradually expanded as time progressed. Thus the Blue Coat School, established in 1710, which had 180 pupils in 1851, had 371 at the end of the century.

Fig. 13.22 Parts of Hereford are prone to flooding. Although the great flood of February 1795 has never been equalled, there were other notable floods in February 1852 and January 1899, as well as many of a lesser nature. On rare occasions the Wye froze over in the winter to an extent that skating could take place. The photograph shows activity on the ice during a freeze that set in on Christmas Eve in 1892 and lasted to 25 January 1893.

New educational foundations include the St Peter's School, of which the foundation stone was laid in 1837, and which opened 1839; Scudamore School, Friar Street (1852); Holmer School, founded 1857 and rebuilt in 1874; St Martin's School (1859); Tupsley (1867); St John's School, Church Street (1868); All Saints' Schools (1870); and St James's School (1896).

There was also a Roman Catholic School, established in 1835, which was held in varying locations within the city. In 1875 the Sisters of Charity settled in a property in Berrington Street, where the school was developed, and which, by 1890 had 210 pupils.

In addition to these there were a number of fee-paying schools, including the Cathedral School. In the 1830s this was in low water, with only about 30 pupils, but by the end of the century this had risen to 110, with much improved facilities. Also offering a public school education for boys at moderate cost was the Hereford County College, built 1877-81, although the original design was not fully implemented. In 1890 the fees were £40 p.a. for boarders, £10 p.a. for day boys. Not so pretentious was Clyde House School at 2 Moorfields, Edgar Street, a boarding and day school for the sons of farmers and the commercial classes, the object being a good commercial education. For girls, there was the Hereford Ladies College, founded in Widemarsh Street in 1860, which was dissolved in the 1890s, perhaps due to competition from the Hereford High School for Girls. The latter was established in 1885 at premises in St Owen Street, with the bishop of Hereford as chairman of the council, and the religious education was naturally directed towards the Church of England. In addition there were a number of smaller private schools for both boys and girls.

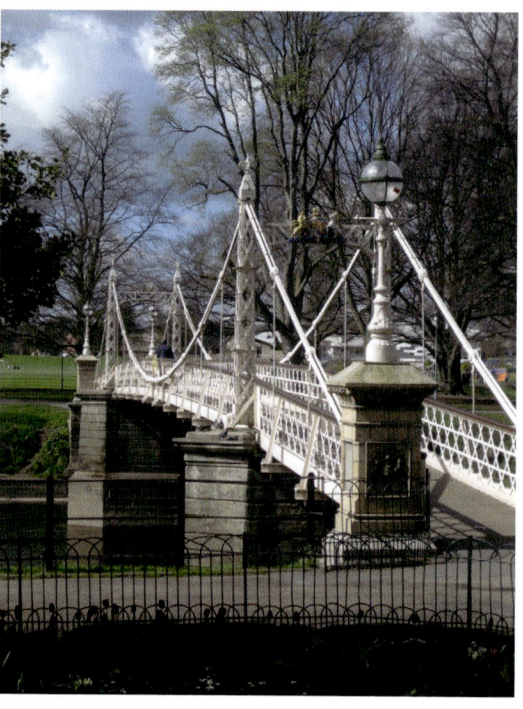

Fig. 13.23 The Victoria Suspension Bridge, built by public subscription to celebrate Queen Victoria's Diamond Jubilee, and formally opened in September 1898.

14 Literature and the Arts

Although well away from major centres of population, nevertheless Hereford had – and has – an intellectual life with its own individual character, some aspects of which are discussed in the following pages. Artists and photographers have left their individual legacies in works that survive in local archives and museum collections. The legacy of the great institutions such as the Public Library in Broad Street is more difficult to quantify, but nevertheless is important, and should be appreciated and enhanced even in these financially difficult times. One remarkable survival is the Woolhope Naturalists' Field Club which has flourished since 1851. It encompasses all aspects of the study of Herefordshire, and its annual *Transactions* contain a wealth of information on the city and county of Hereford. There were, of course, a number of institutions which were important in their day, and these too are discussed in the pages below.

Hereford Permanent Library

The first permanent library in Hereford, as distinct from a circulating library, was the aptly named Hereford Permanent Library, established in 1815 with 190 books and 123 subscribers, who held shares in the library. Its initial premises were in Widemarsh Street, then it was moved to St John Street. By 1838 the library had expanded to contain some 3,400 books and there was a proposal that it should merge with the newly formed Philosophical Society. Although a meeting of shareholders was in favour, a vocal minority were against and the proposed merger was abandoned.[1] The number of books continued to grow, reaching over 7,000 by December 1876, when Henry Graves Bull, MD was librarian. In 1900 it was decided that the library was no longer viable and accordingly it was wound up and the stock was gifted to the Hereford Free Library (see below).

Hereford Literary and Philosophical Society

At the end of the 18th century and the beginning of the 19th, there was a strong 'Literary and Philosophical' movement, with various bodies being established across the country, and an emphasis on natural philosophy and the study of scientific subjects. That for Hereford was set up at a meeting in the City Arms Hotel in December 1836. Activities began on 2 January 1837 with a *soirée*, during which a lecture was given, at the society's rooms in Widemarsh Street, in a house owned by Mr Bullock, the secretary, which about 100 people attended. A second *soirée* followed on 23 January and a third, this time in the Great Room at the City Arms Hotel, on 17 February.

The society was forward-looking in that ladies could be subscribing members, and after the first year, were admitted without a ballot. A pattern of meetings was soon established, with a series of *soirées* during the winter months, and a break during the summer. The basic pattern of sedentary meetings continued until 1848 when Dean Merewether, an active antiquarian and a very active member of the society, proposed excursions to places of interest during the summer months, an idea based on the meetings of the Cambrian Archaeological Society. The first of these, to the Golden Valley, took place on 22 June 1849 in carriages hired for the occasion. It was a success, and a second excursion was organised for the following month, when 28 members of the society went by carriage to Wigmore, and dined in Leominster on the way home. Excursions continued to be held most years during the 1850s. In 1854 the society used the newly opened railway to travel to Abergavenny, continuing their journey by carriage to view Raglan Castle, and dining in Abergavenny on their return. The latest excursion of which a record has been traced, was in July 1860 when the participants travelled to Shrewsbury by train, then to Wroxeter by hired conveyances, returning to Shrewsbury to dine and view the museum and abbey church. It is assumed that the excursions than lapsed.

It had always been the intention for the society to have its own museum and library, and whilst initially the room in Widemarsh Street was adequate, as the society developed, it was no longer large enough to house its growing collections. Following the rejection of the proposed merger with the Permanent Library in 1838, in June 1839 the museum and reading room of the Philosophical Society were moved to premises in Harley Place (now Harley Court). *Soirées* continued to be held in the City Arms Hotel until 1845 when they were transferred to a new Assembly Room at the Green Dragon. Two years later the Philosophical Society moved to

Fig. 14.1 An early 20th-century postcard of the buildings at the south-west corner of Castle Green. In 1824 a committee of citizens took over the maintenance of Castle Green, and the cottage with the pedimented alcove was built to the designs of Robert Smirke in 1824-6, to house a constable to look after the open space, replacing an earlier summer house built by the Society of Tempers. Adjoining this, on the south side, premises were built for the Castle Green Reading-Room and Baths Society, the baths opening in 1829. After the amalgamation with the Philosophical Society in 1858, the building over the reading room and baths was raised another storey to house the museum, and the pediment on the left was added.

premises on the corner of High Street and Broad Street, then the north wing of the City Arms Hotel. This move seems to have caused financial problems, for the initial rent of £53pa was reduced to £50, and the assistant librarian, who actually ran the library, had his salary reduced from £25pa to £20.

In 1852 there was another proposal to amalgamate the Philosophical Society with the Permanent Library, together, this time, with the Mechanics' Institute (see below), a proposal which also came to nothing. There followed a plan to raise money for the society to build its own premises, a prospectus for which was launched in the *Hereford Journal* on 21 December 1853. This proposal seems to have been unsuccessful, for in 1856 negotiations took place about the possibility of sharing premises with the Woolhope Naturalists' Field Club, which had been formed in 1851 (and for which see below). In the event, the proposed cost was too much for the Woolhope Club and the matter was shelved. The matter of premises was finally solved two years later by the amalgamation of the Philosophical Society with the Castle Green Reading-Room and Baths Society. The Castle Green premises of the latter, in the south-west corner of the Green (Fig. 14.1), were heightened so that the Philosophical Society's museum could be housed over the reading room and baths. The new premises nevertheless proved inconvenient for lectures, so the *soirées* continued, first back at the City Arms and then in College Hall. In 1862 discussions about merging the new combined society with the Woolhope Club again took place, but the idea was shelved by the latter.

From then on it was a slow decline for the Philosophical Society. Further abortive discussions on a merger were held, this time with the Permanent Library, which again came to nothing. The last known *soirée* took place on 15 February 1870, a day before a meeting was held to discuss whether to wind up the society. The result of this meeting was not reported, but subsequently the premises were shut up and the subscriptions went uncollected so that the interest on the mortgage on the premises was not paid. Consequently the mortgagee foreclosed and early in 1875 the secretary, W.J. Humphrys, came to an agreement that the premises and contents would be sold to the town council for a sum that would cover the debts of the society.

St Peter's Literary Institution
Clearly such institutions as those above were not designed for the working man, and there was little encouragement to betterment until the formation of the St Peter's Association (later the St Peter's Literary Institute), another pioneering effort by Revd John Venn. Its object was stated to be to improve former pupils of the Sunday School, by establishing a library and reading room. In a report in the *Hereford Journal* on 14 December 1836 it was stated that 150 people had already signified their intention to belong, and went on to say that it 'must prove highly beneficial in affording the means of acquiring religious and scientific knowledge to the humble classes of the city…'. The library, housed in a room over St Peter's Vestry, and with a stock of about 400 volumes, opened on 2 January 1837.

The activities gradually expanded to include lectures of an educational nature. By June 1851 it had outgrown its premises and moved to a house in Bye Street, now Commercial Road. In addition to the library (open from 7am to 10pm), the new premises had a newsroom where both London and provincial newspapers and magazines could be read (open from 6am to 7pm), a museum and a coffee room. Membership then stood at about 340, in addition to 30 life and honorary members.

The institute continued to flourish, with John Venn as president, until 1874, when the Hereford Free Library was opened. The institute library was then transferred to the Free Library (see below) and the Commercial Road premises no longer used.

Hereford Mechanics' Institute

The first Mechanics' Institute in Britain was founded in 1821, the object being to give an opportunity for the artisan class to better itself. A letter advocating the setting up of such an institution for Hereford appeared in the *Hereford Journal* on 14 August 1839. Others followed, and a meeting of supporters of the idea was called by the Mayor, Nicholas Pateshall, for 13 January 1840. However, there was some opposition from Revd John Venn, who thought that the new institute would adversely affect the St Peter's Reading Association, which then had 250 subscribers. In the ensuing discussion a claim that the St Peter's Reading Association was denominational was made, but refuted. In the event, a resolution to form a mechanics' institute was passed. A list of subscribers appeared in the *Hereford Journal* on 22 January 1840, a list which included the names of most of the notable citizens of Hereford. One firm supporter was Dean Merewether, and it was probably through his good offices that the institution obtained premises in the Cathedral Close, which were opened on 2 March 1840: at that time there were said to be about 126 ordinary members. The premises were large enough to hold a library and a reading room. The first year of the institute was celebrated with a *soirée musicale* in the Great Room at the City Arms, which was addressed by Mr Doffnore, a celebrated (and eccentric) promoter of such institutions.

The first president was Dean Merewether, who resigned after a dispute in 1843 at a time when the institute was in financial difficulties. It was fortunate that Sir Samuel Rush Meyrick accepted an invitation to become president and the business of the institute continued, with a series of lectures each year. However, the institute's future remained precarious: there was a crisis meeting to discuss the financial position in February 1848; Sir Samuel Meyrick died shortly after but the bishop of Hereford became president; while another financial crisis occurred in 1852, resolved by a successful appeal for donations which discharged current debts. In March that year the institute managed to move to new premises in East Street, but financial problems soon resurfaced. In February 1856 the Dean and Chapter offered the institute premises at the south end of Church Street rent-free if its problems could be overcome, which they must have been as the institute subsequently moved there. There is little sign of any activity by the institute thereafter, until the *Hereford Times* on 20 February 1858 carried a small advert for the sale by auction of the institute's library of books and household furniture. Thus the institute ended, although there was one final twist. Although it seems that the institute was insolvent, a letter in the *Hereford Times* on 12 June 1858 reported a rumour that there was money left over, but that it had been dissipated at an event on Dinedor four days earlier.

Whatever the truth of the rumour – and it seems likely to have been untrue – the St Peter's Literary Institute outlasted the Mechanics' Institute by many years.

The Woolhope Club, Hereford Free Library and Museums

The institutions discussed above were essentially sedentary, with information disseminated by lecture or the printed word. In the middle of the 19th century there was a spirit of enquiry which led to the formation of societies the purpose of which was to actively investigate the local environment. In the winter of 1851 one such was formed in Hereford, entitled the Woolhope Naturalists' Field Club, still its formal title, although now usually referred to as the Woolhope Club.[2] The name was chosen because of the Woolhope Dome, a Silurian geological feature, and the object of the club was the practical study of the natural history of Herefordshire and the districts immediately adjoining. As it was a field club, the rules stated that it should hold three field meetings each year, the first of which, naturally enough to the Woolhope area, took place on 18 May 1852. Although the main object of study of the club was natural history, from the beginning sites of archaeological and architectural interest were also visited, but it was not until 1893 that this fact was officially recognised by amending the rules to add the study of archaeology to that of natural history.

To bring the knowledge gained by the club to a wider audience, in 1856 a volume of transactions was published for the first time. Five further parts were issued, spasmodically, until 1865, after which annual volumes of transactions were – and still are – published.

The greatest publishing achievement of the club in the 19th century was *The Herefordshire Pomona*, commissioned in 1874 and published in seven parts between 1878 and 1885. It was illustrated by many remarkable chromolithographic plates, taken from drawings made by Alice Ellis and Edith Bull. The latter was the daughter of Dr Bull, the general editor of the work and a great name in the Woolhope Club, while the technical editor was Dr Robert Hogg.

Fig. 14.2 Designed by the local architect, F.R. Kempson, the library and museum building has been described as 'Anglicised Venetian Gothic' and features an intricate coloured stone façade of animal, foliage and zodiac carvings.

As a consequence of the investigations carried out by members, the club gradually amassed a collection of specimens, the storage of which was problematic. It has been shown above that there were two flirtations between the club and the Philosophical Society; these were in part about finding space for a combined museum. The problem of accommodation was finally solved by Mr (later Sir) James Rankin, who was president of the Woolhope Club in 1869. He offered to put up £4,000 for a library and museum, the library to be free and the museum to contain systematically arranged exhibits, with a view to providing popular instruction. A meeting in early 1871 supported this proposal, and in July the Public Libraries Act was adopted, by which rate support was given. The next month James Rankin bought the site in Broad Street and the new Free Library was opened with a reception on 8 October

1874. Part of the provision in the library building was for a room where the Woolhope Club could keep its library and hold its indoor meetings, and after the completion and occupation of the building the club settled into its new premises, called, naturally enough, the Woolhope Room, where it has remained ever since. Although the Woolhope Room has remained largely unaltered, except for extending the glazed cabinets, the Club has moved on. Initially membership was limited to gentlemen only, but happily ladies were admitted to full membership in 1954. The Club continues to flourish.

While the Woolhope Room has altered but little, the library building itself has been extended and altered. Thanks to a bequest from Sir Joseph Pulley and a gift from his nephew Charles Pulley, extensions at the back of the building enabled a new lending library, reference library and art gallery to be opened in 1912. By the late 1950s space was at a premium and a mezzanine floor was added above the old lending library in 1963 and another in the reference library in 1974.

When the library building was opened in 1874, the museum was augmented by artefacts transferred from the defunct Philosophical Society museum, and by collections given by members of the Woolhope Club. With additions over the years, and with extra pressure on space due to the closure of the Churchill Gardens Museum in 2002, a new Museum Resource and Learning Centre was developed in Friar Street, in a building purchased by Herefordshire Council in 2000. This was opened in 2008, to provide proper storage and access to the museum's collection.

A museum of a different kind is to be found in High Town. When Lloyds Bank moved to its new site next to the Butter Market in 1928, it presented its former premises, The Old House, to the city. The building was turned into a museum and furnished on three floors in the Jacobean style.

Yet another variety of museum is the Waterworks Museum, which was opened to the public in April 1975, following the installation of a new pumping station by Welsh Water in 1974, thus making the old pumping station redundant. The old steam engines and Lancashire boiler were recommissioned and in steam by the end of September 1975. Since then, the museum has expanded with the arrival of additional pumping engines, some installed in a new building. The Museum has achieved its aim of telling 'the story of drinking water supplies and distribution in Wales and the Marches from pre-industrial revolution to the present day'.

The building that houses The St John Medieval Museum at Coningsby Hospital, Widemarsh Street dates from the 13th century and includes the chapel and hall of the Knights Hospitaller of St John of Jerusalem. The chapel has some Jacobean heraldic glass and furniture and contains a museum showing fine armour, blazons, documents, medals and models connected with the Order of St John during the 300 years of the Crusades. Upstairs the infirmary has a window into the chapel from which the sick could follow the services and has been arranged with life size models in period dress showing how the sick pensioners of the hospital were cared for.

Finally, mention should be made of the former Churchill Gardens Museum. This was developed after the purchase in 1966 of a house on a prominent position on Aylestone Hill – previously known as Penn Grove – and housed, among other things, an extensive collection of costume, as well as a gallery of the works of the local artist Brian Hatton. Despite some protests it closed in 2002, and its contents were subsequently housed in the resource centre in Friar Street.

Theatre and Cinema

By the beginning of Victoria's reign, the theatre in Hereford was in decline, and the building, on a site to the north of the present library in Broad Street, which had been opened in 1786, was clearly in a poor state. In 1836, after the theatre had been reroofed and repainted, it was leased to Messrs Rogers and Turnbull, who managed a chain of theatres elsewhere. However, it is clear that this was for a limited period, and generally the management changed every year. Adverts in the Hereford papers show that the theatre was not used very much, and the usual offerings were perhaps a melodrama and a farce on the same evening. Other entertainment included a ventriloquist show put on in January 1840 by Mr Dyott, who had just taken over as manager. At that time advertisements described the refurbished theatre: 'Good Fires constantly kept. Thoroughly cleaned throughout, and entirely Re-decorated.' The inference is that it needed it!

In March 1843 it was advertised that Mr Wade Clinton was the new manager of what was then called the 'Theatre Royal', and this name was used occasionally until the theatre was closed. Then, in September 1845 it was announced that the theatre would open for a season under the management of Messrs Poole and Charles. For this a new backdrop had been painted by Mr Gill, the interior had been renovated, and the box seats had been recovered. In 1847 the theatre opened for a short season under the management of Mr James Rogers, and he continued as manager until 1850. After that things went quiet, the theatre not being mentioned in the press until 6 July 1853, when an advert in the *Hereford Journal* stated that the theatre was reopening for a season under the management of Miss Faulkland. On 6 August 1853, in an advert for the theatre that appeared in the *Hereford Times* stated: 'A Police Officer always in attendance to keep the strictest order'. The following year the theatre was managed by a Mr Dale, but by the time of the summer season the following year the managers were Messrs Robson and Pattinson. It was stated that the theatre had been newly decorated and that there was a new backdrop and scenery. In September 1855 the theatre opened for a short season under the management of Edward Miles, who, on 12 August 1855 advertised in *The Era*, a theatrical newspaper, for professional ladies and gentlemen for the Hereford and Torquay theatres. He, too, didn't last long, as in November the theatre opened under the management of Mr W. Peters, with a three-day performance by the English Opera Company.

A couple of other managers followed, until a proposal to build a Corn Exchange on the site came to fruition. Until his death in Leicester on 18 December 1839 the theatre had been owned by John Boles Watson, who also owned the theatres at Gloucester and Warwick. Subsequently the Hereford theatre came into the possession of William Bosley, who sold it to a board of trustees. The final performance at the theatre took place on 20 March 1857, the comedy *London Assurance* and a farce, *An Object of Interest*. The theatre was then demolished, and foundation stone of the new Toll-Free Corn Exchange was laid by Lady Emily Foley on 4 May 1857. Building went on apace, and it was opened to the public on 6 January 1858. As part of the provision in the new building there was a large lecture room, which Littlebury's directory of 1867 states was used for 'concerts, lectures, entertainments, &c'.

Despite the provision of a lecture room at the Corn Exchange, it was evidently felt that there was still a need for a theatre, and what was advertised as the New Theatre opened in the large room attached to the Cattle Market Tavern on 21 August 1858, under the management of Messrs Donald and Neele, for the Three Choirs Festival week. A report in the *Hereford Times* a week later indicated that it could seat about 300 or 400. Then, in October 1858, the New

Fig. 14.3 Broad Street painted by Kenneth Rowntree in the 1930s. The Kemble Theatre is shown on the left. (© Herefordshire Museum Service, ref: 8693/1)

Theatre was under the management of a Mr Atkinson, replaced early next year by Mr George Bolton. Thereafter it opened spasmodically, usually for race nights and a steeplechase in March. Although in 1867 Littlebury's directory stated that 'theatrical performances now take place in a large concert-room situate at the New Cattle Market', it seems that this theatre lapsed at about this time, perhaps not being able to compete with the lecture room at the Corn Exchange or the Alhambra music hall. The latter was situated behind the Royal Oak in Bridge Street and opened in September 1867. This, despite its cheap seats, did not flourish, became a lecture hall, capable of seating about 700, and finally closed in 1892, the building surviving as a storage depot until demolition in 1936.

In 1908 the trustees of the Corn Exchange acquired some property to its rear and developed the overall space into a theatre, whilst retaining the activity of a corn exchange (Fig. 14.3). It opened in 1911 as the Kemble Theatre and survived until 1963 when it was demolished and replaced by Kemble House.

Towards the end of the 19th century two further halls were built in which plays and other entertainments were held. The first was St George's Hall, at the west end of Bewell Street. Built c.1880, the proposed grand design was never fully implemented. Plays and other entertainments were held here, but it may well have been unsuccessful, since early in the 20th century it was turned into a skating rink, to satisfy what was a craze at the time. The second was the Forester's Hall at 29 Widemarsh Street, which, in 1882, was used for a theatrical entertainment. In 1890 it was leased to Arthur Henderson, who used his skills as a former scene painter to completely remodel the interior so that it became a proper theatre, designed to seat 650. First renamed The Athenæum, then The Theatre Royal, it became known by some as the 'Blood Tub' due to the many gruesome murders staged there. In 1905 it was renamed the Garrick Theatre after David Garrick, who was born at the Angel Inn, 22 Widemarsh Street, and baptised at All Saints church in 1717, and who brought about the revival of interest in Shakespeare. In 1916 it became known for a real-life horror, when eight small girls were burnt to death whilst performing in a charity concert for the troops. The theatre was rebuilt and subsequently had a variety of uses, including as a cinema, wartime ARP headquarters and latterly as the County Library. It closed in 1974 and eventually the building disappeared, along with its immediate neighbours, to clear the way for the Garrick House council offices (also since demolished to make way for the new shopping development) and multi-storey car park.

Cinema also came to Hereford at what had been a Countess of Huntingdon's Chapel, built for the evangelist George Whitfield. The chapel's rules railed against 'a vain conformity to the world in card-playing, dancing, frequenting playhouses and places of carnal amusement', but nevertheless it was converted into a cinema in 1912, then into a theatre in 1939 with a capacity of 600 seats, was renamed The County Theatre in 1947 as which it survived for a further ten years before showing films, then was used for roller-skating and as a restaurant cabaret. It became the Regal Cinema in the 1960s and by 2000 was a bingo and concert hall.

The earliest true cinema in Hereford opened soon after the First World War at 74 St Owen Street. From 1919 until 1923 it was called The Kinema, then became The Pavilion in 1924 but closed in 1926, never to show a 'talking movie' (Fig 14.4).

The Odeon, the city's second cinema, was designed in the art deco style and was built on the site of the former Judges' Lodging at 5 Commercial Street. It opened in 1937 and was demolished in 1985, to be replaced by the Commercial Street portion of the Maylord Orchards redevelopment.

The Ritz cinema opened in January 1938 on the Commercial Street frontage previously occupied by the gaol. Later becoming the ABC cinema, declining audiences meant some space was used for bingo then a series of night clubs. A reversal in the fortunes of cinema in the 1990s meant that by 1998 the new Courtyard theatre was showing films. Then the cinema, renamed the Odeon in the 1980s, relocated to its new multi-screen premises at the Old Market development in 2014.

Fig. 14.4 What was once The Kinema and then the Pavilion has been a launderette for many years.

In March 1979, the old Edgar Street swimming baths reopened as the 350 seat Nell Gwynne Theatre and Arts Centre, largely run by enthusiasts. In 1984 management passed to a private company and the name changed to the New Hereford Theatre, Arts Centre and Cinema. A studio theatre was added in 1989, intended for 'workshop' and smaller productions and especially directed towards the encouragement of youth theatre. After eight years, differences in approach and style, especially in attitudes towards local amateur productions, led to the management being taken over directly by the council in the early 1990s. However the cost of upgrading facilities to meet new public entertainment licence standards, led to the building being closed shortly afterwards.

Fig. 14.5 The Courtyard Centre for the Arts

In 1995 the Arts Council offered £3 million towards a completely new centre and the Courtyard Centre for the Arts came into being (Fig. 14.5).

Artists and Photographers

The two most famous artists usually associated with Hereford are David Cox (see opposite) and Brian Hatton (see p.257). Another name connected with Hereford was that of the Gill family, consisting of Edmund Ward Gill (1794-1854) and his sons Edmund Marriner Gill (1820-1894), William Ward Gill (1823-1894) and George Reynolds Gill (1827-1904). E.W. Gill was born in Aylsham, Norfolk, and went to work in Clerkenwell as a japanner, but that trade being unhealthy, commenced practice as a portrait and animal painter. His eldest son, E.M. Gill was born there. In 1823 he decided to travel to Ludlow, and his son W.W. Gill, was borne *en route* at Bridgnorth. After about three years in Ludlow he settled for a short while in Hereford, where his son G.R. Gill was born. Gill senior specialised in portraits of animals, a specialism suited to a country area, and he exhibited portraits of ponies and dogs in an exhibition of pictures held at Ross in 1828. In the 1830s and '40s the family divided their time between Ludlow and Hereford, with the sons also spending time studying and working in London.

There is some evidence of the artistic work that was carried out in Hereford by the members of the family, which also gives an idea of the cost of their work. On 19 February 1842 the *Hereford Times* reported that E.W. Gill had painted a portrait of Tom Tug, winner of the Hereford Grand Steeple Chase. In the summer of 1850 it was advertised in the Hereford papers that E.W. Gill had nine oil paintings of dead game to dispose of by lottery, inviting 200 persons to take shares at 10s 6d each. These clearly took some time to sell, as the draw was not held until 5 March 1851. A lottery was also held in 1841, of 200 shares at 10s, for five oil paintings by E.M. Gill; the first, an original, had already been painted, the others, after various Old Masters, had yet to be completed. The original oil painting, together with watercolours of the others, could be inspected at Mr Gill's in Berrington Street. Another lottery involving three

David Cox

The most famous artist who worked in Hereford was David Cox, who moved to the city late in 1814 to take up a post as a drawing master at a school set up that year by a Miss Croucher. Initially in New Street (a short-lived name for Commercial Road), by the time David Cox arrived in Hereford the school had been moved to Widemarsh Street. Since this post was only two days a week he also obtained a post at the College School, as the Cathedral School was then called, and took a number of private pupils as well. This flexibility was just as well, because Miss Croucher became insolvent early in 1818, her furniture was sold, and the school closed.

On his arrival in Hereford, David Cox and his family lived for a few months in a primitive cottage at Lower Lyde, then in the spring of 1815 they moved to a cottage on the north side of Aylestone Hill at Baynton Wood (Fig. 14.7). In 1817 the family moved again, to a picturesque thatched cottage in what is now Venn's Lane, a cottage which is always associated with his name and which he extended by building a studio-cum-parlour, a somewhat inconvenient arrangement, partly at his own expense and partly at the expense of Mr Parry, his landlord. These moves reflect his improving fortunes, as his talent developed and matured, and was no doubt helped by various journeys he made in the locality, and further afield to places including north Wales, Devon and Bath. In 1826 he also ventured onto the Continent.

Fig. 14.6 Portrait of David Cox attributed to the artist himself. (© Herefordshire Museum Service, ref: 4327)

Such was his increased prosperity that in 1824 he built his own house, called Ash Tree House, on a prominent position on Aylestone Hill. This has previously been identified as the building that is now called Abbey Grange, in Venn's Lane, but was in fact the house now known as Danesmere, on Aylestone Hill, being renamed when it was radically remodelled in the 1880s. However, despite building his own residence, Cox was unsettled, and two years later a chance meeting with William Reynolds, a lawyer from the colony of Berbice (part of British Guiana) who was wishing to return to Hereford, resulted in William Reynolds buying David Cox's new house, which he promptly renamed Berbice Villa. David Cox's later career lay elsewhere, and early in 1827 he moved to London: the advert for the third edition of Rees's *Hereford Guide* that appeared in the *Hereford Journal* on 28 March 1827, and which informed prospective purchasers that the work was illustrated with 12 engravings on wood taken from drawings by David Cox, was almost a postscript to his time in Hereford.

Fig. 14.7 David Cox's Cottage at Baynton Wood, 1885, painted by William Ward Gill. The cottage burnt down in April 1923. (© Herefordshire Museum Service, ref: 393)

members of the family took place on 1844, when 20 paintings in oils were to be disposed of, with 120 shares of 10s each. Other work was of a more mundane nature, and which member of the family painted the scenery for the theatre is not known. One other work was a model of the round chapel at Ludlow Castle, exhibited at a reception in October 1850, the report in the *Hereford Journal* stating that it was made by 'G.W. Gill, artist, of this city.' This could either be W.W. Gill, who was known for making models, or G.R. Gill. In 1851 both of the brothers were lodging in Ludlow, and their careers thereafter lay away from Hereford.

Despite their somewhat spasmodic residence in Hereford, the family evidently made a strong impression, and an exhibition of their work was held in the Free Library in 1888, when some 187 works were exhibited. Most, if not all, of these were owned locally. The exhibition illustrated the skills of the various members of the family – E.W. Gill as a painter of animals as well as a portrait painter, E.M. Gill in studies which included waterfalls (he was known as 'Waterfall' Gill), and W.W. Gill and G.R. Gill as landscape artists, although the latter was also well-known as a portrait painter.

While the Gill family moved into Hereford, another artist of some celebrity who moved out was Charles Lucy. He was born in Hereford *c*.1814, and was a self-taught artist, first coming to notice in 1832. In that year a lithographic print was published by Mr Child, of Eign Street, and a report in the *Hereford Times* on 1 December 1832 stated that he was preparing to study at the Royal Academy. Eighteen months later the same paper reported that he was then pursuing his studies in London, and that he had been awarded a silver medal at a recent exhibition. Once Lucy had left Hereford he made only the occasional return visit – short visits in 1837 and 1842 being reported in the local papers. An attempt was made to capitalise on his local celebrity in November 1842, when paintings by Lucy were advertised to be sold by lottery, under the auspices of the Hereford Art Union, with 325 shares at one guinea each. There were eight paintings to be balloted for, ranging in value from 120 guineas for a large historical painting exhibited at the Royal Academy, down to a small composition of value 5 guineas. There was a free exhibition of the paintings at Messrs Wilson and Philip's, book sellers, High Town. Although the advert continued to appear until August 1843, there is no report of the draw taking place, and it must be assumed that Hereford was not ready for such works! It is not surprising that Lucy's career as a painter of historical subjects lay in London, where he died in May 1873 and was buried in Highgate Cemetery.

Somewhat younger than Lucy was Henry Quintin, whose career in Hereford just overlapped with that of the Gill family. Son of C.F. Quintin, who in 1836 opened a school in Hereford which taught deportment and other gentlemanly attainments, Henry was born about the year 1829. He first comes to notice in Hereford in November 1842 when he appeared in

Brian Hatton

The most noted Hereford-born artist was Brian Hatton, born in a house in Whitecross in 1887, who showed early promise as an artist. As a result of poor health in his earlier years, he spent some years living with friends in Swansea. In 1895 the family moved to Mount Craig,

Fig. 14.8 Brian Hatton (self portrait).
(© Herefordshire Museum Service, ref: 1975-7/569)

at Broomy Hill, where he created his own studio in 1908. In that same year he accompanied an expedition to Egypt, which was led by Flinders Petrie, the noted archaeologist.

From 1912 he shared a studio in London, where he worked on commissions for portraits. On 4 September 1914 he enlisted in the Worcestershire Yeomanry, and he was killed in action in Egypt on St George's Day, 1916.

In 1966 the city council bought Churchill Gardens and established a museum in which the Brian Hatton Gallery, devoted to his work, was added in 1973, the inspiration of his younger sister Marjorie. Regretfully this museum was closed in 2002 and the Brian Hatton collection was transferred, first to the city museum and subsequently to the Resource Centre in Friar Street.

Fig. 14.9 The Lugg Meadows by Brian Hatton. (© Herefordshire Museum Service, ref: 1975-7/578)

court with his brother Charles, charged under the Hereford Improvement Act after drawings were made on a stable door in Berrington Street. He evidently developed his artistic skills, and in 1851 was working as an animal painter in St Nicholas Square. Still in Hereford in 1856, he soon moved away but maintained connections. Drawings by him were used as a basis for the plates in the fifth volume of the Hereford Herd Book issued in 1862, and by 1867 he had moved back, Littlebury's directory recording that he was then working as a portrait and animal painter at 4 St Owen Street. However, he seems to have soon moved on and for good, subsequently working in Gloucester.

When photography began to be developed from the late 1830s, citizens of Hereford were kept up-to-date by reports in the press. Locally, Dr Kidley, of Byford, was experimenting with photo-sensitive paper and some of his work was exhibited at a meeting of the Philosophical Society on 24 April 1840. The first photographic studios in Hereford proved to be of a temporary nature, and the first permanent studio seems to have been that of Edmund Stowe, opened in 1855. He subsequently took Thomas Ladmore into partnership, and eventually Ladmore became full proprietor.[3] Richard Bustin, founder of a famous studio in Hereford, started this in 1858, and it eventually became the best-known studio in Hereford. In parallel with the professionals, there were 'amateurs' who experimented, and the greatest of these was Alfred Watkins, who began his work about 1876. He became extremely interested in the technical side of photography, so much so that he invented what became a very popular exposure meter.[4]

In November 1885 Alfred Watkins, together with some of his friends, founded the Herefordshire Photographic Society, with Mr (later Sir) James Rankin as first president. From

1892, with a new president (Thomas Blake, of Ross) the activities of the club expanded from indoor meetings in the winter to field meetings in the summer, which must have been a labour of love, as the heavy photographic equipment then in use would have been difficult to carry about. A higher profile was given to the society in 1898, when the first exhibition of members' work was held. Unlike the Woolhope Club, ladies could join and at the second exhibition in 1899 there was a ladies' competition. Numbers increased, and at the turn of the century the membership was about 100, so the society was in a healthy state when it went forward into the next century. Its standing was such that in 1907 the 22nd annual meeting of the Photographic Convention of the United Kingdom was held in Hereford, with Alfred Watkins as president for the day. However, difficult times followed, and with the society in debt, despite fundraising efforts, it ceased activities in 1927.

Fig. 14.10 Price's Almshouses on Whitecross Road. The three photographs on this and the following page are all by Alfred Watkins and show not only the quality of his photography but also the invaluable record his images provide of Hereford in the late 1800s and early 1900s.

In 1937, two years after the death of Alfred Watkins, the society was revived, and it prospered despite the problems encountered during the Second World Ward, so much so that a series of Alfred Watkins Memorial Lectures was begun, with an inaugural lecture being given on 23 July 1943. Since then it has had a continuous existence, and in 2009 Joy Davies celebrated 60 years of membership by being appointed lifetime president of the society.

With the historic connection of photography with Hereford, exemplified by Alfred Watkins, it was appropriate that an annual Hereford Photography Festival was established in 1991, supported by a grant from the Arts Council. This was very successful, and was of a high standard. However, funding was reduced for the 21st Festival in 2011 and then completely withdrawn, a victim of government cutbacks. As yet the festival has not been revived.

Fig. 14.11 The ivy-clad bastion next to what is now Greyfriars' Surgery, the ground and buildings on the left being under the inner ring road near the bridge over the Wye.

Fig. 14.12 Harley Court and the cathedral seen from the Town Hall.

Three Choirs Festival

One of the notable musical events that takes place in Hereford is the Three Choirs Festival, albeit only once every three years. This is one of the oldest classical church music festivals in the world. It is not certain when the meetings of the three choirs of Hereford, Gloucester and Worcester cathedrals first began, but in 1724 it is recorded that Dr Thomas Bisse, chancellor of Hereford, preached a sermon at the Gloucester meeting, promoting a charitable collection, in part for members of the three choirs. At the Gloucester festival in 1736 a setting of the *Te Deum* by Handel was performed, and subsequently his work dominated the festival's programme. In 1757, at Gloucester, Handel's *Messiah* was performed at a festival for the first time.

After 1762 concerts were generally held in the purpose-built Music Room (also the School Room), which stood in the Lady Arbour on the south side of the cathedral (see pp.75-6 & Fig. 12.15). This building was paid for by a subscription levied on the gentlemen of the county. Occasionally, different venues were used and in August 1776 the orchestra and a large audience took to the river and were rowed up to the meadows below Old Hill (late renamed Belmont), where tents were pitched, music and dancing performed and a 'cold repast' provided. In 1798 it seemed unlikely that the Hereford festival would take place, until the Duke of Norfolk made an offer to subsidise the charity, but with the number of stewards, who bore the cost of setting up the festival and covered any losses, to be increased from one.

In 1837 there was talk that Hereford could drop out of hosting the festival, since there is much less space for seats in Hereford Cathedral than in those of Gloucester and Worcester making hosting the event less viable. It was rumoured that Warwick might take its place. However, intercessions were made to the new queen, Victoria, who became patron of the charity, six stewards were found who were prepared to guarantee any loss, and the 114th Three Choirs Festival duly took place in Hereford.[5] The *Messiah* was one of the pieces performed; it was a firm favourite during the 19th century and continues to be so today.

Because of the repairs to the cathedral, the 1843 festival was held in All Saints' church, reverting to the cathedral in 1846 even though the repairs had not been completed. Meanwhile the secular concerts were held in the Shire Hall, for which Townshend-Smith, organist at the cathedral and so conductor of the Hereford festival, was pushing to have the acoustics improved. In 1846 the stewards lost about £100 each, so in 1849 their number was increased to eight. In 1852 the stewards made a considerable loss, despite an increased attendance, and in 1855 their total outlay was about £700-800, so in 1858 the number of stewards was further raised to 25, and for 1861 their liability was limited to £25 each. In that year the provision of secular music was extended by the addition of chamber concerts, another innovation of Townshend-Smith.

Townshend-Smith died in 1877. In his latter years he would have known William Elgar and his brother Henry, who both played in the festival orchestra, and may have known William's son, Edward, although Edward did not join the orchestra until 1878 (at Worcester). Elgar was more associated with Dr George R. Sinclair, organist at Hereford from 1889, and a close personal friend. Up until 1897 the festival was held mid-week, starting with a service on a Tuesday: in that year the Festival began with a full orchestral service on Sunday 12 September, during which a new composition by Edward Elgar, commissioned by Sinclair, had its premiere. Such was the closeness between the two men that Sinclair and his bulldog Dan were the subjects of the 11th of Elgar's *Enigma Variations*.

One composition that became a favourite at the festivals was Elgar's *Dream of Gerontius*. After a shaky first performance at Birmingham in October 1900, it was first performed at the festival in Worcester in 1902, and then at Hereford in the following year. By 1905 Elgar's music was as popular at the festivals as the established classics such as the *Messiah*. There was a closer connection when he moved to Plas Gwyn, a house in Hampton Park Road, Hereford, in 1904, the year in which he was knighted. He spent much time cycling around the county (as portrayed in his statue in the Cathedral Close, Fig. 14.13), often in the company of Dr Sinclair. Compositions made during his stay in Hereford include the oratorio *The Kingdom*, the *Wand of Youth* suite, the *Introduction and Allegro for Strings*, much of his *Violin Concerto* and also his *Second Symphony*. He left Hereford at the end of 1911 to move to Hampstead.

After the Gloucester Festival of 1913 the outbreak of the First World War caused a break in the continuity of the festivals, until its resumption at Worcester in 1919, when some 300 stewards had to be found. Prior to 1913 the festivals had been numbered from 1724 but Ivor Atkins, organist of Worcester Cathedral, rather arbitrarily decided on 1715 as the starting year, and this has been used ever since.

In the 1920s Elgar's music, although declining in popularity generally, was still as popular as ever at the Three Choirs Festival, many performances of which he conducted himself. His last appearance was in 1933 and he died the following year.

Although arrangements for the festival at Hereford in 1939 were well advanced, the outbreak of war caused this to be abandoned for the duration, and the next festival took place in 1946 at a time of post-war austerity, with a programme based on that arranged for 1939. Since then the festival has taken place uninterrupted, and in 1992 Anthony Boden wrote that 'Three Choirs continues to expand musically, to commission new work and to engage musicians of the highest international reputation.' Many of the famous names of the 20th century have had work premiered at the festival.

Fig. 14.13 A sculpture of Sir Edward Elgar was commissioned by the Elgar in Hereford Group for Hereford Cathedral and unveiled on 25 September 2005. The work of Jemma Pearson, it depicts Elgar with his Sunbeam bicycle – nicknamed Mr Phoebus.

15 Hereford in the 20th and 21st centuries

HEREFORD HAS undergone considerable expansion during the 20th and early 21st centuries, with the building of a munitions factory during the First World War and subsequent industrial estate and enterprise zone, and several new housing estates on the city's edge and on the previous site of the SAS base – and with more estates set to follow. In addition the heart of the city has seen much change, from a rebuilding of the west front of the cathedral at the beginning of the 20th century to a redesign of the Close in the early 21st century; a new cathedral library and exhibition space for the Mappa Mundi; considerable expansion of the cattle market and then its move out of town and redevelopment of the site; the arrival of supermarkets; an inner ring road and continuing debate about a bypass.

Cathedral

A slight earthquake in 1896 destabilised the pinnacles and upper parts of Wyatt's west front of 1786, and the Dean and Chapter decided it was an opportune time to replace what was regarded as a rather plain façade with something more elaborate to reflect the Decorated style of the late 14th century. This was built between 1904 and 1908 to the design of John Oldrid Scott, son of Sir George Gilbert Scott. Many find it difficult to quarrel with George Marshall's judgement in 1951 that it 'is fortunately not seen in close juxta-position to other parts of the cathedral; for it fits against the nave, as seen from either side, as if it were an entirely separate creation pushed against it without any attempt at incorporating the earlier work. It would have been better had it been built of a local stone, such as was used in the Norman period, and not of the red stone from Hollington in Staffordshire. It is irregularly overloaded with

Fig. 15.1 New Town Hall under construction. The city council was offered land in St Owen Street for a new town hall as a gift by the daughters of the former Town Clerk, Richard Johnson. They accepted the offer and obtained a loan of £25,000 to erect a building to the design of Mr H.A. Cheers of Twickenham and built by a local firm. It opened in June 1904. (© Derek Foxton Archives)

*Figs. 15.2 (left) Wyatt's west front of the cathedral as drawn by T.H. Clarke in 1830
(© Herefordshire Museum Service, ref: 1988-99/1) and
15.3 (right) an early 20th-century postcard showing Scott's partly finished replacement.*

ornament, the sculpture is good in some instances, but in others had better be passed over in silence.' It includes a memorial window for Queen Victoria known as the 'shilling window' as it was partly paid for by a collection of 30,000 shilling coins (totalling £1,500) made by women across the diocese.

A range of buildings had long stood on the east side of Broad Street on what is now part of the Cathedral Close. A central part was occupied by the Globe Tavern, open from at least the late 1830s, when it brewed its own beer, till the 1860s when it closed and the building was converted into apartments. A fire in one of the adjoining buildings in April 1935 led to Colonel George Heywood paying £5,000 to have these 'offending buildings' demolished just a month later. Railings were erected along the edge of the Close, but were removed during the Second World War when metal was needed for armaments. Between 2009 and 2011 the Close underwent a restoration project that included extensive archaeological excavations, replacement paths, a stone mosaic 'apple tree of life' designed by Canon Sandy Elliott (Fig. 15.4) and new railings.

Fig. 15.4 The Apple Tree of Life, designed by Sandy Elliott, outside the west front of the cathedral. (Photograph by Gordon Taylor, © Hereford Cathedral Library)

Fig. 15.5 (top) The corner of King Street and Broad Street with Wyatt's west front of the cathedral in the late 1890s
Fig. 15.6 (lower) The range of buildings that was demolished in 1935. (© Derek Foxton Archives)

15.7 Part of the chained library when it was in a room above the north transept aisle

The Mappa Mundi had never found a settled home, whilst the cathedral's chained library of some 1,500 books, dating from the 8th to the 19th centuries and the largest in existence, had not been on display in its entirety since 1842. In that year the Lady Chapel, which had housed it since the early 17th century, was restored as a place of worship. After that, only part of the library was displayed in a chamber above the north transept aisle and only those prepared to mount a spiral staircase of 54 steps could see it (a scene of two fatalities in the last 15 years of use). When in 1988 the world's spotlight turned on Hereford at the proposed sale of the medieval map to help provide funds for repair work to the cathedral, protests led to its withdrawal from Sothebys and the eventual building of a permanent home which was opened in 1996. This is now shared with the chained library and over 300 volumes from All Saints church, (most of the latter not currently on display).

Other changes at the cathedral include two new windows in the Audley Chapel commemorating Hereford-born Thomas Traherne, poet, spiritual writer and vicar of Credenhill in the late 17th century. The windows were designed by Tom Denny and dedicated on 25 March 2007 (Fig. 15.8).

The shrine of St Thomas Cantilupe in the north transept was restored to something approaching its former glory in 2008 (Fig. 11.2). His bones were in the shrine between 1287 and 1349, though probably in a reliquary on top of the shrine rather than in its base. In 1349 they were moved to a new reliquary in the Lady Chapel. This was destroyed in the Reformation in 1530, but the original tomb in the north transept remained unscathed.

Fig. 15.8 Thomas Traherne is commemorated by four stained glass windows by Tom Denny in the Audley Chapel in Hereford Cathedral. The images are based on passages in Traherne's Centuries of Meditations. *That on the right shows Hereford.*

Electric Light

The electric light works in Widemarsh Street were erected in 1899 and electric light gradually began to replace gas light, but was initially only taken up by the most well-to-do residents, and even some of them were only induced to switch with the offer of free installation. Even so, by 1910 the plant was still operating well below capacity. That soon changed with the siting of the munitions factory in Rotherwas during the First World War resulting in it having to be enlarged.

The introduction of the National Grid greatly increased the areas of the county that could be served by electricity and shortly after the Grid was fully integrated in 1938, the Widemarsh Street power station ceased to be used. In 1947 Electricity Boards were created under the Electricity Act and the industry was nationalized. The new Midlands Electricity Board used the Widemarsh Street site (now part of the site of the multi-storey car park) as its Hereford depot. In 1979 a small power station using heavy oil was opened on the edge of the Grandstand Road Estate. It also supplied Bulmers and Sun Valley with steam. In 1990 the electricity industry was privatised.

City Prison

Located in Commercial Road on the site of St Guthlac's Priory and adjacent to the workhouse; its cells could accommodate 105 prisoners. The last execution in Hereford took place here on

Fig. 15.9 This photograph shows the prison just before demolition when, during a May Fair, it was opened to the public. The sign announced: 'See the old gaol before demolition – try going to gaol of your own accord'. The entry cost 6d. (© Derek Foxton Archives)

Fig. 15.10 Hereford was part of the Oxford Assize Court circuit, and when the judge was seeing cases in Hereford he stayed at lodgings reserved for his own use at 5 Commercial Street. The building was demolished to make way for a cinema, itself demolished as part of the Maylord Orchards redevelopment (© Derek Foxton Archives)

11 December 1903 (12 years after the previous case). The defendant was William Hayward, a roadman aged 61 from Yarpole, accused of murdering his wife Jane. He was known as a drunkard and of violent temper. One evening his wife had gone to the local inn to try and get him to come home for his dinner, but he had refused. When he did return home later he clubbed his wife to death in a fit of rage, but was then spotted trying to remove her body by wheelbarrow. The execution took place in a secluded site in the prison coachhouse (public executions had been banned in May 1868), and even those working on the roof of the nearby Merton Hotel were forbidden to mount their ladders before 8.15am so as to prevent any unauthorised sightseeing.

Cattle Market

The new cattle market, which covered 6 acres and provided space for sales not just of cattle, but also of sheep, pigs and horses, opened at Newmarket Street on 17 October 1856. As from that day the market ceased in the streets, although animals continued to be walked in and out of the market for another hundred years. New facilities were added in 1888, and by the end of the 19th century the animal 'throughput' had reached over 150,000 a year. A wholesale fruit market was established in 1894 and extended in 1910. A railway siding had been provided at Moorfields Station for ease of transporting stock, and in 1914 a rail link was laid across Edgar Street by the Great Western Railway. A remodelling took place in 1956, on the centenary of the market's opening, with the construction of a new sale ring, a new pig market and two new lairages, which helped cope with an annual throughput which had risen to almost 270,000 animals. Just over ten years later the inner relief road works claimed some land on the western side of the market for the widening of Edgar Street, and further developments took place to fit in with the new road pattern. These included a poultry market, furniture sale and showroom, agricultural implement showroom, sheep penning extensions, alterations to the pig market and auction offices and a weighbridge. Sales, held on approximately 260 days each year, regularly reached an annual throughput of almost 440,000, (in one year made up of 74,549 cattle; 24,503 calves; 320,409 sheep; 18,014 pigs and 1,797 horses and ponies). Business became more difficult for all markets in the 1990s as agriculture moved into recession, and was not helped by the BSE crisis and tuberculosis affecting beef and dairy cattle. In 2000, of a total annual 'throughput' of 325,000 beasts there were just 7,400 cattle and 6,000 calves, most of the remaining 94% being fat and store sheep and cull ewes, with very few rams and pigs.

On 20 February 2001, Herefordshire's first confirmed case of Foot and Mouth disease occurred on a farm near Llancloudy. The disease became rampant, movement of stock was tightly restricted and cattle markets ceased to operate, with that in Hereford becoming almost a ghost town. At the same time plans began to take shape to redevelop the market area for an expanded city centre and increased housing provision, and for the market to move out of the city centre, thus also helping to reduce traffic congestion.

After 150 years in central Hereford, the city's new cattle market opened on 21 June 2011, on a 16-acre site on the Roman Road, where, as a sign of greener times, all effluent is treated on site through a seven pond wetlands bio-degrading system. In 2014, 369,000 sheep, 8,000 cattle and 2,000 pigs were sold.

The Cattle Market. (© Derek Foxton Archives)
Figs. 15.11 (top left) In 1925-6, with the electricity works top right
Fig. 15.12 (bottom left) In the late 1940s
Fig. 15.13 (above) In 1995
Fig. 15.14 (below) In 2010

Fig. 15.15 Inside H. Godwin's cider works c.1930s. (© Derek Foxton Archives)

Fig. 15.16 An 'aerial' depiction of Bulmers' cider factory c.1920s. (© Derek Foxton Archives)

Fig. 15.17 William Evans delivery lorry (when cider was delivered by the tanker load!) on Widemarsh Common c.1948. (© Derek Foxton Archives)

Cider

The first cidermakers based in Hereford were the firms of William Evans and Co., established near Widemarsh Common in 1850, and Mr H. Godwin, who opened his cider works at Tillington Road in Holmer in 1898. Both had ceased trading by the second half of the 20th century. Rather more modestly, Henry Percy Bulmer, younger son of the Revd C.H. Bulmer, Rector of Credenhill, heeding his mother's advice to make a career in either food or drink 'because neither ever goes out of fashion', had tried making some cider from apples in the Rectory orchard. Percy Bulmer's efforts were so successful that a year later, in 1888, he engaged in cidermaking on a larger scale. Starting in Maylord Street he then took an acre of land in Ryelands Street, Hereford where he was joined as marketing manager by his brother, Fred Bulmer. Percy Bulmer returned from a visit to Germany in 1904 armed with several ideas: to float the apples in water before crushing, which would both wash them and make it easier to transport them to the milling plant; to improve bottling; and to dry the discarded pomace so that it could be sold as a cattle food, rather than dumped in the countryside till it had sufficiently rotted to be spread on the ground as manure. Later, Bulmers used the pomace to produce pectin, an even more valuable by-product. The business grew steadily, more land was purchased in Ryelands Street and then at Moorfields, and eventually the factory sites covered over 80 acres. The company was floated on the Stock Exchange in 1970 but ran into financial difficulties early in the new millennium and in 2003 was taken over by Scottish & Newcastle Breweries and subsequently be Heineken in 2008, resulting in several job losses in Hereford and the loss of a business that had seemed part of the county's infrastructure.

The original Bulmers' factory buildings at Pomona Place, off Whitecross Road, now houses the Cider Museum.

Suffragettes

The suffragettes held a number of meetings in Hereford, including one in St Peter's Square in 1908. Other open air meetings followed in 1909 and in May there was a debate in the Town Hall on the motion that votes for women be conceded on the same terms as for men. Opposing the motion, Mr R. Brown spoke sarcastically of 'unsexed fanatics' and forecasted that if women got the vote England would be soon be dominated by them. He was supported by Mrs Chapman, who believed women 'were born to rock the cradle' and referred to 'the already declining manners of democracy now that working classes had the franchise'. The audience supported the suffragettes and the motion was carried with an overwhelming majority. After women obtained the vote in 1928, the next mayor was Louise Luard, who was awarded both the MBE and the OBE for her public work.

Fig. 15.18 Suffragettes meeting in St Peter's Square in 1908. (© Derek Foxton Archives)

Supermarkets

On 21 November 1960, Herefordshire's first 'supermarket', called Maypole, opened in Commercial Street, followed by Tescos, also in Commercial Street. As a result of pressure of space at the Tescos store and changing shopping patterns, additional land was released for retail development. This resulted in the construction of the much larger Tescos store on the edge of the inner relief road, as well as the Maylord Orchards development where the first shops opened in October 1987. With the Tescos site, the line of the medieval city defences (actually buried beneath the relief road) was reflected by a sandstone masonry wall almost as high as the original fortification. Sainsburys subsequently built a store on the site of the Barton railway station, to be followed by Safeways who chose the site of the city's first gas works and Canal Wharf timber yards, saw mill and pits. This supermarket is now a branch of Morrisons. The Co-op for a while ran a non-food store in Widemarsh Street before moving out of the city centre and opening a supermarket in Bobblestock (which operated for a while under the name Leos). Another large Tescos was built alongside the A465 Abergavenny Road in Belmont and then, in 2006, after trying to get a foothold in Hereford for 20 years, ASDA opened its store on 22 acres of land at the former Causeway Farm. Meanwhile, in 1998, Lidl opened its store just off Commercial Road, followed by Aldi adjacent to Great Western Way footpath and cycle-way. In 2014 they were joined by Waitrose on the Old Market site.

City Centre Refurbishment

In July 1997 All Saints church opened its café in High Street following a £1.7 million restoration scheme of the church. Regular services still take place and the Lady Chapel is available for prayer and quiet.

In 2000 farmers' markets were reintroduced into High Town. All produce has to be 'grown, reared, caught, brewed, pickled, baked, smoked or processed' within 30 miles of the market.

Fig. 15.19 High Town painted on 5 August 1960 by John Ward. (© Herefordshire Museum Service, ref: 7388)

Fig. 15.20 The new development on the market site (compare with the photographs on pages 270-1).
(© Derek Foxton Archives)

Arguments for and against an extension of the shopping centre onto the cattle market site and whether such a development would have a beneficial or harmful effect on the existing shops, continued for many years, and still continue even after the new development has opened. This it did in May 2014 after 18 months of building work and at a cost of £90 million. Debenhams and Waitrose were the 'anchor' stores, and the site also includes a new state of the art multi-screen cinema and several restaurants.

Railways
In 1914 tracks, ramps and pens for livestock was provided by Great Western Railway at Canonmoor on what became known as the Worcester Down Sidings. The rail service was later extended by a single track across Edgar Street, through the market, to fuel the Electricity Generating Station. As time went on other sidings were constructed for Watkins Flour Mills, Painter Brothers, the Gas Works, H.P. Bulmer, Henry Wiggin and some smaller companies. During the First World War, considerable installations were built to serve military ammunition factories at Rotherwas and Credenhill. With the introduction of the National Grid and increased use of road transport for cattle and perishable goods, the cattle market line ceased to be used. During the Second World War buildings near the line were commandeered by the army for unloading, storing and forwarding foodstuffs for the military camps and hospitals scattered throughout the area.

During the First World War the 120 different railway companies operating in Britain were placed under a measure of state control and subsequently 'rationalised' into four companies nationwide. From 1923 the three companies then operating at Hereford merged to two and until after the Second World War the carriage livery to be seen at Barrs Court Station was the 'Crimson Lake' of the London, Midland and Scottish Railway and the 'Chocolate and Cream' of the Great Western Railway.

The railways were nationalised in January 1948, but with falling revenues a major review was carried out in 1963 under the chairmanship of ICI's Dr Beeching which led to the closure of many lines. By 1966 the only stations remaining in the county were at Barrs Court, Leominster, Ledbury and Colwall: the Hereford to Hay, Leominster to Kington, Leominster to Bromyard and Hereford to Ross lines were either being taken up or had already gone. In 1994 the process of re-privatisation began and now once more Hereford is served by several private railway companies.

Cars and Congestion
One of the country's first cars was built in Hereford by an engineer, Mr J. Naylor, and a carriage builder, Mr Charles Jones and was tested on the city's roads in mid-January 1897. By 1900, cars were being assembled by the Smooth-Geared Auto-Car Syndicate of Commercial Road, who became Connelly and Sons. The new vehicles were all carriage-built by hand, in some cases at the premises of craftsmen of the horse-drawn era. One example was at 20 Bridge Street, now part of the Left Bank Village, where Richard Sully – 'Carriage and Motor Body Builder; Rubber tyres fitted in a few hours' – succeeded John Watkins, who in 1876 had been listed in a trades directory as one of three builders of horse-drawn coaches and carriages. To begin with, the motor car was affordable only by the well-off, but by 1903 Herefordshire had formed its own Automobile Club which organised an annual hill-climb at Dinmore and later at Fromes Hill, attracting 112 entries in 1907. Number plates were first issued on 1 January 1904 and in August that year the first National Light Car Trials were being held in and around Hereford. These were to test the endurance of vehicles costing less than £200 and each day their drivers drove over six different routes, covering two non-stop laps of 50 miles. Although some vehicles were used for day-to-day travel, they were not to displace local horse-drawn transport until the 1920s and there was still plenty of work for blacksmiths, farriers and wheelwrights for some time afterwards. (Between 1946 and 1949 the firm of Aero Parts assembled 64 Westland-Healey motor cars in the city.)

By 1938, the daily number of vehicles using the Wye Bridge had reached an average of almost 5,500. Studies showed that some 80% of all drivers had reason to stop in the city; at certain times of the week barely 15% of vehicles could be classified as 'by-passable'. Thus in 1939, to relieve congestion at the bridge, a new bridge was proposed just yards upstream. It was to be aligned with a new north-south dual carriageway along Victoria Street running parallel with the western medieval wall-line.

The Second World War put an end to these plans, and after the war the problem grew worse. By 1954 the average daily traffic flow over the old bridge had risen to almost 9,500 vehicles. Meanwhile Hereford's population was continuing to grow, encouraged by the arrival of new industrial companies, particularly Henry Wiggin and Company Ltd, who were eventually to employ up to 3,500 people at Holmer, on the north side of the city. Between 1951 and 1961 the city's population rose from 32,490 to 40,431 and by 1971 it amounted to 46,503. In 1965 more than 24,000 vehicles per day were crossing the Wye Bridge, with firms such as AEI /Thornes /BTH on the Rotherwas site. Debate ensued as to whether the original plan for a new bridge so close to the old and alongside the city walls was the correct solution, but an ultimatum from the Ministry of Transport that money should be used for the proposed scheme or withdrawn and allocated elsewhere meant that the scheme that Hereford currently has was constructed. Work started in late 1964 and was undertaken in stages, the new Greyfriars Bridge being opened to traffic in January 1967, and the road completed by November 1969.

Fig. 15.21 This page and opposite; two aerial views before the construction of the new bridge and inner ring road. Above: the junction of Commercial Street and Bath Street with a roundabout (lower left), with Maylord Street curving up towards the top left of the photograph, and Blueschool Street towards the top right. (Photograph courtesy of Donovan Wilson & Graham Roberts)

Fig. 15.22 The cluster of buildings that would be demolished along Victoria Street between St Nicholas' church and where Tescos would be built can be seen at top left-centre of this photograph. (Photograph courtesy of Donovan Wilson & Graham Roberts)

It was not long before 30,000 vehicles a day were crossing the new bridge, but few would have predicted that the number would rise to 57,000 vehicles by 1995 and 78,000 (almost 10% of them heavy-goods vehicles) by 2010. This trend has given rise to renewed discussions and plans for an actual bypass, and the benefits and drawbacks of either a western or an eastern route, or some combination of traffic management and park-and-ride schemes. In 1988 a western route was proposed by the Ministry of Transport, but after consultation the proposal was changed to an eastern one, which the local authorities preferred. This eastern route was subject to a public inquiry in 1991 and 1992, but the inspector advised ministers against the chosen route and recommended a western one, for ministers to reject both options. A revised eastern route was proposed in 1995, and was given a degree of priority by the government but no funding, only for a subsequent government to bin the scheme entirely. The current favoured option is a route to the west of Hereford as this would open up tranches of land for increased housing which would, in part, pay for the road. Such a route would save despoliation of the Lugg Meadows, but mean that any traffic coming from the more populated east to join the A49 would still have to first come in to Hereford.

On 30 January 2015 plans were published for the proposed Southern Link Road, which would be the first stage in a western bypass. Its southern end would be at the A49 Rotherwas roundabout from where it would run west through Grafton Wood, cross Grafton Lane by a bridge, then start to swing north-west, crossing the railway line by a bridge and going under the lane at Haywood to reach the A465 Abergavenny Road near the end of Hayleasow Wood, where a new roundabout would be constructed. A road would also link the B4349 Clehonger road to the roundabout.

Buses

The city council acquired the disused city gaol in the late 1920s and, after everyone was given the opportunity of taking a last (6d) look round, all the buildings except for the Governor's House, which was converted into a waiting room and offices for the bus companies, were demolished. A cinema and café were constructed along the Commercial Road frontage. The city centre branch of Tescos is the terminus for all Hereford City bus services, while the bus station remains the county and nationwide bus station.

Rotherwas Munitions Factory

The Rotherwas estate at Dinedor, the seat of the Bodenhams for well over three centuries, comprised Rotherwas House, an 11-bay mansion built on the site of an earlier mansion by Charles Bodenham to the design of James Gibbs in 1732, and over 2,500 acres of land on the south side of the River Wye. After the death of Count Louis Bodenham-Lubienski in 1912 it was broken up into 76 separate lots and sold. The house was demolished in 1925 following a fire, leaving only the chapel. At the auction of 1912, Herefordshire County Council bought an area of 185 acres overlooked by Dinedor Hill and bordered by the Wye meadows as part of a scheme to provide smallholdings. But the land quickly turned out to be unsuitable and seemed likely to become a costly 'white elephant'. It was, however, well served by the Hereford, Ross and Gloucester Railway and could draw on an ample water, gas and electricity supply. In 1916 it was acquired by the Ministry of Munitions as a site for a factory filling shells with lyddite, made chiefly from fused picric acid, and amatol, an explosive mixture of ammonium

Fig. 15.23 Study for 'No.14 Filling Station, Hereford' c.1918 by Charles Ginner.
(© Charles Ginner estate)

nitrate and TNT, as an insurance in case of accident or mishap elsewhere. Production started in November 1916 and quickly built up, especially after the appointment of Winston Churchill as Minister of Munitions in July 1917. The amatol section went into production with the filling of its first shell in June 1917. At the height of its activity in October 1918, there were 5,943 employees, 1,966 of them men and 3,977 women.

After the signing of the Armistice the Hereford factory was given the task of breaking down the huge quantity of munitions that remained unused. In 1920 the factory was mothballed, only to be reopened at the start of the Second World War. By the autumn of 1940 some 3,700 people, mainly women, were employed at what was then the Royal Ordnance Factory. Early in the morning on 27 July 1942, in Hereford's only air raid of the war, a lone aircraft dropped two bombs, the first exploding on impact killing 19 workers and injuring many more, whilst the other travelled some distance before penetrating the factory perimeter fence and killing all but one of the occupants of the police superintendent's house. Three workers had already been killed and six injured by an accidental explosion the previous September and on 30 May 1944 a 2,000 pound bomb exploded in a filling house which set off other munitions. The filling house was demolished, a sheet of flame shot 2,000ft into the air, two people were killed and

Fig. 15.24 (above) Rotherwas Munitions Factory site and subsequent industrial park photographed from the air in February 2006. The remaining shell store of 1916 can be seen towards the top left-hand corner of the scrubland at the top of the site. (© Derek Foxton Archives)

Fig. 15.25 (below) Photographed in 1990, the shell store is centre right. Wooden huts would have stood in the areas marked off by blast walls in which the shells would have been filled, the blast walls intended to protect workers and munitions on the rest of the site should something go amiss during the filling process. All of these blast walls and the remains of the decauville railway trackway which serviced the huts have now been cleared to make way for new factory buildings, one example being retained on the edge of the site. (© Derek Foxton Archives)

another 30 injured. Action by emergency services and employees at the factory in averting a major catastrophe led to the exceptional award of five George Medals and many other bravery decorations.

For a further 20 years after the end of the war, Rotherwas reverted largely to its former 'white elephant' state – until it was chosen in the 1970s as the site for the expansion of Hereford's sewage disposal system, then based at the Eign Works across the Wye. Herefordshire County Council then began a phased programme of industrial development which was continued and expanded upon reorganisation of local government in 1974 by Hereford and Worcester County Council. By the end of the 1990s, 127 local and international companies occupied working space and gave employment to over 2,000 people.

Following further reorganization of local government in 1998 Rotherwas Industrial Estate, still with over 100 acres of available developable land, was transferred to the new Herefordshire Council.

A 2 mile access road was completed in 2008 to avoid a low bridge and the risk of the estate being cut off from the A49 at times of severe flooding, and so disrupting businesses. In August 2011 the 72-hectare Rotherwas Enterprise Zone was designated to encourage the establishment of firms involved in defence and security, advanced technology, environmental technology or food and drink, offering business rates relief for five years, automatic planning permission for certain categories of development within certain design limits, and ultra-fast broadband. The enterprise zone now is called Skylon Park after a futuristic-looking, cigar-shaped steel structure made by Painters in their Holmer factory for the Festival of Britain held in London in 1951. By March 2015, five plots totaling 114,000 sq ft had been sold with a further nine sales in train. Two new high quality workshops and offices are being built for rent.

Another new building at Rotherwas is that for Herefordshire Records Office. Part forms the three-storey main archive store constructed to meet modern requirements for storing records and preventing their deterioration, the other part houses the offices, public search rooms and education facilities. It opened in the summer of 2015.

In 2013 a new greenway cycle and pedestrian route to Rotherwas was completed, which includes a bridge over the River Wye near the Eign railway bridge.

Wiggins

In 1835, a partnership between a Mr Evans and Mr Askin began in Birmingham the refining of nickel and the manufacture of German Silver (an alloy of nickel and silver much used at the time for cutlery), and were joined in 1842 by Mr Henry Wiggin. Come 1950, the Ministry of Supply, wishing to disperse strategic production, selected Crossway Farm at Holmer as a site for the development of a new generation of metals for the aircraft industry. The firm, by then named after Henry Wiggin, joined the Ministry's scheme and established a factory in Hereford. In 1962 the firm invested heavily in the factory and withdrew from their other sites in Birmingham and Glasgow, from where many workers relocated. By the late 1960s the factory employed over 3,000 people. Since then Inco Alloys, the parent firm and the world's largest producer of nickel, has based its European headquarters and manufacturing and research centre at Hereford. By the end of the century the name of the company had changed again, to Special Metals (Wiggin) Limited, part of The Special Metals Corporation.

Water supply

With increasing population came increasing demand for water and so the need for reservoirs situated on high ground to provide the required pressure. Early in the 1900s a new reservoir was constructed at Bobblestock and this allowed the area of Westfields to be connected to the mains supply, and later to the sewerage system to avoid residents burying their effluent in their front gardens. The need for further capacity as the city grew and the need to serve a wider catchment area was met by constructing an underground storage reservoir close to the Breinton Road works entrance from where pumps deliver water to a reservoir at Ridge Hill south of the city, from where, in turn, pumps move water to a higher reservoir at Aconbury Hill. Another large main runs northwards to a reservoir at Upper Lyde.

Municipal Cemetery

By the beginning of the 20th century the case for a public cemetery for citizens of all shades of belief and opinion was still being made, and in 1908 the town council bought additional land, adjacent to the existing cemetery, from the Church and built a mortuary chapel. During the early 1920s the council took over responsibility for the adjoining Parochial Burial Grounds and subsequently extended the cemetery westwards along Westfaling Street. In 1956 a crematorium was opened on the site, followed by a replacement in 2009. In 2014 there were 1,465 cremations.

Hospitals

The First World War created a pressing need for the treatment of crippled veterans and in 1919 a physiotherapy department was opened at the General Hospital. This was followed in 1927 by an open-air orthopaedic unit, and a pathology department in 1934. Being a voluntary hospital, fundraising was always an issue.

Hereford Municipal Borough Infectious Diseases Hospital had been erected at Gorsty Lane, Tupsley in 1893 with initial provision for 12 patients, expanding to 24 in 1898. In 1902 this was followed by an isolated smallpox hospital, built of corrugated metal in a field to the east of Hollywell Gutter Lane. Its 12 beds were rarely used and it eventually closed in a state of some neglect in 1948.

The Union Workhouse had become the responsibility of the council and renamed the Public Assistance Institute, but the council had responsibility for the care of any sick inmates.

After much wrangling between the council, professional bodies and the trades council (which considered that 'an isolation hospital in the middle of the city was obnoxious', seemingly having no qualms about the central abattoir), it was agreed to develop a new County Hospital, as it became known, and in 1937, Queen Mary laid the foundation stone of the three storey '1930 block'. There would be no operating theatre and no provision for acute cases – in deference to the roles of the General Hospital.

The Second World War brought many new demands, but also antibiotics. An additional 10 hutted wards were constructed to help provide for evacuees, each providing for 36 patients. These 'Canadian' huts were intended to last for 10 years, but lived on into the 21st century. The new '1930 block' opened in stages during 1941, but has since been demolished to provide space for the new hospital access.

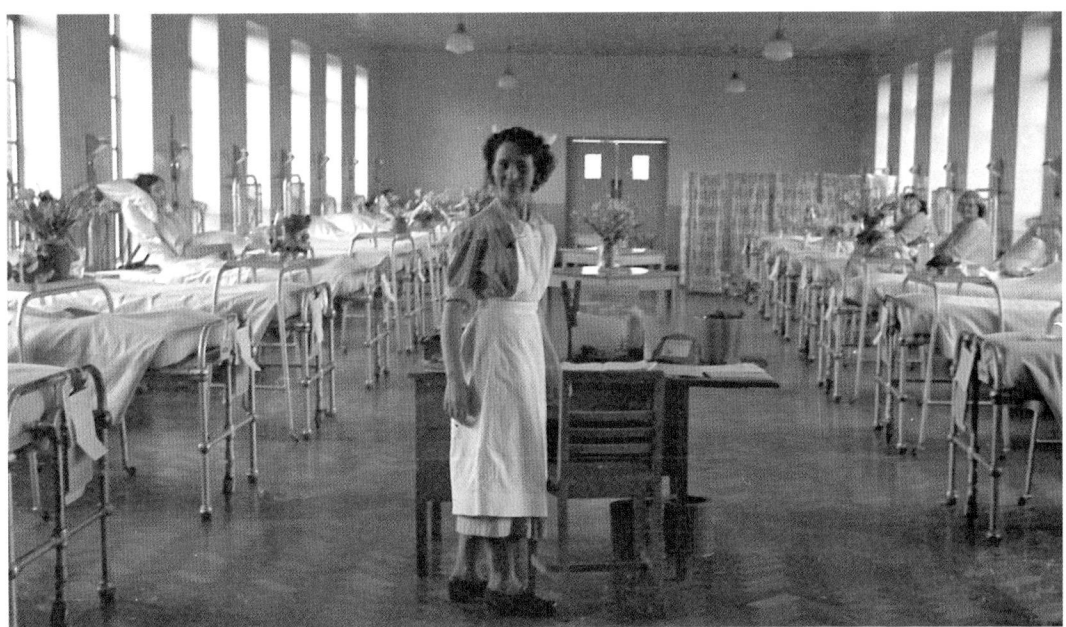

Fig. 15.26 A Hereford ward, probably at the County Hospital, in the 1940s. (© Derek Foxton Archives)

With the advent of the National Health Service in 1946 the County, General, Victoria and all other remaining Hereford hospitals became the responsibility of the Ministry of Health. Though now a unified service, there was little agreement on where a new hospital, recommended in 1948, should be built, nor its size and facilities as medical advances called for continual rethinks. By 1973 the County Hospital contained about 385 beds, mainly for acute patients, whilst at the General Hospital there were 156 beds, also for acute cases. At Tupsley, 25 of the 31 beds were allocated to geriatric patients, the remainder for TB and chest cases, but this hospital later closed and a satellite GP surgery and pharmacy was established on part of the site. The Victoria Eye Hospital (see p.237) continued to be fully used as a separate unit with 25 opthalmic beds.

In 1996, Hereford became one of 13 Private Finance Initiative (PFI) hospital projects authorised across the country by the government in a large scale testing of the model, and in April 1999 a plan was put forward to rebuild much of the County Hospital as a new £65 million 'state of the art' District General Hospital. Compared to the then capacity of 390 beds in the County and General hospitals, the new hospital would provide 250 beds, supported initially by a further 90 from refurbished hospital stock at the 'Canadian' huts, with a greater emphasis on primary and community care. Work began in September 1999 and it opened in 2002, when the old General Hospital was closed.

Under PFI the hospital is paid for by private money and leased back for 30 years. Allowing for income from the disposal of the General and Eye Hospital sites, the full development cost of the new hospital (including fees, financing and interest charges) was estimated at £85 million by the time it opened. The ultimate overall cost during the rental period is expected to reach an estimated £470 million, partly due to the cost of services that have to be purchased over that period under the PFI contract.

Housing

In 1909 Hereford City Council went ahead with a proposal to build a new suburb on the principles of the Garden City pioneered by Ebenezer Howard. It acquired land at Barrs Court, constructed roads and sewers, planted trees and laid down the conditions for building houses. The land was leased to the Hereford Co-operative Housing Company who, with government finance, built 85 houses for rent at a density of no more than 12 houses to the acre. Arranged in 15 blocks of five and three houses and eight blocks of semi-detached houses, each house had three bedrooms and two living rooms. There was an inside W.C. and coal-store in all the houses, an upstairs bathroom in 16 of them and an iron bath in the scullery in others.

Few local authorities provided social housing until after the First World War, despite further powers granted by the Housing and Town Planning Act of 1909. To its credit, Hereford had built 67 new homes between 1902 and 1914. They were to form part of an eventual total of some 8,550 dwellings to be built for sale or rent by the city council during the next 80 years. At one period during the 1960s the city council came to own more than one third of all the houses in Hereford.

Early post First World War council houses appeared in Portfields, Breinton Road, Ross Road, Hunderton, Link Road, Westfields, Mostyn Street, College Road and Stonebow Road, amounting to over 550 in all. From 1920, the increased use of the motor car led to the growth of classic 'ribbon development' extending beyond the White Cross along King's Acre Road towards the long established (in 1785) nurseries close to the junction for Credenhill. Ribbon development also took place along the east side of Canon Pyon Road beyond the municipal boundary, as it did for some distance along the north side of Roman Road.

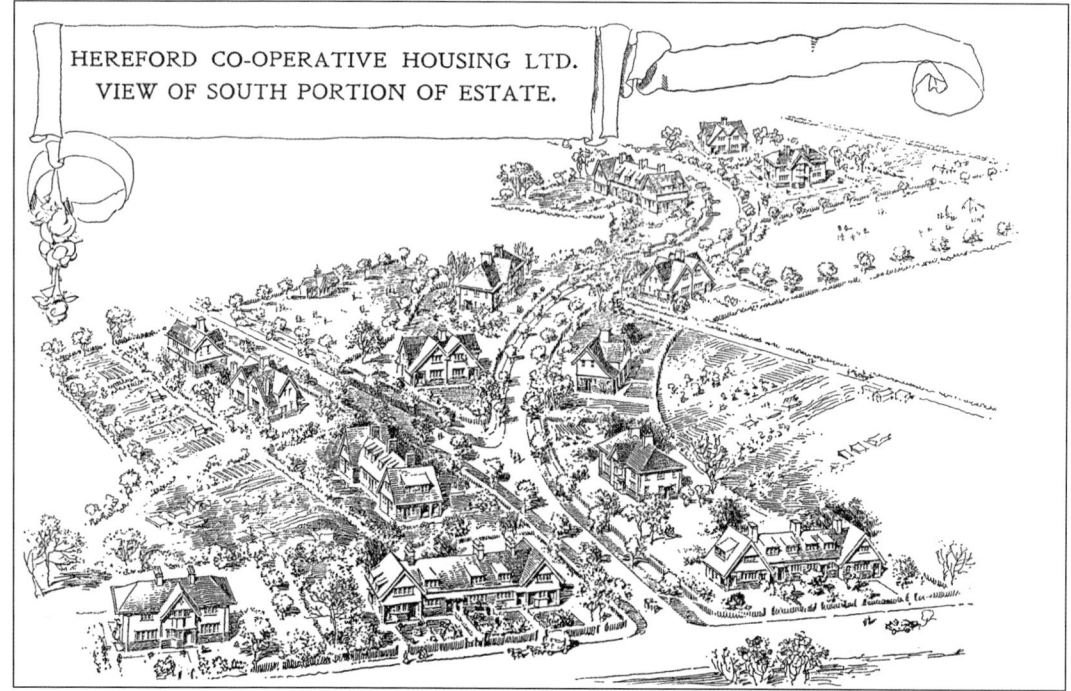

Fig. 15.27 A drawing promoting the Garden City suburb built shortly before the First World War. (© Derek Foxton Archives)

Fig. 15.28 Housing in the Garden City suburb   *Fig. 15.29 Housing in the Portfields*

From 1930, more than 500 houses and 64 flats were built at College Hill, 391 homes at Hinton Court and 16 aged persons flats at St Owen's Place, a grand total of approximately 1,600 since the first council house tenancy in 1902.

After the Second World War, a vigorous programme saw the building of over 1,800 new council homes, including numbers of pre-fabricated 'Cornish Units'. The largest developments were a first phase of 464 houses and flats at Newton Farm, 471 at New Hunderton, 146 at Redhill and 216 at Holme Lacy Road. The programme continued to gather pace during the late 1950s, the '60s and '70s as further phases of rented accommodation were added at Newton Farm and Redhill, and new estates formed with the building of 431 houses and bungalows at Green Lanes, 537 units at 'Whitehouse' and 'Prospect' Farms at Tupsley, 200 houses and 80 four-storey maisonettes and 25 warden-assisted flats at the 'Moor' Farm, north of the White Cross. Here, the listed 17th-century timber-frame and brick farmhouse was carefully restored and converted into two flats.

It wasn't just council houses that were being built. Some 80 acres of Church farmland existed at Bobblestock in an area approved primarily for residential purposes in 1960 and intended for council housing. After some discussion this was amended in 1969, clearing the way for a private sector housing scheme covering the entire acreage up to the south side of Roman Road, which would include a primary school, shops, a public house and open space. By the time all the houses were completed in 1988, the area included a small supermarket and two lock-up shops near the Three Elms Road junction, but nothing came of the original proposals for a school or a public house and the amount of open space was hardly as 'considerable' as had been anticipated. Across the city, much private sector building took place in Tupsley.

House completion rates reached their peak between 1962 and 1966; in 1963 alone, 572 new private and local authority houses were completed, to be followed by 509 in 1964. The building rate for all new housing was, however, easing towards the end of the 1960s, partly as a result of various government 'squeezes'. Between 1971 and 1981 it fell away to a rate little more than half its former level, averaging only 262 per year.

Fig. 15.30 Several decades of new housing, showing different attitudes to density and layout, in the area to the north of the Royal National College for the Blind, seen in the top left-hand corner. Bottom left is Loader Drive, built in the 1970s. Top right is Victoria Park built in 1980. Between them is Campbell Close built in 2008. (© Derek Foxton Archives)

By 1991, 73% of the 20,829 houses in the city were privately owned, 24% managed by the local authority and 3% by Housing Associations. These increases in the city's housing stock did not, however, lead to a commensurate increase in population, since average household sizes had fallen from 3.07 people per dwelling in 1971 to 2.47 in 1991.

In 2002, Hereford City Council transferred its existing housing stock and associated land to Herefordshire Housing Ltd, a housing association created for the purpose. Today it has over 5,000 units and over 300 employees and is carrying out some much needed refurbishment and reconstruction work in Newton Farm. Other Housing Associations working in Hereford include Kemble, formed as the result of a small charitable donation, which now manages over 1,000 homes in the county, many of them in Hereford, and Fortis Living, formed recently as the result of a merger by Elgar Housing which itself had taken over the council housing previously owned by Malvern Hills District Council.

Post-16 Education
Provisions of the Education Act of 1944, to compel local authorities to secure an education for people over compulsory school age, had been anticipated by 42 years in Hereford, with the opening of the country's first ladies' training college for elementary school teachers in College Road in 1902 in what had been Hereford County College (see p.244). The Hereford College of Education quickly expanded after the war to admit men and women over the age of 18 years,

Fig. 15.31 Hereford County College, then Hereford College of Education and now the Royal National College for the Blind. (© Derek Foxton Archives)

but in 1977 the college was closed when much teacher training was transferred to universities rather than specialist colleges. The following year the buildings were taken over by the Royal National College for the Blind and by 1980 the number of its students had reached 160, the majority boarding in halls of residence in Venn's Lane. This number has since declined and the early buildings designed by Frederick Kempson are now used by the College of Arts.

In 1950 the Herefordshire Technical College was founded and moved in 1954 into the first phase of purpose-built new premises at Folly Lane. It quickly expanded until in 1993 it became independent of local authority control, becoming one of the top six employers in Hereford, with a staff of over 700 (most part-time).

Herefordshire College of Art and Design developed from early beginnings in 1852 and in 1969 the Hereford School of Arts and Crafts at Castle Green moved to purpose-built accommodation next to the Technical College at Folly Lane.

In 1973 the campus at Aylestone Hill was further extended with the opening of the Sixth Form College with about 250 students. They were taught in cramped conditions in Broadlands, formerly a private house, and in terrapin huts, but in 1974 it moved to purpose-built buildings in Folly Lane. It took over post-16 education from the secondary schools in the city and some adjacent areas and by 2000 had more than 1,000 students.

In March 2015 plans were announced to create a New Model in Technology and Engineering (NMiTE) college which would specialise in manufacturing, defence engineering and agri-technology. It is expected to be based across the city, mainly using existing buildings. The institution was granted some match funding by central government in November 2015, and it is hoped that it will take its first students in the autumn of 2017, eventually catering for up to 5,000 students who will need accommodation around the city. Some 500 jobs directly connected to the college might be created.

The Fair
St Ethelbert's or the Nine Days Fair had been the social and entertainment highlight of the year for many people, but as with all fairs throughout history, it had a sleazy side and was not all just good clean fun. It could attract criminals and lead to drunkenness and debauchery and,

believing that many citizens could pinpoint former nine-day visits which marked the abandonment of their virtue, the council reverted to the three-days' limit decided by Henry I. Passed in the first year of the reign of Queen Victoria, an Act of 1838 provided that the fair would normally be held on the Tuesday after the first Monday in May and on the next two days (so excluding the modern May Day bank holiday).

But not everyone was fond of the fair, and Victorian concern for propriety added to the annual disruption of local trade and chaos in the streets, produced regular pressures to have the fair stopped, or at least removed elsewhere. In 1911 'the citizens appear to be resigned to this old custom, mainly because it provides a fund of amusement for country folk and children'. It lives on into the 21st century, but is now just a shadow of the great event it once was.

Looking to the Future

In the past few years the development of the old cattle market site has radically changed Hereford city centre, but it is only one of a few developments stretching back over the past 60 years which have done much to alter Hereford: the building of new housing on the site of the SAS camp at Bradbury lines; refurbishment of the Cathedral Close; the building of the new cathedral library and exhibition space for the Mappa Mundi; expansion of the Art College complex; flood prevention works, less visible to the eye but nevertheless having a major effect on the city; extensive housing development at Belmont and before that at Bobblestock; new industries appearing on the Rotherwas munitions factory site and a new link road joining the site to the A49 south of Hereford; supermarket development at many locations; the Left Bank; the Maylord Orchards shopping centre; the building of the Greyfriars Bridge and inner relief road and the more recent link road from Edgar Street to Commerical Road. These are just some of the major developments, but there have been many smaller projects which have effected neighbourhoods or streets.

These will soon be joined by new housing near the football ground whilst debate about a bypass continues. The world moves on and Hereford with it, but the hope must be that we seek to use the best of what is new to help create a Hereford that cares for its past, cares for its residents and cares about the future.

Fig. 15.32 Sign of the times. Restoration of All Saints church by Rod Robinson Associates in the 1990s included work on the upper part of the spire, which had become twisted, and internal work including a new raised floor in the western half of the building with underfloor heating as part of the Café @ All Saints. The work also included 'pods' for the vestry, kitchen, servery, office and toilets, all without damaging the earlier floor which remains sealed below the platform.
(© Derek Foxton Archives)

References

Abbreviations

Aylmer (2000)	Aylmer, G. and Tiller, J., *Hereford Cathedral: A History*, The Hambledon Press, 2000
Boucher *et al* (2015)	Boucher, A., Craddock-Bennett, L. and Daly, T. *Death in the Close: A Medieval Mystery*. Headland Archaeology Ltd., Edinburgh, 2015
Duncumb (1804)	Duncumb, J. *Collections towards the History and Antiquities of the County of Hereford* (1804)
HMC	Historical Manuscripts Commission
HRO	Herefordshire Record Office
Lobel (1969)	Lobel, M.D. 'Hereford', in *Historic Towns Atlas* (Volume 1), 1969
TWNFC	*Transactions of the Woolhope Naturalists Field Club*
LOWV	Landscape Origins of the Wye Valley project, 2008
Pevsner (2012)	Brooks, A. and Pevsner, N. *The Buildings of England: Herefordshire* (2012)
RCHM	Royal Commission on Historic Monuments in England
Shoesmith (1980)	Shoesmith, R. *Excavations at Castle Green* (Hereford City Excavations, Volume 1), Council for British Archaeology, CBA Research Report 36, 1980
Shoesmith (1982)	Shoesmith, R. *Excavations on and close to the defences* (Hereford City Excavations, Volume 2), Council for British Archaeology, CBA Research Report 46, 1982
Shoesmith (1985)	Shoesmith, R. *The Finds* (Hereford City Excavations, Volume 3), Council for British Archaeology, CBA Research Report 56, 1985
Thurlby (2013)	Thurlby, M. *The Herefordshire School of Romanesque Sculpture (with a History of the Anarchy in Herefordshire* by Bruce Coplestone-Crow), Logaston Press, 2013
Whitehead (2007)	Whitehead, D. *The Castle Green at Hereford: A Landscape of Ritual, Royalty and Recreation*, Logaston Press, 2007

Chapter 1 Prehistoric and Roman 'Hereford'

1. This chapter is based upon the period studies on the prehistoric period and the Romano-British period that the author undertook for the English Heritage-sponsored *Hereford Archaeological Research Framework* produced in 2011, when he was employed by Herefordshire Council as County Archaeologist. Thanks are due to Dr Nigel Baker, the overall editor and author of that Framework document for inviting me to contribute to the framework, and to Roger Thomas of English Heritage for his support of the work.
2. Courtesy of Herefordshire Council's former informatics team. The image is a digital terrain model (DTM) generated using the raw Light Detection and Ranging (LIDAR) imaging data. Its creation not only strips out all modern buildings, but also uses colour toning to indicate relative heights, the vertical scale of which is exaggerated. This is why the banks surrounding Castle Green (next to the River Wye at lower right-centre) appear cone-like. The straight line along the flood plain margins at lower right is the Bartonsham Rowe Ditch.
3. A somewhat larger Mesolithic flint 'point' was also found at Victoria Street. As with all the flints of Mesolithic type found in the city, these were not found where they had first been dropped or buried. Rather, they had been re-deposited in later levels or site contexts such as pits.
4. See Thomas, A. and Boucher, A. *Further Sites and Evolving Interpretations* (Hereford City Excavations, Volume 4), Logaston Press, 2002, pp.46-50; McNabb, J. 'The flints', in *ibid.*, pp.149-50 nos. 10 & 11. The discussion of stray or redeposited finds of worked flints here is derived from published reports, and not from a systematic trawl of 'grey literature' reports.
5. *ibid.*, pp.27-39; McNabb in *ibid.*, p.150 nos. 35 & 36.
6. *ibid.*, pp.54-7; McNabb, *ibid.*, nos.16-34.
7. 95% probability; WK-9688.
8. And so probably to be dated to around the late 14th century: *Further Sites and Evolving Interpretations*, *op.cit.*, pp.43-4.

9. Wilkinson, K. and Watson, N. 'Geoarchaeology' in Jackson, R. and Sworn, S. *Investigations along the route of the Rotherwas Access Road, Herefordshire*, Worcestershire Archaeology Client report (v1), WA1968, 2014, pp.72-7; Jackson, R. in *ibid.*, pp.80-2. Brown, T.G., Carey, C. and Dinnin, M. 'The geomorphology, geo-archaeology and alluvial history of the Frome Valley', 62-78 in White, P. *The Frome Valley, Herefordshire: Archaeology, Landscape Change and Conservation*, Herefordshire Council: Herefordshire Studies in Archaeology, **3**, 2011, pp.62-78.
10. See Stead, I. and Hoverd, T. 'The Prehistory of Dinedor and Rotherwas', in Ferris, B. *et al (Dinedor Heritage Group) Dinedor and Rotherwas Explored*, Logaston Press, 2014, for a detailed description of Dinedor hillfort, and the finds made during Kenyon's excavations there. For the original report on the excavations, see Kenyon, K.M. 'Excavations at Sutton Walls, Herefordshire, 1948-1951' *Archaeological Journal*, **110**, 1954, pp.1-87.
11. Detailed discussion of either Credenhill Fort, or indeed of the Roman town at Kenchester, lies outside the geographical scope of this chapter. For in-depth treatment of both sites, and their important hinterlands during both the Iron Age and Roman periods, see Ray, K. *The Archaeology of Herefordshire: An Exploration*, Logaston Press, 2015, Chapters 4 and 5.
12. A length of more than 400m of this road was uncovered and carefully recorded in an archaeological excavation in advance of road improvement works on the A4103 north of Swainshill to the north-west of Hereford in 2004. A future publication by Worcestershire Archaeology will provide details of this work.
13. The existence of the place-name 'Portway', often denoting Anglo-Saxon awareness of the presence of a former Roman road, a kilometre to the *south* of the 'Watling Street West' turn towards Kenchester, further reinforces this possibility.
14. Stone, R. and Appleton-Fox, N. *A View from Hereford's Past: A report on the archaeological excavation in Hereford Cathedral Close in 1993*, Logaston Press, 1996.
15. The potential significance of this alignment is evident when it is appreciated that a direct continuation of the alignment of 'Watling Street West' south from Badnage on the A4110 would extend precisely to the only point at which, historically, it has been possible to cross the Yazor/Eign Brook marsh at the northern end of Widemarsh Street. Having crossed here, an alignment towards the historic ford by the Bishop's Palace would exactly reproduce the alignment of the early ditch on the 'Mappa Mundi' site.
16. This again has added significance if there was a Roman road traversing exactly this area.
17. Henig, M. and Booth, P. *Roman Oxfordshire*, Tempus 2000, pp.68-72.

Chapter 2 Anglo-Saxon Hereford
1. Opinions vary as to the extent of Saxon Hereford, especially among those archaeologists who have so far reviewed the evidence: Shoesmith (1980); Shoesmith (1982); Stone, R. and Appleton-Fox, N. *A View from Hereford's Past: A report on the archaeological excavation in Hereford Cathedral Close in 1993*, Logaston Press, 1996; Shoesmith, R. 'Architecture and Furnishings: The Close and its Buildings', pp.293-321, in Aylmer (2000); Thomas, A. and Boucher, A. *Further Sites and Evolving Interpretations* (Hereford City Excavations, Volume 4), Logaston Press, 2002; Baker, N. *An Archaeological Research Framework for the City of Hereford*, Herefordshire Council: Herefordshire Archaeology Report 310, January 2013, pp.58; Boucher *et al* (2015). See also, Whitehead, D. 'Historical introduction', pp.1-6 in Shoesmith, R. (1980); Keynes, S. 'The History of the Foundation: Diocese and Cathedral before 1056', pp.3-20 in Aylmer (2000); Blair, J. 'The Anglo-Saxon Church in Herefordshire: Four Themes', pp.3-13 in Malpas, A., Butler, J. *et al*, *The Early Church in Herefordshire: Proceedings of a Conference held in Leominster in June 2000*, Leominster Historical Society, 2001; Whitehead (2007); and Bassett S. 'The Middle and Late Anglo-Saxon Defences of Western Mercian Towns', in Crawford, S. and Hamerow, H. (eds), *Anglo-Saxon Studies in Archaeology and History*, **15**, Oxford University School of Archaeology, 2008, pp.180-239.
2. In October 1055 the outlawed Earl Aelfgar joined forces with Gruffudd ap Llywelyn, defeated an Anglo-Norman force based at Hereford under Earl Ralph, and went on to sack the city (Keynes *op.cit.*, pp.18-19).
3. Shoesmith (1980), pp.52 & 55. Whitehead (2007), pp.5-9, connects the pre-Conquest landed estates held by St. Guthlac's with a putative British and later royal Saxon district of 'Lydas' (Lyde) to the north of Hereford.

4. 'Roman' period road: see Chapter 1, above. Metalled road: see Stone and Appleton-Fox *op.cit.*, pp.31-2.
5. Boucher *et al* (2015), p.59.
6. This excavation, overseen in the field by Philip Rahtz on behalf of the Hereford Excavation Committee, was nonetheless written up by Ron Shoesmith (1982), pp.28-35. It followed the excavation of a section across the defences which indicated pre-defensive occupation. Shoesmith, R. 'Hereford – The Western Rampart', *TWNFC*, **39**, 1967, pp.51-62.
7. Shoesmith (1982), p.30
8. The dating of the kilns depends upon a single radiocarbon sample from a burnt wooden stake retrieved from the infilling of one of the flues. This produced a date of 760 +/- 85 years AD (Shoesmith [1982], pp.31, 90; but it has been recalibrated to the mid-late 8th century (S. Bassett, 'The Middle and Late Anglo-Saxon Defences of Western Mercian Towns', *op.cit.*, pp.187-8). Given the isolated nature of the single sample, it is wisest to regard such dating as provisional, and indicative of a use-life for the kilns sometime in the 8th century, although some uncertainty will continue to attach to the date. The recalibrated date provides a span of approximately 780-850AD. However, both Shoesmith (1982, p.77) and Bassett (*op.cit*, p.186-91; p.235 n.61, 62) have suggested that although a mid-9th century date for the first-phase bank and ditch cannot be ruled out, a late 8th century date probably fits the observed sequence better.
9. Shoesmith (1982), p.91, and Thomas and Boucher *op.cit.*, p.3, respectively.
10. See, for instance, Whitehead, D. in Shoesmith (1982), p.13 (quoting the evidence of the Llandaff charters and the Welsh Annals). However, this is possibly stretching the evidence too far at present. There is nonetheless also the legend that the event recorded in the Anglo-Saxon Chronicle for 794AD to the effect that Offa caused the head of the relatively young King Ethelbert of East Anglia to be struck off took place at Sutton near Marden, north of Hereford, giving rise to the new, or additional dedication, of the cathedral to the king-martyr (for the basis of the cult, see Rollason, D. 'St Aethelberht of Hereford and the Cults of European Royal Saints' *Cantilupe Journal* 18, 2008, pp.8-28; see also Ray, K. and Bapty, I. *Offa's Dyke: Landscape and Hegemony in Eighth-Century Britain*, Windgather Press, 2016, pp.283-5).
11. Shoesmith (1982), pp.31-4.
12. Nigel Baker (pers. comm.) suggests that this may, however, be simply an example of an early orientation setting a pattern simply followed, at intervals, by later activity; and that the ovens could just be an example of ecclesiastical investment.
13. The dating and characteristics of the earliest Anglo-Saxon activity in Hereford is an urgent research concern, more especially in light of the recent discovery of early sunken-floored buildings in Shrewsbury. The activity relating to Offa's presence could have been related to the creation of the great linear earthwork that descends to the Wye near Bridge Sollers to the west of Hereford. As John Blair has put it, 'if Offa did indeed transfer the Magonsaetan see from *Lidebiri* (Lydbury North or Ledbury) to the defended frontier site at Hereford, it was probably in the context of a defensive and administrative reorganisation connected with the building of his Dyke', Blair, J. *The Church in Anglo-Saxon Society*, Oxford University Press, 2005, pp.287-8. Discussion of the 'pre-Mercian' origins of Anglo-Saxon Herefordshire and its bearing upon the early history of Hereford is provided by other writers (see especially, Sims-Williams, P. *Religion and Literature in Western England, 600-800*, Cambridge University Press, 1990). There is little tangible evidence upon which to base a comprehensive understanding of the origins of the Magonsaete (a people documented for central and northern Herefordshire only from the 9th century on).
14. Miller, D. Archaeological work at Rotherwas Industrial Estate, Herefordshire (Rotherwas Futures), Historic Environment and Archaeology Service, Worcestershire County Council, internal report 1837, 2011.
15. *ibid.* The enclosure could have been a cattle-corral or was just conceivably part of a temporary military encampment.
16. Heys, F.G. 'Excavations at Castle Green 1960, a lost Hereford Church', *TWNFC*, 36, 1960, pp.343-57; Shoesmith (1980).
17. Shoesmith (1980), pp.24-32. The more reliable dating of cist burials in the cathedral precincts places them mostly in the early 12th century (Boucher *et al* (2015), pp.76-9). The earliest date from one of the Castle Green burials was AD500-800; it would be useful to refine this further using modern techniques.
18. Shoesmith (1980), pp.9-17; Figure 7 (plan); p.39 (dates).
19. Whitehead (2007), p.24.

20. *ibid*, pp.12-18.
21. It has been estimated by extrapolation from the section across the (later) Saxon defences at 5 Cantilupe Street (see below) that the first phase clay and turf rampart could have been up to 8.5m in width, so there was clearly a step-change in the character of the early enclosure at Hereford in this possible late-8th or early 9th-century phase.
22. Watkins, A. 'Foundations of Buildings in Hereford castle', *TWNFC*, 1933, pp.36-40.
23. Drawn by M.G. Boulton reproduced as Figure 2 in Shoesmith (1980).
24. Shoesmith (1982), p.98; Figure 145.
25. Boucher *et al* (2015), p.172.
26. Shoesmith (1982), pp.67-8. Friars' Gate was the former name for St Nicholas Street.
27. Shoesmith, R. 'Hereford City Excavations, King's Head Site 1968', *TWNFC*, **30**, 1968, pp.348-53, 'Shoesmith, R. 'Hereford City Excavations, 1970', *TWNFC*, **40**, 1971, pp.225-40.
28. See *An Archaeological Research Framework for the City of Hereford, op.cit.*, p.25, concerning hints of the local existence of the former east ditch at Harley Court; and Whitehead (2007), p.16, for the parish boundary line. The parch-mark is visible on aerial photographs.
29. Apparent lack of Saxon defences south of the Wye: Shoesmith (1982), pp.74-83; Thomas and Boucher *op.cit.*, pp.5-11. Bedford is an example of a late Saxon period *burh* established with a defended area extending each side of a strategically-important, but vulnerable, river-crossing. However, other defended riverside settlements/*burhs* lacking transpontine suburbs featured a north-bank *burh* enclosure, with a south bank defended bridgehead, as now recorded archaeologically at both Southwark and at Bristol (Nigel Baker, pers. comm.).
30. Keynes *op.cit.*, p.8. The case for and against the first bishop being Putta, according to Bede expelled from his former see at Rochester following the attack on Kent by the Mercian king, Aethelred, in 676 has been examined at length by Keynes in the same publication *(ibid*, pp.5-7). See also *The Church in Anglo-Saxon Society, op.cit.*
31. William of Malmesbury claimed to have seen, *c.*1140, a stone cross standing by the cathedral: 'On a fine cross erected by Cuthbert, Bishop of Hereford, Milfrith, king (*regulus*) of the Magonsaete, and his Queen were commemorated with three earlier bishops of the diocese' (Lobel [1969], p.1, quoting from the Gesta Pontif., Rolls Series, ed. Hamilton, p.299).
32. Keynes *op.cit.*, pp.10-12.
33. This record is to be found entered onto a page of the still-surviving late 8th-century Hereford Gospels. It was written down at the request of Thurkil the White who deliberately 'rode to St Aethelberht's minster' at the request of one of the appellants to ensure that the judgement was properly recorded. (For this and other actions of Athelstan in defence of episcopal holdings, see Keynes, *op.cit*, pp.16-20.)
34. Keynes, *ibid*, p.19. It has been pointed out, however, that there is no evidence for rebuilding and that it was not likely that Aethelstan would have been buried 'in the church which he himself had constructed from the foundations' if it really was a complete ruin (Barrow, Julia 'The History of the Foundation: Athelstan to Aigueblanche, 1056-1268', pp.21-47 in Aylmer (2000); Boucher *et al* (2015), p.7).
35. Barrow (*ibid*) regards this as a reflection of Hereford being both poor and 'not in any way notable for cultural achievements'. A more charitable view sees it simply as innately more conservative. Mention of the canons here serves also to highlight another puzzle concerning the topography of late Saxon Hereford and the developmental history of the environs of the cathedral. In the introduction to a forthcoming book on the early secular buildings of Hereford (Hughes, Morriss and Baker, forthcoming), Nigel Baker has suggested that the canonical residences bordering the cathedral precinct, that are a unique feature of the topography of the medieval city, might just possibly date back to the later Anglo-Saxon period.
36. This was first pointed out in Shoesmith in 'Architecture and Furnishings' in Aylmer (2000), pp.297-8. The alignments are discussed in detail also in Boucher *et al* (2015), pp.176-9. According to the Anglo-Saxon ecclesiastical architectural scholars, H.M. and Joan Taylor (1965) *Anglo-Saxon Architecture, Volumes I and II*, Cambridge University Press, 1965, p.295, the only surviving (north) wall of Bishop Robert's double chapel was built partly up from the remains of an earlier, Anglo-Saxon, stone wall.
37. 'As was often the case with major Old English foundations, there were several churches at Glastonbury, built in a line on an east-west axis. The oldest, called "Ealdchirche" by the English, had allegedly been built of wattle by twelve disciples of the apostles Philip and James, and was later extended in wood; the newest, built on to the "Ealdchirche" by King Ine of Wessex in the 8th

century, had been greatly extended by Dunstan in the 10th. William of Malmesbury's description of the four churches evokes the English sense that the very buildings were to be cherished as relics. Whenever possible, old churches were extended or adapted. When this was impossible, they were not demolished, but reverently preserved.' (Garnett, George *The Norman Conquest: A Very Short Introduction*, Oxford University Press, 2009, pp.99-100).
38. Rodwell, W., Hawkes, J., Howe, E. and Cramp, R. 'The Lichfield Angel: A spectacular Anglo-Saxon painted sculpture' *The Antiquaries Journal*, **88**, 2008, pp.48-108.
39. Boucher *et al* (2015), pp.45-7.
40. Quoted in Duncumb (1804), p.523.
41. Stone and Appleton-Fox *op.cit.*, pp.34-41; pp.22-4. The possible post-Conquest date for the burials and pit is the suggestion of Derek Hurst who is writing up the library building excavations.
42. Boucher *et al* (2015), pp.64-70; 76-87; 195-6.
43. Given that the charter of this date for an estate at Staunton-on-Arrow 'in the territory of the Magonsaete' specifies the holding also of a tenement in Hereford (Lobel [1969],p.2).
44. Ralph was also known as 'Ralf of Mantes' (after his birthplace), or 'Ralph the Timid' due to his apparent inability to act decisively in times of crisis.
45. For the Welsh dimension, see Charles-Edwards T.M. *Wales and the Britons 350-1064*, Oxford University Press, 2013, pp.565-6. It has been suggested that Ralph 'almost certainly built the castle…before 1052, and established a Norman garrison in it' (Lobel, 1959, 2), but the case is circumstantial.
46. Anglo-Saxon Chronicle, C Version, entry for 1056.
47. *ibid*: Herefordshire was seemingly at this time part of a separate Earldom of Gloucester.
48. Boucher, A. 'Ewyas Harold Castle: Archaeological Surveys' (www.ewyaslacy.org.uk/Ewyas-Harold/Ewyas-Harold-Castle-Archaeological-Surveys/2007), Archaeological Investigations (Hereford) Ltd, 2007.
49. Lobel (1969), p.2. Duties which the king required of his burgesses included providing guards for his hall, and beaters when he went hunting. Mention of the duty of the king's burgesses specifically to contribute to the harvesting of grain 'on the king's manor at Marden' provides some substance to the notion that Offa had a 'villa' at Sutton close by. Specification that the villeins of Kingstone had to carry venison back to the city indicates the likely Anglo-Saxon origin of hunting forests at Treville and the Hay (*haga*) of Hereford.
50. Shoesmith (1982), pp.35-44; 77-85; Figure 130. Ron Shoesmith (pers. comm.) has suggested that differences in the form of the bank as between Cantilupe Street and Victoria Street might also be explicable if St Guthlac's monastery had been surrounded by its own (early) defensive circuit, subsequently absorbed within the eastwards extension of the burh in which the cathedral stood. This might also explain the somewhat eccentric configuration of the plan of this later eastwards extension to the overall defended enclosure.
51. *ibid*, pp.36-8; Figure 41.
52. Crooks, C. 'Hereford Flood Alleviation Scheme: Archaeological excavation and watching briefs', Archaeological Investigations Ltd: Hereford Archaeology Series, 827, 2009; Boucher *et al* (2015), pp.8-9.
53. Shoesmith (1982), p.99.
54. Boucher *et al* (2015), pp.37-42, 173-5.
55. *ibid*, p.32. Bone from this burial, and a charred emmer wheat seed from the post-pit, produced a date range for this structure of *c*.850-950.
56. *ibid*, pp.31-5.
57. As such, and perhaps ironically, it very much returns us to the model proposed by Lobel and her Hereford-based Woolhope Naturalists' Field Club informants in 1969.

Chapter 3 The first years of the Norman Conquest
1. Five men had been recognized as king in some part of England during 1066. The Confessor was still king at the beginning of the year, dying in January. Harold had then seized the throne. Harald Sigurdsson 'Hardrada' had briefly been recognised as king in York after his defeat of Earls Edwin and Morcar at Fulford on 20 September and before his own defeat by Harold at Stamford Bridge five days later. In London in October, when the news from Hastings arrived, the Witan hailed Edward the Aetheling as king. To contemporaries, the coronation of William on Christmas Day may not have appeared the permanent settlement that a retrospective view casts in stone.
2. The sons of Aelfgar, who had, with Gruffudd ap Llywelyn taken Hereford in October 1055, and was himself the son of Leofric of Mercia and Godgifu (Godiva).
3. The office of earl became equated with the Norman 'count': Latin *comes* plural *comites*.

4. Probably on the death of Earl Ralph. There is an alternative view that Ralph had been deprived of this earldom after his defeat by Aelfgar and Gruffudd outside Hereford in 1055.
5. Domesday records that in the time of the Confessor, Edric held six manors in Shropshire and one in Herefordshire. It is possible that other, unmarked Edrics, are the same man. (Reynolds, S. 'Eadric Silvaticus and the English Resistance' *Historical Research*, Volume 54, May 1981, Issue 129, pp.102-105.
6. Lewis, C.P. 'Richard Scrob (*fl*.1052-1066)', *Oxford Dictionary of National Biography*, Oxford University Press, 2004 (http://www.oxforddnb.com/view/article/23505, accessed 4 April 2015).
7. '*Eadric cild þa Bryttas wurdon unsehte wunnon heom wið þa castelmenn on Hereforda, fela hearmas heom dydon.*'
8. '*multos e suis militibus et scutariis perdiderunt.*'
9. About the feast of the Assumption of St Mary (15 August).
10. According to William of Poitiers fitz Osbern was left in charge of the city of *Guenta*, which might ordinarily be Winchester, *Venta Belgarum*, fitz Osbern's normal base, but *Guenta* is described as being 14 miles from the sea which 'divides the English from the Danes', so the place is *Venta Icenorum*, Norwich. (Stenton, F.M. *William the Conqueror and the rule of the Normans*, G.P. Putnam's and Sons, 1908, p.58).
11. Hillaby, J., 'The Norman New Town of Hereford: Its Street Pattern and its European Context,' *TWNFC*, **53,** 1983, pp.181-95.
12. Dickinson, R.E. 'The Town Plans of East Anglia: a study in urban morphology', *Geography* Vol.19, No.1, March 1934, pp.37-50.
13. The triangular Corn Market at Worcester appears to owe its shape to random topographic factors rather than a deliberate plan (Baker, N. and Holt, R. *Urban Growth and the Medieval Church, Gloucester and Worcester*, 2003, p.170).
14. Stone, R. 'The Development of Widemarsh Street, Hereford. An Archaeological Perspective', *TWNFC*, **59,** 1997, pp.85-100.
15. Stone, R. 'Archaeological Excavation at 46 Commercial Street, Hereford', *TWNFC*, **59,** 1998, pp.182-214.
16. Shoesmith, R. 'Hereford City Excavations: King's Head site', *TWNFC*, **40,** 1968, pp.348-53.
17. '*Hereford non grandis, quae tamen fossatorum praeruptorum ruinis ostendat se aliquid magnum fuisse*', *Gestis Pontificum Anglorum* of William of Malmesbury, 298, Available from Gallica, the Bibliotech Nationale Francais website at http://gallica.bnf.fr/ark:12148/bpt6k50285r.image.r-malmesbury.f331.langEN; accessed 11 March 2015.
18. Garmonsway, G.M. (ed.) *The Anglo Saxon Chronicle*, Everyman, 1972, pp.185-6, 200; Thorn, F. and C. (eds) *Domesday Book: Herefordshire,* Phillimore, 1983, 179a, note 2, C1-15; Lobel (1969), pp.2-3.
19. Lobel (1969).
20. *Domesday Book, Herefordshire, op.cit.,* 179a.
21. Lewis, C.P. 'Lacy, Walter de (*d*.1085)', *Oxford Dictionary of National Biography*, Oxford University Press, 2004; online edn, May 2011 (http://www.oxforddnb.com/view/article/15863, accessed 6 April 2015).
22. Capes, W. *Charters and Records of Hereford Cathedral*, p.14; Smith, B. *A History of Malvern*, 1964, pp.44-45; Harvey, J. *English Medieval Architects*, 1987, p.193.
23. William fitz Osbern would clearly have been expected to work with anyone who had interests in the county and was prepared to support the Norman regime in smoothing the transition from English to Norman rule in Herefordshire. Richard Scrob and his son Osbern, Alfred of Marlborough and Bishop Walter would have been of particular importance (Lewis, C.P. 'The Norman Settlement of Herefordshire under William I', *Anglo-Norman Studies*, **VII**, 1984, p.211).
24. Barrow, Julia 'Walter (d.1079?)', *Oxford Dictionary of National Biography*, Oxford University Press, 2004 (http://www.oxforddnb.com/view/article/28629, accessed 27 Oct 2015).
25. HMC *The Manuscripts of Rye and Hereford Corporations etc.* 13th Report, Appendix, Part IV, 1892, p.292.

Chapter 4 The early Castle, the City Walls and Gates

This chapter is based on 'Chapter 8, The Later Medieval Defences' by Shoesmith, R. & Morriss, R.K. in Thomas, A. and Boucher, A. *Further Sites and Evolving Interpretations* (Hereford City Excavations, Volume 4), Logaston Press, 2002, pp.169-182.
1. *Gesta Pontificum* of William of Malmesbury (ed. N.E.S.A. Hamilton) *Rolls Series,* 1870, p.298.
2. Turner, H. *Town Defences in England and Wales,* 1970, p.13.
3. Christie, N. and Creighton, O., with Edgeworth, M. and Hamerow, H. *Transforming Townscapes:*

From burh to borough: the archaeology of Wallingford, AD 800-1400, The Society for Medieval Archaeology, 2013, p.149.
4. Mahany, C. 'Excavations at Stamford Castle, 1971-6', *Château Gaillard. Etudes de castellologie médiévale VIII, Actes du Colloque International tenu a Bad Muenstereifel,* p.233.
5. Armitage, E.S. *The Early Norman Castles of the British Isles,* 1912 (New Edn. 1971).
6. Davison, B.K. 'Early Earthwork Castles: a new model', *Chateau Gaillard,* **3,** 1969, pp.17-47; Bouard, M. de 'Quelques données francaises et normandes concernant le problem de l'origine des mottes', *Chateau Gaillard,* **2,** 1967, pp.19-26.
7. I am grateful to Professor David Crouch for clarifying problems of dating Robert's creation as Earl of Leicester.
8. Whitehead (2007), pp.29-30; Pevsner (2012), p.324.
9. Walker, D. (ed.) *Charters of the Earldom of Hereford, 1095-1120,1* Charter 18, p.21 grants land outside the gate of St Owen '*extra portam apud sanctum Audoenum*'. Camden Miscellany, **22,** 1964. In previous works the date of the construction of the extended northern defences was given as 1189.
10. Shoesmith (1982).
11. Shoesmith (1982) p.83.
12. HMC *The Manuscripts of Rye and Hereford Corporations etc.* 13th Report, appendix 4, 1892, p.284. Hereford was not and had never been 'in Wales', and presumably it is a geographical meaning which is implied in the charter.
13. Appleby, J.T. (ed.) *Chronicle of Richard of Devises,* 1963.
14. *Pipe Rolls,* 1190, p.49
15. *Rotuli Literarum Clausarum in Turri Londinensi Asservati,* 2 Vols., 1833-44, I, p.131.
16. Note ix, *Rot. Litt. Claus.,* p.263.
17. *Town Defences in England and Wales, op.cit.,* p.24.
18. Lloyd, J.E., *A History of Wales,* 2 vols., 1911, ii, p.662.
19. Crooks, C. 'Hereford Flood Alleviation Scheme: Archaeological excavation and watching briefs', Archaeological Investigations Ltd: Hereford Archaeology Series, 827, 2009.
20. Thomas, A. and Boucher, A. *Further Sites and Evolving Interpretations* (Hereford City Excavations, Volume 4), Logaston Press, 2002, pp.51-4, note i.
21. Shoesmith, R., *The Civil War in Hereford,* Logaston Press, 1995.
22. *Calendar of Close Rolls,* 1247-51, PRO, p.534.
23. Shoesmith (1982), pp.85-7.
24. Shoesmith (1982), p.44.
25. Pilley MSS (Manuscript volumes, newspaper cuttings and other notes collected by Walter Pilley (in Hereford City Library); Watkins, A., 'Hereford City Walls', *TWNFC,* **23,** 1919, pp.159-63.
26. Cave's Testimony during the Civil War quoted in *The Civil War in Hereford, op.cit.,* p.60, note xv.
27. Morgan, F.C., 'Trade in Hereford in the 16th century', *TWNFC,* **29,** 1936, pp.1-20 esp p.16.
28. Morriss, R.K., *The Timber-framed Buildings of Hereford,* forthcoming.
29. Watkins, A., 'Hereford City Walls', *TWNFC,* **23,** 1919, in note xvii.
30. Taken from Shoesmith, R., & Crosskey, R., 'Go to Gaol … In Hereford', *TWNFC,* **48,** 1994, 97-139
31. Morgan, F.C., 'Hereford Poor and Prisons in Olden Days', *TWNFC,* **38,** 1966, pp.220-35.
32. Minutes of the Hereford City Council (HCC) 1699. Notes from the Minutes concerning gaols are in Hereford Record Office (HRO) K38/Cd/6Box2.
33. HCC Minutes 26 November 1792. Collins, W., *Modern Hereford, with special reference to the development of the Municipality, Part 2,* 1911, p.10.
34. HCC Minutes 29 March 1797; *Modern Hereford, op.cit.,* p.12.
35. Order Book of the Commissioners of the Hereford Paving Act, 1778-1810, f272 (HRO); *Modern Hereford, op.cit.,* p.12.
36. Nield, J., Letter XLIX, 'Remarks on Hereford County Gaol,' *Gentleman's Magazine,* April 1908, pp.289-91.
37. Brayley, E.W. & Britton, J., *A topographical and Historical Description of the County of Hereford,* 1805, p.489.
38. Shoesmith, R., *The Civil War in Hereford,* Logaston Press, 1995, p.36.
39. Shoesmith, R., *The Pubs of Hereford City,* Logaston Press, 3rd. edn., 2004, pp.212-5.

Chapter 5 The Castle post Anarchy to the eve of the Civil War
1. *Reg. Regnum* II, 150, 165; *Pipe Rolls* (*PR*) 1163, 7.
2. *PR* 1165, 110; 1173, 39; 1174, 121 – for brattices see Cathcart King, D.J. *The Castle in England and Wales,* 1988, pp.53-4; Higham, R. and Barker, P. *Timber Castles,* 1992, p.362.
3. Warren, W. *Henry II,* 1973, pp.129, 141; *PR* 1177, 52; 1178, 100; 1179, 39.

4. Colvin, *King's Works* II, p.674; *Timber Castles*, *op.cit.*, pp.138-9.
5. Whitehead, D. 'Historical background to the City Defences' in Shoesmith (1982), pp.18-21.
6. Appleby, J.T. (ed.), *The Chronicle of Richard of Devizes*, 1963, p.30; *PR* 1190-91, 45; 1193-4, 86-7.
7. *Ibid.*, 85-6; *PR* 1201, 264; 1202, 272-3.
8. *Turris* as a free standing stone tower is discussed in Pounds, N.J.G. *The Medieval Castle in England and Wales*, 1990, pp.21-4; Coulson, C., *Castles in Medieval Society*, 2003, *passim*, Higham and Baker, *Timber Castles*, pp.122, 132, 142 all suggest that a *turris* could also be constructed of timber.
9. Warren, W. *King John*, 1997, pp.103, 108, 121-2.
10. Martin, S.H. 'St Guthlac's Priory and the City Churches', *TWNFC*, 1954, p.226; Whitehead, D. 'Some Connected Thoughts on the Parks and Gardens of Herefordshire', *TWNFC*, 1995, pp.197-8.
11. Harvey, J. *Medieval Gardens*, 1981, p.80; *Inq. Miscellaneous 1251-61*, p.315; Charles & Emmanuel *Cath. Muniments* III, p.1178; *Pat. Rolls 1258-1266*, 431; Bannister, A.T. 'The Possessions of St Guthlac's Priory, Hereford', *TWNFC*, 1918, p.38.
12. Warren, W. *King John*, pp.217-19; Colvin, *King's Works* II, p.119.
13. *Close Rolls 1237-42*, 254; *Liberate Rolls 1226-40*, 488; Colvin, *King's Works* II, pp.674-5.
14. *Liberate Rolls 1240-45*, 38, 260, 296; *Close Rolls 1237-42*, 254; *1242-3*, 443.
15. *Inq. Miscellaneous 1392-1399*, 69; Lloyd, *History of Wales* II, p.696.
16. *Close Rolls 1247-51*, 436; Shoesmith, R. *Castles and Moated Sites of Herefordshire*, Logaston Press 2009, p.152.
17. Pounds, H.J.G. *The Medieval Castle in England and Wales*, 1990, pp.109, 125; Robinson, C.J. *The Castles of Herefordshire*, 1869, p.75; Duncumb (1804), **I**, pp.234-5.
18. *Cal. Pat. 1258-1266*, 478; *Liberate Rolls 1260-67*, 173, 175.
19. *Liberate Rolls 1267-72*, 88-9; *Close Rolls 1264-8*, 19, 59, 68; *Cal. Pat. 1258-66*, 610.
20. Duncumb (1804), **I**, pp.238-9.
21. *Cal. Pat. Roll 1324-7*, 337.
22. Despenser's remains, or at least the greater part of them, may have ultimately been buried at Hulton Abbey, in Staffordshire, where a burial exhibiting unusual bone injuries consistent with hanging, drawing and quartering was excavated. (Lewis, M.E. 'A Traitor's Death: the identity of a drawn, hanged and quartered man from Hulton Abbey, Staffordshire', *Antiquity*, 2008, **82**, pp.113-24.
23. *Cal. Pat. 1343-49*, 418; *Cal. Pat. 1281-92*, 514.
24. Cooke, W.H. (ed.), *Duncumb's Collections towards the History and Antiquities of the County of Hereford*, IV, 1892, p.96.
25. Robinson, *op.cit.*, p.73; McKisack, M. *The Fourteenth Century*, 1959, pp.465-7; Johnson, M. *Behind the Castle Gate*, 2002, pp.139-42.
26. *Liberate Rolls 126-40*, 247; *Hist. MSS. Comm, 13th Report*, App. 4, 1892, pp.286; *Cal. Pat. 1391-96*, 213; *Lib. Rolls 1260-67*, 175.
27. *Cal. Pat. 1385-89*, 280.
28. This account is based on Hodges, G., *Owain Glyn Dwr and the War of Independence in the Welsh Borders*, Logaston Press, 1995.
29. *Cal. Pat.1391-96*, 591.
30. Colvin, *King's Works*, p.676.
31. *Ibid.*, **VI**, p.47.
32. *The Letters and Papers of Henry VIII 1509-13*, **I**, p.896.

Chapter 6 The Norman cathedral, Bishops and Churches

1. I am indebted to the many publications on the cathedral which are the basis for this section. They include Marshall, G., *Hereford Cathedral: its evolution and growth*, 1951, which also cites earlier works by various 19th-century writers including Britton, Willis and Scott; RCHM, *Herefordshire, Vol. 1,* 1931, pp.90-120; Morris, R.K., 'The Architectural History of the Medieval Cathedral Church' and Whitehead, D., 'The Architectural History on the Cathedral since the Reformation', and Reardon, M., 'The Restoration of the Modern Cathedral', all in Aylmer (2000), pp.203-240; 241-285; 286-292; Thurlby, M., 'A Note on the Romanesque Sculpture at Hereford Cathedral and the Herefordshire School of Sculpture', *Burlington Magazine,* **126**, 1984, pp.233-34; Thurlby, M., *The Hereford School of Romanesque Sculpture,* Logaston Press, 2013; Pevsner (2012), pp.270-306; and, of course, *The Cathedral Guide*.
2. Thorn, F. & C., (eds), *Domesday Book, Herefordshire,* London, 1983, 2.27.
3. RCHM, *Herefordshire, Vol. 1, South-west*, 1931, p.93.
4. Morris in note 1, p.208.
5. Marshall in note 1, pp.52-66.
6. Morris in note 1, p.210.

7. Morris in note 1, p.214.
8. Whitehead in note 1, p.243.
9. Boucher *et al* (2015), see Illus 10, p.18 and p.55.
10. Capes, W.W. *Charters and Records of Hereford Cathedral*, **I**, 1908, p.84.
11. Stone, R. and Appleton-Fox, N., *A View from Hereford's Past*, Logaston Press, 1996.
12. *op.cit.*, p.22.
13. Suggestion by David Whitehead.
14. Boucher *et al* (2015), pp.76-8.
15. Sometime between 1163 and 1186 'Bishop Robert' ordered the Chapter to remove a house which had been built on the burial ground. It is not certain which Bishop Robert: Robert de Melun (1163-67) or Robert Foliot (1174-86). (Capes, W. *Charters and Records of Hereford Cathedral*, 1908).
16. *A View from Hereford's Past, op.cit.*
17. Morgan, F.C. undated pamphlet, p.17.
18. Coplestone-Crow, B. 'The Anarchy in Herefordshire' in Malcolm Thurlby (2013).
19. Pearn, A.M. 'Origin and Development of Urban Churches and Parishes: A comparative study of Hereford, Shrewsbury and Chester', PhD Thesis, Cambridge 1988, p.134.
20. RCHM, *Herefordshire, Vol, 1*, pp.120-2 and Plate 64 (Stalls); *A Short History of St. Peter's Church, Hereford*, Gloucester, nd but probably 1960s.
21. Barrow, J. ('The canons and citizens of Hereford, c.1160- c.1240', *Midland History*, 1999, **24**, p.9) considered that it had probably been built in the 12th century.
22. RCHM, *Herefordshire, Vol.1,* pp.122-6.
23. At Winchester the parishes appear to have been reorganised after fire-damage in 1141 during fighting between rival armies in the city (Pearn, *op.cit*); Gozo: Barrow, J. (ed), *English Episcopal Acta VII, Hereford 1079-1234,* Oxford University Press, no.16.
24. Barrow, J. *Episcopal Acta*, no.16.
25. Duncumb (1804), pp.426-7.
26. RCHM, *Herefordshire, Vol, 1,* pp.130-1.
27. Watkins, A., 'St. Giles Chapel, Hereford', *TWNFC*, 1927, pp.102-5.
28. Pearn, 1988, *op.cit,* p.152 and Knowles and Hadcock, *Medieval Religious Houses*, Longmans, Green and Co., 1953, p.363.
29. Pearn, 1988, *op.cit,* p.151.
30. Swinfield dined with the Hereford Greyfriars on Palm Sunday 1289. As the friars were mendicants, he paid for the food himself. The meal did not include meat as it was Lent: the wine, however, does not seem to have been stinted. Webb, Revd J. (ed.) *Roll of the Household expenses of Richard de Swinfield.*
31. Capes, W. (ed), *The Register of Bishop Thomas de Charlton*, pp.173-7.
32. Crooks, C. and Eisel, J.C. *Greyfriars, Greyfriars Avenue, Hereford; An Archaeological Evaluation*, Archaeological Investigations Ltd, 1999.
33. Capes, William, *Charters and Records of Hereford Cathedral*, 1908, p.85.
34. *ibid*, p.112.
35. Bannister, A.T., 1929, *A Transcript of 'The Red Book', a Detailed Account of the Hereford Bishopric in the Thirteenth Century*, Camden Miscellany 1929, **XV**, Camden Society, p.4.
36. Marshall, G., 'The Blackfriars Monastery and the Coningsby Hospital, Hereford' *TWNFC*, 1920, **XXIII**, part III, pp.239-48.

Chapter 7 Hereford as a Centre of Medieval Learning and Art

1. Daniell, C. *From Norman Conquest to Magna Carta,* 2003, p.193.
2. *ibid*, p.192.
3. Edwards, K. *English Secular Cathedrals*, 2nd edition 1967, pp.192-93.
4. Bradshaw, H. & Wordsworth, C. (ed.) *The Statutes of Lincoln Cathedral,* 1892-1897, **ii**, p.57.
5. Also called Robert of Losinga, or of Lorraine (= Lotharingia).
6. Mason, E. *William II: Rufus, the Red King,* 2005, pp.76-77.
7. Welborn, Mary C. 'Lotharingia as a Centre of Arabic and Scientific Influence in the Eleventh Century', *Isis* 16/2, 1931, pp.188-199.
8. Barlow, F. *The English Church 1066-1154: A History of the Anglo-Norman Church*, 1979, p.15.
9. Liège was Lotharingia's principal centre of learning, and the use of the abacus was taught there. See Metlitzki, D. *The Matter of Araby in England,* 1977, p.16.
10. *ibid*, p.17.
11. *ibid*.
12. *ibid*, p.18.
13. His dates are given as c.1062-1110 by Roth, C. *A History of the Jews in England,* 1941.
14. Haskins, C.H. *Studies in the History of Medieval Science,* 1924, p.117.
15. *The Matter of Araby in England, op.cit.*, p.21.
16. *The English Church 1066-1154, op.cit.*, p.247.
17. *ibid*, pp.72 & 259.
18. Runciman, S. *A History of the Crusades,* 1951-54, **iii**, p.492.

19. British Library, Arundel MS 377
20. *Studies in the History of Medieval Science, op.cit.*, p.125. Arin was a contribution to the cosmological learning of the West first introduced by Petrus Alfonsi in his *Dialogus* and in his climate-map, *c*.1110. That schematic map shows the mythical city of Arin set on the zero meridian of Hindu astronomy, where it was held by medieval Arab geographers to be the navel of the world; on den Brincken, A-D. 'Centre of the Earth: Arin' in Friedman, J.B. & Figg, K.M. (eds) *Trade, Travel and Exploration in the Middle Ages: An Encyclopaedia*, 2000, p.103.
21. Moreton, J. 'Roger of Hereford and Calendar Reform in Eleventh- and Twelfth-Century England', *Isis*, **86**, 1995, pp.562-86, especially p.562.
22. Morey, A. & Brooke, C.N.A. *The Letters of Gilbert Foliot*, 1967, p.291: index to the three charters Roger witnessed for Gilbert as Bishop of London.
23. Thorndike, L. *A History of Magic and Experimental Science*, 1923, **ii**, pp.182-83.
24. *Studies in the History of Medieval Science, op.cit.*, pp.124-25.
25. Wright, T. *Biographia Britannica Literaria: Anglo-Norman Period*, 1846, p.90.
26. See *Preface* reprinted in Jourdain, A. *Recherches critiques sur l'âge et l'origine des traductions latines d'Aristotle*, 1843, app. N. xxi, p.430.
27. Robert Grosseteste, *Summa Philosophiae*, **i**, ed. L. Baur, 1929-30, p.280. It has to be said that there is some doubt about whether Grosseteste wrote this *Summa*, and today it often appears as *Pseudo-Grosseteste*. Other circumstantial evidence clearly links the men whether this citation from Grosseteste stands or falls.
28. *The Matter of Araby in England, op.cit.*, p.40.
29. Although one sometimes sees the presence of this manuscript in the cathedral library cited as proof of Alured's connection with Hereford, it has to be recognised that the manuscript arrived in that library as a result of the Reformation, the evidence strongly suggesting that it came from Cirencester.
30. *The Matter of Araby in England, op.cit.*, p.40.
31. Butterworth, C.E. *The Introduction of Arabic Philosophy into Europe*, 1994, p.50.
32. Bacon, R. *Compendium Studii Philosophiae*, *c*.1271.
33. Baeumker, C. *Die Stellung des Alfred von Sareshel (Alfredus Anglicus) und seiner Schrift De motu cordis in der Wissenschaft des beginnenden XIII*, 1913, in *Sitzungsberichte der bayerischen Akademie der Wissenschaften, philos.-hist. Klasse*, p.24.
34. Orme, N. *Medieval Schools*, 2006, p.80; most of the poem is printed in Brewer, J.S., Dimock, J.F. and G.F. Warner (eds) *Giraldi Cambrensis opera*, Rolls Series, 21, 1861-91, volume i pp.382-84.
35. *ibid*, pp.409-21.
36. NLI 700.
37. The tale of this book's double loss by Hereford Cathedral is told by Birkholz, D. *Hereford Maps, Hereford Lives*, in Lilley, K.D. (ed.) *Mapping Medieval Geographies: Geographical Encounters in the Latin West and Beyond, 300-1600*, 2013, pp.225-231.
38. Lefèvre and Huygens, *Speculum Duorum*, 1974, pp.168-9 ('To Master William, Chancellor of Lincoln').
39. *The Introduction of Arabic Philosophy into Europe, op.cit.*, p.48.
40. Roger of Wendover, *Flores Historiarum*, *c*.1220: '... they left Oxford empty, some engaging in liberal studies at Cambridge and some at Reading'.
41. Lewis de Charleton in 1361 and Thomas Chaundler in 1453; also Thomas Cantilupe (although he had been chancellor of Oxford in 1262 before he became a canon in 1273, and then bishop in 1275).
42. A fuller account of the Mappa Mundi is given in Arrowsmith, S. *Mappa Mundi, Hereford's Curious Map*, Logaston Press, 2015, from which much of this information is drawn.
43. Hereford Cathedral Library MS P.1.7. Gameson, R. 'The Insular Gospel Book at Hereford Cathedral', *Scriptorium*, **56**, 2002, pp.48-79; Alexander, J.J.G. *Insular Manuscripts 6th to the 9th Century*, Survey of Manuscripts illuminated in the British Isles, 1978, pp.63-4.
44. MS 302. Temple, E. *Anglo-Saxon Manuscripts, 900-1066*, A Survey of Manuscripts Illuminated in the British Isles. 1976, pp.112-3; Morgan, N. and Panayotova, S. (eds) *A Catalogue of Western Book Illumination in the Fitzwilliam Museum and the Cambridge Colleges*, Illuminated Manuscripts in Cambridge, Pt 4, **1**, 2013, pp.151-7.
45. Barrow, J. 'Robert the Lotharingian' *Oxford Dictionary of National Biography*, **47**, 2004, pp.4124-6.
46. 'Mathematics and Astronomy in Hereford and its Region in the Twelfth Century', in Whitehead, D. (ed.) *Medieval Art, Architecture and Archaeology at Hereford*, 1995, pp.50-59.
47. Gullick, M. 'The English-Owned Manuscripts of the *Collectio Lanfranci* (s.xi/xii)', in Dennison,

L.(ed.) *The Legacy of M.R. James*, 2001, pp.99-117.
48. MS O.2.7, a collection of canon law texts, includes chronological lists of popes, patriarchs and Roman emperors, and MS O.2.9 includes extracts from Isidore and Eutropius.
49. Webber, T. 'Monastic and Cathedral Book Collections in the Late Eleventh and Twelfth Centuries', in *The Cambridge History of Libraries in Britain and Ireland*, **1**, 2006, pp.109-25.
50. Barrow, J., 'The Canons and Citizens of Hereford c.1160-c.1240', *Midland History*, **24**, 1999, p.6.
51. See especially the poem of Canon Simon du Freisne: Hunt, R.W. 'English Learning in the Late Twelfth Century', in Southern, R.W. (ed.) *Essays in Medieval History*, 1968, pp.110, 121-2.
52. Russell, J.C. 'Hereford and Arabic Science in England about 1175-1200', *Isis*, **18**, 1932, pp.14-25; Burnett, C. 'Hereford, Roger of', *Oxford Dictionary of National Biography*, **26**, 2004, p.765.
53. Thomson, R.M., *Books and Learning in Twelfth-century England: the Ending of 'Alter Orbis'*, 2006, pp.47-8, 77-84; Gullick, M. 'The Bindings', in Mynors, R.A.B and Thomson, R.M. *Catalogue of the Manuscripts of Hereford Cathedral Library*, 1993, xxvi-xxxii; Pollard, G. 'The Construction of English Twelfth-century Bindings', *The Library*, 5th series, **17**, 1962, pp.1-22.
54. HCL MS P.9.7. The obits in the Kalendar provide post and ante quem dates.
55. Ker, N.R. *Medieval Libraries of Great Britain: a List of Surviving Books*, 2nd ed. 1964, pp.96-100; 3rd ed. http://mlgb3.bodleian.ox.ac.uk; *Catalogue of the Manuscripts of Hereford Cathedral Library, op.cit.,* xv.
56. Ker, N.R. 'The Medieval Pressmarks of St Guthlac's Priory, Hereford, and of Roche Abbey, Yorks.,' *Medium Ævum*, **5**, 1936, pp.47-8.
57. HCL MSS O.3.8, O.3.9, O.4.10 and Magdalen College Oxford MS lat. 226.
58. James, M.R. 'The Library of the Grey Friars of Hereford,' *Collectanea Franciscana*, **5**, 1914, pp.114-23.
59. Williams, J. *The Chained Library at Hereford Cathedral*, 1996), p.24; Ker, N.R. 'Sir John Prise', *The Library*, 5th series, **10**, 1955, pp.1-24.
60. HCA 7031/2, f.140v, Chapter Acts, 16 Feb 1590.
61. HCA 4642.
62. HCA 3395.
63. Morgan, F.C. 'Hereford Cathedral: the Vicars Choral Library', *TWNFC*, **35**, 1955-57, pp.222-55, with a transcription of the first 52 pages of the donors' book. The College was dissolved in 1937 and the books transferred to the Cathedral Library in 1947.
64. HCA 1135; for more on the library's construction, see Charles, B.G. and Emanuel, H.D. 'Notes on Old Libraries and Books', *Cylchgrawn Llyfrgell Genedlaethol Cymru = The National Library of Wales Journal*, **6**, 1950, pp.361-72.
65. Bowen, G. 'The Jesuit Library in Hereford Cathedral', *Bulletin of the Association of British Theological and Philosophical Libraries*, **20**, Feb. 1965, pp.13-34; **21**, Aug. 1965, pp.17-27; Thomas, H., 'The Society of Jesus in Wales, c.1600-1679: Rediscovering the Cwm Jesuit library at Hereford Cathedral', *Journal of Jesuit Studies*, **1**, 2014, pp.572-88.
66. HCL MS P.9.15, with fair copy made from it R.3.2.
67. HCA 3974i.
68. Morgan, F.C. 'Dr. William Brewster of Hereford (1665-1715): a Benefactor to Libraries,' *Medical History*, **8**, 1964, pp.137-48. In 1994 this library, with its two book presses, was transferred to the cathedral.
69. Williams, J. 'Old Books in New Buildings: the New Library Building at Hereford Cathedral', *Library History*, **14**, 1998, pp.17-22; Tiller, J. 'The New Library Building', in Aylmer (2000), pp.311-3.
70. Thurlby, M. 'Hereford Cathedral: The Romanesque Fabric', in Whitehead, D. (ed.), *Medieval Art, Architecture and Archaeology in Hereford: British Archaeological Association Conference Transactions,* **XV**, 1995, pp.15-28.
71. On the Anarchy see Bruce Coplestone-Crow in Thurlby (2013), pp.1-36.
72. Whitehead, D. 'The Mid-Nineteenth-Century Restoration of Hereford Cathedral by Lewis Knockalls Cottingham, 1842-1850', in *Medieval Art, Architecture and Archaeology at Hereford, op.cit.*, pp.176-86. The restoration was commenced in 1842 by L.N. Cottingham and continued in October 1847 by his son Knockalls Johnson Cottingham.
73. Thurlby (2013), pp.40, 58-59. See also, *The Ecclesiologist*, **IX**, No. LXXII June 1849, pp.345-7, on evidence for the correct restoration of the nave piers.
74. Thurlby (2013), p.39.
75. Zarnecki, G., Holt, J. and Holland, T., *English Romanesque Art 1066-1200*, Exhibition Catalogue, Hayward Gallery London, 5 April - 8 July 1984, pp.154-5, cat. 105.

76. Francis, K. 'The Romanesque Crossing Capitals of Southwell Minster', in Alexander, J.S. (ed.) *Southwell and Nottinghamshire: Medieval Art, Architecture, and Industry*, The British Archaeological Association Conference Transactions, **XXI**, 1998, pp.13-23.
77. Nichols, S. and Thurlby, M. 'Notes on the Romanesque Capitals from the East Arch of the Presbytery of Hereford Cathedral', *The Friends of Hereford Cathedral Fifty-First Annual Report*, 1985, pp.14-26; *English Romanesque Art 1066-1200*, *op.cit.*, pp.154-5, cat. 109.
78. Zarnecki, G. *Later English Romanesque Sculpture, 1066-1140*, Alec Tiranti, 1953, p.29; Stone, L. *Sculpture in Britain: the Middle Ages*, Penguin, 1955, p.49.
79. Thurlby, M. 'A note on the Romanesque sculpture at Hereford cathedral and the Herefordshire school of sculpture', *Burlington Magazine* cxxvi, **973**, 1984, pp.233-4. The New Minster charter is illustrated in colour, in Wilson, D. *Anglo-Saxon Art*, Thames and Hudson, 1984, pl. 261. For Nether Wallop, see Gem, R. and Tudor-Craig, P. 'A "Winchester school" wall painting at Nether Wallop, Hampshire', *Anglo-Saxon England*, **ix**, 1981, pp. 11536.
80. 'Notes on the Romanesque capitals', *op.cit.*, pp.14-26, at 16; Temple, E. *Anglo-Saxon manuscripts, 900–1066*, Miller, H. 1976, cat. 97, fig.294; Thurlby (2013), fig.247. A Troper is a book of liturgical music containing tropes or sequences, used during services in the medieval Church.
81. Hills, G.M. 'The architectural history of Hereford cathedral', *Journal of the British Archaeological Association*, **xxvii**, 1871, pp.46-84, at 52.
82. Thurlby (2013), fig.318 (Bredwardine), figs 209, 217 (Shobdon), fig.272 (Hereford, St Giles).
83. *ibid*, figs 14, 17, 28, 31 and 51.
84. Thurlby, M. and Kusaba, Y. 'The Nave of St Andrew at Steyning and Design Variety in Romanesque Architecture in Britain', *Gesta*, **XXX/2**, 1991, pp.163-75.
85. For further discussion, see Thurlby, M. 'Articulation as an expression of function in Romanesque architecture' in Jill A. Franklin, J.A., Heslop, T.A. and Anderson, C. (eds) *Architecture and Interpretation: Essays for Eric Fernie*, Boydell and Brewer, 2012, pp.42-59.
86. Thurlby (2013), pp.95-132; Baxter, R. 'St Mary, Kilpeck, Herefordshire', *The Corpus of Romanesque Sculpture in Britain and Ireland*, http://www.crsbi.ac.uk/site/810/.
87. Hart, W.H. (ed.) *Historia et Cartularium Monasterii Sancti Petri Gloucestriae*, 3 vols, Rolls Series, **I**, 1863-1867, p.16.
88. Thurlby (2013), figs 12-15, 36 and 37.
89. *ibid*, figs 22 and 23.
90. *ibid*, figs 20 and 21.
91. *ibid*, figs 229, 267, 326 and 367.
92. *ibid*, pp.46, 240-42.
93. *ibid*, pp.152-4, figs 235-6.
94. On the Eardisley font, see Wood, S. *The Eardisley Font*, Eardisley History Society, 2012; Thurlby (2013), pp.195-9; figs 28-33 for details of the interlace at Chaddesley Corbett, Eardisley and Hereford.
95. Thurlby (2013), figs 245 and 247.
96. *ibid*, pp.210-1, figs 329 and 332.
97. *ibid*, pp.215-24, 263-6,
98. *ibid*, pp.75-81, figs 94-97.
99. *ibid*, pp.174-5, figs 270 and 271; *Romanesque Architecture and Sculpture in Wales*, Logaston Press, 2006, fig. 95.
100. Zarnecki, G. 'St Michael, Moccas, Herefordshire', *The Corpus of Romanesque Sculpture in Britain and Ireland*, http://www.crsbi.ac.uk/site/490/.
101. Gethyn-Jones, E. *The Dymock School of Sculpture*, Chichester, 1979; Zarnecki, Jerzy (G.) 'Regional Schools of English Romanesque Sculpture', unpublished PhD thesis, University of London, 1950. Zarnecki, G. 'St Peter, Bromyard, Herefordshire - Hereford', *The Corpus of Romanesque Sculpture in Britain and Ireland*, http://www.crsbi.ac.uk/site/867/.
102. Thurlby (2013), figs 61, 64 and 65.
103. *ibid*, figs 71-3.
104. Drake, C.S. *The Romanesque Fonts of Northern Europe and Scandinavia*, The Boydell Press, 2002, p.15.
105. RCHM, *An Inventory of Historical Monuments in Herefordshire, II, East*, 1932, pl.54.
106. Thurlby, M. 'The Abbey Church, Pershore: An Architectural History', *Trans. Worcs.Arch. Soc.* 3rd Ser., **15**, 1996, pp.146-209 at 156.
107. On the Gloucestershire lead fonts, see Zarnecki, G. *English Romanesque Lead Sculpture*, Alec Tiranti, 1957, pp.10-14, 32-4, ills 28-31, 33, 35 and 36.
108. Thurlby (2013), pp.92-94, fig.107.
109. *ibid*, pp.240-242, fig.378.
110. *ibid*, fig.39.
111. *ibid*, pp.65, 240-2.
112. RCHM, *An Inventory of Historical Monuments in Herefordshire, I, South-West*, 1931, p.90.

113. Brakspear, H. 'A West Country School of Masons', *Archaeologia*, **81**, 1931, pp.1-18.
114. Morris, R. 'The Architectural History of the Medieval Cathedral Church', in Aylmer (2000), pp.203-40 at 209-10.

Chapter 8 Trade and Commerce in the Middle Ages

1. Hillaby, J. 'The Norman new town of Hereford ...', *TWNFC*, **44**, 1983, pp.191-3; Johnson, *Ancient Customs*, pp.32-3.
2. Hillaby, J. 'Hereford Gold: Irish, Welsh and English Land: the Jewish Community of Hereford and its clients, 1179-1253', *TWNFC*, **44**, 1984, pp.358-419.
3. List in Johnson, *Ancient Custom*, pp.229-37; Martin, S.H. 'St Guthlac's Priory and the City Churches', *TWNFC*, **34**, 1954, p.220.
4. Described in Lobel (1969), p.7; Johnson, *Ancient Customs*, pp.34-37.
5. Whitehead, D. 'The King's Acre Lime', *TWNFC*, **56**, 2008, pp.31-36.
6. Capes, W. *Charters and Records of Hereford Cathedral*, 1908, pp.130-32.
7. The early history of Widemarsh remains to be written but elements of its history can be found in Johnson *Ancient Customs*, pp.155-6; Charles, B.G. and Emmanuel, H.D. *Calendar of the earlier Cathedral Muniments* 3 vols., 1955, *passim*; Duncumb (1804), **I**, pp.410-12; Rhodes, J. (ed.) *A Calendar of the Registers of the Priory of Llanthony by Gloucester,* Gloucestershire Records Series 15, (Bristol and Gloucester Archaeological Society, 2002), pp.207, 361, 459, 481.
8. Whitehead (2007), p.18; *An Archaeological Research Framework for the City of Hereford* Herefordshire Archaeology Report 310, 2012, RP37.
9. Brian, A. 'The Tenurial History of the Lugg Meadow', *TWNFC*, **52**, 2004, pp.61-8.
10. *Calendar of the earlier Cathedral Muniments, op.cit.,* **III**, 1126, 1206.
11. Barrow, J. *English Episcopal Acta VII: Hereford 1079-1234*, 1993, pp.1-2; Whitehead (2007), pp.36-7; *Charters and Records, op.cit.*, p.36; Dew, *Extracts from the Cathedral Registers*, 1932, p.37.
12. Glassock, R.E. 'England *circa* 1334' in Darby, H.C. (ed.) *New Historical Geography,* 1976, p.184.
13. Around 200 names have been exploited, principally from the *Cathedral Muniments*.
14. Webb, J. (ed.), *The Roll of Household Expenses of Richard de Swinfield* **I** (Camden Society, 1855), p.91.
15. HMC *The Manuscripts of Rye and Hereford Corporations etc.* 13th Report, Appendix, Part IV, 1892, p.292.
16. *Household Expenses, op.cit.,* **II**, 1854, c.
17. *Ibid,* **I**, 1853, pp.89, 188, 192, 70, 68, 146; for Adam *Pictoris* see *Pipe Rolls*, 5 John (1203), 55.
18. Bacon, O. 'Brecon Priory Church: Rebuilding the Nave'. *Brycheiniog*, **27**, 1994/5, pp.43-52.
19. Harvey, J. *Medieval Architects*, p.207.
20. *Charters and Records, op.cit.*, XXXII-III.
21. *Cal. Pat.* 1247-58, 40.
22. *The Manuscripts of Rye and Hereford Corporations, op.cit,* pp.284, 279.
23. *Charters and Records, op.cit.*, pp.4, 13; *Extracts from the Cathedral Registers, op.cit.,* p.7.
24. *Close Rolls*, 1227-31, 537; *Pat. Rolls*, 1258-66, 196, 208.
25. *Register of Thomas Cantilupe*, 1906, pp.83, 91; *Regesta Regum* **II**, p.159.
26. Dyer, C. *Making a Living in the Middle Ages,* 2002, pp.228-51; Horrox, R. and Ormrod, W.M. (eds) *A Social History of England 1200-1500*, 2006, pp.1-30.
27. *Register of Thomas Charlton*, 1913, pp.8-9 – notices the 'great multitude of Welshmen (who) flow daily towards (England)'.
28. Langford, A.W. 'The Plague in Herefordshire', *TWNFC*, **35**, 1956, p.48; Lobel (1969), p.8, note 27.
29. *Cal. Pat.* 1381-85, 216, 225, 328; *Cal. Inquisitions Miscellaneous* 1348-77, 261; Johnson, *Ancient Customs*, pp.52-3.
30. *The Manuscripts of Rye and Hereford Corporations, op.cit,* p.286.
31. All the references in this section come from *Calendar of the earlier Cathedral Muniments, op.cit.,* **I-III**.
32. Johnson, *Ancient Customs*, 29.14.
33. *Register of Adam of Orleton*, 1907, pp.76-7, 131; Marshall, G. 'The Shrine of St Thomas de Cantilupe in Hereford Cathedral', *TWNFC*, 1930, pp.40-43.
34. *Ibid;* Morgan, P. 'The Effect of the Pilgrim Cult of St Thomas Cantilupe on Hereford Cathedral', pp.145-52.
35. *Making a Living in the Middle Ages, op.cit.,* pp.240-3.
36. *Extracts from the Cathedral Registers, op.cit,* p.9.
37. Williams, D.H. 'The Abbey of Dore' in Shoesmith, R. and Richardson, R. (eds) *The Definitive History of Dore Abbey,* Logaston Press, 1977, pp.31, 35.
38. *Cal. Pat.* 1354-58, 262; *Register of John of Trillek*, 1910, p.227.

39. Hereford Cathedral Library, HCA 2393.
40. *Cal. Inquisitions Miscellaneous* 1399-1422, 150; *Calendar of the earlier Cathedral Muniments, op.cit.*, **III**, 1123.
41. *Extracts from the Cathedral Registers, op.cit.*, p.81.
42. Williams, D.H. *White Monks of Gwent and the Border*, 1976, pp.49-50.
43. Watkins, A. 'Three Early Timber Halls in the City', *TWNFC*, 1919, pp.165-8; Lobel (1969), p.8.
44. Pevsner (2012), p.327.
45. *Extracts from the Cathedral Registers, op.cit.*, p.123.
46. *Ibid, pp.*84-5.
47. *Cal. Pat.*1391-6, 591.
48. *Extracts from the Cathedral Registers, op.cit.*, p.111; *Calendar of the earlier Cathedral Muniments, op.cit.*, **III**, 1095.
49. Shoesmith (1980), see also note 2 above.
50. *Charters and Records, op.cit.*, **X**, p.197.
51. *Cal. Pat.* 1377-81, 120.
52. Charles and Emmanuel, *Cath. Muns.* III, 1064; Capes, *Charters and Records*, 251-2; Dew, *Extracts*, 91.
53. *Calendar of the earlier Cathedral Muniments, op.cit.*, **III**, 1141-2.
54. *Ibid.*, **III**, 1246, 1223, 1082; HRO, *Records of Hereford City: Muniments of Title*, pp.194, 216.
55. *The Manuscripts of Rye and Hereford Corporations, op.cit.*, pp.298-9.
56. *Calendar of the earlier Cathedral Muniments, op.cit.*, **III**, 1028-9
57. Dyer, A. *Decline and Growth in English Towns 1400-1640*, 1991, pp.12-13.
58. Johnson, *Ancient Customs*, 116.
59. Pinches, S. *Ledbury – a market town and its Tudor heritage*, 2009, pp.35-39.
60. *The Manuscripts of Rye and Hereford Corporations, op.cit.*, p.322.
61. HRO, CF50; Bannister, A.T. 'The Possessions of St Guthlac's Priory, Hereford', *TWNFC*, 1918, pp.34-42.

Chapter 9 The Medieval Buildings of Hereford
This chapter owes much to the research carried out for Baker, N., P. Hughes and R.K. Morriss *The Houses of Hereford 1200-1700*, forthcoming.
1. Olver, P. 'Geology and Building Stones' in Pevsner (2012), pp.3-10; Kendrick. F.M., 'Some Reflections on the use of Natural Products in Herefordshire' (Presidential Address), *TWNFC*, 1967, **39**, pp.7-10.
2. Vince, A.G., 'The Ceramic Finds' in Shoesmith (1985), pp.34-83.
3. There is some confusion about the dates of these clergy. *Fasti Herefordensis* places Viall's death in 1513 but his will is clearly dated 6 July 1525.
4. This section is based on the work of Kathryn Davies in *Artisan Art, Vernacular wall paintings in the Welsh Marches, 1550-1650*, Logaston Press, 2008.
5. Swanson, R. and Lepine, D. Aylmer (2000), pp.54-5.
6. Radford, R., Tope & Tonkin, J. 'The Great Hall of the Bishop's Palace at Hereford', *Medieval Archaeology*, **4**, pp.83-86.
7. Blair, J. 'The Twelfth-Century Bishop's Palace at Hereford', *Medieval Archaeology*, **XXX1**, 1987, p.65.
8. 'A Contract and Schedule of Works supplied to the builder', HRO HD 8/17.
9. RCHM *Herefordshire* Vol I, 1931, p.114.
10. Aylmer (2000).
11. Shoesmith, R. 'A Brave & Ancient Priviledg'd Place – The Hereford Vicars Choral College' in Hill, R. and Stocker, D. (eds) *Vicars Choral at English cathedrals – Cantate Domino*, Oxford, 2005.
12. Heref Cath Lib. 7003/1/1 p.13.
13. HRO K11/3796.
14. 'A Brave & Ancient Priviledg'd Place ...', *op.cit.*
15. HCA 3996.
16. Hereford Cathedral Muniments Vol. I, p.466.
17. Hereford Cathedral Muniments Vol III, p.1104.
18. Heref. Cath Lib. Chapter Act Book Vol 1, 1515.
19. Watkins, A. 'Three early timber framed halls in the city of Hereford, *TWNFC*, **23**, 1919, 164-71. The 18th- and 19th-century title deeds for Harley Court can be found at Heref. Cath. Lib. 4520 (i –xxxvi)
20. RCHM *Herefordshire* Vol I, 1931, p.141.
21. *ibid*, p.142.
22. Capes, W.W. *Register of Thomas de Charlton*, Hereford, 1912.
23. The use of surnames at the period was not fully established. John was known both by his surname and his trade.
24. Capes, W.W. *Register of John Trefnant 1389-1404*, Hereford, 1914, p.145.
25. Bannister, T. (ed.) *Registrium Thome Spofford*, Hereford, 1917, p.112.
26. The inventory was found in the HRO Hereford City Misc. papers VI 42. A printed slip dates it erroneously to 1514/15.
27. HCL 7031/4 f.96v; HCL 7031/4 f 196/7; *ibid.* 395
28. See census records 1861, 1871, 1881.
29. Aylmer (2000), p.34.

30. Shoesmith, R., 'Hereford Cathedral Barn', *TWNFC*, **59**, 2011, pp.125-146.
31. *ibid.*
32. Tyers, I., 'Tree-ring analysis of six secular buildings from the City of Hereford', Ancient Monuments Laboratory Report 17/96, Historic Buildings and Monuments Commission for England, interim report.
33. Unpublished report for their visit HCA 6526.
34. Chapter Act Book, Hereford Cath Lib. 1571 p.34v. The marginal note has been added to this earlier volume in a hand similar to that used for such notes until *c.*1640.
35. HRO HD 10/47.
36. Aylmer (2000)*,* pp.566-78
37. Shoesmith, R. *Hereford: History and Guide*, Alan Sutton, 1992, p.20.
38. Although there are no early title deeds for the property, it has been possible to track the occupants back via the assessments for poor rate in the series of St Peter's parish rate books (1696-1720). From these there is sufficient correlation and overlap to identify the properties in the Hearth Taxes of 1664 and 1665. For more detailed information see Baker, N. *et al The Houses of Hereford* (forthcoming).
39. HRO Hereford City Archives Lawday 1625.
40. HRO Hereford City Archives Lawday 1661.
41. Much information concerning the Booth Hall can be found in Watkins, A.'The Boothall Inn', *TWNFC*, 1919, p.165; Powell, H.J. 'The Booth Hall', *TWNFC*, 1959, p.206; Watkins, A. 'The Freemen's Prison', *TWNFC*, 1934, p.49*;* Report, 'Dinner at the Booth Hall' *TWNFC*, 1921, p.xxxv.
42. Most of the early records for the Booth Hall come from HRO Corporation Archives Box 1. The loose accounts are endorsed Sack 3 Bundle 6.
43. HRO GH 1.
44. From Deeds and abstract of title Hereford Corporation deeds box 1.
45. HRO Transcripts of Sacks 15-19 p.31.
46. Shoesmith, R. *The Pubs of Hereford City*, Logaston Press, 2004, pp.46-54
47. Sacks 1624.
48. HRO AM 29/1.
49. HRO Transcripts of Sacks 17-19 p.353.
50. HRO Transcripts of Sacks 17-19 p.353.
51. HRO AP39/183 also BH22/1; BH22/3; HA 31/3; Hereford Corporation deeds box 1
52. Hereford Cath. Lib. 7031/f.7031.
53. HRO Hereford City Archives Lawday 1478 & 1499.
54. HRO P1/5 f.276 Great Black Book.
55. HRO AC 7/22.
56. HRO William Bullock 16th March 1709.
57. Hereford Cath Lib 5253, 5254, 6442; Hereford Charity Commissioners p.298.
58. HRO Corporation deeds box 1.
59. HRO HA 31/344.
60. HRO Hereford City Documents transcripts volume 16-19.
61. Hereford City Documents transcripts volume 16-19. HRO Transcripts of Sacks.

Chapter 10 The Civil War

1. Much of the text for this chapter is taken from Shoesmith, R. *The Civil War in Hereford*, Logaston Press, 1995. David Whitehead's help with the latter part of the chapter is acknowledged. There are many general works on the Civil War; the following are relatively recent and were also used in the preparation of this chapter. Downing, T. and Millman, M. *Civil War*, London, 1991; Porter, S. *Destruction in the English Civil War*, Stroud, 1994; Sherwood, R., *The Civil War in the Midlands,1642-1651*, Stroud, 1992. More local sources specifically concerning the war include: Webb, J. (ed.), T.W. Webb *Memorials of the civil War between King Charles I and the Parliament of England as it affected Herefordshire and the adjacent counties*, 2 Volumes, London, 1879; Webb, J. (ed.); T.W. Webb *Military Memoir of Colonel John Birch ... written by Roe, his secretary ...*, Camden Soc., New Series, **VII**, London, 1873; Whelan, B., 'Hereford and the Civil War', *The Dublin Review*, July-September 1926, pp.44-72; Duncumb (1804), **1**; Heath-Agnew, E. *Roundhead to Royalist, A Biography of Colonel John Birch*, Hereford, 1977.
2. N. Wharton, Letter IX in 'Letters from a Subaltern in the Earl of Essex's Army ...', *Archaeologia*, **xxxv**, Society of Antiquaries, London, 1853, pp.331-3.
3. Webb, J. 'Some Passages in the Life and character of a Lady resident in Herefordshire and Worcestershire during the Civil War ... collected from her Account-book ...', *Archaeologia*, **XXXVII**, 1857.
4. Lewis, T.T., *Letters of the Lady Brilliana Harley ...*, Camden Society, 1854.
5. Watkins, A., 'Roaring Meg', *TWNFC*, **23**, 1919, pp.172-4.

Chapter 11 Faith and Religion

1. Finucane, R.C. 'Cantilupe as Thaumaturge: Pilgrims and their "Miracles"', in Jancey, M. (ed.) *St Thomas Cantilupe, Bishop of Hereford*, 1982, pp.137-144.

2. Finucane, R.C. *Miracles and Pilgrims. Popular Beliefs in Medieval England*, Dent, 1977, p.98. This is a book to which the present account is greatly indebted.
3. Shoesmith, R. & Morriss, R.K. 'The Hereford Blackfriars', Nov. 1988, Hereford Archaeology Series, 38. (Herefordshire Through Time ref: SHE 10321).
4. This section owes much to S. Martin, *The Black Death*, Chartwell Books, 2009.
5. Benedictow, O.J. *The Black Death 1346-1353: The Complete History*, Boydell & Brewer, 2004.
6. Dew, E.N. (trans.), *Extracts from the Cathedral Registers, AD 1275-1535*, Hereford Times, 1932, p.120.
7. For the English Reformation in general see especially Dickens , A.G. *The English Reformation*, London, 1964, 2nd edn., London 1989, and Haigh, C. *English Reformations: Religion, Politics, and Society under the Tudors*, Oxford University Press, 1993. For the continental Reformation, see Cameron, E. *The European Reformation*, Oxford University Press, 1991, and Chadwick, O. *The Penguin History of the Church, The Reformation*, 1990.
8. For the history of the school see Tomlinson, Howard *Hereford Cathedral School, A History over 800 years*, Logaston Press, 2018 and Orme, N. 'The cathedral school before the Reformation', in Aylmer (2000), pp.565-78.
9. For medieval bishops in general, and the life of the cathedral in the middle ages, see Aylmer (2000), and Moir, A.L., 'The bishops of Hereford', *TWNFC*, 1955-57, pp.117-33 and *The Bishops of Hereford their Cathedral and Palace*, Hereford Cathedral, 1964.
10. For a general history of the churches in England in the period 1660-1833, see Hylson-Smith, K. *The Churches in England from Elizabeth I to Elizabeth II*, vol. I, 1558-1688, and vol. II, 1689-1833.
11. For the history of the Dissenters in England from the Restoration to 1837, see Watts, M.R., *The Dissenters. Vol I: From the Reformation to the French Revolution*, Oxford University Press, 1978 and *The Dissenters. Vol II: The Expansion of Evangelical Nonconformity*, Oxford University Press, 1995.
12. For the history of the Roman Catholics in Herefordshire in the period from 1660 to 1837 see Blacklock, F.G. *The Suppressed Benedictine Minster and other Ancient and Modern Institutions of the Borough of Leominster*, Leominster, 1897, p.271; Coleman, D. *Orcop. The Story of a Herefordshire Village from Pre-history to Present Times*, 1992, p.226; Cummins, J.L. *Catholic Martyrs of Herefordshire*; Holt, T.C. 'The Jesuits in Hereford from 1760 till 1857', *Worcester Recusant*, June 1983, p.41; Reeves, N. *The Leon Valley. Three Herefordshire Villages Kingsland, Monkland and Eardisland*, Phillimore, 1980, pp.33-4, 110-11 and *The Parish of Saint Ethelbert*, Leominster, 1873, pp.11-3; Salt, A.E. 'The church in Herefordshire. The Restoration (1660) to the Georges (1714)', *TWNFC*, 1946-8, pp.176-7.
13. Pevsner (2012), p.312.

Chapter 12 Georgian Hereford
1. This chapter was written at a time when the Hereford Record Office was closed. The city records were thus, inaccessible and the content of the chapter was therefore based upon earlier research carried out for different purposes in the 1970s and '80s. Moreover, some of the records may have been reclassified since that time. The referencing of this chapter has been fairly light since the context often indicates the sources, which for a large part of the chapter were the council minute books from *c*.1690-1775. From 1770 the *Hereford Journal* becomes a particularly valuable source of information.
2. Parker, G. *Global Crisis: War, Climate, Change and Catastrophe in the 17th Century*, 2013; Henshall, Nicholas *The Zenith of European Monarchy and it Elites: The Politics of Culture 1650-1750*, 2010.
3. Jancey, E.M. *The Royal Charters of the City of Hereford*, 1973, pp.8, 25; HRO, Minutes and Proceedings of the Common Council of the City of Hereford, 1693-1707, 1729-36, ff.39-97.
4. Williams, W.R. *Herefordshire Members 1213-1896*, 1896, pp.92-103.
5. HRO, Minutes 1673-1736, *passim*.
6. Collins-Baker, C.H. & M. *The Life and Circumstances of James Brydges, First Duke of Chandos*, 1949, p.27.
7. HRO, Minutes, 1693-1736, ff.77, 78, 84, 100.
8. *ibid,* ff.99, 108, 117, 120-1.
9. HRO, Records of Hereford City: Muniments of Title: a Calendar, *passim*.
10. HRO, Minutes, 1693-1736, *passim*; HMC 13th Report, Appendix, Part IV, *The Manuscripts of Hereford Corporation*, 1892, pp.346-9; *Charity Commissioners' Report*, 1838, *passim*.
11. HRO, Minutes, 1693-1736, ff.65; *Charity Commissioners' Report, op.cit.*, pp.57-9.

12. HRO, Minutes, 1755-78, f.191; Shoesmith, R. & Crosskey, C., 'Go to Gaol in Hereford', *TWNFC*, 1994, pp.101-3.
13. HRO, Minutes, 1693-1736 and 1755-78, *passim*.
14. *ibid*; HRO, F.C. Morgan transcripts, sacks 24-27, 101; for Moor House see *Place: Hereford Civic Society Newsletter*, Spring, 2015, p.6.
15. Ellis, J.M. *The Georgian Town, 1680-1840*, 2001, 148-9; Lobel (1969), p.10.
16. Defoe, D. *A Tour Through ... through Great Britain*, Everyman, 1962, p.50; Morris, C. (ed.) *The Journeys of Celia Fiennes*, Cresset Press, 1947, p.44.
17. Duncumb (1804), **I**, p.18; HRO, Minutes, 1693-1736, f.179; Catalogue of Hereford City Mss., **I**, p.30.
18. HMC *Portland* **II**, 1893, p.292; Simpson, S. *The Agreeable Historian*, 1746, p.226; Whitehead, D. & Shoesmith, R. *James Wathen's Herefordshire*, Logaston Press, 1994, pp.1-2.
19. Price, J. *Historical Account of the City of Hereford*, 1796, pp.64-5; Duncumb (1804), **I**, p.354; Whitehead, D. *The Book of Worcester*, 1976, p.129.
20. Duncumb (1804), **I**, pp.381-4.
21. HRO, Minutes 1755-78, f.291; *The Hereford Guide*, 1806, 48; *Historical Account, op.cit.*, p.65.
22. HRO, Minutes, 1693-1736, *passim*; Calendar of the Guildhall Collection, HA108/77; HMC *Portland* **II**, 1893, p.292; Spicksley, J. *The Business and Household Accounts of Joyce Jeffries*, 2012, p.20.
23. *The Georgian Town, op.cit.*, pp.10-24.
24. *Hereford Journal* 17 June 1779, 13 January 1780, 8 May 1777.
25. HRO, Minutes, 1693-1736, *passim*.
26. *ibid*; Hereford Cathedral Library, Fabric Accounts, 1721-2, 1727-8, 1737-8 – ex. inf. Rosalind Caird. Simon Fisher's paintings can be found in the houses mentioned, except Holme Lacy in the British Library and Hampton Court in a private collection; HRO, Minutes, 1708-54, f.472; Minutes 1755-78, f.100; Watkins, C. and Cowell, B. *Uvedale Price*, 2012, pp.30, 159, 160, 184.
27. HRO, Order Book of the Commissioners of the Hereford Paving Act, 1778-1810, f.94; Guildhall Coll. 1, 550.
28. *ibid*, Guildhall Coll. HA/108,178, 11/1; *The Manuscripts of Hereford Corporation, op.cit.*, p.352; HRO, Paving Commissioners, f. 27.
29. *The Manuscripts of Hereford Corporation, op.cit.*, p.351; Macray, W.D. (ed.), *Ms Papers, Proclamations and other Documents of the City of Hereford*, 1894, p.31.
30. Thompson, E.P. 'Hunting the Jacobin Fox' in *Past and Present* **142**, 1994, pp.112-15.
31. HMC *Portland* **II**, p.292; HRO Minutes, 1755-1778, f.40; LC Deeds 3594 (i); Guildhall, HA 11/4; Paving Commissioners, f.159.
32. Connor, H. 'Mistress Joyce Jeffreys and her physician, Dr. Bridstock Harford (1607-1695)', *Journal of Medical Biography* (Online First), 18 December 2014; *The Manuscripts of Hereford Corporation, op.cit.*, p.339; Langford, A.W. 'Some Herefordshire Medical History', *TWNFC*, 1958, p.62; HRO, Paving Commissioners, f.24; Minutes, 1693-1736, f.103.
33. HRO, LC Deeds 7595 (i); *Hereford Guide*, 1806, p.44; HRO, Guildhall GH 2/40; HA 11/7; for Bird HRO, M26.
34. Whitehead, D. & Budd, A. *St Martin's, Hereford 1560-1640*, 1977, 12-16; Lobel (1969), p.30.
35. *The Manuscripts of Hereford Corporation, op.cit.*, pp.348, 351; HRO, Minutes, 1693-36, *passim*; on Malvernian brick see Whitehead, D. 'Brick and tile making in the woodlands of the West Midlands in the 16th and 17th centuries' in *Vernacular Architecture* **12**, 1981, pp.44-46; Aylmer (2000), p.119.
36. Davey, E. & Roseff, R. *Herefordshire Bricks and Brickmakers,* Logaston Press, 2007, pp.15-20; Dyer, A. 'Wood and Coal: a Change of Fuel', *History Today,* September 1976, pp.598-607.
37. Nef, J.U. *The Rise of the British Coal Industry*, **I**, 1932, pp.215-21; Hughes, P. & Leech, A. *The Story of Worcester*, Logaston Press, 2011, pp.68-9; Kingman, M. 'The Adoption of Brick in Urban Staffordshire, 1665-1760', *Midland History* **35** (I), 2010, pp.89-106.
38. HRO, Guildhall, HA 111/3; F.C. Morgan transcripts, sacks 15-19, 93, 101, 110; *The Manuscripts of Hereford Corporation, op.cit.*, p.346; Whitehead, D. 'The Sack Warehouse, Wye Street, Hereford', *Hereford Civic Trust Newsletter*, **30**, May 1983, pp.1-3.
39. Oliver, R.C.B. 'The Hartstonges and Radnorshire: Part I', *Rads. Society Trans.* **XLIII**, 1973, pp.40-48; Duncumb (1804), **I**, pp.563, 598.
40. HRO, Minutes 1693-1736, f.77, 80-81; Minutes 1755-78, f.275; Quarter Sessions Minute Book, 1792-97, f.43.
41. Henshall, N. 'Kingdom, Power and Glory', *History Today,* **63**, (II), 2013, pp.12-13; Whitehead (2007), pp.56-58.

42. HRO, LC Deeds, 3594(i) – Mansion House; Paving Commissioners Order Book, *passim*.
43. The work of Thomas Symonds is listed in Colvin, H. *A Biographical Dictionary of British Architects 1660-1840*, 2008, p.106; his monuments in Roscoe, I. *A Biographical Dictionary of Sculptors in Britain 1660-1851*, 2009, p.1218; his career as the surveyor of the fabric at the cathedral in Whitehead, D. 'A Goth among the Greeks', *Friends of the Cathedral Annual Report*, **57**, 1991, pp.35-8; his interest in gothic architecture also Whitehead, David 'Artisan Attitudes of Gothic in Georgian Herefordshire', *Georgian Group Journal*, **XVII**, 2009, pp.68-75.
44. 'Goth among the Greeks', *op.cit.*, pp.36-8; Whitehead in Aylmer (2000), pp.259-64.
45. Whitehead, D. 'Historical background to the city defences' in Shoesmith (1982), pp.23-4; Bruyn-Andrews, C. (ed.) *The Torrington Diaries*, **I**, 1934, pp.127, 316.
46. HRO, Minutes 1708-54, f.478; 1755-1778, ff.65, 76, 86; Whitehead, D. 'John Nash and Humphry Repton: an Encounter in Herefordshire, 1785-98', *TWNFC*, 1992, pp.228-31; for Gethin *Hereford Journal*, 25 October 1826.
47. Wye & Lugg Navigation Act 1695 HCL.
48. Wye and Lugg accounts 1696-1700 HRO K12/33.
49. Hurley, H., *Herefordshire's River Trade*, Logaston Press, 2013, chapter ten.
50. Kissack, K, *Monmouth*, 1975, p.287.
51. LOWV, Barge accounts.
52. *Herefordshire's River Trade, op.cit*, chapter five.
53. Hereford Corporation HRO G.H. 1/146-183.
54. from HRO AA20/D/Viol 6.
55. Eisel, J. 'Life on the River', *Herefordshire Miscellany*, Woolhope Naturalists' Field Club, 2000, pp.52-53.
56. Waters, I., *The Port of Chepstow*, 1977, p.28.
57. 1822 Directory, Pulling's accounts HRO BB77, Farr, G., *Chepstow Ships*, 1954, LOWV barge accounts.
58. Hurley, H. *River Trade, op.cit.*, chapter two.
59. LOWV barge accounts.
60. *Herefordshire's River Trade, op.cit.*, chapter ten.
61. Shoesmith, R. *Hereford: History and Guide*, Alan Sutton, 1992, pp.77-8.
62. Info John Eisel 2011, Woodhouse accounts HRO L24, Leech account HCA 5715-3.
63. LOWV barge accounts; Pulling accounts HRO BB77.
64. *History of Tyberton Church*, 2004.
65. *Herefordshire's River Trade, op.cit.*, chapter eleven; *Hereford Journal* 13 Feb 1772.
66. LOWV barge accounts; *Hereford Journal* 5 May 1824.
67. Directories 1844, 1851, Pulling accounts BB77 (uncatalogued).
68. HRO, Minutes 1693-1736, f.26.
69. *The Manuscripts of Hereford Corporation*, *op.cit.*, p.349; HRO, Minutes 1693-36, f.142.
70. HRO, Minutes 1755-78, passim.
71. Nehemiah Wharton (1642) in *Cal. State Papers Dom.* **XVIII**, p.399; Eisel, J. 'Notes on the former Hereford Market Hall', *TWNFC*, **53**, 2005, p.27.
72. Whitehead, D. 'Goths and Vandals: Restoring Historic Buildings in Georgian Herefordshire', *Georgian Group Jnl.*, **XVIII**, 2010, pp.115-123.
73. HRO, Minutes 1755-78, f.354; Market Hall Account Book, 1811-12.
74. Whitehead (2007), pp.67-70; 'John Nash and Humphry Repton', *op.cit.*, pp.212-13; 'Go to Gaol', *op.cit.*, pp.108-24.
75. Martin, S.H. 'Ullingswick, the Infirmary and Dr. Johnson', *TWNFC*, **XXXV**, 1957, pp.293-8; Duncumb (1804), pp.433-6; Langford, A.W. 'The History of Hereford General Hospital', *TWNFC*, 1959, pp.149-54; *Hereford Journal* 8 August 1776; 23 December 1793, 25 July 1794; HCL, Pamphlets 34, f.54.
76. Hurley, H., *The Old Roads of South Herefordshire*, 2nd edition 2007, p.24.
77. Ledbury Road Act 1721 HCL, Gloucester Road Act 1726 HRO K38/Ce/vi/6, Hereford Road Act 1729 HCL.
78. Hereford Road Act 1729 HCL, *Old Roads, op.cit.*, pp.36-41.
79. Hereford Trust Tolls *c*.1850 HCL fp LC386.
80. *Old Roads, op.cit.*, p.104.
81. HRO, Q/A5/15; Q/AS/1-12; *HJ* 24 August 1814-26 April 1815; Eastnor Castle Muniments, Smirke correspondence.
82. Eastnor, Smirke correspondence; for Heather – see Pickford, C. 'The County Surveyors of Herefordshire', *TWNFC*, **58**, 2010, pp.181-3 and Whitehead, D. 'Rebuilding a career: John Nash in Herefordshire 1790-1800' in Tyack, G. (ed.), *John Nash: Architect of the Picturesque*, 2013, pp.31-2.
83. HRO, Q/A5/15; *Hereford Journal* 21 August 1816 - 3 September 1818.
84. Borsay, P. *The English Urban Renaissance*, 1989; see *The Georgian Town, op.cit.*, pp.79-86 for a more critical view. *Hereford Journal*, 10, 17 & 24 September 1800.

85. This section is based principally upon the advertisements in the *Hereford Journal* from 1770 to *c.*1790; Lysons, D. *The Origin and Progress of the Meeting of the Three Choirs*, 1895; for Leeming see http://streathambrixtonchess.blogspot.com/2011/03evert-picture-tells-a-story-ThomasLeeming; Cox in Solly, N.N. *Memoir of the Life of David Cox,* 1873, 34-50 and *Hereford Journal* 25 February 1818.
86. Haig, R. *A History of Theatres and Performers in Herefordshire*, Logaston Press, 2002, pp.35-43, 47-9, 85-6.
87. *James Wathen's Herefordshire, op.cit.,* p.3, quoting Warner, R. *Literary Recollections* **I**, 1830, pp.387-8; Wilson, B. *The Making of Victorian Values,* 2007, *passim*.

Chapter 13 Victorian Hereford
1. Norfolk Terrace does not appear on H. Price's map of Hereford, surveyed in 1802 and published in 1803. The first reference to Norfolk Terrace so far traced in the *Hereford Journal* occurs in an advert of 22 June 1808.
2. *Hereford Journal* 31 July 1799. Jones, *The Visitor's and Resident's Guide to the City of Hereford, … ,*1866, pp.39-40. Initially a charitable institution, on 23 December 1801 an advert in the *Hereford Journal* stated that it was then open to all patients on terms adapted to their circumstances.
3. This is often called the Lamp Act. The official title was 'An Act for paving, repairing, cleansing, and lighting, the Streets and Lanes in the City of Hereford, and Suburbs thereof, and removing Nuisances and Annoyances thereof, and for creating a Fund towards the Expences thereof, by inclosing divers waste Grounds within the Liberties of the said City, and for the better Application of Charity-money for setting the poor People of the said City to Work, and to enable Bodies Corporate to alienate their Houses and Lands within the said City.' The Act was amended 1816 and then in 1838 as part of the Act that reduced the length of St Ethelbert's Fair in May each year.
4. *Hereford Times* 24 May 1845.
5. This section is based on Wood, G. *Railways of Hereford*, 2003, and Smith, W.H. *Herefordshire Railways*, 1998.
6. The three connected tram roads that linked Hereford to Abergavenny were bought by the Newport, Abergavenny and Hereford Railway, but because of financial problems the sale was not completed until February 1852 (*Hereford Times* 28 February 1852). The line was closed temporarily from 30 Nov. - 30 Dec. 1852 (*Hereford Times* 6 November 1852), and then finally on 1 May 1853, at which time the cast-iron tram plates, tie-bars and chains were offered for sale by tender (*Hereford Times* 16 April 1853).
7. Summarised from Hadfield, C. *Canals of South Wales and the Border*, 1960, pp.206-8. Also Bick, D. *The Hereford and Gloucester Canal*, New Edition 2003), p.58.
8. The cost would include not only the cost of the land, but a charge for legal work, fencing, and making up the roads on the estates. The word allotment did not have the connotations that it does today, and merely means an allocation of land, whatever its subsequent use.
9. The history of the activities of the Hereford Freehold Land Society is considered in Eisel, J.C. 'The History of the Hereford Freehold Land Society and the expansion of Hereford in the Nineteenth Century,' in *TWNFC* (forthcoming).
10. One of the lots has a meadow on the north side of the building plots which lined Broomy Hill, and this subsequently was bought by the Hereford Freehold Land Society, on which it developed the Barton Estate, by building Tower Road, and allotting to members the building plots which lined it.
11. *Hereford Journal* 13 Sept, 1862, *Hereford Times* 13 Sept. 1862.
12. Overbury House was advertised as being to let, *Hereford Journal* 1 December 1842; and Athelstan Hall advertised as being to let *Hereford Times* 21 July 1860. The date for Broadlands is given in Pevsner (2012), p.354.
13. The first reference to North Villas in the local press is in *Hereford Times* 20 Nov. 1858.
14. A mistake was made in drawing up the 1854 Act, concerning the relation between the scope of the Act and the Turnpike Act then in force, and in 1855 an Act to correct that oversight had to be brought into law.
15. Summarised, with additions, from O'Donnell, J. *John Venn and the Friends of the Hereford Poor*, Logaston Press, 2007.

Chapter 14 Literature and the Arts
1. For a discussion of the debate, see Eisel, J.C. 'The Herefordshire Philosophical Society', *TWNFC*, 2011, p.65.
2. Although no definite evidence has been found, there is strong circumstantial evidence to suggest

that a date late in 1851 is correct. For instance, R.M. Lingwood, first president of the Woolhope Club, was a member of the Philosophical Society, but on 7 July 1851 he gave notice that he would withdraw from that society with effect from the end of the year. This rather suggests that the proposal for a new club had reached the planning stage, and that he anticipated becoming a member, he being a man of wide scientific attainment and interests. For Lingwood's full story see *TWNFC*, **57**, 2000, pp.103-9.

3. For a full discussion of early Herefordshire photographers see Eisel, J.C. 'Early Herefordshire Photographers', in *Essays in Honour of Jim & Muriel Tonkin*, 2011.

4. A full discussion of Alfred Watkins' life and work is given in Shoesmith, R., *Alfred Watkins, A Herefordshire Man*, Logaston Press, 1990.

5. A collection in aid of the widows and orphans of the clergy was first implemented in 1724, which was thus counted as the first in this series. However, there had been annual meetings of the three choirs prior to this date.

Chapter 15 Hereford in the 20th and 21st centuries
Much of the information for this chapter is owed to Roberts, G. *The Shaping of Modern Hereford*, Logaston Press, 2001.

Index of Personal Names

Abbott, Edward 205
Abel, John 141, 155
Adelard of Bath 83
Addis, Thomas 199
Aelfgar of Mercia 22
Aelfnoth, Sheriff 22
Aelfstan, Ealdorman 19
Aelfwig, moneyer 33
Aethelbald, King 12, 13, 15
Aethelstan, King 21
Æthelstan, moneyer 33
Aethelwulf, Bishop 19
Aldwyn, Prior 33
Alexander IV, Pope 80
Alderne, Captain 156, 158
Alfonsi, Petrus 82
Alfred of Shareshill 83, 91
Allen, John 197, 198-99
Alice 'of the kechyn' 126
Andrews, Bridget 198
    Richard 120
Apperley, John 191, 201
Aquablanca, Bishop Peter d' 69-70, 71, 110, 171
Aquinas, St Thomas 71
Aristotle 83-84
Ashby, Canon 128
Aston, John 175
Atforton, Alice de 79
Athelstan, Bishop 19, 21, 61, 89
Atkins, Ivor 262
Atkinson, William 215
    Mr (theatre manager) 252
Aubrey, John 163
Audland, John 183
Audley, Bishop 74
    James 58
Avicenna 84

Bacon, Roger 84
Baker, William (glover) 190
    William (barge owner) 207
Ballard, Stephen 223
    Lt 158
Banister, Thomas 196
Barlow, Elizabeth 185
    John 179

Bar(n)ard, Mary 48
Barnold, Col 150
Barrett, Robert 238
Baskerville, Thomas 194, 195, 199
Beauchamp, Earl Thomas de 58
    William de 171
Beauclerk, Bishop Lord James 163, 195
Beaufort, Edward, Duke of Somerset 112
Bec, Robert de 36-37
Becket, Archbishop Thomas 70, 84
Bell, Stephen 176
Bennett, Charles 239
Benny, Philip 182
Benson, Dean George 185
Bernard, chaplain 71
Béthune, Bishop Robert de 61, 65, 78, 93
Beonna, Bishop 19
Berewe, John 128
Berrow, 'constable' 156-58
Birch, Col John 156-62
Bird, Thomas 200, 209
Biss, James 207
Bisse, Dr Thomas 261
    Bishop 121
Black, Edward 203
Blake, Thomas 259
Blethyn 29
Boden, Anthony 262
Bodenham, Charles 280
    Sheriff John 59
Bodenham-Lubienski, Count Louis 280
Bodley, Sir Thomas 92
Bolton, George 252
Booth, Bishop Charles 74, 91
Bonner, Bishop Edmund 179
Bosley, William 251
Boulers, Bishop Reginald 112
Boure, William 110
Bowen, William 135
Bradford, George 195
Brakspear, Sir Harold 99
Brecon, Walter de 104

Brewster, Dr William 92, 204
Brian, Count 30
Bridges, Sir John 156
Briouze/Braose, Bishop Giles de 66
    William de 66
Bromwich, family 137
    Richard & Matilda 137
Brown, Mr R. 274
Brugge, Simon & Isabella de 110
Brunel, Isambard Kingdom 225
Brut, Walter 176
Brydges, James, Lord Chandos 188, 204
Buck, Samuel & Nathaniel 192-93
Buckle, George 207
Bull, Henry Graves 245
    Edith 249
Bullock, Mr 245
Bullock, William 138
Bulmer, Revd C.H. 273
    Fred 273
    Henry Percy 273
Bunning, Mr 207
Burnett, Charles 89
Bustin, Richard 258
Butler, Bishop James 204
Buyton, Henry 131

Cachepole, Henry 134
Cadwallador, Roger 180
Cam, John 199
Camm, John 183
Cantilupe, Bishop Thomas de 71, 85, 109, 165-68
    canonisation of 168
Carpenter, John (*see also* Meynsere) 128
    Thomas 179
Carter, John 85
    Mayor William 155
Carwardine, James 135
Catchpole, Henry 110
Cave, Sir Richard 146-48, 150
Caxton, William 75
Chapman, Mrs 274
Charles I 143, 155

Charles II 163, 187
Charlton, Bishop Lewis de 106, 174
Cheers, Mr H.A. 263
Chippenham, John 112
    Thomas 111
Church, Thomas 45
Clare, Earl Gilbert de (k.1314) 57
Clarke, Anne 182
    T.H. 264
Clarks, James 155
Clayton, John 140, 225
Clehungre, Roger de 123
Clifford, Roger 71
Clinton, Mr Wade 251
Cocks, Charles Somers, Lord Somers 217
Coenwulf, King 19
Coke, Bishop George 181
Coningsby family 114
    Col Fitzwilliam 146, 174
    Lord Thomas 187
    Sir Thomas & Philippa 172, 174
Cooke, Mr 207
Cooks family (of Moor House) 191
Cooper, Lt 158
    William 197
Corbett, Mr 147
Cormeliis, Walter de 103
Cornewall, Henry, MP 188
Cottingham, Lewis Nockalls 93, 232
Courtenay, Archbishop 74
Cox, David 108, 218, 254
Cranmer, Archbishop Thomas 178
Cranston, James 196
Croft, Dean then Bishop Herbert 92, 155, 159, 182, 184, 185
Crompton, Adam 207
    George 208
    Jonathan 207, 209
Cromwell, Oliver 149-50, 187
Croucher, Miss 255
Crowley, Robert 128-129
Crumpton, John 207
Cule, John 135
Curley, Timothy 76, 231, 234
Curtis, Thomas 138
Cuthbert, Bishop 19
Cuthwulf, Bishop 19

Dale, Mr 251
Dan the bulldog 261
Daniell, David 138
    Sir John 171
Darnell, Catherine 123
Davies, Arthur 186
    Joy 259
Day, Charles 185
Dayes, Edward 172
Defoe, Daniel 193
Denny, Tom 266, 267
Despenser, Hugh the Elder 57
    Hugh the Younger 56-58, 72
Devereux, Robert, 3rd Earl of Essex 144, 145
    Walter 112
Dingley, Thomas 85, 125
Docwra, Sir Thomas 169
Doffnore, Mr 248
Dominic, St 170
Donald & Neele, Messrs 251
Drew, Edward 138
Duckham, Thomas 231
Duncumb, John 194, 195, 203
Dyott, Mr 251

Eadric the Wild (*Sylvaticus*) 30, 35
Eadwig, moneyer 33
Ealdgyth (dau. of Aelfgar) 22
Earnwig, moneyer 33
Easton, John 207, 208
Edith, wife of Edward the Confessor 65
Edith, wife of Robert the iron-monger 165
Edgar, King 22
Edward the Confessor, King 22, 29, 33
Edward I (as prince and king) 54, 55, 56, 71
Edward II 56-58, 72, 109, 171
Edward III 72
Edward IV 75, 112, 113
Edward V 75, 113
Edwards, Augustus Charles 137, 138, 239
    William 118, 126
Edwin, Earl of Mercia 29, 30
Egerton, Bishop 61
Eleanor of Provence 54, 71
Elizabeth I 91
Elizabeth, wife of Edward IV 75

Elgar, Sir Edward 129, 261-62
    Henry 261
    William 261
Elliott, Canon Sandy 264
Ellis, Alice 249
Elyott, George 134
Ethelberht, St 11, 19, 22, 95, 165
Evans, Thomas 136
Exton, James 184
Eyton, Emily 50

Fairfax, Sir Thomas 150
Fallowes, Benjamin 217
Fauconberg, Philip de 165
Faulkland, Miss 251
Felton, Thomas 183
Fiennes, Celia 193
Fisher, Matthew & William 196
fitz Osbern, William 29-31, 33, 35, 104, 131
Foley, Lady Emily 251
    Paul Henry 92
    Paul, MP 188
    Thomas, MP 188
Foliot, Bishop Gilbert 80, 83
    Bishop Hugh 80
    Archdeacon Ralph 91
    Bishop Robert 80, 122
Forde, Richard de la 80
Foxe, Bishop Edward 178
Francis of Assisi, St 170
Freisne, Simon de 84

Gardener, Dr 189
Garrick, David 219, 252
Gatesby, John 125
Gaunt, John of 58
Gaunter, John le 109
Gaunther, John 101
Geers family 204
    Timothy, MP 188
George, Edward 223
Gerald of Wales 84
Gerard, Bishop 65, 81, 82
Gethin, John 206
Gibbs, James 280
    William Moore 230
Gill family 254, 256
    Edmund Marriner 254, 256
    Edmund Ward 254, 256
    George Reynolds 197, 254, 256
    William Ward 254, 256

Ginner, Charles 281
Glyn Dwr, Owain 59
Godgifu (Godiva) 22
Godwin, Earl 22
Godwinson, Earl Harold 19,
    22-25, 29, 35, 40
Godwinson, Earl Sweyn 22
Goodier, Francis 135
Goodman, Francis 207
Gorge, Henry 188
Gough, Richard 85
Gozo, priest 79
Greene, Canon 124
Greenland, George 238
Greenway, Griffith 133
Grey, Henry, Earl of Stamford 144
Griffiths, Francis 183
Grosseteste, Bishop Robert 83-84
Grove, William 230
Gruffudd ap Llywelyn 22
Gurney, Alfred 133
Guthlac, St 11, 15
Gwynne, Nell 163

Hackluit, Sergeant 149
Haddon, G.C. 235
Hammond, Captain/Colonel 145, 157
Hamo 102
Hampden, Bishop 235
Harding, Richard Morris 239
Hardwick, Philip 123
    Thomas 215, 217
Harford, Bridstock 199
    Bridstock II, MP 188
Harley, Brilliana 148
    Edward 163
    Edward, 4th Earl of Oxford 215
    Bishop John 179
    Sir Robert 148, 149, 162
Harold I Harefoot 33
Harold II (*see also* Godwinson, Harold) 33
Harold, son of Earl Ralph 23
Hartstrong, Sir Standish 203
Hatton, Brian 250, 257, 258
    Charles 194
    Marjorie 257
Havergal, Francis Tebbs 92
Hawkins, Francis 236
Haworth family (of Moor House) 191, 203

Hayward, William & Jane 269
Hearne, Thomas 158
Heather, Charles 217
Henderson, Arthur 252
Henry I 36, 82, 105
Henry II 37, 40, 51, 70
Henry III 41, 52, 53, 54, 55, 58, 70, 71, 106, 110
Henry IV 59
Henry V (as prince) 59
Henry VI 112
Herbert, Lord (Henry Somerset) 146
    Sir William 112
Hereford, Nicholas 175
Heywood, Col George 264
Hodges, Mary 182
Hogg, Dr Robert 249
Holyn, Roger 80
Hood, Robin 71
Hopkins, Evan 208
Hoskins, William 207
Howard, Ebenezer 286
    John 48, 214
Howarth, Captain 156, 158
Huck, William 48
Hugh & Roger, wheelwrights 105
Hughes, Luke 207
    W.C. 141, 212
Hugyn, Thomas ap 60
Humphrys, W.J. 247
Huntingford, Bishop 121
Hutchinson family 236
Hyde, family 138, 140
    John 138, 140
    Thomas 140
    Mrs 154
Hyde, George, Earl of Clarendon 144

Innocent IV, Pope 80
Isabella, Queen, wife of Edward II 56-58, 72

James II 187
Jearrad, Robert W. 79
Jeffries, Joyce 145, 146, 150, 195
John, King 51-52, 66
John of Worcester 22, 29
John, son of Rudolph 104
Johnson, Richard 263

Jones, Charles 277
    John and Mary 133
    Mr 199
    Thomas 207
Jukes, F. 214

Kayes, Margeria 80
Kemble, St John 184, 185
Kempson, F.R. 231, 249, 289
Kenyon, Kathleen 6
Kerr, William, Earl of Lothian 153
Kerry family 197
Kidley, Dr 258

Lacock, John 196
Lacy, Hugh de 52
    Walter de 33, 131
Ladmore, Thomas 258
Lanfranc, Archbishop 89
Laud, Archbishop William 143, 180, 181
Lawdey, Sir Richard 145
Lawrence, Mayor James 119
Leche, David 128
Leeming, Thomas 218
Leigh, Dean James Wentworth 92
Leland, John 12, 53-54, 60
Lewis, George Robert 213
    John 191
    Richard 208
Leofgar, Bishop 22
Leofric of Mercia 22
Leslie, Alexander, Earl of Leven 149, 151
    Sir David 153
Lettson, Dr 48
Lewis, Thomas 210
Lindsay, Mr F.W. 237
Lingen, Sir Henry 148, 156, 160-61
    Dr 230
Livingstone, James, Earl of Callender 151
Lloyd, Canon Owen 91
Llywelyn the Great 54
Llywelyn ap Gruffudd 41, 55, 71
Locke, Matthew 163
Losinga, Bishop Robert de (the Lotharingian) 20, 61, 65, 81-82, 89, 94, 121
Luard, Mayor Louise 274
Lucy, Charles 256-57

Maddy, Benjamin 196
Mann, Thomas 208
Margaret of Anjou, wife of Henry
　VI 75, 112
Marlowe, Christopher 72
Marshall, George 263
Mary, Queen (mother of George
　VI) 284
Mascall, Bishop 176
Massey, Col 147, 149
Matthews, William 189, 203
　Col (of Belmont) 217
Matilda, Empress 36-37
Matilda, wife of Henry I 65
Maund, Thomas 208
Maurice, Prince 145
Mayhew, Bishop 74
Mayo, Thomas 197
Melun, Bishop Robert de 70
Merewether, Dean 232, 246, 248
Meynsere, John 111, 128
Meyrick, Sir Samuel Rush 248
Miles of Gloucester, Earl of
　Hereford 36-37, 38, 51
Miles, Edward 251
Milfrid 95
Montfort, Simon de 54, 55, 71
Moore, Col Samuel 162
Morcar, Earl of Northumbria 29
Morgan, James 188
　Penelope 109
　Sir Thomas 156
Morris, John 2356
　Philip 240
　Richard 99-100
Mortimer, Catherine 58
　Edmund 59
　Joan 58
　Roger (d.1282) 54, 55, 56
　Roger (ex.1330) 56, 57-58, 72
Moxley, William 207
Moxon, William 234
Musgrave, Bishop 121
Mylling, Bishop Thomas 75, 113

Nash, John 204, 206, 214, 215,
　217
Naylor, Mr J. 277
Nicholson, Thomas 136, 231
Nield, James 48
Nott, Walter 171

Oates, Titus 184
Odo of Bayeux, Bishop 30, 31
Offa, King 12, 13, 15, 19
Orleton, Bishop Adam 57, 72,
　109, 111
Osbert son of Theobald 33

Packwood, James 208
Parfew / Purfoy, Bishop Robert 179
Parker, John 235
　William 198, 199, 215, 219
Paris, Matthew 33, 71
Parry, Thomas 135
　Mr (David Cox's landlord) 255
Partridge, Margaret 134
Pateshall, Mayor Nicholas 248
Paul VI, Pope 184
Payens, Hugh de 169
Pearce, Daniel 207
　George 208
Pearson, Jemma 262
Pember, John 239
Pembridge, Sir Richard 170
　Sir William 171
Pembrugge, Sir William 80
Percy, Harry (Hotspur) 59
Perling, R.F. 190
Peters, Mr W. 251
Phillips, Mayor Richard 189
Phippotts, Nicholas 123
pictoris, Ade 105
pistore, Samson 105
Pitt, Moses 48
Poole & Charles, Messrs 251
Pount, William 80
Powell, John 206
　Mary 78
　William 219
Pralph, John 149
Prath, John 80
Price, Edward 183
　John 195, 213
　Mayor William 144, 145
　Mr (merchant) 209
　Uvedale 196
Prichet, Maud 150
Priest, Nathaniel 197
Primrose, George 185
　Maud 182-83
Prise, Sir John 91
Pritchard, Richard 136
　Thomas Farnolls 212
　William 240

Probert, William 136
Pudge, William 240
Pugin, Augustus Welby 185
Pulley, Charles 250
　Sir Joseph 250
Pulling, William and John 196,
　207, 209, 210
Purfoy / Parfew, Bishop John 179
Purvey, John 175
Pychard, Sir Milo 165
Pytts, Samuel 188

Quarrell, Edmund 182
Quintin, C.F. 257
　Charles 258
　Henry 257

Radenor, John 128
Radford, Captain William 207,
　208, 238
Ralph, Earl of Norfolk 31
Ralph, first dean 61
Ralph of Mantes, Earl of Hereford
　22, 29
Rammell, Thomas 234
Rankin, Sir James 249, 258
Ravenhill, John 189
Rawlins, John 120
Rawlinson, James 92
Reginald the Smith 105
Reinhelm, Bishop 61, 65, 93
Repington, Philip 175
Repton, Humphry 196
Reynolds, Michael 92
　William 255
Rhys ap Gruffydd 39
Rhywallon 29
Richard I 34, 38-39, 40, 51, 102,
　169
Richard II 58, 74, 107, 111, 123,
　171
Richard of Holdingham 85
Richard of Devizes 40
Richard of York, Duke 112
Robert of Gloucester, Earl 36
Robert of Leicester, Earl 36
Robert the Deacon 29
Robson & Pattinson, Messrs 251
Robyns, James 80
Roe, Secretary 156-57
Roger, son of Miles, Earl of
　Hereford 37, 38, 51
Roger of Breteuil 31

Roger of Hereford 83-84, 91
Rogers, James 251
    Captain Wroth 163
    & Turnbull, Messrs 251
Robinson, W.W. 126
Rowntree, Kenneth 252
Rudhale, Archdeacon Richard 91
Rupert, Prince 144, 148, 150

Samuel, George 43, 44, 47
Sancto Colano, Tomas de 80
Saye and Sele, Lady Caroline 92
Scobie, Col 237
Scory, Bishop 190
Scott, George Gilbert 232
    John Oldrid 263
    Michael 83
Scotus, Marianus 82
Scrob, Richard 29
Scudamore, Col Barnabus 149-56, 158
    George 114
    John 155, 184
    Viscount John 148, 190
Seaborne, Peter 135
    Richard 138
    Thomas 183
Seward, Henry Hake 213
Simpson, Samuel 194
Sinclair, Dr George Robertson 129, 261, 262
Skidmore, Francis 232
Skippe, Bishop John 178-79
Slingsby, Sir Henry 150, 155
Swerdon, Mr 238
Smirke, Robert 217, 246
Smith, Bishop Miles 92
    Samuel Snr 183
Somerset, Lord Arthur 188
Speed, John 53-54, 129
Spofford, Bishop 71, 111
Spring, Thomas Winter 136
Stanford, Maurice de 80
Stanbury, Bishop John 74, 186
Stanway, John 128
Stephen, King 36-37
Story, Bishop John 179
Stowe, Edmund 258
Streeter, Canon B.H. 92
Streona, Edric 29
Stukeley, William 171
Sully, Richard 277

Swift, Thomas 207, 208
Swinfield, Bishop Richard 80, 85, 104, 169, 170, 171
Swynderby, William 175-76
Symonds, Philip 207
    Thomas 198, 204, 212, 214, 215

Talbot, Geoffrey 36-37, 78
    Revd Dr 215
Taylor, Isaac 192
    Maurice 110
    Rowland 179
    Silas 21, 163
Temple, Captain 157
Thelwell, John 198
Thomas & Philip the Smiths 105
Thomas, Francis 212
    Joseph 208
Thornton, Thomas 92
Thorpe, Elizabeth 136
Tirri, John 109
Tomkins, John 191
Tope, Thomas 105
Torrington, Viscount 206
Townshend-Smith, Mr 261
Traherne, Thomas 183, 266, 267
Traunter, Henry 201
Trefnant, Bishop Thomas 71, 74, 176
Trehearne, James 189
Trilleck, Bishop 174
Tringham, John 201
Trumper, Joseph 207
Tudor, Jasper 112
    Owen 113, 171

Vale, W.H. 213
Varley, John 213
Vavasour, Sir William 148
Venn, Revd John 233, 241-42, 247-48
Vere, Bishop William de 65, 69, 81, 95, 98, 121
Viall, John 118, 126
Vincent, Richard 133
Vitalis, Orderic 31

Walcher, Abbot, of Malvern 82
Walden, Humphrey 199
Wall, James 191
Waller, Sir William 146, 147-48

Walter of Lorraine, Bishop 31, 33, 65
Walter the *Piscator* 105
Waltheof, Earl of Northumberland 30, 31
Walton, Thomas 163
Ward, John 275
Wardroper, John 126
Wathen, James 43, 44, 45, 194-95, 198, 199, 200, 203, 220
Watkins, Alfred 47, 79, 106, 126, 135, 138, 142, 161, 201, 258-60
    John 277
Watson, John Bowles 219, 251
Weave, William 194
Wellington, Mr 193
Welsh, Edward 179
    William 207
Werour, John le 105
Westfaling, Henry 126
Weston, Sir John 169
Wharton, Bishop John 179
    Nehemiah 144-145
White, Mr 238
Wiggin, Henry 283
Wilde, John 183
William I 29, 31, 33, 65
William of Malmesbury 21, 32, 33, 35, 116
William of Poitiers 30
William the Dyer 105
William the Goldsmith 104
William the Painter 105
Williams, Roger 197
    William 207
Willim, George 136, 196
Wolston, Canon 124
Wood, John 221, 222
Woodcock, Thomas 218
Woodhouse, Mr J. 208
Woore, Philip 208
Worthyn, Thomas 111
Wren, Bishop Matthew 181
Wulfheard, Bishop 19
Wulfstan, Bishop of Worcester 65
Wyatt, James 204
Wyclif, John 175

Younge, John 171

GENERAL INDEX

abacus 82
Above Eign 228
Alban House 138
aldermen 187, 189, 221
allotments 241, 243
almshouses 190, 240-1
    Coningsby Hospital 172, *173*, 192, 241
        St John Medieval Museum 250
    St Giles 79
    Price's 201, *259*
    Trinity 3
Anarchy, the 36-7
Anglo-Saxon
    city 11-28
    defences 8, 15, 17-19, 21, 22-4, 35
    domestic settlement 24-6
    ironworking 26
    market area 28, 32
    remains 7
    royal residence 26-8
Arabian learning, connections with 81-4
astrology & astronomy 82
Auretone 29
Aylestone Hill 203, 231
    Ash Tree House, *see* Danesmere
    Athelstan Hall 231
    Baynton Wood, David Cox's cottage 255, *256*
    Berbice Villa 255
    and brick-making 203-4
    Broadlands 231, 289
    campus 289
    Danesmere (once Ash Tree House) 231, 255
    Overbury Lodge 231

bailiffs, royal 111
banks
    Bodenham's 200
    building societies 227
    City and County *199*
    Lloyds 133, 199
    Worcester City and County 133
Baptists 183
barges 207
    built at Hereford 207
Barroll House 204
Barton
    Station 225
    Tower Road 228

Bartonsham 103, 110, 228
    St James 231
battles
    Bryn Glas 59
    Marston Moor 149
    Naseby 150
    in Offa's reign 12
    Powick Bridge 144
Belmont 261, 290
Bewell House *202*
bishops
    authority of 23, 28
Bishop's Meadow 24, 40
Black Death 77, 106-7, 174
Black Friars 79, 80, 170
Blackfriars Monastery 146, 171-3, *173*, 192
Bobblestock 287, 290
book sellers 197
    Wilson and Philip's 257
Boothall/ Booth Hall 48, 58, 110, 116, 118, 134-7, *135*, 196
Bradbury Lines 7
Brampton Bryan 148
Breteuil-sur-Iton 32
    laws and customs 101
Bridewell, the 48, 163, 191, 214
bridges
    construction 33
    Greyfriars 277, 280, 290
    Lugg 107, 206
    Mordiford 34
    rebuilding in 1490
    Wye 33, 151, *151*, 186, 205, 206, *206,* 210
        heavy traffic 277
    repair 107, 186
Bronze Age 4-5
Broomy Hill
    Belvedere 230
    Mount Craig 257
    waterworks 211, 234
buildings
    internal decoration 118-9
    medieval 115-42
    open hall plan 138, *139*
    roof timbers, decoration *121, 139*
    roofing material 118
        crown post 128
    stone 115-6

timber-framed 118
   wall paintings 119
Bullinghope 14
burgage plots 32, 117
burgesses
   community of 102
   French 32-3, 105
burnt stones 5
Bye Street suburb 35

canal, *see under* transport
Canon Frome
   in Civil War 150-1, 155-6
Canon Moor 102
canons, secular 33
Capler
   quarries 115
cartography 84
castle 37, 51-60, *53*
   bailey 78
   barbican 191
   in Civil War 147, 162
   'council chamber' 51
   county hall 58
   in disrepair 144
   first reference to 29
   established by fitz Osbern 31
   gatehouse 163
   Great Tower 147
      demolition of 163
   hangings at 58
   king's great chamber 54
   king's garden/orchard *52-3*, 103
   'king's house' 51
   motte 37
      tower on 52, 53, 162
   Norman 14, *16*
   repairs 159
   St Martin's chapel, *see under* churches
   'shire hall' 52, 110
   in 12th century 35-6
   warehouses on site of 207
Castle Cliffe House 12, 162, 163, 214, *214*
Castle Green 12, 14-15, *14*, 16, *16*, 37, 163, 188, 191, *214*, 215, *246*
   cemetery 78
   estate 228, 230
   Reading-Room and Baths Society 246, 247
Castle Hill 37, 163
cathedral 120-31, *206, 214*
   administration, commission of inquiry 91
   aisles 70
   Audley Chapel 73, 74, 266
   Bishop's chapel 20, 61, *61*, 75, 94, 121

Bishop's Cloister 76
Bishop's Palace 118, 121-3, 159
canons 83, 84, 120, 160, 176, 186
   bakehouse 102, 129
Cantilupe Shrine 74, 165-8 *166, 167*, 266
   destruction 177-8
   stealing from 111
Cathedral Barn 129-31, *130*
   restoration 75
cemetery 21, 76-8
centre of learning 81
chapter 176, 179
Chapter House 71, 75, *158*, 159
choir/quire 63
   vaulting 69
   and the city 111
   in Civil War 75
clerestorey 69, 71
Close 75-8
   Apple Tree of Life *264*
   buildings on east side of Broad Street 264, *265*
   canonical houses 111, 125-9
   as cathedral cemetery 76-8
   Deanery 125
   Elgar statue 262, *262*
   Harley Court (once Harley Place) 118, 125-6, 131, 246, *260*
   Harley House 127, 131
   as market-place 111
   Mechanics' Institute 248
   monumental mason 204
   No.1 128, 131
   No.2 *127*, 128
   precinct wall 75
   restoration, 2009-11 264, 290
College of Vicars Choral 91, 115, 118, 123-5, *124*, 160, 163
College Hall 219
Cottinghams' restoration 93
crossing 65, 71, *98*
   tower 70, 71
crypt 69, *70*
Dean Leigh Library, see library
   dedication to St Mary 19
double-chapel, *see* Bishop Robert's chapel
Early Gothic Sculpture 98-100
font 65, 97
Hereford Gospels 89, *90*
Lady Arbour 76
Lady Chapel 69, *69*, 98, 99, 266
library 76, 89-92
   chained 92, *266*
   New Library Building 92
Mappa Mundi 85-8, *86*, 266, 290

Music Room 76, *205*, 261
nave 65, *68*
Norman 61-74
pilgrimage 85, 165-8
post-Reformation 180
prebendaries 120
rebuilding/repairs 32, 204, 231-3
Reformation, changes during 178
retrochoir 98
Romanesque sculpture 71, 93-8
Saxon 19-21, 61
St John's 'church' 69
St John's Quad excavations 20-1, *20*, 26-7
school 76, 81, 131, 177, 244
    in Civil War 177
shrine of St Thomas, *see* cathedral, Cantilupe Shrine
Skidmore screen 232-3
Stanbury Chapel 74, *186*
transepts *62*, 63, 70, 71
vicars choral 120
    expulsion of 182
west front *264, 265*
    collapse of 75, 204, *205*
    destabilised by earthquake 263
    Romanesque *64*
windows
    'shilling' 264
    Traherne *73*, 266, *267*
cellars, medieval 109, 115-6
cemetery
    municipal 235, 284
    crematorium 284
census, 1801 192
Centuries of Meditation 183
Chandos House 204
charity funds, use of 195
charters 34, 55, 107, 189
    Charles II's 187
    Queen Elizabeth's 187, *188*
    Richard I's 38-9
Church of England 185-6
churches and chapels
    All Saints 32, 78-9, *203*, 208, 261
        café 275
        library 92
        restoration *290*
    Baptist chapel, Commercial Road 233
    Bye Street baptist chapel 183
    Christadelphian Hall 233
    Countess of Huntingdon's Connexion chapel 233, 253
    Eignbrook Congregational chapel 233
    Friar Street Quaker meeting house 184
    Holy Trinity, Whitecross Road 231
    Plymouth Brethren
        Barton Hall 233
    Primitive Methodist chapels
        Chandos Street 233
        Clifford Street 233
        St Owen's Gate 233
    Quakers 183-4, 233
        Quakers' Lane (Friar Street) Meeting House 233
        King Street Meeting House 233
    St Candida's chapel 80
    St Eligius chapel 80
    St Francis Xavier Roman Catholic 185, 233
    St Giles 79, *79*, 169
    St James, Bartonsham 231
    St John's Methodist church, St Owen Street 233
    St Martin's 15, 54, 60, 78-9, 151, 162, 231
    St Nicholas 79, *190*, 208, 231
    St Owen's 33, 49, 79, 152
    St Paul's, Tupsley 231
    St Peter's 102, 112, 131, *215*, 241
    United Reform Church 233
    Wesleyan chapels
        Bridge Street 233
        Holmer Road (Venn's Lane) 233
cider 172
    Bulmers' factory *272*, 273
    H. Godwin's works *272*, 273
    museum 273
cinemas 233, 253
    ABC 253
    Kinema 253, *253*
    Pavilion 253
    Regal 253
    Ritz 253
citizens 103-4
Civic Trust 202
Civil War 75, 143-64
    causes 143, 180-1
    Hereford captured by Stamford, 1642 144
    Hereford captured by Waller, 1643 147-8
    Hereford captured by Col Birch 156-8
    removal of Birch's regiment from castle 162
    'Roaring Meg' 161-2, *161*
    siege of Goodrich Castle, 1646 160
'Civitas' 23, 33
clay 191
coal, *see under* trade and commerce
cockfighting 135
coffee house
    Woodcock's 199, 218, *219*
commissioners 222
Common Council 187, 189, 221
    landholdings 189-91

Coningsby Hospital, *see under* almshouses
Conservative Land Society 228, *229*, 230
corn-drying ovens 12-13
county hall 58
Credenhill fort 10, *10*
crusades 169, 174
Cry of the Oppressed, the 48
Cuckold's Green 192
Cwm, The, Monmouth, Jesuit province of 92

Declaration of Indulgence, 1687 183
defences
    Angevin 38
    bastion towers 41, *42, 260*
    gravel ramparts and ditch 38
    repair of 34
    Saxon 8, 15, 17-19, 21, 22-4, 35
    south of the river 40
    stone face added 40-1
    walls, city 35, 37, 38-50, 144, 193, 205
Dinedor/Dunre 5, *6*, 154
Dinmore preceptory 169
Dissenters 179, 182-4, 187
dissolution of the monasteries 171, 178
Dobunni 6
doctors 199
Domesday Survey 23, 27, 31, 32, 61, 65
Dominicans 79, 80, 170, 171
Dore Abbey, monks of 110
Drybridge House 28
duel 188
dyeing 105

Early Cotswold ware 27
earthquake, 1896 263
education, *see* schools
Education Act, 1944 288
Eign 103
Eign Brook 32
Eign Hill 191
Eign quay 196, 210
electricity
    electric light works, Widemarsh Street 267, *270*
elite, power of 187-9
enclosure 191
Enigma Variations 261
Ergyng, kingdom of 15
excavations
    Berrington Street 2, 17, *17*, 24-5, *27*
    Bewell Street 3, 26, 28
    Broad Street 8, 9
    Cantilupe Street 3, 23-4
    Drybridge House 28
    Eign Gate 8

    King Street 26
    Old Market 3-4
    Rowe Ditch 24
    Sack Warehouse 3
    St Ethelbert's Street 25
    St Giles *79*
    St John's Street 9
    Victoria Street 2, 3, 7, 9, 12-3, 17
    Wall Street 3
    Widemarsh Street 8
executions 57, 58, 267, 269

fairs 34, 238, 289-90
    feast of St Denys 105, 109
    St Ethelbert (Nine Days) 105-6, 110, 186, 238, 289-90
famine (1314-1321) 106
Farmers' Club 45, 117
Fayre Oaks
    discovery of bronze sword 4, *4*
fees
    city's division into 33-4
    erosion in importance of 102
    tension between king's and bishop's 34
fire engine 188, 201
    house 211
fire precautions 200-1
First World War 280-1
floods *243*
    Great Flood of 1795 206
    prevention 290
Foot and Mouth disease, 2001 269
Franciscans 170, 171
Franklin Barnes House 239
'free bush' 188, 189
freedom
    fines 189
    purchase of 104, 195
freemen 187, 189, 190, 196, 204
freemen's chamber 135
French community 103

gaol 46, 48, 54, 58, 60
    Freemen's Prison 134
    city prison 267-9, *268*, 280
    new 204, 214
Garnons 145
gas manufactory 221
gates, city 40, 144, 205
    Bye Street/Byster's Gate 40, 43, 46, *46*, *47*, 50, 147, 154, 157, 197
        gaol 48
        statues 46, *47*
        workhouse in 191
        from Church Street to Close torn down 111

demolition 189, 206
Eign Gate 40, 42-3, *43*, 50, 116, 147
Friars' Gate 40, 41, 42, 50, 152, 170, 194, 206
North Gate 32, 120
St Owen's Gate 34, 38, 40, 49-50, 152, 154, 192, 205
    magazine stored 143
    Primitive Methodist chapel 233
Widemarsh Gate 40, 43-4, *44*, *45*, *47*, 147, 206
Wyebridge Gate 34, 42
Georgian Hereford 187-220
    rebuilding 200-6
gin distillery, Pulling's 196
glaziers 105
Glorious Revolution 197
Glyn Dwr rising 60
Goodrich Castle, siege of, 1646 160
governance 33-4
Governor's House/Lodge 162, 163, 280
Green Lanes 287
Grey Friars 80, 170
guard house 211
guildhall 110, 134, 211
guilds
    craft 141
    Merchants Guild 134

Hampton Bishop 103, 154
Hampton Park
    brickworks 231
    estate 231
Haywood/Haye, royal forest 52, 54, 106
    Lodge *193*
hearth tax 192, 200
Hereford
    and Breteuil laws and customs 101
    Breviary 91
    City and County Benefit Building Society 227
    in Civil War, *see* Civil War
    centre for malting 196
    coat of arms *154*, 155
    commercial city 131-42
    compared to other towns 103, 115, 191
    Co-operative Housing Company 286
    council 204-6
    County College 244
    decline in prosperity 113, 115
    derivation of name 13
    destruction of city in 1055 11, 22, 32
    division into four fees 33-4
    effect of crusades on 169, 174
    Freehold Land Society 227
    Garden City 286, *286*

Georgian 187-220
    service centre 196-200
Gospels 89, *90*
governance 102-3, 221-2
High School 244
High School for Girls 244
Improvement Act, 1854 222, 234
Photography Festival 259
refurbishment 275-6
season 218
see of 19
Simon de Montfort at 54-5
Theatre 200
Victorian era 221-44
    move from Georgian 220
Waterworks Museum 235
Herefordshire Friendly Society 241
Herefordshire Pomona 249
Herefordshire School of Romanesque Sculpture 95-7
Hermes, bronze 8
Hinton 55
Hogg's Mount 37
Holmer 154
    Crossway Farm 283
    Hall 133, *140*
    Wiggins 283
hospitals 235-7, 284
    'Canadian' huts 284, 285
    County Hospital *240*, 284-5, *285*
    Dispensary 236-7
    General Hospital/ Infirmary 199, 215, 221, 230, 235-6, *236*, 284, 285
    isolation hospital (Municipal Borough Infectious Diseases Hospital) 237, 284
    lunatic asylum 215, 221
    Private Finance Initiative (PFI) 285
    Victoria Eye Hospital (previously Herefordshire and South Wales Eye and Ear Institution) 237, 285
    William's, St Owen Street 199
housing 227-31, 286-8
    associations 288
        Fortis Living 288
        Herefordshire Housing 288
        Kemble 288
    'Cornish Units' 287
    council houses 286
    Garden City 286, *286*
human remains 12
Hunderton 8, 228
    council houses 286
    discovery of Neolithic axe 3
Huntington 55

Improvement Commission 204, 206
inns, pubs, hotels and taverns 197-8
    Anchor 207
    Barrels 50
    Black Lion 119
    Black Swan *198*
    Blue Boar 134, 137-8
    Catherine Wheel 197
    Cattle Market Tavern 251
    City Arms 238, 245, 247, 248
    Crown and Sceptre 199
    Globe Tavern 264
    Golden Fleece 138
    Green Dragon *142*, 199, 238
    Kerry Arms 197
    King's Head 120
    Lamb 50
    Mitre 238
    Pack Horse *197*
    Pippin *116*, 117
    Ship 135
    Swan and Falcon/City Arms *198*
    Wellington Inn 45
Institution of a Christian Man 178
Interregnum 162-3, 187
Iron Age 5-7, 10
ironworking 26

Jacobites 197
Jewish community 101-2, 169-70
Judge's Lodgings 217, 253, *268*

Kemble House 252
Kenchester 7, 10
King's Acre 191
    development 286
    nursery 196
King's Book 178
Knights Hospitaller 80, 169
Knights Templar 79, 169

Lamp Act (1774) 109, 204
Lanfranc's *Collectio* 89
Left Bank 288
Liberty, the 102
libraries
    Hereford Free Library 248
    first permanent library 245, 247
    Public Library, Broad Street 245, 249-50, *249*
lime burners 105
limners 105
Litley Court estate 231
Liverpool & Bristol Company 207
Lollards 74, 175-6

London, Herefordshire Club 188
Lower Bullingham 55
    Broad Green 191
Lower Portfields 228
Lugg Meadow 223, *258*, 280
Lugwardine, royal manor of 103

Magna Carta 66, *67*
Magnis, see Kenchester
malting 196
Mansion House 204, 211
Mappa Mundi, *see under* cathedral
maps and plans 8, 18, 31, 46, 49, 63, 131, 133, 224, 228
    Brayley's map, 1806 121
    John Speed's map 39, 129, 171
    Isaac Taylor's map *43, 122*, 171
    John Wood's Survey *222*
Market Hall 107, 115, 140-2, *140, 141, 155*, 192, 212, *212*
markets 28, 31, 32, 238
    Butter Market 213, *239*
    cattle market 234, 235, 269-71, *270, 271*
    in the Close 111
    corn 104
    Corn Exchange 251
    encroachment 107-9
    at entrance to castle 58-9, 104
    farmers' 275
    Norman 31-3, 38, 131
    Old Market, *see* Old Market
martial law 159
Masonic Lodge 242
mayor 187, 221
Mayor's Parlour 119
medieval
    buildings 115-42
        floor plan 117
        open hall plan 138, *139*
    learning 81-100
mercers 104
Mercians 13, 28
Mesolithic 2, 3
metal working 32
mills 56
    Bartonsham 110
    Castle 211, 235-6
    corn 196, 242
    fulling 110, 114
    Leather, Monkmoor 193, 194
    Lugg Mill 110
    Scutt Mill, Eign 103, 104, 204
    walking 110
    water 102
mint 33

model farm 243
moneyers 23, 32-3, 101
Monkmoor 194, 221
Moor House 201, 203
Moorfields 30, 221
    Bulmers 273
    Estate 230
    Place 228
    Station 225
Mordiford 154
Municipal Corporation Act, 1835 221
murage grants 40
museums
    Churchill Gardens 250, 257
    Cider 273
    city 249-50
    St John Medieval 250
    Old House 250
    Waterworks 235, 250
Music Meeting 218

NE Prospect of the City of Hereford 192-3
Neolithic 3
New Hunderton 287
Newton Farm 287
Newtown 228
Norman
    Conquest 29-33
    market-place 31-3, 38, 131
Normandy 32
    Cormeilles 103-4
nuns 80
    Sisters of Charity 244

Offa's Dyke 15
Old House, the 117, 119, 132-3, *132*, 250
Old Market 3-4, 253, 276, 290
Oxford University 84, 92, 176

pageant, Corpus Christi 113
Painscastle 39, 54
Parliament
    Long 143, 182
    MPs, 17th & 18th century 188
    'Rump' 163
Paving Act, 1774 222
Phoebus, Mr *262*
Pilgrimage of Grace 60
pilgrims 85, 105, 165-8
    as source of income 109
plague 77, 106-7, 109, 114, 174
pluralism 176-7

poor
    Benevolent Society for relieving the Sick Poor 241
    'deserving' 190
    distribution of coal to 191
    Lying-in Charity 241
    provisions for 240-3
    Public Assistance Institute 284
    Society for Aiding the Industrious 241-3
    Society for supplying Poor Women with
        Needlework 241
    washing baths 242
    and Widemarsh 191
    workhouse 191, 214, *240*, 241, 284
    Working Boys' Home 243
Poor Law Amendment Act, 1834 241
population 106, 107, 191-2, 221, 277
Portfields 30, 103, 171, 193, 286
pre-urban settlement 1-2
prison, *see* gaol
professions 196-200
public health 233-7
    burials 234, 235
    cesspits 233-4
    Public Health Act, 1842 234
    sewage disposal 233-5, 283
    washing baths 242
    water supply 211, 234-5
public works 211-8
Putson 55

Quakers, *see under* churches and chapels

race course 191, 218
railways, *see under* transport
rebuilding
    Georgian 200-6
Redhill 5
    Bradbury Lines 7, 290
    development 287
Reformation 74, 128, 177-80, 266
Restoration 182, 187
Richard's Castle 29
riots
    1691 197
    1698-9 191
    1705 191
river; see also Wye
    barges 207, 210
    boats built 208
    crossings
        Roman period 8
    Pollution Act, 1874 235
    stone quay 54

  trade 207
  warehouses 207
  Water Witch *209*
  wharves 207-8
Roman Catholics 187
  harassment of, 17th & 18th centuries 184
  secret services 184
Romano-British settlement 8, 9, 10
  altars 8, *9*
  roads 9, 12
Rotherwas 290
  Enterprise Zone 283
  House 280
  Industrial Estate 283
  Junction 226
  munitions factory 267, 280-3, *281*
    explosion 281-2
    shell store (1916) *282*
  Ribbon 5
  Skylon Park 283
Rowe Ditch 6-7, 24, 40, 103, 151
royal visits
  Charles I 150
  Edward IV 113
  Henry II 51
  Henry III 52-5
  Henry IV 59
  Henry V 59
  Isabella 56-7
  John 51-2
  Queen Mary 284

Sack Warehouse 3
saffron 195
St Giles's estate 228
St Guthlac's
  cemetery 37, 78
  monastery/Priory 11, 14-15, 16, 25, 27, 35, 53,
    54, 56, 58, 78, 80, 91, 103, 110, 114, 157
St Owen's Nursery 230
schools, colleges and education
  All Saints 244
  Blue Coat 243
  Cathedral, *see under* cathedral
  Clyde House 244
  Miss Croucher's, New Street 255
  Hereford College of Education 288-9, *289*
  Hereford County College 244, 288, *289*
  Hereford High School 244
  Hereford High School for Girls 244
  Hereford Ladies' College 244
  Hereford School of Arts and Crafts 289
  Herefordshire College of Art and Design 289
  Holmer 244

  Mechanics' Institute 247, 248
  New Model in Technology and Engineering
    college (NMiTE) 289
  C.F. Quintin's school 257
  Roman Catholic 244
  Royal National College for the Blind *288*, 289
  St Martin's 244
  St James 244
  St John's 244
  St Peter's 244
  St Peter's Literary Institution 247-8
  Scudamore National School 190, 244
  Sixth Form College 289
  Tupsley 244
science 81-2
Scudamore Charity 188, 190, 195
sculpture
  Dymock/Bromyard School 97
  Herefordshire School 95-7
  West Country School of Masons 99
Second World War 277
  air raid 281
  'Canadian' huts 284
sewage, *see under* public health
Shire Hall *215*, 217, 261
shops and shopping 218, 237-40
  Augustus Edwards 239
  Greenlands 238-9
  Harding Bros. 239-40
  Messrs Heins piano showroom 233
  Marks and Spencer 239
  Maylord Orchards 274
  Philip Morris 240
  W. Pritchard and Sons 240
  supermarkets 274-5
    Aldi 275
    Asda 275
    Lidl 275
    Maypole 274
    Sainsbury 274
    Tesco 28, 274, 275
    Waitrose 275
Skylon 283
slums 221, 227
Smallporse 110
societies
  Castle Green Reading-Room and Baths Society
    246, 247
  Hereford Literary and Philosophical Society 245-7
  Herefordshire Photographic Society 258-9
  Philosophical Society 245, 247, 250, 258
  Society for Aiding the Industrious, *see under* poor
  Society of Tempers 163, 214, 246
Stafford-type ware 27, *27*

stallage 105, 109
stocks and pillory 213
streets, squares and roads
    Aubrey Street 234
    Baggallay Street *229*, 230
    Barrs Court Road 231
        North Villas 231
    Barton Road
        Barton Hall Plymouth Brethren 233
        Turnpike House 226
    Bath Street (once Sally Walk, then Mill Street) 193, 221, *278*
        Hodges iron foundry 240
        mill building *242*
    Berrington Street 2, 24-5, 254
        Countess of Huntingdon's chapel 233
        Roman Catholic school 244
    Bewell Street 3, 26, 28, 108, 196, 227
    Blackfriars Street 8, 235
    Blueschool Street *278*
    Bodenham Road *230*, 231
    Breinton Road 235, 286
    Bridge Street 110, 118, 119, 277
        Wesleyan chapel 233
    Broad Street 8, 9, 80, 185, 198, *203*, 219, 238, *252, 265*
        buildings on east side 264, *265*
        Kemble Theatre 252
        Public Library 245, 249-50, *249*
    Bruton Street 105
    Bryngwyn Terrace 231
    Burcott Row 201
    Butcher's Row *107, 108*, 135, 213
    Bye Street, *see* Commercial Street
    bypass 280
    Cabache Lane, *see* Church Street
    Canal Road 171
    Canon Pyon Road 286
    Cantilupe Street 3, 23-4
    Castle Mill 105
    Castle Street *202*, 204
    Chandos Street
        Methodist chapel 233
    Church Street (Cabache Lane) 111, 118, 127-9, *127*, 128, 184, 200, 248
        Mayor's Parlour 119
    Churchill Gardens 257
    Clifford Street
        Primitive Methodist chapel 233
    Clive Street *227*
    College Hill 287
    College Road 286, 288
    Commercial Road (once New Street) 28, 255
    car manufacture 277
    city prison 267-9, *268*
        Baptist chapel 233
        eye hospital 237
    Commercial Square 240
    Commercial Street (Bye Street) 28, 109, 120, 138-40, 183, 217, 218, 240, 241, *278*
        cinema 253
        Judge's Lodgings 217, 253, *268*
        St Peter's Literary Institution 247
        Tesco 274
    Coningsby Street 171
    Cooken Row (*Cokenrewe*) 107, 108, 213
    Cornwall Street 228, *229*
    corveseresrewe 109, 113
    East Street 218, 248
    Edgar Street 235, 242, 253
        Clyde House School 244
    Eign Road
        The Crozens 233
        eye hospital 237
    Eign Street 108, 133, 195
    Elm Road 231
    Folly Lane 231, 289
        The Folly 231
    Friar Street (once Quakers' Lane) 184, 221, 233
        iron foundry 238
    Gaol Street 50
    Grenfell Road 230
    Grope Lane 50
    Grove Road 230, *230*
    Gruneisen Street 230
    Hafod Road 231
    Hampton Park Road
        Plas Gwyn 262
    Harley Court (once Harley Place) 118, 125-6, 131, 246, *260*
    Harold Street 230
    High Street 118, *213*, 240
    High Town *107*, 108, 115, 116, 117, 120, 134, 163, 197, *213*, 239, *275*
        Alban House *137*, 138
        Greenlands 239
        High Cross 211
    Highmore Street 228
    Hinton Court 287
    Hollywell Gutter Lane 284
    Holmer Road, *see* Venn's Lane
    Ingestre Street *229*, 230
    inner relief road 274
    King Street 4, 26, 184, 195, *265*
        Quaker Meeting House 233
    King's Acre Road 286

King's fishboordes 108
Kyrle Street (once Venn Road) 242
Link Road 286
Llanbleddian Terrace 230
Loader Drive *288*
Lyde Street 228
Maylord Street 102, 113, *278*
    Bulmers 273
mercerierewe 109
Meyrick Street 230
Middle Row 108-9
Mile, Mill or Milk Lane *121*
Mill Street, *see* Bath Street
Mostyn Street 286
Norfolk Terrace 221
Packers Lane 137
Park Street *227*, 229
Portfield Street *227*
Prospect Terrace 221
Quakers' Lane, *see* Friar Street
Ranelagh Street 230
Richmond Place 221
Ross Road 286
rows 107-9
Ryelands Street 228
    Bulmers 273
St Ethelbert Street 25, 204
St James Road 230
St John Street 9, 127, 218
St Martin's Street *200*, 221
St Nicholas Square 258
St Owen Street (formerly Hungery Street) 117, 123, 199, 204, 258
    cinema 253
    Hereford High School for Girls 244
    St John's Methodist church 233
    library 245
St Owen's Place 287
St Peter's Square 211, 214, *274*
St Peter's Street 116
Sally Walk, *see* Bath Street
Southbank Road 231
Southern Link Road 280
Station Approach 5
Stonebow Road 286
Three Elms Road 287
Union Street dispensary 237
Venn Road, *see* Kyrle Street 242
Venn's Lane (once Holmer Road) 231
    Christadelphian Hall 233
    Royal National College for the Blind 289
    David Cox's cottage 255
Victoria Street 2, 3, 7, *279*

Wall Street 3
Westfaling Street 284
Westfields Street 228
Whitecross Road 226, *259*
    Holy Trinity church 231
    Toll House 226
Widemarsh Street 32, 113, 117, 119-20, 145, 146, 150, 171, 198, 199
    electric light works 267
    Hereford Ladies' College 244
    library 245
    Mansion House 204, 211
    Philip Morris 240
    school 255
    toll gate *216*
suburbs
    burnt by Talbot 36
    Georgian 192
    housing 286-7
    robbed by Roger Mortimer 54
    Victorian 227-31
suffragettes 274
Sutton 19-20
swimming baths 242, 253

tallage 55
Tan Brook 171, 194
theatres and entertainment 251-4
    Alhambra music hall 252
    the Athenæum 252
    Broad Street 219, 251
    County 253
    Courtyard 253, *254*
    Forester's Hall 252
    Garrick Theatre 252-3
    Hereford 200
    Kemble Theatre 252
    Nell Gwynne Theatre and Arts Centre 253
    New Hereford Theatre, Arts Centre and Cinema 253
    New Theatre 251
    St George's Hall 252
    skating rink 252
    Theatre Royal 251, 252
Three Choirs Festival 261-2
Toledo, connections with 82
Toleration Act, 1689 182, 184
toll gates 216
tolls 34, 189
Tolsey 105, 134, 141, 163, 211
town hall 211, *263*
trade and commerce 131-42
    SEI/Thornes/BTH 277
    armour 113

barge-building 207
boats built 208
brick-making 201-4
car manufacture 277
    Aero Parts 277
    Connelly and Sons 277
    Smooth-Geared Auto-Car Syndicate 277
    Westland-Healey motor cars 277
carpets 195
cloth industry 110, 115, 195
coal, price of 201, 210, 242
dyers 195
flax dressers 195, 200
George and Tudor 223
guilds 113-4
Inco Alloys 283
iron foundry 221, 238
    Hodges 240
leather trade 109, 113
masons 105
Middle Ages 101-114
Nash's Warehouse *202*, 203
Painters 283
Price and Co. 223
Rod Robinson Associates 290
smiths 105, 113
Special Metals (Wiggin) Limited 283
tanners 194
    Hatton's tannery *194*
    Leather Mill, Monkmoor 193, 194
warehouses 223
weavers 195
Henry Wiggin and Company 277, 283
wool-mart 110
woollen manufactory which employed the poor 190, 195
transport
    buses 280
    cars
        made in Hereford 277
        National Light Car Trials 277
    congestion 277-80
    Hereford and Gloucester Canal 210, 222-3, *223, 224*
        end of 226
    railways 224-6, 276-7, 280
        Barrs Court Station 224, *225*, 226, 276
        Barton Station 225
        Moorfields Station 225, 269
        Rotherwas Junction 226
    tramroad 210
treaties
    Winchester, 1153 37
trows 192, 207

Tupsley 55, 103, 191, 230, 287
    discovery of hand-axe 2, *2*
    Gorsty Lane isolation hospital 237, 284
    Prospect Farm 287
    St Paul's 231
    Whitehouse Farm 287
turnpike
    gates 226
    trust 206, 216

United Parishes Burial Board 235

Vicars Choral, *see under* cathedral, College of Vicars Choral
Victoria, Queen 261
Victoria Park 288

walls, city, *see under* defences
wards 102, 221
Wars of the Roses 112-3
Water Witch *209*
water supply 234-5, 284
    waterworks 211
    Waterworks Museum 235, 250
Watling Street West 7
Weobley
    castle 36
Westfields 30, 228
    council houses 286
wheelwrights 105
White Cross *106*, 174
    Moor Farm 287
Whitecross 228, 257
Widemarsh 55, 191
    Brook 110, 194
    Common 201
    enclosure 191
    Moor 102-3
wine merchants 196
    Tanners 196, 203
witchcraft 182
Wood's survey *222*, 231
Woolhope Naturalists' Field Club 245, 247, 249
workhouse, *see under* poor
Wye
    Bridge 33, 151, *151*, 186, 205, 206, *206, 210*
        heavy traffic 277
        repair 107, 186
    Horse Towing Path 207
    Navigation 188, 191, 192, 195, 196, 201, 207
    sewage in 235
    skating on *243*